IMPACT

Dr. George Kozmetsky receives the National Medal of Technology from President Clinton at the White House on September 30, 1993.

IMPACT

How IC^2 Institute Research
Affects Public Policy
and Business Practices

Edited by
W. W. Cooper, S. Thore,
D. Gibson, and F. Phillips

The IC^2 Management and Management Science Series, Number 6
Edited by W. W. Cooper and George Kozmetsky

QUORUM BOOKS
Westport, Connecticut • London

Library of Congress Cataloging-in-Publication Data

Impact : how IC² Institute research affects public policy and business practices /
   edited by W. W. Cooper . . . [et al.].
       p.   cm. — (IC² management and management science series, ISSN
   1058–5036 ; no. 6)
   Includes bibliographical references and index.
   ISBN 1–56720–030–3 (alk. paper)
   1. Research, Industrial—Economic aspects—United States.
   2. Technological innovations—Economic aspects—United States.
   3. Community development—United States.   4. Urban policy—United
   States.   I. Cooper, William W. (William Wager), 1914–
   II. Series.
   HC110.R4I48   1997
   338′.064′0973—dc20   95–50748

British Library Cataloguing in Publication Data is available.

Library of Congress Catalog Card Number: 95–50748
ISBN: 1–56720–030–3
ISSN: 1058–5036

First published in 1997

Quorum Books, 88 Post Road West, Westport, CT 06881
An imprint of Greenwood Publishing Group, Inc.

Printed in the United States of America

The paper used in this book complies with the
Permanent Paper Standard issued by the National
Information Standards Organization (Z39.48–1984).

10 9 8 7 6 5 4 3 2 1

Contents

PART II NEW METHODOLOGIES

PART III NEW SCIENCE

Tables and Figures

TABLES

FIGURES

Preface

INTRODUCTION

In September 1993, George Kozmetsky, founding director and current chairman of the board, IC^2 Institute, The University of Texas at Austin, received the National Medal of Technology from President Clinton, with Vice President Gore in attendance. The awards ceremony is pictured at the front of this book. To quote from the *Fact Sheet* prepared by the United States Department of Commerce,

The National Medal of Technology is the highest award bestowed by the President of the United States for extraordinary achievements in the commercialization of technology or the development of human resources that foster technology commercialization. This Presidential award is presented annually at a White House ceremony to individuals and companies. The award was established by the Stevenson-Wydler Act. (Public Law 96-480)

The citation celebrates Dr. Kozmetsky's "commercialization of various technologies through the establishment and development of more than 100 technology-based companies that employ tens of thousands of people and export over one billion dollars world wide." This description is incomplete, however, in its omission of Dr. Kozmetsky's role as a professional—helping to found societies like The Institute of Management Sciences or more recently the Society for Design and Process Science, or as an academic administrator—where, under his leadership as Dean, the College and Graduate School of Business Administration, The University of Texas at Austin became a world-class and highly ranked school in business and management education and research. After finishing his service as Dean in 1982, George and his wife, Ronya, decided to find a way to "give back" what they believed they had received from society. They wanted to do this in the creative and innovative manner that has distinguished their professional lives. These events are described and put in context in the book *Making It Together* (The Free Press 1981), which was jointly authored by George and Ronya as well as in the volume *Creative and Innovative Management* (Ballinger 1984), subtitled *Essays in Honor of George Kozmetsky* edited by A. Charnes and W. W. Cooper.

The editors of the present volume believed that the recognition provided by the Presidential Award of the National Medal of Technology provided an appropriate occasion for another volume in honor of George Kozmetsky. For this purpose they decided to focus on the activities of IC^2 Institute Endowed Fellows, who were invited to contribute to this volume. Each of the contributed chapters is based on the authors' own research or educational activities and each is accompanied by a summary indicating relevance for the public and private sectors.

THE IC^2 INSTITUTE AND RELATED ACTIVITIES

George and Ronya Kozmetsky formed the "RGK Foundation" as a family foundation and established the "IC^2 Institute" at The University of Texas at Austin. This was followed by founding IC^2's Austin Technology Incubator (ATI), which offers business "know-how" assistance and facilities to "start-up" technology firms. Subsequently, the Texas Capital Network (TCN) was brought into existence as a non-profit development organization to bring potential investors into contact with promising new ventures for start-up firms like those at ATI as well as others nationwide.

ATI and TCN complete an IC^2 trio: Innovation, Creativity, and Capital (IC^2), where Innovation and Capital are needed to bring Creativity into successful application. ATI and TCN are directed mainly toward theory application, whereas IC^2 is centered more on developing theory and encouraging creativity at the University of Texas and elsewhere. The mission of the IC^2 Institute is to enhance understanding of the processes of economic wealth creation and prosperity sharing. The IC^2 Institute accomplishes its mission through

- defining and conducting an integrated, interdisciplinary program of research and education on the enterprise system
- developing a synthesis of research, education, and practice that mutually reinforce and enhance each other
- disseminating knowledge through a systematic program including classes and a full curriculum for a Masters' Degree in Science and Technology Commercialization, publications, workshops, seminars, and conferences
- engaging the University of Texas and universities around the world in dialogue and initiatives directed at contributing to society's economic, social, and cultural well-being.

Examples from each of these activities will be found in the chapters that follow. Here we only need to note that the activities and influence of the IC^2 Institute are not confined to the University of Texas and they are not confined to academia. Indeed, a major orientation of the IC^2 Institute is pointed toward encouraging interactions between practitioner organizations and academia to help provide a two-way flow that will encourage relevance and widen the horizons for research and its uses. This flow in both directions is carried on locally, nationally, and internationally.

CONTENTS OF THIS VOLUME

With this brief description of the IC^2 Institute as background, we now turn to the contents of this volume. As prepared by the Fellows—or, more precisely, by the Endowed Centennial Fellows of the IC^2 Institute—papers in this volume extend over a range that we have divided into the following three groups: (1) New Programs, (2) New Methodologies, and (3) New Knowledge. The first category refers to descriptions or discussions of new programs with which the authors have been associated. These include new programs designed to deal with social problems (e.g., juvenile delinquency) or needed educational developments and opportunities (for engineers, managers, and medical practitioners), and these papers also report some of the research accompanying these developments. The second category deals with newly developed capabilities in the form of computerized methods and mathematical models and concepts for planning managerial activities or evaluating the performances of ongoing social programs or economic behavior. Finally, category three deals with new research that is yielding new substantive knowledge in areas ranging from botany to pharmacology.

In each case the author(s) was asked to prepare his or her write-up to make an important contribution to the literature dealing with the topics addressed, and also to accompany this write-up with a summary that could make its intended contributions to science or society understandable in lay language. No attempt at coordination was imposed on any of the authors—the above tri-partite classification is due to the editors. In the following section, we summarize each chapter in a manner that can provide further guidance to readers.

CHAPTER SYNOPSES

NEW PROGRAMS

Chapter 1: "The Austin Project, 1989–1994: Interim Report on an Ongoing Innovation" by Walt W. Rostow

We begin our chapter summaries with The Austin Project (TAP), a new program developed under the guidance of Walt W. Rostow and his wife, Elspeth, who have turned their energies from scholarly research and high level advising of governments (on international politics and policies) into new channels directed to problems involving the lives and conduct of juveniles in American society. The need for creative thought and innovative activities in this area is evident from, for instance, the accelerating increase of violent crime in this segment of our population—an acceleration that has now reached a point where it has more than compensated for decreases in violent crime rates among other sectors of the population.

As Dr. Rostow notes, TAP was preceded by more than two years of research undertaken in close cooperation with officials and experts involved in these problems. This research identified the fact that $54 billion is being spent annually on such programs but in a manner that is primarily directed to "damage limitation." No coherent strategy is used to guide these vast expenditures and no systematic basis of accountability has been provided to evaluate the effects of these numerous programs—which have been spawned in a "reactive manner" over many years to deal with the increasingly urgent problems of youth crime, delinquency, and violence.

Instead of adding one more program to deal with the immediate emergency, Dr. Rostow proposes a longer range strategy based on a principle which he refers to as "continuity of intervention" identified with (1) bringing young children from prenatal care into the school system in good health, with a sense of self-worth, (2) linking their subsequent schooling to an enlarged range of future possibilities in the work force and professional life, and (3) seeing them into the working life of society at the highest level that their talents, ambition, and energy permit.

This is, indeed, only a set of objectives intended to guide constructive approaches to a longer range program at national levels. However, Dr. Rostow also provides for shorter range considerations, including tests of various possibilities that can be used to guide (and correct) the longer range course of developments. The various ways in which this is done are described in this chapter, which discusses some of the programs developed and carried out locally in concrete form in Austin, Texas.

Chapter 2: "Telemedicine: Its Place on the Information Highway"
by Frederick D. Williams and Mary Moore

Our society is confronting severe problems, such as the ones we just noted in delinquent behavior and violence among juveniles. It is also being presented with large opportunities, such as those in telemedicine—which is defined in this chapter by Frederick Williams and Mary Moore as "uses of telecommunications technology to facilitate healthcare delivery." Even some of the words and usages in this medium are new (e.g., words like "geekspeak") so that our language must struggle and change to describe these developments—which include "networking of services to expand and improve such things as the availability and use of electronic libraries for education, research, and practice." The discussion of telemedicine opportunities in this chapter also covers rapid and accurate feedback and response capabilities so that a patient in Appalachia, for example, can 'visit' a specialist in Chicago via a video link showing x-ray damage of a lung while the specialist can consult with 'Medline' to call up the results of recent research for its possible bearing on diagnosis and treatment—all of this being done in real time while consulting with the patient's primary care physician.

Chapter 3: "Pricing of Services on the Internet" by Alok Gupta, Dale O. Stahl, and Andrew B. Whinston

It is of interest to note that the roots of the networks described by Williams and Moore are to be found in ARPANET—so named because the Advanced Research Project Agency of the Department of Defense developed this network with various academic institutions. Growing like "Topsy" this subsequently became the NSFNET—with infrastructure support provided by the National Science Foundation—and it has now grown into the Internet and WWW (World Wide Web) which are actually networks of networks.

Internet, NSFNET, and WWW continue to evolve currently supporting thirty million users growing at a rate that has sometimes approached 100 percent annually. As might be expected, congestion, with resulting delays, is beginning to make an appearance just as NSF is beginning to withdraw its support of the infrastructure, which forms the backbone of Internet. A search for alternatives to present methods of support and management must therefore be made and this forms one focus for research being conducted by the Center for Information Systems Management at the University of Texas.

One may ask whether a governmental or private entity, or some combination, should now be empowered to manage this previously unmanaged system or at least its infrastructure. An alternative is to examine whether prices and like mechanisms might be used in a manner analogous to the way our economic system manages itself.

This topic forms the focus of discussion in this chapter by Gupta, Stahl, and Whinston. With adaptations from economic theory, this research examines possible uses of pricing mechanisms to manage infrastructure capacity. Simulation studies like those described in this chapter promise enough improvement over the present practice of "free access" to justify further research and development along these lines. Finally, as noted in this chapter, this can (and should) include research into new accounting and billing arrangements as well as the use of "smart agents" and like devices (from artificial intelligence) to handle adjustment dynamics that are likely to be required as this system continues to evolve.

Chapter 4: "Needed Innovations in Capital
Expenditure Planning"
by Richard L. Tucker and G. Edward Gibson, Jr.

The Construction Industry Institute (CII), headquartered at the College of Engineering at The University of Texas at Austin, was founded in 1983 by a consortium of construction (engineering) firms in order to conduct research in engineering and construction and, concomitantly, to identify where new programs and activities need to be undertaken. In recognition of the importance of this work, the Construction Industry Institute recently was awarded $2 million by the Sloan Foundation.

This chapter reports results of a study undertaken for CII by Tucker and Gibson that focuses on important changes needed in the 450–500 billion dollar construction industry. In a manner akin to the "Takaguchi principles" (for integrating design and operations for quality management in manufacturing) the authors find that major improvements are needed in pre-project planning for construction undertakings. They also find that bringing this about will require closer coordination and team arrangements that will involve engineering and business managers in new organizations and approaches that can assume flexible and changing forms in response to client needs and opportunities. Mere conformance to specifications no longer suffices, so methods of project management must be devised that will make it possible to *anticipate* client needs and opportunities and this, in turn, will require new methods of managing. It will also require changes in engineering education in which core engineering courses will be augmented or complemented with courses in business and management so that students will (a) be able to fit into these newer kinds of managerial environments more quickly and easily and (b) be able to create and implement new managerial methods to meet the still further changes that will occur in the future.

Chapter 5: "Interdisciplinary Research in Materials
and Devices for Electronics and Photonics"
by John M. White and Ben G. Streetman

This chapter describes interdisciplinary programs involving faculty and students in chemistry, physics, and engineering actively involved in advanced research in electronic materials and devices. Many of these activities are organized in centers such as the Microelectronics Research Center at the University of Texas. With support from organizations like the National Science Foundation and the Department of Defense, these activities are being arranged (and rearranged) in response to national needs, but without losing sight of the need for educating the next generation of young people to work on these problems. This education extends to experience in working across disciplinary lines in ways that might be absent from education developed only along more traditional departmental (within-discipline) lines. One can also see in this chapter the great flexibility of university environments and their ability to respond to opportunities in research almost as soon as new advances are made elsewhere in the world and one can also sense the excitement that accompanies activities in contexts like those described by White and Streetman—contexts in which education as well as research are oriented so that both can be responsive to social needs as well as scientific progress—for example, in cross-disciplinary activities that can be built around centers like those discussed in this chapter.

NEW METHODOLOGIES

Chapter 6: "The Unreasonable Effectiveness of Management Science for Solving Management Problems"
by Gerald L. Thompson

The methodologies discussed in this part of the book represent ongoing research in developing new tools for use in planning and evaluating management activities and social programs and extend to improving our ability to understand the performances of economic systems. The chapter by Gerald Thompson reports some of the mathematical models and methods that he and others have developed in response to needs in management for improved planning of day-to-day operations.

The descriptions that Professor Thompson supplies have an attractive simplicity. This simplicity belies the ingenuity that was needed to develop these new methods and makes it possible to portray the contributions to management in a direct manner by means of concrete examples. The second example in the article is illustrative of his point. Dramatic reduction in the costs of changing from one color to another on cars leaving a production line were obtained by (a) arranging the assigned colors in a "snake line" and then (b) cutting across the contours of the snake to obtain the order in which the colors are to be applied. Assurance is then provided that the resulting order requires changing colors no more than one less than the total number of colors. The procedure resulted in a dramatic reduction in annual costs.

The methods Professor Thompson devised can be used in many other applications. They form part of an interrelated body of developments that have affected mathematics, generally, as well as other sciences and management practices. Indeed, these kinds of developments have led to a body of new disciplines that are collectively referred to as "management science."

Chapter 7: "Using Computer Intensive Technologies
to Aid Insurance Regulators: Early Detection of
Insolvency and Fraud"
*by Patrick L. Brockett, Linda L. Golden, and
Xiaohua Xia*

This chapter focuses on newly developed methods for detecting aberrant
behavior in data that may be indicative of either insolvency in an insurance
company or fraud in one or more of the claims being processed by an insurance
company. The methods covered are Data Envelopment Analysis (DEA), Expert
Systems, Neural Networks (Computer Codes), and Self Organizing Feature
Maps. Before moving to our discussion of these topics, however, it is worth
noting that the emphasis in this chapter is shifting to inferences from data
generated from past behavior (*ex post*). This emphasis differs from the planning
(*ex ante*) methodologies emphasized by Thompson.

IRIS (Insurance Regulators Information System) provides a set of financial
ratios that were developed for the NAIC (National Association of Insurance
Commissioners) and have been used for many years by State Regulatory
Agencies to monitor the behavior of insurance companies. However, tests
(conducted by one of the authors of this article) revealed serious shortcomings in
the use of the IRIS ratios for Early Warning Systems. In contrast to other
techniques that have now been essayed—including the current "risk-based capital"
adjusted version of these ratios recently adopted by the NAIC—the alternatives
described by Brockett, Golden, and Xia have pattern recognition capabilities that
can be exploited with the high-speed information processing capabilities that are
now available.

DEA provides capabilities for evaluating performance of individual entities
in a way that replaces statistical (or other) *averages* with evaluations conducted
by reference to best practices of *individual* entities. Multiple inputs and outputs
can be dealt with while obtaining an overall "figure of merit" to evaluate the
performance of each of many entities. This is accomplished without recourse to
weights and so forth, even when the inputs and outputs are measured in different
units. Physical and social (e.g., demographic) as well as financial variables can
therefore be used in any combination and, unlike customary regression methods,
DEA avoids the necessity of specifying the relations between inputs and outputs.

Brockett, Golden, and Xia next explore how Expert Systems (which are
already in use by some insurance companies) with their pattern recognition
capabilities might be joined with DEA for use by regulatory agencies. This
naturally leads to Neural Networks, which represent yet another computer
implemented approach that proceeds, in a manner analogous to the human brain,
to identify patterns by (1) learning from experience, (2) generalizing from
examples, and (3) abstracting "essences" from input data.

The above approaches are elucidated with illustrative examples. One neural
network model using NAIC data is found to compare favorably with other

approaches such as the use of A. M. Best & Co. ratings for use in insurance company Early Warning Systems. Another neural network model, when applied to detect automobile insurance claim fraud, is found to outperform the human experts in the industry.

Chapter 8: "A Two-Stage DEA Approach for Identifying and Rewarding Efficiency in Texas Secondary Schools" by Victor L. Arnold, Indranil R. Bardhan, and William W. Cooper

This chapter moves to a public sector application of DEA that is developed in more technical detail than in the chapter by Brockett, Golden, and Xia. This use of DEA formed part of a study by a three-University consortium working with the Texas Education Agency (TEA) and the Legislative Education Board (LEB) of Texas that was directed to improving accountability and methods for reevaluating public school performance in Texas. Statistical regressions applied to TEA data on secondary schools at an early stage yielded unsatisfactory results. Recourse to DEA then yielded a surprising result. None of the schools rated as "excellent" on state mandated levels of achievement were also efficient. In the terminology defined in this chapter these "excellent" schools were found to be "effective" but not "efficient" because they used excessive input amounts to achieve the outputs (such as math scores) which enter into these mandated levels of excellence. Other schools were found to be performing efficiently but had failed to achieve these state-mandated excellence levels because of the difficult conditions they confronted—such as large numbers of economically disadvantaged and low-English-proficiency students. As noted in the concluding portion of this chapter, there appears to be a need for new ways to accord recognition to efficiently performing schools. This can include new ways of budgeting or reallocating incremental resources along with some of the other possibilities explored in this chapter.

Chapter 9: "A Management System for Monitoring and Analyzing the Productivity of Armed Forces Recruiting" by David B. Learner, Fred Young Phillips, and John J. Rousseau

This chapter derives from work done by its authors (with others) as part of an engagement with the Office of the Assistant Secretary in the U. S. Department of Defense. Examples built around Rosetta (one of the commercially available computer codes for use with DEA) illustrate some of its graphic capabilities. Emphasis is on flexibility in response to "what if" questions that are contrasted with the kinds of "what if" questions that can be addressed when statistical regressions or other types of *averages* are used. This can be done because DEA focuses on *individual* observations and the (possible) shortcomings or inefficiencies relative to other observations in *each* input (such as advertising dollars and recruiting personnel) and *each* output (such as number of high school graduates recruited). Finally, the issue of "effectiveness" (as distinguished from "efficiency") is addressed by evaluating performances on subsets of the variables (such as Army Contracts Negotiated) as they relate to other subsets (such as Stated Intentions to Enlist) in studies of force sizes and enlistments.

Chapter 10: "The Competitiveness of Nations" *by Boaz Golany and Sten Thore*

The meaning of "international competitiveness" and its uses in national policy have been hotly debated in the popular literature and in economics—as well as in the halls of governments. One source of disagreement is the multiple dimensions that enter into considerations of relative advantages with, possibly, one nation being ahead in some of these dimensions and behind in others. Another source of disagreement is the absence of an agreed upon measure that can take each of these dimensions into account.

Golany and Thore bring DEA to bear on this problem in an illustrative application that uses data for the so-called G-7 nations over the twenty-one-year period 1972–1992 as obtained from the National Council of Competitiveness. The following results are obtained: Japan and Italy systematically outperform the other countries consisting of France, Germany, the U.K., the U.S., and Canada—with Canada consistently at the bottom. Perhaps even more important is an additional finding that the summary DEA scores used to evaluate competitiveness of each of these nations have been systematically falling over this period. In other words, later performances for each of these nations is worse than their earlier ones.

There are those who argue that improving relative competitive position is less important than other considerations such as improving the standard of living within a country or taking account of longer range needs by investing in education. However, outputs like improved standards of living and inputs like investment in education are some of the multiple components that are used to obtain these DEA ratings. Moreover, as illustrated in this chapter, the DEA printouts can be called upon to show output shortfalls and input excesses. These same printouts show the reference group used to obtain these estimates so that DEA also supplies needed "benchmarking," without extra effort, for each country in every year.

Chapter 11: "Instability, Complexity, and Bounded Rationality in Economic Change"
by Ilya Prigogine, Ping Chen, and Kehong Wen

This chapter turns to methods and concepts directed to a deeper understanding of the sources of instability in economic systems. Attention is directed to whether unstable behavior, when observed, can lead to permanent changes in underlying structure. As might be expected, the methods and concepts differ from the ones described in the immediately preceding chapters. The theory of chaos (to which Professor Prigogine has been a major contributor) is used to guide a search for relations—or changes in relations—that can determine the nature of the economic behavior that might (or might not) be predictable in the future. The methodologies used take the form of nonlinear differential equations (and like approaches) which represent the kind of mathematics that is best suited to uncover relations that would otherwise not be apparent from, say, an inspection of pertinent data.

The theory and methods used are illustrated by applications to data in which Prigogine, Chen, and Wen show the different effects of the 1973 Arab oil embargo and the 1987 stock market crash. The oil embargo is found to have produced a structural change in the economy whereas this was not the case for the stock market crash.

No straightforward "inspection of the data" will suffice to identify these distinctions, as will be clear from the data plots and diagrams provided in this article. Theoretical concepts and methodologies like those used by Prigogine, Chen, and Wen are required. The resulting findings are intended to set new directions for research in economics. However, these findings can also have other consequences. For instance, the break (or discontinuity) associated with structural changes due to the "oil-price shock"—itself a consequence of the Arab oil embargo—should make it clear that large and expensive economic and econometric studies like Project Lincoln used to guide the formation of Federal policy in the 1970s were based on erroneous assumptions of stability. Their methodology, in its use of statistical models based on historical data and concepts of smooth equilibrating behavior (on which econometrics and economics have long depended) were also not up to doing what was required to deal with these problems. Instead, new concepts and new methods of analysis. like those described in this chapter, are required to better understand how our complex and dynamically changing society organizes itself.

Chapter 12: "Diversification Strategy, Strategy Change, Performance and State-Defined Risk: Some Longitudinal Evidence"
by Timothy W. Ruefli, Donde P. Ashmos, and James M. Collins

Using data from 236 Fortune-500 companies that had changed strategies during the period 1949–1969, Professors Ruefli, Asmos, and Collins review and extend past studies on causes and effects of changes in corporate strategy. Most of the published studies have been confined to static analyses (or, comparative statics) and do not provide any way of analyzing and evaluating the risks that are likely to accompany changes in strategy.

As noted in this chapter, treatment of the latter two topics required recourse to methodologies that differ from the ones used in past studies. Ordinal time series, as recently originated by Professor Ruefli, was therefore brought to the task by the authors and entropy measures were adapted to these tasks so they could be used to obtain ordinal measures of the risks associated with changes of strategy states. These states, in turn, were identified with a taxonomy for different types of strategies so that results from this study could be compared with earlier work.

Using "Return on Assets" and "Return on Sales" as criteria, the following results were obtained: (1) Consistent with earlier studies, troubled firms are the ones most likely to change their strategies. (2) In general, strategy changes resulted in relatively poorer performances and higher risks for both troubled and untroubled firms. (3) However, particular strategy changes did not produce superior economic performances in both the risk and return dimensions and therefore did not conform to this general pattern.

This certainly is not the end of the line for this research, or even for the kinds of methodologies and concepts that will need to be developed, since, as Ruefli, Ashmos, and Collins note, change is no longer merely something that management must confront. An increasing number of firms are coming to view change itself as a tool that management can use for positive competitive advantage. Inferences from data on past behavior will not be enough for these kinds of managerial uses. Increasingly, there will be a need for new developments in the *ex ante* modeling methods discussed in connection with Professor Thompson's chapter at the beginning of this section.

NEW SCIENCE

Chapter 13: "The Role of Basic Research in Developing New Treatments for Parkinson's Disease"
by Creed W. Abell and Sau-Wah Kwan

This chapter covers recent research on neurotransmitters, such as dopamine, which relay messages between neurons that, in turn, are made up of different but related subsystems of nerve cells referred to as "neuronal pathways." One of these pathways, which is responsible for the control of movement, has been shown to be defective in Parkinson's disease. Alterations in this pathway are also responsible for movement disorders commonly observed in schizophrenic patients. Another pathway in the dopamine system has been linked to brain functions that control emotion.

This chapter reviews much of the recent work in this area of research. Some of this work was stimulated after Parkinsonian like effects were found to occur with use by dope addicts of some of the neurotoxants for synthesizing heroin, after with subsequent studies showed how they destroyed cells in the portion of the brain that makes dopamine. This research was helped by more rigorous diagnostic classifications that have recently been developed by psychiatrists. At a more basic level Professor Abell was able to put to rest some long-standing controversies by showing fundamental differences in some of the enzymes involved. This showing now makes it possible to design drugs that are targeted to treatment of neurological and psychiatric disorders like Parkinson's disease as well as pointing to other drugs that can be targeted to the treatment of depression. *Inter alla* this finding can also eliminate some of the drugs now used, some of which can produce life-threatening side effects such as hypertensive crisis.

Chapter 14: "Drugs as Probes for Intrinsic and Protein-Induced Bending of DNA"
by Laurence H. Hurley and Daekyu Sun

This chapter provides an example of the kind of research that leads to improved states of knowledge for use in the design of new drugs for deeper understanding in molecular biology and for use in genetic engineering. It is directed to the effects of drugs associated with protein-induced bending of DNA. Each DNA molecule is a two-stranded chain in which nucleic acids are sequenced as represented by the symbols—A (Adenine), C (Cylosine), G (Guanine) and T (Thymine)—which appear in the formulas contained in the Appendix to this article by Hurley and Sun. This sequence determines the genetic code with the strands coiled in a double helix in which each subunit in one strand is connected to a subunit in the other strand in the forms A–T or G–C bondings. A change or replacement of any of the sequences changes the genetic code. More recent work has shown, however, that even *bending* of the DNA molecule may also affect its properties. The evidence for such induced bending is summarized in this chapter and results from recent research—by the authors, among others—is described and evaluated.

The writing in this paper, which is highly technical, is representative of research in this area. For those who may not wish to (or be able to) follow these technical developments, the authors summarize the significance of what is being covered so that it can be appreciated by a broader audience. However, the significance of the research described in this paper can readily be appreciated from the fact that it has already led to the development of three new anti-cancer agents that are currently undergoing field tests and trials.

Chapter 15: "Potential Agents for the Commercialization of Virus-Resistant Transgenic Plants"
by Maureen S. Bonness, Nilgun E. Tumer, and Tom J. Mabry

It has been two decades since the first transgenic organism was engineered genetically. Attempts to produce new crop plants that could not be generated by conventional breeding are now proliferating with impacts extending from agronomy to the treatment of diseases in humans and a revolution is now under way with effects that are being felt in both industry and academic research.

Industry and academic research are joined in this chapter by Bonness, Turner, and Mabry that discusses research into an antiviral protein in pokeweed that can enter and kill virus infected cells and thus prevent a virus from spreading. This protein has already been cloned and transferred to tobacco and potato plants at Monsanto (Dr. Tumer's company) and it also appears to have antiviral properties for animal cells that are presently in clinical trials for the treatment of HIV, leukemia, and cancer. To provide a better basis for understanding this antiviral behavior, laboratories at the University of Texas have developed a method for screening pokeweed cells and have now been able to identify a line that does *not* produce antiviral cells. Tumer and colleagues proceeding with their experiments at Monsanto have also genetically engineered several other crop species to produce antiviral protein.

As pointed out in this chapter, the possibilities from this kind of research are enormous. They create new economic opportunities, to be sure, but they raise many important ethical questions as well as questions on the possible need for new institutional arrangements and regulatory safeguards.

Robert S. Sullivan
Director
IC^2 Institute

Part I

NEW PROGRAMS

1

The Austin Project, 1989–1994: Interim Report on an Ongoing Innovation

Walt W. Rostow

This interim report covers the first five years of the Austin Project (1989–1994). Its goal, as announced on May 6, 1992, is to bring the men, women, and children of Austin's eastside into the mainstream of American society over the next generation.

The report is set out as an exercise in innovation in public policy involving four stages: (i) defining a strategy, which took two years; (ii) applying that strategy to a given time and place in the form of a plan; (iii) bringing the initial plan to life at the appropriate scale; and (iv) modifying the initial plan in the light of unfolding experience.

Right now the plan is at stage (iii)—that is, in the midst of the struggle for resources to permit the problems of the inner city to be matched by the level of preventive investment.

The inner cities were found to be caught up in an economic-social vicious circle. Most of the resources going to them were for damage control rather than prevention. The strategy for reversing the vicious circle involves: sustained support by the city's political leaders; continuity of intervention over the whole span from prenatal care of pregnant women to entrance of properly trained young men and women into the workforce or professional life; investment in prevention elevated to match the scale of the problems to which it is addressed; effective mobilization of the business community, colleges and universities, religious institutions, and relevant social service agencies around this strategy; and, most important of all, development of steady working partnerships with the Hispanic and African-American neighborhoods.

On the basis of this strategy a 350-page plan for Austin was written in four months by fourteen men and women of vastly different backgrounds and experience but a common view of an appropriate approach to the task.

After some fifteen months of operation with this plan—detailed in the text—the Austin Project was ready to go to scale. At a meeting on December 13, 1993, the board of directors approved a systematic effort to mobilize the resources necessary to match the problems of inner city. The strategy for this sustained effort, rooted in the plan for Austin, called for a tripartite, linked community-neighborhood strategy: work with small children and their families; a program from school to workforce and the professions; and a direct assault on three of the central-city districts to which the Austin Project would apply this strategy with great intensity.

On March 4, 1994, at the initiative of the Domestic Council of the President, the Austin Project was presented at the White House by nine members of the board of directors. As a result of that meeting, the city and the Travis County governments, assisted by the Austin Project, applied for designation as an Empowerment/Enterprise Zone.

To the social scientist this project is of interest both as a test of whether a comprehensive preventive strategy will work in the inner city and as a prototype of innovation in public policy.

THE STAGES OF THE AUSTIN PROJECT

The Austin Project (TAP) is a nonprofit private foundation. Its existence was formally announced on May 6, 1992, by the mayor of Austin (Bruce Todd), the Travis County judge (Bill Aleshire), and the president of the board of directors of the Austin Independent School District (Beatriz de la Garza). Its objectives were then defined as follows.

"The Austin Project aims to mobilize the public and private sectors of the Austin Community for two purposes.

- To reverse the decline of the disadvantaged inner-city neighborhoods in the next several years; and
- to set in motion a process which would bring the men, women and children who live there into the mainstream of American society over the coming generation."[1]

This essay is, therefore, an account of the first few years of an innovation not expected to achieve its ultimate objective until well into the next century. As such, it must be regarded strictly as an interim report.

The Phases of Innovation

Innovations in public policy almost always proceed in four phases[2] (i) the posing of a question leading to a period of analysis—often an interval filled with confusion and uncertainty—out of which, with luck, a reasonably lucid answer emerges, permitting a strategy to be defined; (ii) applying that strategy to a particular time and place in the form of an initial plan for action; (iii) bringing the initial plan to life amid the complexities of the active world; and (iv) modifying the initial plan in the light of unfolding practical experience. Thus, innovation is not a once-for-all event but a living, unfolding, circular working process.[3] Indeed, with the passage of time and changing circumstances, a fifth stage may be required: the generation of a quite different innovation.

The following account seeks to state and explain the question posed; the answer that emerged; the strategy to which that answer led; the initial plan built on that strategy; and the first phase of the effort to implement the plan, including problems encountered and changes made.

The Question

The Austin Project arose from a suggestion of my wife, Elspeth Davies Rostow. I had just turned in to my publisher a long book on theorists of economic growth since David Hume and Adam Smith. Elspeth observed that I did not appear pregnant with another book of seven hundred pages and that we might consider working on a subject of common interest. She dubbed the search The Joint Venture, a name that soon found its way onto the inevitable gray boxes.

After some exploration of alternatives we settled on the nation's urban problem. We began with a painful question: Why, after the devoted effort of many hundreds of social scientists and many thousands of public and private social workers, and the application of many billions of public and private dollars, was the condition of America's inner cities worse in 1989 than it was when Watts blew up on August 11, 1965?

I would underline the importance of this question, for in both science and public policy the answers one generates are heavily determined by the questions posed. In the world of urban analysis and policy formation this question is only occasionally confronted, usually in the context of welfare reform. The more conventional question is what are the "needs" of the community. The implication of seeking the causes of progressive deterioration rather than the needs will emerge. Here I would merely note that our approach via causes rather than needs arose from extensive work in developing countries. In fact, the Austin Project can be understood as the application of development theory and experience to the inner-city problem in the United States with the caveat that the inner city has many economic advantages over a developing country but one great disadvantage, a gravely weakened family structure.

After two years' reading in a voluminous literature, consultation with experts, and direct observation of a good many American cities from a development perspective, we concluded that we understood the basic reason for the nation's monumental failure.

The Answer

We have failed to solve the inner-city problem in the United States since 1965 because we lacked (and still lack) a coherent urban strategy. Lacking a coherent strategy, we have applied our skills and resources overwhelmingly to limiting or mitigating the symptoms of prior failure—from neonatal clinics to prisons. An exact categorization of the content of social expenditures with respect to primary prevention, secondary prevention, or damage limitation is, of course, impossible. But a 1992 evaluation of social expenditures during the Bush administration is suggestive. Increases of $54 billion were cited: 85 percent were damage limitation (Medicare and food stamps), mandated by law and the product of rising medical costs and unemployment; or income from work so low as to force families below the poverty line. Only 15 percent might be regarded as investments in prevention (elementary education, school nutrition, Head Start.) Something like that proportion is probably typical of American cities.[4]

In Austin the title of a key urban public service program was changed in 1992 from "Youth at Risk" to "Opportunities for Youth," but the damage-control character of the enterprise and its fragmentation by symptom are apparent in the following list of areas addressed

Unhealthy Infant	Child Abuse
Physical and Mental Disabilities	Low Self-Esteem and Poor Physical Fitness
Teenage Pregnancy	Hunger
Illness	Substance Abuse/Addiction
Drop Out/Insufficient Education	Inadequate Child Care
Unemployment	Youth Crime

Fragmentation has been exacerbated by two further factors: First, the almost incredible multiplicity of worthy private social agencies at work in our cities, drawing on public as well as private funds. In Austin about 300 are engaged in "Youth" programs. Second, the current highly specialized nature of the social sciences in the United States, which reinforces these tendencies. The field of urban studies has its experts on young children and families, dropouts and gangs, drugs and crime, teenage pregnancy and health, education and the inner-city economy—and a good many even narrower specialties, many designed to distinguish the relative situation of particular minorities. The proportion of creative effort devoted to intellectual or policy synthesis—to viewing the inner city as an intimately interacting dynamic system—is low.[5]

The upshot of all this is that the de facto American policy toward its inner cities consists in a massive array of fragmented, ill-coordinated, mainly damage control (or secondary prevention) programs. There was never any reason to believe that a strategy of this sort could reverse the vicious circle at work in our inner cities. Preventive programs of real promise do exist in every city, but none exists on a scale that matches that of the problem to which it is addressed.

The Deeper Roots of the Problem: How the Vicious Circle Came About

Like many major phenomena, the present deteriorating state of the inner cities results from the convergence of a number of independent forces, in particular the following.

- World War II and the postwar period witnessed a large-scale migration of African-Americans from the rural south to northern cities and an accelerated flow of immigrants from Latin America. On the whole, both groups were predominantly poor and not well educated.
- Nevertheless, until the coming of the microelectronics revolution in (approximately) the mid-1970s, a good many of these migrants commanded sufficient skills to find places in the manufacturing work force. The new technologies widened the gap in required areas of competence (and in wage rates) between skilled and unskilled labor and raised the skill requirements even for a good many service jobs.
- As this process proceeded, the average level of unemployment in the United States rose from 4.7 percent in the 1950s and 1960s to 7.1 percent for the 1970s and 1980s. As Table 1.1 and Figures 1.1 and 1.2 demonstrate, "Black and Other" unemployment ran at about twice the level of "White"; for males 16-19, who generate a good deal of antisocial behavior, the "Black and Other" proportion more than doubled over this period relative to "White."

Table 1.1

Cyclical Behavior of Black and Other Relative to White Civilian Unemployment, 1948–June 1991

	Average All Workers	White	Black and Other	Black[a] and Other/White	Males 16–19 White	Black and Other	Black and Other/White
P 1948	3.8%	3.5	5.9	1.7	—	—	—
T 1949	5.9	5.6	8.9	1.6	—	—	—
P 1953	3.0	2.7	4.5	1.7	—	—	—
T 1954	5.5	5.0	9.9	2.0	13.4	14.4	1.1
T 1957	4.3	3.8	7.9	2.1	11.5	18.4	1.6
T 1958	6.8	6.1	12.6	2.1	15.7	26.8[a]	1.7
P 1960	5.5	5.0	10.2	2.0	14.0	24.0	1.7
T 1961	6.7	6.0	12.4	2.1	15.7	26.8	1.8
P 1969	3.5	3.1	6.4	2.1	10.0	21.4	2.1
T 1971	5.9	5.4	9.9	1.8	15.1	28.8	1.9
P 1973	4.9	4.3	9.0	2.1	14.2	27.8	2.0
T 1975	8.5	7.8	13.8	1.8	18.3	38.1	2.1
P 1979	5.8	5.1	11.3	2.2	13.9	34.2	2.4
T 1982	9.7	8.6	17.3	2.0	21.7	48.9	2.2
P 1989	5.3	4.5	10.0	2.2	13.7	31.9	2.3
T 1991[b]	7.0	6.2	11.4	1.8	—	—	—

Note: P = cyclical peak; T = cyclical trough
[a]"Black" after 1972
[b]Tentative (June)

- The adjustment of the inner-city workforce to the imperatives of the new technologies was gravely impeded by the sluggish response of the public school system to the new environment, and by the almost equal sluggishness of private and public employers to recognize their vital interest in cooperating intimately with the school systems in training the young for good entry-level jobs upon graduation from high school. Under these circumstances, the verdict of inner-city youth was overwhelmingly that their schooling was dull and irrelevant, unrelated to any credible path to an attractive future.
- This complex of circumstances heightened in the inner city the pressures on previously conventional family life induced throughout the advanced industrial world by a change in sexual mores and the increased role of women in the workforce. In different ways these circumstances tended to reduce the inhibitions to teenage pregnancy and to increase the attractiveness of gangs as a substitute for gravely weakened or nonexistent families.
- To an extent difficult to measure when multiple forces are at work, welfare policies may have compounded inner-city problems (as well as cushioned their impact) by providing what appeared to some a subsidy for creating a single-parent household and, more generally, by strengthening a sense of neocolonial dependence, humiliation, and bitterness, and by weakening a sense that self-help was necessary and that a greater control over one's destiny was possible.
- A further compounding difficulty is the understandable but costly flight of successful men and women from the inner city, reducing the number of resident and visible role models who made their way into the mainstream of American society.

Figure 1.1
Unemployment Rates of White Compared to Black and Other[a]

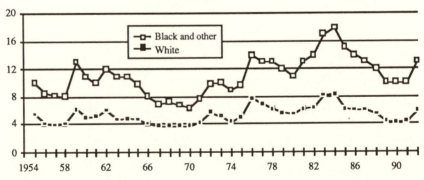

[a]Percent of civilian labor force
Data from Citicorp Economic Database, Household Survey, May 1991.

Looked at in this way, the vicious circle can be stated as follows. A powerful converging set of economic forces sharply raised the level of unemployment in the inner city and simultaneously reduced in the minds of young men and women future prospects for good jobs. This perceived narrowing of realistic options, along with concurrent social forces, led to an increase in teenage pregnancies, a good many of which resulted in low-birthweight babies. More generally, inexperienced and hard-pressed young mothers did not provide their children with the physical care, continuity of affection, and stimulation required for proper development in the early, critical years. As a result the children often entered school with little self-esteem or confidence. In schools dominated by the principle that time should be the independent variable, learning the residual, many ill-prepared students fell further behind. This lag plus the gathering sense that school was dull, irrelevant, and offered no credible, attractive future yielded a decision to drop out and surrender to the real-enough attractions of the streets: gangs, crime, sex, drugs. For some the attractions included money—for cars, gold chains, Reeboks, and so forth. The surrender to street life, in turn, constituted a powerful negative feedback. It not only added to the flow into the system of teenage mothers but also enlarged the pool of young people ill equipped for decent entry-level jobs in an increasingly high-tech world. And so the vicious circle continues.

Figure 1.2
Relative Unemployment Rates for Black and White Teen Males

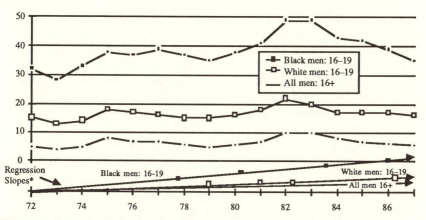

[a]These are linear regressions on the data for each of the three graph lines.
Data from *Labor Force Statistics Derived from the Current Population Survey, 1948–87.* U.S. Department of Labor Bureau of Labor Statistics, August 1988.

While the tragic vicious circle ground down, there were those with a vision of how it might be reversed—or, perhaps, who simply felt a personal moral duty to struggle against the tide—in the inner city neighborhoods, in government agencies, and in the Anglo community. The bulk of the population in the disadvantaged neighborhoods was weighed down with rhetoric never fulfilled; the bulk of the Anglo population was convinced that social policy was not the answer and expenditure of funds, except on police and prisons, was not the answer. The Austin Project was built initially on the residual minority who, for intellectual or moral reasons, had decided to gear their efforts to a strategy of prevention.

The Strategy: How to Reverse a Vicious Circle

Putting aside details for later consideration, the strategy that emerged to reverse the vicious circle had these five components:

- First, sustained support by the city's political leaders.
- Second, continuity of intervention over the whole span from prenatal care of pregnant women to entrance of properly trained young men and women into the work force or professional life, all conducted so as to engage and reinforce families.
- Third, investment in prevention elevated to match the scale of the problems to which it is addressed.
- Fourth, effective mobilization of the business community, colleges and universities, religious institutions, and relevant social service agencies around this strategy.
- Finally, and most important of all, development of steady working partnerships with the Hispanic and African-American neighborhoods.

The principle of continuity of intervention breaks into three large human objectives (1) bringing young children from prenatal care forward into the school system in good health, with a sense of self-worth, and with their natural curiosity alive within them; (2) linking their subsequent schooling to an enlarged range of future possibilities in the workforce and professional life— possibilities which they come to regard as credible and which turn out to be credible; and (3) seeing them into the working life of the society at the highest level their talents, energy, and ambition permit and, along the way, narrowing the terrible gap between average and inner-city unemployment.

The principle of prevention also changes its character as early childhood gives way to youth and young adulthood. The fact is that teenagers who are clearly bound for a professional career or a job which holds promise of advancement don't have babies. Nevertheless, we cannot be wholly satisfied with a policy that merely builds up promise of a more fulfilling working future. Teenage pregnancy is a reality. Prevention begins, of course, with prenatal care; that is, by efforts to influence the behavior of the mother. And in the early years external intervention is primarily addressed to parents and parenting with the aim of encouraging early immunization, a healthy diet, continuity of affection, intellectual stimulation, constructive socialization, and so forth. As the child moves forward the parental role remains important, but prevention increasingly takes the form of widening the options the young person perceives as realistically available for the expression of his or her curiosity and talent.

From Strategy to a First Phase Plan: 1991–1992

The elements of the strategy briefly summarized above were contained in a paper written by my wife and me in the summer of 1991 and sent out as a draft for criticism. It was entitled "Reflections on How to Bring People in the Disadvantaged Communities into the Mainstream."[6]

Newly elected Mayor Todd heard we were working on the paper and asked that we send it along to him when finished. This was done on August 29. In September the Mayor decided to proceed with a project based on the proposed strategy for reasons he later expressed as follows:

When Walt first outlined the concept several months ago, it struck a familiar chord. As one of six children from a poor, single-parent household, I benefited from many of the programs he envisioned. That informal support came from my mother, grandparents, caring neighbors and civic leaders in the small Texas town where I grew up. But in a large, modern day city, that support structure is not always present. Families are geographically disbursed, school finances and budgets strained, and civic groups hard-pressed to meet demand much less provide for additional recipients. The cracks in the social fabric are tearing at the cloth itself.

Although substantial assistance is necessary for many of our youth, sometimes the small things make the difference—adult encouragement at a critical emotional time, or directed and positive education about life threatening effects of early teen-age pregnancy or AIDS. While expansion of proven existing programs such as Head Start is necessary, innovation is also called for. And the underlying critical factor to ensure success is community involvement. We must restructure a community network to replace the one that made the difference between success or failure for me over three decades ago.[7]

Mayor Todd did not state in print his second major reason for backing the Austin Project, perhaps because it would have sounded self-serving. He felt that his gift as a politician was to bring together disparate elements in the community, and that it was imperative that something like the Austin Project be started if Austin (and most other American cities) were not to go the way of Los Angeles, where the Anglos, the Hispanics, the African-Americans, and the Asians all regard themselves in different ways as endangered minorities.

In short, the Austin Project was meant to prevent the rise of tribal minority sentiment and to heighten the sense of community.

The following seven months were devoted to three activities. In part, it was known in the family as the Willy Loman period; that is, like the salesman in Arthur Miller's play, the Mayor and I talked individually or in small groups to virtually every elected official and church leader, and to college presidents, a good many business executives, the social service community, and, above all, the neighborhood leaders of the Hispanic and the African-American communities. The upshot was a fragile consensus that the Austin Project ought to be tried. Dropouts from school were reaching an alarming level, prison expenditures were rising, and the inner city was deteriorating; and the gulf between the Anglo community and the minority communities was deepening.

Second, statisticians were at work in the university and in the excellent Auditor's Department of the City of Austin documenting the costs of inner city unemployment and poverty (at least $390 million per annum) and the fact that the bulk of social expenditures was going to damage control rather than prevention.

Third, these interim months were used to assemble a small volunteer task force and a board of directors of about fifty covering a wide range of the Austin community.

Thus, when the announcement was made of the Austin Project on May 6, 1992, we were ready to go.

In four months the all-volunteer task force of about fourteen produced a strategy and a First Phase Plan of some 350 pages which it laid before the directors on September 8, 1992.[8]

The task force was a strong-minded crew of extremely varied background and experience. It embraced three experts on young children, a former acting police chief with thirty years experience as an officer of the law, a doctor who was expert on both pediatrics and adolescent sexuality, five public officials, and academic experts of one kind or another. We were able to come to agreement around the five principles set out and write a first-phase plan that, we hoped would produce a turn in Austin's affairs in (say) five years and would level the psychological, income, employment, and educational barrier across I-35[9] in a generation's time—I-35 being in fact and in symbol the rough dividing line in Austin.

The Meeting of December 13, 1993

By December 13, 1993, on the basis of fifteen months of practical experience, the task force of TAP presented to the board of directors an operational plan that set forth a linked community-neighborhood strategy for the time ahead, a clear cut role for TAP in the neighborhoods, and a strategy for financing the enterprise. We were, in short, clear enough about the nature of our job to attempt to fulfill the third injunction, "Investment in prevention elevated to match the scale of the problems to which it is addressed."

I would underline a curious fact which may (or may not) apply to other innovational exercises. Those who carried out TAP's operational plan were the same individuals who wrote it. As operators of a plan in which they were catalysts, not service providers, they established networks which came to include literally hundreds of people who shared in their domain, the main tenets of the strategy.

A Linked Community-Neighborhood Strategy

First, we decided, in close working cooperation with the City of Austin, Travis County, and the Austin Independent School District (AISD), to supplement what might be called our community strategy with a systematic neighborhood strategy. The latter was foreshadowed by the city's Self-Reliant Neighborhood Plan, by widening collaboration of public and private agencies with neighborhood organizations in Dove Springs in recent months, and earlier by the discussion on neighborhoods in Chapter 8 of our First Phase Plan of September 1992. Martin Gerry, who in mid-1993 was taken on as executive director of the project, also was responsible for the planning of the neighborhood work and the initial contacts with the neighborhoods.

What is now envisaged is a wider and more systematic effort in five neighborhoods, engaging both public and private agencies. The City of Austin will concentrate on the underserved areas in northeast and southeast Austin. TAP's participation in that effort is proposed to focus mainly on portions of the Blackshear, Campbell, and Zavala areas, which constitute the heart of the inner city and a high proportion of its social pathology.

Stripped to essentials, TAP's neighborhood strategy had four institutional roots: maternal and child care centered on clinics devoted to these aims; early care—including educational reform centered on the elementary school system; youth opportunity centers which would provide a wide range of services designed to keep the young people on track to good jobs as opposed to the life of the streets; and local centers devoted to paths to work and the professions. These neighborhood enterprises were designed to strengthen families and to give substance to these critical disadvantaged neighborhoods. They would be fully backed by the community-wide enterprises dealing with the various phases of childhood and the whole complex reaching from school entrance to the workforce and the professions.

The plan for the neighborhood programs has been extensively described in three TAP documents.[10] Here is how that role was initially defined:[11]

Partnership in development is, indeed, possible; but economic and social progress cannot go forward without the assumption of responsibility by those who wish to progress. Such authentic partnership obviously requires that those who live in the neighborhoods play an important role in planning programs designed to deal with their problems. . . .

Ultimately, perhaps the most important result of the neighborhood programs could be a growing sense among their men, women, and children that increased control over their destiny is possible as well as dignified partnership with all sectors of the Austin community.

THE COMMUNITY-WIDE FUNCTIONS OF THE AUSTIN PROJECT

The December 13 meeting of the board of directors also reviewed the community-wide functions of the project:

- To define a strategy of preventive investment which, if implemented, would radically reduce the current abnormally high levels of social pathology in Austin.
- To persuade the Austin community to adopt such a strategy.
- To develop plans, in increasing detail, to implement that strategy.
- To play a catalytic role, working with both public and private institutions, to implement the projects and policies the strategy requires, including the generation of external funding. TAP is not and, in our view, should never become a service provider.

With respect to the diffusion and acceptance of the strategy of preventive investment, it is probably fair to say we have had some success, although the hard facts of rapidly mounting prison costs and of a skilled labor shortage may have accomplished more than the logic and rhetoric of TAP's argument. In any case the actual allocation of public resources has moved toward support for healthy child development and widening the paths to work and the professions. The following specific community-wide enterprises are under way in which the Austin Project is significantly involved.

Healthy Child Development

This work, which has been designated by the Austin City Council a priority area, requires intimate collaboration among public and private agencies and institutions throughout the Austin community. Members of TAP's task force chair four such sharply focused collaborative units.

Linda Welsh: Perinatal Coalition (prenatal care and the child's first year)
Peggy Pryor: Immunization/Wellness
Emily Vargas Adams: Shared Information System (SIS)
Jeannette Watson: Early Care and Education (being formed)

The following notes are designed merely to suggest the range and direction of their work.

Perinatal Coalition

- A planning work group is developing a strategic plan (including funding requirements) to increase early access to perinatal care and improved birth outcomes.
- A special group is designing a Memorandum of Understanding with the State of Texas which will permit medicaid funds to be used for case management.
- The program of the Perinatal Coalition will also coordinate closely with the Immunization/Wellness Task Force as well as the neighborhood programs as they unfold.
- KLRU-TV and the Austin *American Statesman* have worked in concert to heighten public awareness of the critical importance of prenatal care and early childhood and to provide educational materials.

Immunization/Wellness Task Force

• A steering committee has been established for this task force that includes some forty public and private service providers: Dr. Donna Bacchi, Dr. Robert Bernstein, Marie Jones, Rafael Quintanilla, and Diana Resnik; chaired by Peggy Davis Pryor of TAP.

The Immunization/Wellness Task Force (IWTF) started its community-wide, long-term efforts with Austin Immunization Week (AIW), April 23–30. During this week twenty-three public and private sites were open on weekends and in evening hours to provide free, walk-in immunizations. At the end of the week, 1,880 children and family members had received free immunizations at the sites during the publicized hours. Several hundred more were screened to ensure up-to-date immunization status. In addition, increased demand for immunizations has been reported throughout the regular city clinics.

Over four hundred volunteers worked to educate and publicize AIW and to assist at clinic sites. Intensive and extended media coverage was provided by all major and minority news sources. Neighborhood walks and door-to-door outreach were conducted in several zip code areas.

The success of the AIW efforts have served not only to educate and increase awareness of the problem but also to solicit ongoing involvement of community members with the task force. The task force has collaboratively created an Immunization Action Plan to the year 2000 for Travis County which defines action steps for private and public health care givers, community based organizations, and schools, as well as the structure and role of the task force.

The task force envisages a broader future role in helping the community come to understand the importance of preventive health care for children and to act on that principle. It views the immunization program as a route to this wide field of action and is drawing up practical plans to move in this direction. In that spirit it has formulated a longer-run immunization plan for Austin/Travis County with targets set to the year 2000, underpinned by a better tracking system than is now available.

The Shared Information (SIS) Task Force

The basic goal of the Shared Information System (SIS) is to share information among public and private nonprofit agencies, hospitals, clinics, schools, churches, and others to enhance the functioning and availability of health and human services. The potential components of the SIS include:

• Interactive resource directory of health and human service information;
• Automated intake, case management, and referral; and
• Interagency communications link to facilitate referrals, shared case management, and integrated service provision.

The task force, now including over thirty public and private agencies, conducted an initial survey which revealed a strong interest in the automated intake, referral, and communications system on the part of most agencies contacted. Agencies whose program participants would profit from an integrated system were especially interested in serving as pilot sites. Some concern was expressed about confidentiality, but new and effective security methods which enable the limited sharing of data should permit the sensitive handling of these important matters.

In July 1993, the planning group of the SIS prepared an initial outline of a funding proposal to move strategic and program planning forward which will e taken up in the larger Austin/Travis County system which TAP hopes to move forward in the course of 1994.

Early Care and Education Task Force: Status Report

The Austin Child Care Council has begun planning for the establishment of an Early Care and Education Task Force in collaboration with the Austin Project. The task force will deal with child care and development from the age of two through the adjustment to the early grades of elementary school.

The three active task forces include 30–40 public and private agencies. The following list of agencies participating in the Perinatal Coalition illustrates the unifying potential of this method: Any Baby Can; Austin Child Care Council; Austin Independent School District Health Services; Austin Travis County Health Department–WIC, Public Health; Austin Travis County Pediatric Home Care; Blackstock Family Health Center; Brackenridge Hospital; Capital Area Easter Seals; CEDEN Family Resource Center; Child, Incorporated; Children's Hospital Specialty Care; CIDC; Communities in Schools; Community Advocates for Teens and Parents; Community Representatives; Creative Rapid Learning Center; Del Valle ISD PEP Program; Homespun-ECI; Lutheran Social Services; March of Dimes; Marywood Maternity Services; MHMR Infant Parent Program; NHIC; P.R.I.D.E.; PCA Health Plans; People's Community Clinic; Planned Parenthood; Public Health Region I; Seton East Clinic; Seton Hospital; Seton Northwest Teen Center; St. David's Hospital; TDH WIC Program; TDHS–Coordinated Care; Teenage Parent Council; Texas Department of Health; Travis County Human Services; University of Texas–Department of Special Education, Department of Human Ecology; School of Nursing. This grouping of public and private social service agencies is no small thing. It represents a long-sought recognition that the Austin Project is not a competitor of the social service agencies, but a unifier. It is now quite natural that Austin Project task force members should chair these four groups.

Although TAP is not formally involved, work on healthy child development in Austin will be significantly strengthened by the doubling of capacity of the People's Community Clinic and by the expansion of Head Start already underway.

TAP's role in strengthening the work of AISD and the A+ Coalition's efforts to bring to bear modern technology in the education system evidently belongs in the following section (*Paths from School to the Work and*

Professional Life). It should be noted, however, that accelerated learning methods with the use of computers in the classroom have produced promising results in a few Austin elementary schools[12]; and such schools can help avoid the often traumatic letdown of children as they make the transition from kindergarten or Head Start to early years in the public school system. On the principle of continuity, the successful accelerated-learning elementary school is the appropriate link between healthy child development and entrance on a successful journey to the workforce and professions.

Paths from School to Work and Professional Life

The following brief notes suggest the complex pattern of associations in which this work moves forward with the public school system, the community college, the City of Austin, Austin's colleges and universities, private nonprofit agencies concerned with education, and the private business sector.

A Mobile Manufacturing Technology Laboratory

TAP made its operational debut on the Austin scene in an unlikely way. At the suggestion of George Kozmetsky and with substantial support from his family foundation, TAP helped finance and transferred to AISD a mobile manufacturing technology laboratory developed by National Center for Manufacturing Sciences. It contains state-of-the-art computers, a robot, and computer-controlled machine tools. Traveling from one middle school to another for two-to-three week periods, it permits students to carry out preplanned, hands-on experiments. Its larger purpose is to demonstrate to students at an early stage that they can handle high-tech manufacturing equipment and thereby widen their vision of the realistic options open to them in the future.

The 36-foot van is now completing its first rounds of Austin's middle schools. From all accounts the students and teachers are enthusiastic. TAP is developing plans to buy a second mobile van devoted to the electronics industry.

Career Academies

As of 1992 AISD had two magnet schools (academies): one in Science, the other in liberal arts. TAP in association with AISD is developing a series of academies directly linked to jobs in particular fields or the professions. We are intent that students maintain up to the time of final decision the flexibility to enter the workforce from secondary school or proceed to college.

The first new academy TAP helped foster is devoted to training in health care with support from Austin's hospitals. It opened in September 1992 with twenty-five students enrolled at Crockett High School.

Planning and development move forward on a second academy addressed to Technology and the Performing Arts. This will embrace a middle school as well as a high school. This academy is supported by the Performing Arts Center and faculty of the University of Texas.

Other academies are likely to develop as a result of the apprenticeship program described below.

Tech-Prep

TAP's Secretary-Treasurer Robert Rutishauser also serves as Executive Director of Tech-Prep in Austin, a linking of a high school curriculum with two years focused on technical training in the community college. With formal state approval achieved, this program is about to gain momentum.

Youth Apprenticeships and Work-Based Learning

Under the leadership of the City Council a task force has been formed to develop an industry driven apprenticeship program. The City Council appropriated $230,000 for use in this fiscal year to get a program of work site learning opportunities underway in Austin, and a plan to that effect was presented to the Council on April 27.

The principal recommendation was the establishment of a Construction Gateway Pilot Training Program which will provide ten weeks of training to qualify up to thirty participants for entry level and apprenticeship positions. This program was developed by a group led by Frank Peters and which included representatives from the Associated Builders and Contractors, Associated General Contractors, Austin Building Trades Council, Texas Capital Area Builders, Austin Community College, AISD, Del Valle ISD, SER (Service, Education, Redevelopment) Jobs for Progress Inc., PIC (Private Industry Council), and several local companies. This was a truly remarkable group to reach an operating consensus. The presentation included data showing the benefits of partnership, as the private sector is making significant contributions of resources to supplement those from the city.

This Construction Gateway program will be supported by two complementary efforts: (1) a summer program to qualify ten AISD and Del Valle teachers to teach the ABC (Associated Builders and Contractors) curriculum this fall, and (2) a construction industry awareness program for twelve to twenty high school students this summer. These are starting on a small scale and will be expanded as experience is gained.

We would underline the great importance we attach to this linkage in its own right and as a precedent. There is every reason to believe that Austin will experience a powerful construction boom over the next decade and perhaps beyond. The boom will be dependent on the expansion of plant as opposed to the transient tax breaks of the 1980s. The conversion of Bergstrom Air Force Base to a commercial airport and the conversion of Mueller Airport to some combination of industrial, commercial, and housing use will cost something like a billion dollars over the next ten years. In addition, decisions have already been made to expand industrial capacity, requiring further construction outlays of at least two billion dollars. The multiplier effects of a sustained construction boom on this scale are likely to keep the average unemployment level in Austin low for a decade at least.

Average unemployment in Austin is now under 4.5 percent. But unemployment remains high in our disadvantaged neighborhoods: perhaps 10 percent on average, 20–30 percent for young men 16–19 years of age. There is little doubt that this chronically high level of unemployment is a major—some believe a dominant—cause of the high level of social pathology in these neighborhoods.

It is our conviction, therefore, that a major task for the Austin community is to assure that the occasion of this boom be used to bring down permanently the level of unemployment in Austin's disadvantaged neighborhoods. This requires, however, that a maximum number of the unemployed in these neighborhoods be trained and otherwise rendered job-ready. Then a "hire Austin policy" would be useful and appropriate.

The place to start is clearly with a training program linked to the jobs opened up by the conversion of Bergstrom. To this end the substantial but fragmented vocational training capacity of Austin must be unified and sharply focused on the larger task ahead. TAP is addressing itself to this problem and is in touch with those charged with the Bergstrom conversion.

Summer Finance Institute

Members of the Austin Project have been working with local financial institutions led by Smith Barney Shearson on a Summer Finance Institute. Each participating financial institution will have one or two interns for seven weeks this summer. The program is aimed at talented juniors from low- and moderate-income families. The students will be together for a seminar one afternoon each week and will spend the rest of the week working at their sponsoring organization.

A Community Bank

One of the first initiatives of TAP, even before our First Phase Plan was completed in September 1992, was to set in motion work on a development bank. With the city government taking the lead, the development bank is at last now moving into operation, with capital supplied by a consortium of thirteen local banks. Within TAP the bank has been viewed as a critical part of a concerted program to stimulate and support entrepreneurship in the disadvantaged neighborhoods—a program including a business academy, links to the Austin Incubator, and support for young entrepreneurs from retired executives. The University of Texas Business School is firmly committed to assisting such an effort and already has a program in being. With the bank in place, headed by Tim Stack, an experienced banker dedicated to urban development, TAP is activating this whole program which, among other things, should reinforce our neighborhood programs.

Technology Support for Education

AISD has allocated an additional $900,000 to expand computer-assisted learning, and TAP is working with AISD to expand the supply of used but usable computers.

Computer Recycling Program

The Travis High School repair and recycling program, initially a volunteer enterprise, has been moved from an after-school activity into the regular daily schedule. Junior Achievement is considering taking over this program and scaling it up eventually to include all AISD high schools.

University of Texas

President Berdahl has launched a program to raise the retention rate of minority students at the University of Texas, as well as a broader program to explore ways of bringing the university into larger and more effective support of urban development in Austin and beyond. On March 3, 1994, Professor Frank Bean presented to the president a committee report outlining the functions the university might perform with respect to Austin and the state. The UT system has been developing in parallel an urban policy for the state which was outlined to the TAP Task Force on May 19, 1994.

URBAN FINANCING: A POLICY IN TRANSITION

Clearly we knew enough about the job to conceive of 1994 as the year of beginning to go to scale—that is, to fulfill in the time ahead the criterion of matching the scale of the investment to the scale of the problem.

The financing campaign we intend to launch in 1994 will take place in a context of what appears to be an important transition: a transition from external financing of discrete urban projects to the financing by consortia of comprehensive urban plans, based on agreed criteria.

With certain exceptions (for example, block grants), both government and the private foundations have dealt with urban problems by providing categorical grants—that is, resources were provided for narrowly specified purposes. These grants supported specific projects unrelated to any coherent, comprehensive urban plan. In fact, it has been obvious for some time that America's inner cities constitute an interconnected system, caught up in a vicious circle, yielding a self-reinforcing sequence of damaged children, a public education system incapable of preparing youth for the modern workforce, and a retreat of the young to the life of the streets and its related pathology: dropouts, teenage pregnancy, drugs, crime, and so forth. It is a system whose final output is a fantastic increase in prisons and prisoners, and a workforce incapable in the long run of sustaining America's position in an increasingly competitive high-tech world. Along the way a variety of preventive projects were financed and showed promise; but, again, there was virtually no effort to scale them up to the size of the problem to which they were addressed.

The categorical, project approach contributed to this outcome because it could not come to grips systematically with the ultimate driving forces in this degenerating system. This approach was inevitably driven to mitigating symptoms of the degeneration, of which the expansion of prisons is the most flagrant result.

There is now evidence that this approach to financing urban projects may have begun to change—at least in the minds of a good many public and private officials. As a program which has stood from the beginning for a comprehensive urban plan committed to prevention, TAP has been drawn into national discussions centered on the need for change—for example, a Robert Woods Johnson meeting in Princeton on July 30–31, 1993, a meeting in Washington sponsored by the National Academy for Public Administration (NAPA), and two other national institutions to which an Austin team was invited, headed by the Mayor. The June 1994 meeting in Chicago of NAPA was devoted in part to urban problems and plans. Most important of all, the federal government appears to be moving towards policies which (i) encourage and provide general criteria for good comprehensive urban plans; and (ii) which provide a consortium approach to financing such plans by bringing together in financial support, after careful review, the major departments and agencies. TAP was invited to participate in such a review which took place on March 4, 1994, before the Domestic Policy Council.

Although this is not the occasion to elaborate, U.S. foreign aid made a similar transition from a diffuse project approach to an international consortium approach in support of national plans starting in 1958. Under the leadership of then-Senator John F. Kennedy and his Republican colleague Senator John Sherman Cooper, a Senate resolution led to a consortium of Japan, Western Europe, and the United States chaired by the World Bank in support of the Indian Second Five Year Plan. That pattern led to at least sixteen such consortia. It has persisted to the present, although a great many developing countries no longer require foreign aid. The donors have maintained control over the use of their funds by a system of detailed annual review in which the year's results were examined against the standards initially agreed.

TAP's Proposed Financing Strategy

In this setting of transition in national urban policy, we plan to present in some detail to about a dozen national foundations our development plan as a whole. We would be pleased to receive support either for the plan as a whole or for some component in which they have a particular interest. At the present time most (but not necessarily all) foundations will be inclined, we believe, to support specific projects in areas where they have developed cumulative expertise—for example, child care, education, vocational training, bringing school dropouts or teenage mothers back to school and the workforce, and so on.

Should the federal government adopt a consortium approach focused on urban plans, it is possible—by no means certain—that the foundations might also move in that direction.

It may be useful, therefore, to share with the reader the vision of an urban financing policy and procedure which we have informally shared with some government and foundation officials.

1. The cities would formulate comprehensive urban plans, varying according to their unique circumstances but incorporating, with heavy emphasis, an increase in investment in prevention, and a maximum concerted effort by the community as a whole.

2. After careful initial review, the federal (and state) governments would agree to contribute a fixed level of total funding (corrected for inflation) in support of the plan for, say, ten years. Performance under the arrangement would be reviewed annually by the relevant public and private institutions.

3. Savings due to investment in prevention will be retained and plowed back into further preventive investment. The time lag between preventive investment and results will be short in some cases—for example, in the effect on low-weight births of inducing pregnant women to accept regular treatment in prenatal clinics in the first trimester. The same will be true of savings from immunization, or from a substantial decline in unemployment on a wide range of social pathologies. The time lag in some cases will be longer, that is, the effect of a good Head Start experience on the high school dropout rate.

One possible mission of the private foundations, acting in consortium against the background of a plan they regard as sensible, and with the commitment of federal and state authorities to steady funding, might well be to cover these time lags. Private foundation support would then spike at the early stage of the enterprise and then decline after, say, five years as preventive investment takes hold and yields its results. Since foundation money is and should be "soft," the arrangement might be attractive to foundations almost always gravely concerned whether the projects they fund will be picked up for consequent public funding.

It should finally be noted that if foundations come to cooperate in consortium arrangements, their respective contributions to the aggregate support effort could still maintain continuity with their traditional sectoral interests— that is, health, education, neighborhood development. That kind of specialization within agreed total support for a given country plan characterized, for example, the contributions of the several agencies supporting the Alliance for Progress in the second half of the 1960s—that is, the World Bank, IMF, the Inter-American Development Bank, and AID.

We concluded that this is the kind of scheme we should like to explore while also pursuing resources in terms of more traditional financing via categorical and project grants.

The Return to the Foundations and the White House Meeting of March 4, 1994

Against this background, on February 15, 1994, we laid out our plans to begin the process of going to scale before the three foundations which had mainly supported us from mid-1993: the Carnegie Corporation, the Annie E. Casey Foundation, and the Robert Wood Johnson Foundation. We shall learn their response in the months ahead.

On March 4, at their request, we presented the Austin Project to the agencies concerned with urban policy, chaired by William Galston of the Domestic Policy Council.

He had instructed us to do three things: to write a paper of not more than ten pages for general circulation; to attach as many appendixes as we wished on aspects of our program; and to bring a delegation of responsible representatives of the Austin community. My deputy Martin Gerry and I were the only task force members present.

The concluding passages of our ten-page paper are worth repeating here.

Support from the Clinton Administration

In order to proceed with the work which has been described above, the Austin Project requires assistance from the federal government in three specific areas.

First, on or before June 30 of this year, the City of Austin will submit an application to the President's Community Enterprise Board (through the Department of Housing and Urban Development) requesting that areas of Austin (including the three so-called ASCEND pilot neighborhoods) be designated as an "empowerment zone" under the Empowerment Act of 1993. ASCEND's strategy for accomplishing the economic and social transformation of Austin's low-income neighborhoods will be a core element of the strategic plan that accompanies that application. The designation of low-income neighborhoods as an Empowerment Zone would greatly aid and undoubtedly accelerate our overall efforts. Your careful consideration of the application which is submitted by the City of Austin will be greatly appreciated.

Second, the successful implementation of several important elements of the ASCEND comprehensive strategy and of ASCEND's long-term approach to shifting the focus of funding to prevention, depends upon the approval of waivers sought under various federal programs. Indeed, our ability to raise 'investment funding' from private foundations for the model-prototype phase of the strategy will hinge on their perception of whether the federal government will look favorably on the waiver requests that will be submitted on our behalf. An expression by the administration of its interest in and general support of the waiver strategy which we are proposing is essential to our continued progress.

Third, we propose that the administration (through an Executive Order or through coordinated actions taken by individual cabinet departments) establish a priority for the award of grants under a large number of discretionary grant programs for local jurisdictions which have taken serious steps to establish a comprehensive program to accomplish the economic and social transformation of low-income urban neighborhoods. We believe such a priority would advance the principles which the President enunciated in his May 7, 1993, statement submitting the Empowerment Act of 1993 to the Congress. It would greatly assist the work of local communities, such as Austin, which are trying to create systems, where only uncoordinated arrays of federal and state programs currently exist.

We approach the Federal government with an acute sense of the fiscal problem the country now confronts. We believe that each of the actions which we are requesting is within the current authorities of the Executive Branch. None would appear to require either legislative authorization or increased budget expenditure.

A National Conclusion

The Austin Project was never targeted to Austin alone—much as we cherish the future of our hometown. No member of the board of directors, no senior member of the task force failed to understand that we aimed to produce a replicable model for the nation. As the original paper said. "The concept outlined here will almost certainly have to be proved viable on a local basis before a President and Congress, . . . and the other relevant institutions in American society commit themselves to it."

Therefore, we have asked how much it would cost roughly to set all our cities in the right direction as measured by bringing the all-too-familiar social pathology down to the average in the community. If all the affected American cities were to formulate and execute plans which roughly conformed to the principles of the Austin Project, one comes to a cost of about $125 billion a year over a ten or fifteen year period, to be shared by local, state, and federal funds. This amount of money represents about two percent of our current annual GNP (approximately $6 trillion), a figure which is now rising at about $180 billion per annum, cleared of inflation.

What do these preliminary, rough, conservative estimates mean? First, as annual estimates, they are not uniform. The steady-state figures are considerably less than the peak figures (that is, those applicable to the pilot neighborhoods). Evidently, adjustments to these estimates will have to be made at least annually.

Second, none of these estimates takes into account the savings envisaged. Savings in the form of increased city gross domestic product, increased revenues to the public institutions of the city, reductions in the costs of safety net expenditures, and decreases in expenditures for public safety and prisons are anticipated. It now costs Austin approximately $390 million per year to contain the city's social pathology, while the bill for prisons expand inordinately. (A bond issue for prisons of $65 million will be presented to voters this year by Travis County.)

Assuming that the costs of urban development plans are shared among local, state, and federal governments, it is evident that a consortium approach to the reduction and elimination of the economic and social pathologies of the urban core is both possible and cost-effective.

The response to our presentation was extremely positive, but it would be wrong to draw conclusions now about the outcome of our submission to the foundations or to the Domestic Policy Council. In short, we do not know whether or not the generosity of the foundations and the policy of the federal and state governments will permit the Austin Project to begin to go to scale in 1994.

CONCLUSIONS

In general, I conclude that the strategy of prevention rather than remediation is the right strategy for the American cities; that the five principles set out for the Austin Project are the correct principles around which to build an urban policy; and that in Austin, Texas, the distinction between prevention and remediation has bitten quite deep.

The immediate goal enunciated by our political leaders on May 6, 1992, was to achieve the beginning of subsidence in the symptoms of social pathology within (say) five years of the beginning of operation of the Austin Project.

In calculating the time necessary to reach our immediate goal, expectation and hope are a large part of the equation. We obviously do not know when the turn-around in Austin's fortunes will begin, nor are we currently in a position to predict with certainty the point in time when the ultimate goal will be achieved (i.e., when the average level of social pathology will be constant across Austin's neighborhoods). Perhaps reversal of the current trend and movement toward the ultimate goal will come sooner than we expect because of new hopes stirred by our work in the neighborhoods. Perhaps, by demonstrating clear paths to gainful employment, we will achieve a marked reduction in dropouts across the community even before our service strategy is fully implemented. Perhaps this same positive spiral will be generated by our work to ensure the development of healthy children, to improve family functioning, or to strengthen the physical and social fabric of our neighborhoods. Most likely, it will be all of these things.

But once a clear turning point has been reached, and progress to our ultimate goal has become steady and evident along a wide front, the availability of both public and private investment capital could be greatly expanded throughout the nation in consequence of TAP's demonstration that our approach can be cost effective—and not an impossible dream.

But we have found out something quite firm in Austin. On the one hand, the conventional instruments of governance cannot by themselves carry out the revolutionary changes required to achieve the goals enunciated on May 6, 1992. The private sector, the colleges and universities, the religious community, the private social services, and, above all, the Hispanic and African-American neighborhoods must play their part. On the other hand, without the consistent leadership and support of the responsible political officials, no progress is possible in the community. In Austin that bonding of the community and the political leaders has taken place to an important degree.

That, I think, is the greatest lesson thus far of the Austin Project.

NOTES

1. Quoted in W. W. Rostow, "The Austin Project, 1989-1993: An Innovational Exercise in Comprehensive Urban Development," unpublished essay prepared for the Institution for Social and Policy Studies, Seminar Series on Inner City Poverty, Yale University, Fall 1993, p. 6.

2. An interesting example is given on p. 8 of the "Manufacturing Technology" article, special survey, in the *Economist* of March 5-11, 1994. The chart entitled Front-Loaded shows "Concept Design," "Concept Verification," "Full Scale Development," "Production," and "Use" set against percent of life cycle cost on the vertical axis, life-cycle phase on the horizontal. This conforms, in the case of the Austin Project, to the original paper and "concept" (1989–1991). The making and testing of the plan (1992–1994) and the full scale development planned for 1994 are described at the end of this paper.

3. A not irrelevant illustration of this four-phase, ongoing process is the work of the land grant universities in relation to American agriculture. Phase one was the basic research on soils, plants, animals, and so forth conducted at those universities. Phase two yielded from this basic research new fertilizers, seeds, and improvements in animal husbandry. In phase three these inventions were brought to the farms by the county agents. In phase four the practical lessons of success and failure were brought back to the scientific laboratories of the land-grant universities to stimulate fresh research. President Robert Berdahl of the University of Texas at Austin has several times related the challenge confronting contemporary American universities with respect to the nation's urban problem to the historic role of the land-grant colleges with respect to agricultural productivity.

4. Martin Gerry has summarized his more precise, disaggregated study of this matter in the following terms: "Of total public expenditures for children services in the United States over the last 5 years, approximately 60% have been allocated for maintenance, 30% for treatment, and 10 percent for prevention. Well over 1/2 of the public funds expended for maintenance are spent on costs which are clearly preventable." Martin H. Gerry, "Estimated annual public expenditures for children's services in the United States during the period 1990–1992" (unpublished paper for the Danforth Foundation. Austin, Texas, July 1993).

5. Let me cite as an example of fragmentation and little synthesis a volume containing a series of admirable, highly professional essays: James B. Steinberg, David W. Lyon, and Mary C. Vaiana (eds.) *Urban America, Policy Choices for Los Angeles and the Nation* (Santa Monica: Rand, 1992).

6. This paper, written jointly by W. W. Rostow and Elspeth D. Rostow, was published with several appendixes, under the title "The Austin Project" in

Proceedings of the American Philosophical Society, vol. 136, no. 3 (1992), pp. 355–409.

7. Ibid., p. 358.

8. We also produced a detailed plan for young children: *An Investment Plan for the Young: The Austin Project, First Phase.*

9. I-35 is the North-South federal highway which roughly divides the more affluent and less affluent districts of Austin.

10. *Report of the Task Force to Board of Directors,* December 13, 1993; *Interim Report of the Austin Project for the Period June, 1993–December 31, 1993,* February 15, 1994; and *A Report to the Domestic Policy Council from the Austin Project,* March 4, 1994.

11. Rostow and Rostow, "The Austin Project." Also see Chapter 8, p. 255, of TAP's *First Phase Plan.*

12. The lead article in the August–September 1993 issue of the national magazine *Teaching Pre K-8* (pp. 41–48) was devoted to one of these schools, Langford. The title of the article is "Wouldn't It Be Wonderful . . . If All Schools Were Like This!"

2

Telemedicine: Its Place on the Information Highway

Frederick D. Williams and Mary Moore

This chapter provides a brief interdisciplinary overview of the salient features of modern telemedicine. Most of the generalizations we make are based on the present researchers' interests and experiences in field studies of telemedicine applications, often with a focus on processes of adoption or the diffusion of technological innovations.

Healthcare is a major candidate for improvement in any vision of the kinds of "information highways" that are now being visualized. The concept of telemedicine captures much of what is developing in terms of technology implementation. In most cases, there are implications for commercialization. Yet even with the breakup of AT&T in 1984, the continuing dead hand of regulation has discouraged business entry into dramatic new telecommunications services because of the threat of government interference or litigation among competing business interests (Williams 1991). Now with the shift of federal interest to telecommunications growth as a major economic goal, we can expect an unleashing of investment in this area. In this period it will be important to maintain a priority for public service applications of telecommunications, lest public interest applications like healthcare be left behind in the rush to build the information highway. A priority for telemedical applications is innovative policy making and the attitude that effective healthcare is good business not only for the population at large but for the many opportunities it offers for business entrepreneurship and technology transfer.

A BIRD'S EYE VIEW OF "TELEMEDICINE"

Some Basics

Although telemedicine may have a variety of specific definitions, depending chiefly on who is writing about it, the concept typically refers to uses of telecommunications technologies to facilitate healthcare delivery. Telemedicine dates back to the 1920s, when radio was used to link public health physicians standing watch at shore stations to assist ships at sea that had medical emergencies. Much later came the large-scale demonstrations in telemedicine involving the ATS-6 satellite projects in the 1970s, wherein paramedics in remote Alaskan and Canadian villages were linked with hospitals in distant towns or cities (see Hudson 1990).

"Medical informatics" is often used in conjunction with modern applications of telemedicine (Kuhn 1988). While the former generally refers to a wide range of information technologies—that is, specialized computing systems, computer work-stations, database designs, software—used in medical practices, the latter refers to the uses of telecommunications to distribute such services. Many telemedical applications include informatics components, making it often difficult to separate the two.

Today there are assorted specific projects representing a wide variety of telemedical or combined informatics applications. Examples of these applications include:

- networking of large healthcare groups, multicampus linking of hospitals and research centers, linkages among rural health clinics and to a central hospital
- physician-to-hospital links for transfer of patient information, diagnostic consultations, patient scheduling, and research literature searches
- video program distribution for public education on healthcare issues
- use of video and satellite relay to train healthcare professionals in widely distributed or remote clinical settings
- transfer of diagnostic information such as electrocardiograms or X-rays
- videoconferencing among members of healthcare teams
- video links between patient and physician for diagnostic interview purposes
- capturing "grand rounds" on video for use in remote consultation or training
- instant access to, and aided search techniques for gathering, information from databases or electronic library collections

Benefits

Simply from the uses of telecommunications for distance-reducing or time-saving, telemedicine can offer many benefits. The following points are drawn from an analysis by Moore (1993a) of recent telemedicine projects.

Improved Access

Telemedicine can provide access to healthcare in previously unserved or underserved areas. These areas include both rural and inner city or barrio locations, which typically have a lower healthcare practitioner-to-population ratio. Access to specialty care is also improved in that those using telemedicine can use the services of specialty practitioners. For example, teleradiology services are often used to provide the services of a radiologist to many remote locations that do not have a local radiologist. Telemedicine can also accelerate diagnosis and treatment by reducing the time required for patients to be first seen by their family physician, then be referred to other locations, travel to those locations, receive specialty care, return home, and revisit their family physicians. With telemedicine, need for travel is reduced; and since the family physician is often present for the telemedicine consultation, the need to revisit the family physician after the consultation is obviated.

Traditionally, a fair amount of time may be required for patient records to be dictated, transcribed, and sent to referring physicians. After the traditional consultation, the referring physician must then dictate his or her own records and send them to the family physician requesting the consultation. This can become a problem; according to the Institute of Medicine, 30 percent of physicians could not access patients' records; 70 percent of hospital records were incomplete, and twenty-two people in hospitals depended on access to patient records at a given time. With telemedicine consultations the referring physician, consulting specialists, and patients often gather together for the consultation. Telemedicine services integrated with electronic medical records can further alleviate these problems by providing enhanced access to the records, and alerting those writing medical records to gaps in information or obvious inconsistencies identified through computerized validity checks (MacDonald and Barnett 1990).

Reduced Costs

One of the most obvious cost reductions is the reduced necessity for travel. Travel costs can apply to patients traveling for specialty care, or to healthcare professionals traveling for continuing education. Both of these services can be provided locally through telemedicine. Telemedicine can reduce costs by decreasing the duplication of services, technologies, and specialists. For example, one pathologist can provide services to a number of locations using telepathology. Rural physicians have been able to reduce the costs of emergency on-call services by using telemedicine. Two or more distantly located physicians have joined together to use telemedicine to provide emergency services, so that each physician does not have to be on call every single night in his or her own location. Instead, each physician takes a turn at being on call through telemedicine services. If emergencies take place that cannot be handled through telemedicine, the local physician is summoned for in-person care. During times of crisis or disaster when the need exceeds the number of physicians available at a location, telemedicine can provide remote physician supervision to paraprofessionals. Further cost reductions are available when healthcare is provided locally in rural hospitals rather than in specialty care centers. Small rural hospitals often have lower overhead costs due to the lack of specialty equipment, and they have lower personnel costs.

Reduced Isolation

Telemedicine has been shown to reduce professional isolation by providing peer and specialist contact for patient consultations and continuing education. Hartman and Moore (1992) found that 76 percent of those physicians, 92 percent of nurses, and 88 percent of allied health professionals participating in telemedicine continuing-education programs reported that their sense of professional isolation was reduced. Not only was their access to continuing education increased but their participation in the programs allowed them a sense of closer contact with colleagues in other locations.

Although many technologies may provide the technical accuracy needed for telemedical diagnosis and treatment, when reduced isolation is the goal, Boor et al. (1981) reported that color, full motion video is critical: "[A]nything short of full-duplex color telecommunications would be viewed as sub optimal for the health professional user. This format allowed the closest replication of the face-to-face communication between colleagues in consultations and between patients and physician, hence, would be, in effect an absolute requirement."

Improved Quality of Care

Telemedicine provides enhanced decision making through heretofore impractical collaborative efforts. These take place when the referring physician, the consulting physician, the patient, and the patient's family meet together through interactive video. Rarely in face-to-face medical care do encounters of this type take place. Instead the patient visits each physician in succession. Patient records may be lost in the process. Because physicians sometimes cannot read the records of other physicians, each visit may take place in isolation, without critical information on past diagnosis, treatment, and outcomes.

With telemedicine, patient visits to referring and consulting physicians can take place simultaneously, providing the synergy derived from a healthcare team approach. Since both physicians and the patient are often present, the patient can relate history and symptoms directly. The result is often greater patient involvement, increased knowledge, and enhanced compliance with treatment, as the patient becomes an active part of the patient-care team. In addition, Furtado (1982) reported social therapeutic applications of telemedicine, when patients who were hospitalized at great distance from their families were provided hospital visits through interactive television. Hartman and Moore (1992) described the potential positive impact on patient care and compliance of the simultaneous presence of the referring physician, the consulting physician, the patient, and the patient's family. Furthermore, the patient visit is frequently recorded on video and can be reviewed repeatedly if necessary. One further benefit to the quality of care occurs with telemedicine. Physicians have reported that quality of care is improved because they are educated by the consultations with specialty physicians, increasing their ability to treat similar cases in the future.

TELECOMMUNICATIONS ADVANCES

Although the "information highway" is a vague term, it does refer to enhancements in telecommunications, and many of these can expand the telemedicine benefits just described. Some of these enhancements represent transfer of advances from military applications, the coalescence of computing and telecommunications technologies over the past twenty-five years, and the burst in new and competitive services following the breakup of AT&T in 1984. There are also many opportunities for technology commercialization in the healthcare area.

The Public Switched Telephone Network

Modern telecommunications networks are both managed by computers (mainly the switches that route messages) and offer a wide range of linkages to computer services. In some respects, modern networks are increasingly taking on the character of giant distributed computing systems, as services from the latter are available to anyone who has access to the network. As computers become more ubiquitous in the network, we tend to call these networks intelligent. In telemedicine, for example, many new network-based services represent a telecommunications link to computer capabilities—that is, intelligent network applications. The largest and most accessible network is the public switched network that is operated mainly by telephone companies, local as well as long distance. The public network is a common carrier, so to speak; it is available to anyone or any organization that can afford to use it. Any information or message can be transmitted without the telecommunications company interfering with content.

Most of the telemedical services using the public network are traditional voice, facsimile (fax), or data transmissions. Because the original public network was designed with only intelligible voice transmission (voice grade) as a requirement, its capacity is limited in both signal complexity and speed. That your voice sounds a bit flat over the phone is an example of the limits of complexity, because the higher and lower frequency ranges of voice are not transmitted. A visible example of speed limitations is that if you connect your personal computer to voice-grade lines, such as to link with a service like Medline™ or connect to the Internet, you are severely restricted to slow data transmission rates (without very expensive modem connections, currently at 2400 baud, only a little faster than you can read). Of course, we do use the voice-grade network for many healthcare applications, including voice consultations and administration, faxing records, exchanging data in batches such as to download research reports from a medical information service, and to exchange billing data over an electronic network. For some years now, it has been possible to transmit electrocardiographic readings or other diagnostic data from a family physician's office or rural clinic to a specialist's laboratory or a distant hospital. Although it is possible to pack more into the voice-grade network, it is both technically and economically desirable to upgrade services.

The most important priority is to promote advances that improve the capacity of the public network and to make these services as easily available as today's dial tone. Enhancements have been bound up in local and federal telecommunication regulations that slow the process of network upgrades in order to keep the price of basic service low for the residential customer. You can purchase more telecommunications capacity (as with a T1 line for example, equivalent to twenty-four voice channels), but it comes at a price considerably above usual costs for traditional business lines. Thus, for example, the costs of maintaining a network of computers linked among several hospitals or medical centers may be as much for special telecommunications services as for operating the computers themselves. Another problem is that an organization desiring special telecommunications services may find it necessary to deal with different vendors in order to put together a single service. This process was so cumbersome in the south Texas area that a database guide to vendors and services, and especially the critical contact person in the company, was developed (Sung 1993).

Ideally, we will have a public network on which we can make a data or video call as easily as we now do a voice one. It should also greatly facilitate the availability of information services. Thus, for example, a patient in a rural Appalachian clinic could "visit" a specialist in Chicago via a high-definition video link, one sufficient for showing a recent X-ray image of lung damage and where the shared video images are of sufficient quality to convey a sense of personalness to the patient-physician exchange. Data service could be used to retrieve any published medical reference, including computer-based services that could provide alternative treatment protocols, given an input of symptoms.

There are, of course, many networks—government, military, multinational industry, financial—that remain private, secure, proprietary, and purposely isolated from public use. Not all telecommunications networks are publicly accessible, although they may operate on leased public lines. What we need is a wholesale upgrade of the public network. Some experts argue that this is the coming of an all digital network, called ISDN.

Integrated Systems Digital Network (ISDN)

In the plans of many telephone companies, the next major upgrade of the public switched network is the integrated systems digital network.[1] In this network, all traffic is digitally coded, which allows for more use of intelligent services as well as a substantial compression of signals so that traditional telephone lines have a much greater capacity. The advantage of this service to the customer is that several services can be operated simultaneously with a single call. For example, two medical researchers could confer by voice on the outcome of a study while sharing linked computer screens showing graphs of numerical results; a fax might be sent in the meantime on the same connection. If ISDN were available in the home, a patient could transmit information from a vital signs monitor while conferring by voice with a nurse in the physician's office. Reasonable quality (but not broadcast quality) video can be transmitted over ISDN, which could make patient interviewing or even psychological counseling more personal and could include visual information. The advantage of ISDN to the residential or business customer is that one call can connect a range of voice, data, and video alternatives, and even some combinations of those. A computer can be plugged in and dialed as easily as a voice call. In fact, we could see some type of communications terminal that combines voice, data, and video replace the traditional telephone.

The advantage to the nation's telecommunications companies is that a basic form of ISDN service does not require replacing all the existing telephone lines; it simply packs more information into them. However, new switching equipment is required, as are interface devices that connect the customer's residential or business equipment with the ISDN system (if the equipment does not already have that capability, which some now does).

Although in the last of the 1980s and early in the new decade we have seen increased availability of ISDN, there are still debates as to whether it will fully develop as the next version of the public network. Some industry watchers are betting that ISDN may be leap-frogged in favor of moving to a broadband network fully capable of switching high-quality video images (along with multiple voice channels, and relatively high-speed data transfer).[2] This may be among the reasons why we have not seen a burst of new ISDN-based technologies for telemedical applications.

Broadband Switched Network

Probably along with all of the publicity given to the coming of the information highway, you have seen examples of a residential customer interacting with a TV presentation like a game show or a news display that can be accessed via branching menus, or a school child doing math interactively on a home TV set. This is based on a telecommunications network with video channels having the capacity to send signals upstream to the cable company or whoever is disseminating the programs. Unlike your current cable service, this system will be digital, capable of transmitting high-definition TV images (roughly the same quality of a 35mm movie film) and will likely combine a wide variety of additional services, including optional telephones. That it can simultaneously provide mixes of voice, text, graphics, and moving image displays qualifies it as multimedia.

The current engineering, as well as business, thrusts in this area are able to offer dial-up multimedia services for the home, business, or school. The programming materials are stored in highly compressed digital form in video file servers that when accessed by the customer can download program material (like an exercise video) in a matter of seconds into the memory of a video receiver. One can then watch the presentation on one's own time schedule, and in some cases interact with it (like a computer program). In some services, one may be interacting directly with a very high-speed remote computer.

It is with interactive broadband and multimedia services that we will probably see the most visible changes in full-scale telemedical applications. High-definition television has many advantages in depicting details of patient appearance, or results of X-ray or ultrasound diagnostic images. Interactive multimedia also has numerous applications for training in medical settings, or fulfilling requests from physicians in widely diverse settings for treatment protocols, and other resource materials.

Multimedia patient records are another area of development (Stead and Hammond 1988). Take one example, say, a patient with a knee injury. The multimedia record would contain a brief video clip of knee movement. This is stored and repeated over the duration of the patient's recovery. Graphic records such as X-rays could be stored along with oral commentary. Hand-held digital communicators could be used for routine entry of verbal commentary or treatment guidance. Links to vital-signs monitors could feed information into the record. Although we now have the capability to do each different application, often with separate technologies, the time is approaching when single communications devices and their telecommunications links will easily accommodate multimedia services. The question in healthcare will be to identify priority areas of applications. There is also much potential for technology commercialization in this area.

Unlike ISDN, the nation's entire public network would have to be rebuilt for switched broadband. Although many advancements in telecommunications technologies build upon one another, as when ISDN can be added to the present network, the move to a fully switched broadband network is not a logical technological step beyond ISDN; it is a much different technology. Industry estimates of the costs of installing a national broadband network vary widely, to a total of as much as $100 billion. Given the limits to government funding of the last several decades and the political restrictions of high taxes, it is unlikely that the federal government can build the network. The former regional Bell companies, AT&T, and other large telecommunications providers assert that they can build it if given incentives, including freedom from regulation. But there are many serious questions—including, for example, that of where the nation's cable TV operators would fit into this picture, how to keep one or several companies from dominating overcontrol of the services (one of the worries with the aborted Bell Atlantic–Telecommunications, Inc. merger); and most of all, how universal availability of services to the entire population can be fostered. Public interest critics are already complaining that plans to build advanced services appear to focus mainly on wealthy areas of cities. Mainly by regulation, telephone services have become virtually universally available; and by regulation and advertising, so has television. Nobody is yet sure about the information highway—and that is a major barrier not only to growth but to assuring that services like healthcare will be a part of this development.

The Internet

The Internet is an interesting parallel telecommunications development compared to the services just described. Beginning in the early 1970s, the U.S. military and various universities began to link their computers, so that data and messages could be communicated among cooperating groups. An early network, ARPANET, was organized by the Advanced Research Projects Agency, a branch of the Department of Defense. An important requirement was to design a network over which computers with different operating systems could share information—a kind of communications standard. This network initiative expanded, eventually being promoted by the National Science Foundation (NSFNET), until finally the interlinking of a large number of networks by a standard known as Transmission Control Protocol/Internet Protocol (TCP/IP) allowed the worldwide growth of a more-or-less network of networks. This is essentially the Internet that has attracted so much attention in the 1990s.

The Internet is unusual for a number of reasons, the main one of which is that, unlike virtually all other major networks, it is not owned by any one entity. It is a cooperative arrangement primarily influenced by its educational, research, governmental, and a growing number of commercial users. By agreeing to a set of operating protocols, users of the Internet have developed many innovations for seeking out information from different databases accessible via the network, methods for sharing documents, and an explosively growing international e-mail system.

Already the Internet is popular among researchers who can readily use e-mail to share information, query one another, or simply communicate about common interests and needs. File transfer options can also be employed for distributing longer documents and reports. Remote medical sites that could not otherwise afford a special data network or extensive long-distance phone charges can use the Internet for management coordination. Also, as described below, file servers can be established for the storage and retrieval of medical information, publications, statistics, or reports.

One example of application is in our projects with the South Texas Health Research Center (STHRC), a unit of the University of Texas Health Science Center in San Antonio (a medical school). STHRC has gained a growing reputation as a repository for information important to healthcare needs, services, and issues regarding the U.S. Hispanic populations, beginning with its service area in south Texas. Although it would be advantageous to link all the hospitals, clinics, and training sites in south Texas in a sophisticated telecommunications network, the cost is prohibitive at this time. So are the costs of having all the dispersed units use long-distance telephone lines to link their desktop computers with STHRC. A shortcut to installing an interim service is to (1) create computer-stored files of the STHRC information often requested in the field, (2) install those files in an STHRC file server (essentially a central computer), (3) connect that STHRC server to the Internet with appropriate menus and file indexes, (4) encourage local clinics and other sites to link their desktop computers via local phone lines or state telecommunications lines to the nearest Internet access point, and (5) develop training so individual users in the field will know the few simple steps for connecting to STHRC via the Internet to request needed information or to exchange e-mail. Once in place, any person or organization worldwide who had access to the Internet could use information services from the South Texas Health Research Center, a specialist in Hispanic healthcare delivery.

Whether the Internet in some advanced version of its current form or in some other enhanced but largely open digital telecommunications network is widely available, many of the current practices and innovations will be the basis for product or service development. With a little patience, the Internet is a usable service for certain telemedical applications as of this writing; but importantly it is an inexpensive and easily available testbed for technology commercialization in telemedicine. There is already a growing array of software and service businesses for improving access to and use of the Internet. A main problem in looking ahead to further development of the Internet is that its operation is mainly subsidized by government grants, industry participation, and support by university computing centers. To survive, it will have to become more commercialized, and the challenge is in how to accomplish this without compromising its openness, democratic quality, lack of regulatory barriers, and attraction to entrepreneurship without high entry costs. There are also widely different thoughts on how or where revenue-producing components could be integrated into the Internet so it could become self supporting. Should there be subscriber and (sometimes) measured service costs as in the telephone business? Should commercial operators be taxed to support public services? Can advertising help to support it, or would it drastically deter further development of public service and other noncommercial uses? Finally, opinions differ widely on how the Internet might fit in with national initiatives for an information superhighway. Surely, the Internet has opened many opportunities for users in telemedicine, but further development will depend highly upon the direction of U.S. policy in advancing digital network services.

Mobility: Digital Radio Links

Advances in digital radio technology are leading to increased portability of terminals, services, and integration of broadcast and wired networks (like paging and voice telephone). Increased portability carries many locational or spatial implications, allowing for increased flexibility and decentralization. Achieving portability requires advances in terminal instruments capable of multimedia uses as well as independence from stationary power sources. One means for achieving portability is to have digital radio links to voice telephone, computer laptop terminals, palm-size terminals, and even fax machines. Increasingly this is called the development of a personal communications network (or PCN), and it is on the planning boards of many telecommunications vendors. There are at least two applications of digital radio services that are immediately relevant to telemedicine. One is the PCN (or PCS for service) mentioned above. This could offer many advantages for healthcare professionals working in the field. A digital terminal could not only provide immediate connections to the voice network but also make it easily possible to exchange text or numeric data or messages between the worker and the home clinic, hospital, or research center. A personal digital communicator could be used to access a specially formatted version of a patient's medical records, insurance eligibility, or even an on-the-spot treatment protocol. We can expect, too, that with medical services being improved for underserved populations, there will be a need for much gathering of field research data. Survey workers equipped with digital communicators could download computer-assisted interview questions, and then enter responses for immediate transmittal to a data collection center. Immediate information on the incidence of certain illnesses or use of immunization services by designated populations has traditionally been hampered by the slowness of survey research methods. With input from hand-held communications units, a survey can begin to generate results almost immediately. Individuals using these communicators can have personal electronic addresses that can locate them anywhere within range of the digital radio transmission–reception facilities.

Another application of digital radio is in the development of wireless information network facilities. This is where a medical campus, a research park, or any large building complex can be equipped for switching digital communications signals among all stationary or mobile units in the immediate area. This means, for example, that a medical researcher carrying a laptop computer or digital communicator can transfer data or messages while located anywhere in the immediate range of the facility—even from an automobile or ambulance. Given connections among wireless information networks, national or regional networks, and PCN networks, it will be increasingly possible to establish mobile dial-up voice, data, text, or simple image connections between any two individuals or stations using the services. We can expect that at some point, translation, speech recognition, and speech interpretation services (all discussed below) could be added to the network.

MEDICAL INFORMATICS

Medical informatics generally represents applications of information technologies and services, some of which are integrated with telecommunications (Shortliffe and Fagan 1989; Greenes and Shortliffe 1990). Although it is not our purpose here to discuss the broad range of informatics applications, it is instructive to envision how developments in this field will further enhance telemedicine. Examples of development can be seen in a large program of research grants funded under the National Library of Medicine's Integrated Academic Information Management System (IAIMS).

Integrated Academic Information Management System

The IAIMS programs grew out of the application of information technologies in medical library settings, dating back to the 1960s, to an expanded role of information management in the 1980s and 1990s. There is an excellent review of these programs reprinted from the *Bulletin of the Medical Library Association* (Lorenzi 1992). As of the date of that report, eighteen organizations were or had been operating IAIMS projects in planning, modeling, or implementation phases.

Among the projects are:

- Baylor College of Medicine (Houston, Texas): An enhanced information services architecture has developed incorporating high-speed networking, improved standards, and improving linking with outside resources; the project includes development of the virtual notebook system, a multimedia hypertext interface for the user (Gorry et al. 1991).
- Columbia-Presbyterian Medical Center (New York, N.Y.): The goal is one stop information shopping, that is, to offer access to all relevant information sources, including e-mail and word processing, through a single work-station; the project includes development of special software for patient chart tracking, surgery scheduling, and other practical tasks (see Clayton et al. 1992).
- Georgetown University Medical Center (Washington, D.C.): The aim has been to create a medical decision support system by combining into a single system a wide range of databases, computers and communications services; the project includes a scholar workstation component for research and training applications (Broering and Bagdoyan 1992).
- American College of Obstetricians and Gynecologists (a national organization headquartered in Washington, D.C.): The project has developed ACOGQUEST, a integrated information system targeted to the specialized needs of obstetricians and gynecologists (research includes a heuristic-based patient management system with interactive operation of patient records).
- Yale University School of Medicine (New Haven, Conn.): An attempt has been made to design an integrated information system specially oriented to the needs of an academic medical center, including development of information maps to aid users.
- University of Washington (Seattle, Wash.): A newer program is attempting to build upon prior IAIMS project findings in designing a broadly integrated information system serving the northwest region and Alaska (including research on developing graphic interfaces for existing databases).

Virtually all of the above and most other developments in medical informatics are closely associated with commercial applications. In fact, many projects are done either with commercial partnerships or entirely by commercial interests. In a broad perspective, the challenge is to diffuse these innovations—often developed in large, high-tech medical facilities—out into the field, encouraging use by individuals who are not traditionally comfortable with technology. A current bibliography of management information research in healthcare is reported by Moore (1993b).

Decentralized Hospital Computer Program

Many advances in informatics are software intensive. Among these is the Decentralized Hospital Computer Program (DHCP) developed and standardized by the U.S. Veterans Administration. It is an integrated system based on a powerful set of software tools with shared data accessible from any of its application modules. It includes many functionally specific application subsystems such as laboratory, pharmacy, radiology, and dietetics. Physicians need applications that cross these application boundaries to provide useful and convenient patient data. One of these multi-specialty applications, the DHCP Imaging System, integrates multimedia data to provide clinicians with comprehensive patient-oriented information. User requirements for cross-disciplinary image access have been studied. Integration approaches are evaluated both for their ability to deliver patient-oriented text data rapidly and their ability to integrate multimedia data objects. There is a steady number of applications projects on DHCP reported in medical research publications. See Moore (1993b) for a current bibliography on the topic.

Artificial Intelligence

Another important area of software development is in artificial intelligence or expert systems. Essentially this is software that can emulate human decision capabilities. It is not just automation but the interpretation of information and posing of decisions, including in some cases an attached probability weighting of alternatives. Some efforts in this area focus directly upon medical decision making as in diagnostic tasks (Barnett et al. 1987; 67–74). Although there is still much progress to be made, especially in making such programs available over a healthcare network, this is a likely direction of software development. For example, INTERNIST-1 was developed to serve as a computer-assisted diagnostic program for internal medicine (Masarie, Miller, and Myers 1985). The goal is to have a consultant program that, based on a patient's symptoms, laboratory tests, and history, can assist a physician in performing a medical diagnosis. The program is built upon a database of literally hundreds of profiles of specific diseases.

Language Translation

Finally, we should note the increasing availability of software that can assist in machine translation of languages. In our work in south Texas and from the healthcare issues raised by the North American Free Trade Agreement, we have seen a need for development of software that can assist in Spanish/English translations of medical reports, correspondence, and even textbooks. There now exist capabilities for integrating machine translation services directly into a telemedicine network, another challenging area for commercialization.

HUMAN AND ORGANIZATIONAL FACTORS

Improved Human Interface

Most researchers agree that the weakest link in modern network services remains the interface between the human and the technology. Keyboards, complex program commands, and complicated screen layouts are a major barrier to full human access to network services. However, just as some computer users have found mouse, pull-down menu, or touch-screen interface an improvement over the entry of keyboard commands, we can expect improvements in how we communicate with the network. One is spoken commands, which is discussed below. Another is the entry of ordinary language by writing on a input screen with a stylus (as with the new digital hand-held communicators). "Hypermedia" techniques are constantly being refined. This is where a text or graphics presentation has buttons for mouse or touch-screen entry to call for further details, sidebars, or other related presentations. Some new multimedia screen designs (e.g., *Compton Encyclopedia* CD-ROM Edition) allow the user to create interim maps of the information they are compiling. The maps can be stored, recalled, or rearranged to control organization of information that will be consulted or communicated. Visualize, for example, an epidemiologist gathering data from several subfiles of different databases, perhaps discarding some and replacing with others in the process. Rather than download and save each of the files, the map can be used to record the design of the intended report. When the final selections are decided, the map can automatically access the desired data sets and place them into one file in a requested standardized format.

We can expect that the network will have an increasing capability to recognize speech, which, for practical purposes, means creating a system for either input of computer commands or for generating text from speech. Both are now technically possible, although the former is more reliable than the latter because of its much smaller operating vocabulary. Both capabilities should have wide use when accessing networks with hand-held devices where typing input is not convenient. A healthcare survey worker, for example, could input data, including brief memorandum entries, solely by speech. There are also many applications for e-mail, including voice input messages text-translated and faxed to a destination. A physician's commentary could be directly dictated at a distance and automatically converted to text for insertion into a medical record held at a central location.

It is one step to transform spoken utterances into text but quite another to have some type of understanding of that text so that it can be acted upon. Typically this means that free speech can be interpreted as more than a set of commands or a limited vocabulary. Currently there is software that, once a specific database is accessed (through limited spoken commands), a combination of agreed-upon commands can be combined with free speech to locate file entries. The agreed commands might be "Search for," plus "and" then free speech is used to communicate individual words or phrases (e.g., "Search for *diphtheria* and *children under three"*). Given feedback on the number and size of files located, a further command could narrow the search (*Delimit to year 1995*). Currently a priority is to develop a system where the network can answer simple spoken questions in a well-defined subject matter area, for example, directory information. It will be increasingly possible for this technology to be used for interrogating databases. For example, selected standard medical references could be put into a database form that could be accessed by spoken requests—as, for example, "list symptoms, *endocarditis*." Again, translation services could also be integrated into the system.

Technology-Assisted Management

Another major opportunity offered by advances in telecommunication are the applications in healthcare management. There are several generalizations of overall importance here. One is that intelligent networks give us new capabilities for management, not the least of which is the ability of individual managers to increase the scope of their supervision. Another is that network services make a much wider range of updated information more readily available for decision makers. However, for these advantages to be gained, it is usually necessary to revise existing management practices, or as some say, reinvent the organization. Much of the current literature on organizational change comes from the reorganization of large businesses (Davis and Davidson 1991). For contemporary views on this concept, let us turn briefly to the works of several of today's management experts.

Business analyst Tom Peters (1988) holds that successful organizations will ride through this revolution by being flatter, populated by more autonomous units with more local authority to define products and set prices, oriented more toward niche markets providing high-value-added goods and services, quality conscious, service conscious, more responsive, faster at innovation, and a user of highly trained flexible people who may not all be employees of the organization. The same holds for most of the analogous components of public services.

Just as major businesses are moving away from a rigid hierarchical bureaucracy to more decentralized operational clusters or forms of project management, public service organizations need to move more of their resources and decision-making authority out into the field. Resources and decision making need to be near the clients they are serving, as a business needs to be close to its markets. The new telecommunications infrastructure allows intelligence to be more accessible to individuals working in the field. We are seeing an evolution from a hierarchical or bureaucratic structure toward matrix forms of organizations (Drucker 1989, 1992; Benjamin and Blunt 1992).

The healthcare delivery organization of the future can use telecommunication-based management to move more resources from the central organization out to the patient. The administrative agency can become more of an information center rather than a concentration of services, because telecommunications permits moving the services closer to the people who need them. The healthcare organization can exist on the network much as a "virtual organization" combining clinics, hospitals, and physicians' offices, as it now does in central facilities. Increasingly, even the home, school, or workplace can be integrated to some degree into that network. Administrators, physicians, researchers, and field workers can be interconnected by intelligent networks that share skills, access to information resources, and financial transaction services in a decentralized and collaborative network organization. This could mean a literal reinvention of the healthcare organization in an era where the demands of underserved populations are gaining increased recognition. Just as healthcare has been a relatively eager adopter of many technologies, it faces the challenge of applying technology-assisted management as a major advance in telemedicine. In fact, the virtual healthcare organization may be the key platform for delivery of medical services in the new century. On the other hand, technology is only as effective as the ability of users to adopt and apply it, our next topic.

Barriers to Technology Adoption

Technological Issues

Although one might speculate that the major barrier to full-scale implementation would be the technology for telemedicine delivery, technology has not been reported as a major problem in the implementation of current individual telemedicine projects (Moore 1993a). However, problems arise when existing items of equipment cannot be integrated to work with each other. The Consensus Conference of the Mayo Telemedicine Symposium (*Proceedings* 1993) recommended that vendors work together to assure that various items of equipment communicate in the future. In order to assure a minimum standard of quality, it was also recommended that professional groups within the medical community develop technology standards.

Those implementing telemedicine projects in the past have protested that they were unable to see and compare equipment being considered for purchase (Moore 1993a). To address this concern the state of Texas has arranged for simultaneous vendor demonstrations, transmitting the same material over the same bandwidth. The publication *Telemedicine Today* has also published comparative information on three telemedicine vendors, VTEL, CLI, and PictureTel ("Telemedicine Rollabout" 1994).

Telemedicine technology is dependent on advanced telecommunications networks. Yet in rural Texas many areas do not yet have fiber optic lines. Instead, there are twisted pair telephone lines installed by the WPA in the 1930s. In some locations it has been difficult even to map where fiber optic lines are located. Lines may run within a mile of each other, yet still the networks are unconnected (Hartman and Moore 1992). Furthermore, when dedicated fiber optic lines must be used for telemedicine, the costs can be enormous. The tariff rates, especially for T1 services within local calling areas, may inhibit rural access to interactive video. Within Texas there have been efforts to provide a 25 percent reduction in fees when lines are used for educational or nonprofit services.

Regulatory Barriers

The fear of malpractice and problems arising from licensing issues have been of concern to some people in implementing telemedicine services. Since studies of teleradiology have shown that it is rarely 100 percent as effective as in-person viewing of radiographs, the concern arises over what might happen if a misdiagnosis were made (Rinde et al. 1993). Those implementing telemedicine have suggested, however, that telemedicine can increase the effectiveness of distant consultation. Since many consultations in the past were performed physician-to-physician over telephone, telemedicine video imaging helps improve the accuracy of diagnosis. There have been no published reports of malpractice judgments against physicians performing telemedicine consultations.

Problems may arise when telemedicine consultations are performed across state lines. Since physicians are licensed to practice on a state-by-state basis, it is conceivable that a specialist in New York providing a consultation to a general practitioner in South Dakota could be prosecuted for practicing medicine without a license in South Dakota. The Consensus Conference of the Mayo Telemedicine Symposium (*Proceedings* 1993) has urged that alternatives to state-specific medical licensing be developed, and that a single national medical licensure examination be developed.

Concerns with patient confidentiality could be a barrier to implementation as well. While none of the directors of successful telemedicine projects have thought that problems with patient confidentiality had significantly hindered provision of services, several were able to relate instances when patients had refused telemedicine services because of fear of lack of privacy. There was also consensus among directors that all forms of patient records, both traditional paper records and information transmitted through telecommunications, could allow breaches of confidentiality (Moore 1993a). In addition, questions must still be resolved regarding the ownership of patient records, especially electronic patient records. These may be more easily distributed to multiple locations than traditional paper records or X-rays, for example. Directors felt that privacy and information dissemination concerns were not so formidable, however, as to inhibit adoption of telemedicine services.

Financial Issues

Telemedicine services are often undertaken to control the costs of healthcare. In rural areas the goal is to control the cost of transportation and distant referral. In urban areas the goal may be to avoid referring patients, and losing the income associated with those patients, to other facilities. Both environments have attempted to use non-physician care providers, supervised by physicians via telemedical links to control costs.

Calculations of the costs of telemedicine must include the one-time expenditure for equipment, recurring expenditures for network services, maintenance and personnel, and intangibles such as time spent learning how to use a new service, inconvenience to healthcare providers when they must leave their offices to use the new service, and lost opportunity costs. Generally, in the past, the cost of equipment was the most serious deterrent to adoption. This is less of a deterrent today, when equivalent equipment costing over $100,000 a few years ago can be obtained for $15,000 or less.

Cost analysis is hampered because telemedicine consultations are rarely reimbursed by Medicare, Medicaid, or third-party insurers. Lack of a reimbursement strategy is a serious barrier to implementation. Recently the Health Care Financing Administration has taken a first step toward a reimbursement policy, considering case-by-case reimbursement for telemedicine consultations conducted in a project in Georgia.

Although there has been no definitive cost-benefit study across projects, several studies have addressed cost issues:

- Georgia's test of thirty patients seen live and then over video showed no changes in their diagnosis between methods. Most of the patients seen (81%) were kept and treated locally—demonstrating increased revenue to local provider, increased revenue to the consultant, and decreased cost of care to the patient.
- Texas Tech MEDNET demonstrated savings of $1000 per patient when the patient was treated locally instead of referred to specialty care centers. In addition, those at one local site attributed the community's restoration of confidence in the local hospital to the telemedicine services, resulting in increased patronage of the hospital.
- Texas Telemedicine demonstrated a break-even analysis in 2.7 years, when the lower costs of treating in rural communities, travel time for physicians and patients, and lost opportunity costs were considered.
- Both Telemedicine Canada (Toronto) and Memorial University (Newfoundland) have demonstrated full cost recovery for educational efforts. The director of the Newfoundland service also reported that, during a trial of slow scan technology to an oil rig, three medical airlifts were saved.

The nature of the healthcare organization has demonstrated potential for reducing manpower costs by allowing support personnel to perform routine diagnosis and treatment and freeing physicians to perform more complex tasks. As healthcare reform proposals emerge, it appears that a re-definition of roles will be an element in the final plan. At an appearance in Austin, Texas, Hillary Rodham Clinton said, "We need to be asking what physicians are doing, and we need to be asking why nurses are not doing more" (Clinton 1993). The potential for non-physician healthcare providers taking increased responsibilities has long been a tenet of telemedicine. Muller et al. (1977) and Cunningham et al. (1978)

described an inner city project in New York with the objective of minimizing costs by using nurses and not making unnecessary referrals. Cunningham et al. examined whether physicians could be replaced with nurse practitioners assisted by telemedicine links, and concluded that pediatric nurse practitioners could function with televised consultation, rather than on-site supervision, 40 percent of the time. Muller determined that, because the physician was needed only rarely for consultations, the addition of a physician devoted to telemedicine consultations was only justified if there were at least five satellite clinics and full network utilization of 1,750 hours per year.

In evaluating costs of telemedicine one must also consider the value of the services. Measuring the effect of telemedicine on costs alone may not be an adequate basis for deciding whether to introduce a telemedicine system. Improvements in healthcare and patient outcomes are difficult to measure financially. There is another consideration as well: "The value of telemedicine systems to individuals and communities can go well beyond the simple calculations of dollars saved and additional care provided. This value includes the creation of markets, which then attracts investment and delivery of goods and services to these new markets" (*Proceedings of the Mayo Telemedicine Symposium* 1993: 8).

Organizational Issues

Since healthcare takes place within an organization, the organization has substantial impact on whether or not telemedicine is successfully adopted. Studies have referred to different usage rates of telemedicine at different locations (Dohner et al. 1975; Hartman and Moore 1992). There are no recent studies on site selection, although Bashshur and Armstrong (1976) wrote, "The choice of demonstration sites for telemedicine projects is a critical factor in the eventual success of these projects." Reports from the directors of telemedicine projects have confirmed this observation. One director of a successful telemedicine project attributed the success solely to the organizational culture and a firm commitment from management to adopt telemedicine. Another said the managers of his healthcare organization almost killed his project before it began. A third director described how organizational support for telemedicine was not a foregone conclusion, even after equipment had been purchased (Moore 1993a).

In addition to organizational support, there are other elements of the organizational culture that may have an impact on adoption. The success of a project often has to do with the efficiency and smoothness of its administration. With Texas Tech MEDNET, problems reported in the project with locating specialists and scheduling telemedicine consultations led one rural site to prefer one medical center to another, altering the existing patient referral patterns (Hartman and Moore 1992). In another project, Grundy et al. (1982) identified that only 30 percent of telemedicine recommendations were acted upon, due to administrative inefficiencies. Physician-to-physician contact with this system was rare. In some cases the consultants' recommendations were not transmitted to the attending physicians. Some recommendations were simply not acted upon, some were partially implemented, and others were lost to follow-up.

It is obvious that even if the technical aspects of telemedicine were flawless, administrative problems could result in frustration and disenchantment. The directors of successful telemedicine projects agreed that one key to success was to simplify everything that could be simplified. Equipment should be user friendly; only critical paperwork should be required; forms should be simplified; and procedures for conducting consultations should be as effortless as possible (Moore 1993a).

Individual Adopters

Just as organizations do, individuals also evince characteristics that lead to the successful adoption of telemedicine. Some individuals are much more willing to accept and use telemedicine services than others (Hartman and Moore 1992; Moore 1993a), leading to question such as:

- Who uses telemedicine the most, and why?
- Why do some individuals never use telemedicine systems?
- What are the individual characteristics of early adopters and heavy users of telemedicine?

Although some individuals embrace telemedicine, others resist. Hartman and Moore (1992) described a radiologist who resisted teleradiology even though it could substantially reduce travel time for him. One explanation for resistance might be fear of the impact of telemedicine on the healthcare system. These fears may include the fear of lost income, perhaps resulting from altered referral patterns, or the fear of increased responsibility of non-physician healthcare providers, which has been an outcome in some projects.

Interviews with ten telemedicine directors led to the following observations about the characteristics of individuals most likely to use telemedicine. In many cases those leading the projects could be described as charismatic entrepreneurs (Conger and Kanungo 1988; Conger 1989). They were articulate, enthusiastic, energetic, self-sacrificing, obsessed with their users, impatient for change, and true believers in their causes. Several directors interviewed discussed the personal characteristics of those referring physicians and healthcare providers who were most likely to use telemedicine services and help make it a success. These individuals were inquisitive, confident enough to ask questions and not be intimidated by specialists, and humble enough to believe that they did not know all the answers. They demonstrated qualities of lifelong learning; often used many sources for information; often were outgoing; preferred personal contact for consultations; and were often, in Morris's (1970) terms, "information influentials" who conducted telemedicine consultations and then often went on to educate other local colleagues about the outcomes of the consultations. Those consulting specialists who provided telemedicine services were characterized as being opinion leaders in their fields, being experienced, providing a high standard of care, being flexible and adaptable, and as being altruistic—since only rarely are these physicians reimbursed for the their services in the consultations. Several directors expressed the view that technical support personnel for telemedicine must be experienced, capable, and flexible, since telemedicine needs vary and may be unpredictable. Successful technical support staff were described as being technically competent, committed, paying attention to detail and accuracy, being obsessed with quality, and having and projecting their recognition of a sense of urgency in many telemedicine applications.

THE NEED FOR COMMERCIALIZATION RESEARCH

A shortcoming of most of the demonstration projects in telemedicine is that they give insufficient emphasis to long-range commercialization. Many never survive after a subsidized developmental and demonstration cycle. This is not so much to criticize earlier studies, because in new applications of technology it is necessary to focus on development and "try-out." However, we are now at a point in telemedicine where we know more about what telemedical application might work under demonstration circumstances than we know about how it will fit into the economics of medical practice. Who will make the necessary investment for development? Who will pay for the technology transfer process of bringing it to market? Once in place, how will the application generate revenues to yield a return on its investment?

Whereas many telemedical studies have placed the emphasis upon one-time demonstrations or adoption-of-innovations paradigms, they have left the commercialization cycle largely to postresearch implications. It is now important to put more emphasis upon commercialization potential as a major up-front priority in research designs. Prospective telemedical applications should be examined initially for commercialization potential, then R&D would not only focus on the technical and medical issues but keep an eye on commercialization from the beginning. What is the market? What are the arguments favoring a technology application? What are the cost-benefit comparisons among technology options? What are the development and marketing costs? What are the potentials for return on investment? Answers to these questions will likely underlie the most successful and self-sustaining telemedical applications for the information highway.

A VIEW FROM THE FUTURE HIGHWAY

Given progress in overcoming these barriers and the national interest in universal healthcare now aroused, it seems clear that there will be a steady growth of applications in telemedicine. Simply the debate over healthcare reform promotes attention to needed improvements in the delivery of services, and it seems a truism of our age that technology is called upon as an agent of change. Some of the enhancements we should expect include:

- There will be an improvement in the overall administration of healthcare in the United States.
- Physicians will have improved access (ease, speed, accuracy) to information vital to diagnosis and treatment.
- Physicians will have easier access to consultative services through enhanced telecommunications links with major medical centers, including remote analyses of diagnostic data.
- Third-party reimbursement for medical cases will extend to telemedical services.
- Expansion of information services into the home will improve opportunities for emergency communications, and remote monitoring of vital signs, as well as public education in health matters.
- Training of healthcare professionals will be more widely available due to advances in distance and on-site instructional media.
- There will be improved diffusion of medical services in traditionally underserved areas by networking rural clinics with each other and with major medical facilities, as well as by improved links for emergency and consultant services directly to homes.
- Public health services can move their intelligence and resources closer to their client populations through administrative decentralization.
- Medical information systems, by improved methods of information gathering, storage, and retrieval, will enhance the efficiency of transferring knowledge from research into training or practice.
- Improved methods for gathering, assembling, and interpreting data from the field will enhance the analytical power and hence medical planning, policy making, and evaluation of programs.
- Many of the most successful applications of telemedicine will be evaluated at the outset for their commercialization potential.

In conclusion, as inviting as the above prospects seem for the future of healthcare, they will not be realized without two major emphases in national policy and attitude regarding telemedicine. One is that although we must face up to building a new national telecommunications infrastructure, it is critical that this be done with an eye toward benefits for the whole range of American citizens. If we have a network only accessible to the "information haves," we will only increase the socioeconomic and political gap between the classes in our society. Like public education or transportation, and the public switched network, the highway must be accessible to all citizens who wish to partake of its services. In a large scale view, this is not only a positive economic policy but also one that can make available new tools for trying to solve our nation's mounting problems in education and healthcare. We hope that our glimpse into an expanded vision of telemedicine is an argument in that direction.

Second, and finally, we should not assume that improvements in telemedicine will necessarily involve only government and big business. There are many areas for technology commercialization, such as developing specialized hardware or software for medical applications, that will likely come from the small-business, technology-based entrepreneurial community. There will be no future view of healthcare improvements from the information highway without a full range involvement. It will need more than government and big business. Critical at the grass-roots level are the individual physician, nurse, administrator, benchtop inventor, and entrepreneur.

NOTES

1. Traditional analog telecommunication involves transmission of an electrical or broadcast (electromagnetic) wave pattern that has the same qualities as an acoustic sound wave. The transmitted wave is an analog of the acoustic wave to be transduced back to its original form at the destination. Digital signal forms are bursts of binary (combinations of a two-state signal like "0" and "1") information that can code as many characteristics of an acoustic wave as are needed to reproduce it at the destination. Digital representations can be highly compressed so as to increase transmission capacity and speed. Another advantage of a digital network is that it is readily compatible to computer codes which are digital. Since video can also be converted into digital form, this means that a single telecommunications channel can carry alphanumeric characters, voice, and video in a single coding and routing system.

2. Bandwidth is the width of an electrical transmission path or circuit in terms of the range of frequencies it can pass. Broadband typically refers to circuits greater than voice grade, and often ones that carry a broadcast quality TV image (like cable TV).

REFERENCES

Barnett, G., et al. (1987). "DXplain: An Evolving Diagnostic Decision Support System." *JAMA*, 258(7): 67–74.

Bashshur, R., and Armstrong, P. (1976). "Telemedicine: A New Mode for the Delivery of Healthcare." *Inquiry*, 13: 233–244.

Benjamin, R. I., and Blunt, J. (1992). "Critical IT Issues: The Next Ten Years." *Sloan Management Review*, 7–19.

Boor J. L., Schaad, D. C., and Evans, F. W. (1981). "Communications Satellites in Health Education and Healthcare Delivery: Operational Considerations." *J. Educ. Tech. Sys*, 9(4): 371–377.

Broering, N. C., and Bagdoyan, H. E. (1992). "The Impact of IAIMS at Georgetown: Strategies and Outcomes." *Bulletin of the Medical Library Association*, 80(3).

Clayton, P. D., Sideli, R. V., and Sengupta, S. (1992). "Open Architecture and Integrated Information at Columbia-Presbyterian Medical Center." *MD Computing*, 9(5): 297–303.

Clinton, H. R. (1993). Presentation at the University of Texas, Austin, Texas, April 6.

Conger, J. A. (1989). *The Charismatic Leader: Behind the Mystique of Exceptional Leadership*. San Francisco: Josey-Bass.

Conger, J. A., and Kanungo, R. N. (1988). "Behavioral Dimensions of Charismatic Leadership." In J. A. Conger, R. N. Kanungo and Associates (eds.), *Charismatic Leadership*. San Francisco: Josey Bass.

Cunningham, N., Marshall, C., and Glazer, E. (1978). "Telemedicine in Pediatric Primary Care." *JAMA*, 240(25): 2749–2751.

Davis, S., and Davidson, D. (1991). *2020 Vision: Transform Your Business Today to Succeed in Tomorrow's Economy*, Chapters 1–3. New York: Simon and Schuster.

Dohner, C. W., Cullen, T. J., and Zinser, E. A. (1975). *ATS-6 Evaluation: The Final Report of the Communications Satellite Demonstrations in the WAMI Decentralized Medical Education Program at the University of Washington*. Prepared for Lister Hill National Center of Biomedical Communications. Seattle: University of Washington.

Drucker, P. F. (1989). *The New Realities. In Government and Politics, in Economics and Business, in Society and World View*. New York: Harper and Row.

Drucker, P. F. (1992). "The New Society of Organizations." *Harvard Business Review*, 95–104.

Furtado, R. (1982). "Telemedicine: The Next-Best Thing to Being There." *Dimensions*, 10–12.

Gorry, A. (1991). "The Virtual Notebook System: An Architecture for Collaborative Work." *Journal of Organizational Computing*, 1(3): 233–250.

Greenes, R. A., and Shortliffe, E. H. (1990). "Medical Informatics: An Emerging Academic Discipline and Institutional Priority." *JAMA*, 263(8): 1114–1120.

Grundy, B. L., Jones, P. K., and Lovitt, A. (1982). "Telemedicine in Critical Care: Problems in Design, Implementation, and Assessment." *Critical Care Medicine*, 10, 471–475.

Hartman, J. T., and Moore, M. (1992). *Using Telecommunications to Improve Rural Healthcare: The Texas Tech Mednet Demonstration Project*. Prepared for the Office of Rural Health Policy, U.S. Department of Health and Human Services. Lubbock: Texas Tech University.

Hudson, H. (1990). *Communication Satellites: Their Development and Impact*. New York: The Free Press.

Kuhn, R. L. (ed.). (1988). *Frontiers of Medical Information Sciences*. New York: Praeger.

Lorenzi, N. M. (ed.). (1992). "Symposium: A Decade of IAIMS." *Bulletin of the Medical Library Association*, 80(3).

MacDonald, C. J. and Barnett, G. O. (1990). "Medical-Record Systems." In E. H. Shortliffe and L. E. Perreault (eds.), *Medical Informatics: Computer Applications in Health Care*, pp. 181–218. Reading, Mass.: Addison-Wesley.

Masarie, F. E., Jr., Miller, R. A., and Myers, J. D. (1985). "INTERNIST-1 Properties: Representing Common Sense and Good Medical Practice in a Computerized Medical Knowledge Base." *Computers and Biomedical Research*, 18: 458–479.

Moore, M. (1993a). *Elements of Success in Telemedicine Projects*. Report of a research grant from AT&T; Graduate School of Library and Information Science, the University of Texas at Austin.

Moore, M. (1993b). *MEDLINE SEARCH: 1. Medical Management Information Systems; 2. Decentralized Hospital Computer Program*. Center for Research on Communication Technology and Society, the University of Texas at Austin, Austin, Texas.

Morris, W. C. (1970). *The Information Influential Physician: The Knowledge Flow Process Among Medical Practitioners*. Ann Arbor, Mich.: The University of Michigan.

Muller, C., Marshall, C. L., Krasner, M., Cunningham, N., Wallerstein, E., and Thomstad, B. (1977). "Cost Factors in Urban Telemedicine." *Medical Care*, 15(3): 251–259.

Peters, T. (1988). *Thriving on Chaos*. New York: Harper and Row.

Proceedings of the Mayo Telemedicine Symposium. Including "Telemedicine and Access to Care," A Consensus Conference to Explore Telemedicine as a Vehicle for Expanding Access to Cost Effective Health Care. (1993). Rochester, Minn.: Mayo Clinic.

Rinde, E., Nordrum, I., and Nymo, B. J. (1993). "Telemedicine in Rural Norway." *World Health Forum* 14(1): 71–77.

Shortliffe, E. H., and Fagan, L. M. (1989). "Research Training in Medical Informatics: The Stanford Experience." *Academic Medicine*, (64)10: 575–578.

Stead, W. W., and Hammond, W. E. (1988). "Computer Based Medical Records: The Centerpiece of TMR." *MD Computing*, (5)5: 48–62.

Sung, L. (1993). *The South Texas Telecommunications Inventory and Database Program for Use in Planning Telecommunications-Based Training for Health Care Applications*. San Antonio: University of Texas Health Science Center in San Antonio.

"Telemedicine Rollabout Units: Battle of the Titans." (1994). *Telemedicine Today*, 2(1): 1, 6–9.

Williams, F. (1991). *The New Telecommunications: Infrastructure for the Information Age*. New York: The Free Press.

3

Pricing of Services on the Internet

Alok Gupta, Dale O. Stahl, and
Andrew B. Whinston

The Internet is by far the fastest growing economy in the world in terms of the number of users and information providers. Currently there are over 30 million users with an estimated 100 percent annual growth. As an economic system we view the information providers—including entertainment, news, and educational services—as producers and the users as consumers. The Internet is already experiencing traffic jams. Given the growth rate of the Internet and the need to provide real-time services in future, this congestion will become a severe problem if proper coordinating mechanisms are not designed and implemented. We have developed a priority pricing mechanism based on general equilibrium theory in economics, and we use a measure based on the collective benefits obtained by the users to evaluate the performance of the system. We have developed a simulation model to test the validity of our approach and to show the gain in efficiency induced by pricing. Based on simulation results with a nonpriority pricing scheme, we show substantial improvements versus a free access policy. Furthermore, we address the issues concerning the development of new accounting/billing methods, cross-subsidization of services, infrastructure investment, development of smart agents for dynamic scheduling and users' job management, and the possible competitive market structures which will evolve over the Internet.

INTRODUCTION

The Internet has become the primary means of communication for most of its users. It is no wonder that individuals who have access to it get more information through Internet than any other source. The Internet currently provides individuals access to e-mail, news groups, free software, data transferring capability, real-time conferencing, and many other services. For virtually any problem one faces, a posting to relevant news group(s) can provide solutions (or at least good suggestions) quicker than ever before possible. Researchers can use the Internet facilities such as telnet, ftp, gopher, and World

Wide Web (WWW) to obtain research articles, software tools, or to conduct a survey. Cronin (1994) appropriately states that "the impact of high-speed global communication on research and education is already so profound that the Internet has been dubbed the second Gutenberg revolution."

However, the use of this massive global network is not limited to academic/research purposes. Businesses, whether large or small, are using the Internet's capabilities for exchanging ideas, customer support, and trouble-shooting, among others. Many businesses have recognized that an Internet connection can open new avenues to international access for business partners, customers, and markets. Companies that did not have resources for personal computer networks earlier no longer need to rely on more expensive and inefficient methods of data transfer and acquisition, that is, using diskettes. A personal computer can now be a node on the Internet and access its vast resources in terms of information and data-transfer capabilities. Multinational companies and companies in the service sector benefit from Internet's ability to provide an efficient, reliable, and inexpensive form of communication. Globalization of markets is forcing almost every business to be more efficient and to search for ways of reducing cost. Businesses must increase their global awareness, monitor the (international) markets, and exploit every possible opportunity.

Volume on the Internet is growing faster than 100 percent a year. At last count the number of Internet users was about 15 million, as a conservative estimate. This phenomenal growth is primarily due to the fact that Internet access is relatively inexpensive, and no fee is charged for using most of the valuable services provided by the servers on the Internet. Until recently, practically no commercial services were available on the Internet; however, this situation is changing rapidly. The Internet already has a variety of services or is being used to access several services. Moreover, the infrastructure of the Internet is itself changing; NSF is withdrawing its support for the NSFNET, the major infrastructure backbone supporting the Internet today in the United States. Many private companies are now interested in providing infrastructure and acting as an access provider to the network (SPRINT, PSINET, AT&T, and so forth). These companies see enormous potential for growth and development of the services provided on the Internet. In effect the Internet will become a worldwide or global economy in itself, with consumers armed with sophisticated access tools and firms providing digital services. In the near future, movies, television, other digital entertainment, news, books, lectures, and videoconferencing, are all candidates for a service on the Internet. In addition, economic transactions such as purchasing products and arranging contracts will also be supported.

"Traffic Jams Already on the Information Highway" was the headline of a front-page article that appeared in the November 3, 1993, *New York Times.* Armed with the ability to join the Internet through personal computers, thousands of new people join this community every day. In the near future, both voice and video services could be provided on the Internet. Obviously, this will induce an enormous load on the Internet infrastructure, and the data will have to be transferred at terabytes rates through many nodes. The fiber-optics technology coupled with modem laser-guided router technology are capable of handling such a load, but as the volume increases the chances for long delays, loss of messages, and blockage can increase faster than they can be handled. Clearly, a mechanism is required which both gives access to users who most value it and minimizes the waste incurred due to loss and delays.

Other issues such as copyright protection, security, and data integrity (to name a few) will be as complex as the Internet structure and culture itself. The technical issues involved in encryption and authentication of users and providers are also quite complex and have to be addressed. However, we concentrate here on the primary force needed to create and sustain a market—the pricing of services. We feel that pricing is one of the most important issues facing the development of commercial Internet services. We argue that appropriate pricing mechanisms will efficiently distribute the load on the Internet and minimize the losses and delays in services. We view the Internet as an economic system which can be analyzed by looking at the appropriate equilibrium conditions, which in turn can often be imposed by choosing appropriate prices. Specifically, we divide the services in two categories: (i) user services, that is, services that users want, such as news or movies, and (ii) network services, that is, the infrastructure services or the vehicle that delivers the user services. In this paper we concentrate on the pricing of network services which are enforced by infrastructure providers. We also discuss the form of the markets that could develop over the Internet and other issues related to user-services pricing.

FUTURE OF THE INTERNET SERVICES AND PRICING ISSUES

Currently, Internet infrastructure is a highway of information paths with no usage-based fee. Typically a connection fee is charged based on the size of the data pipeline connecting a server to the Internet. Whether or not to charge for network services is a complex question. A flat charge for services will result in large inefficiencies in usage, because the services providing low value might require as much bandwidth as the ones providing relatively higher value. In addition, delays and losses might reduce the value of the services considerably. Although a model incorporating fixed seasonal changes in prices (time of the day in the case of the Internet) has a potential to improve the usage, it is far from the best practical solution.

In the near future, the Internet will surely carry voice and video services all over the globe. These developments will provide opportunities for new types of services which potentially need real-time transmission and reception of data. As mentioned earlier, the transmission layer of the Internet, that is, the backbone(s)—will probably be able to carry this amount of data. However, depending upon the number of users or the total load at a server, it might not be able to handle the flow of data at such high rates. Clearly a simple solution to this problem is to have redundant capacity. However, it will be difficult to assess the potential demand, and in most cases redundant capacity will not be cost-effective. Furthermore, servers providing the real-time services, such as interactive videoconferencing, will have to ensure that these services are uninterrupted. In a network environment with nondedicated links,[1] providing uninterrupted services will be impossible without a priority mechanism.[2] A priority mechanism ensures that the jobs in a higher priority are completed before starting the processing of a lower-priority job, regardless of the time of arrival. Thus, if uninterrupted services have to be provided, such as videoconferencing, then a priority mechanism has to be developed so that these real-time services are not interrupted by other jobs which might not require immediate handling.

A well-designed priority pricing mechanism has the potential to handle these problems. The basic idea is to levy tolls on the users of the system's capacity. The priority mechanism ensures that users with higher value, and presumably a greater willingness to pay for services, can be distinguished from the users with lower value. This distinction in turn allows service providers to decide whose needs should be fulfilled first and whose services can be preempted if desired. Ideally, we want to charge higher prices for the services which require higher capacity and impose greater delays on other users. Furthermore, if many users require a service during a certain time interval, general economic principles dictate that prices for those services should be higher during that time interval. However, one potential problem exists with direct applicability of these ideas: the services on the Internet are essentially "public goods,"[3] that is, usage by one user does not preclude its usage by another—even though the quality (in terms of service time) may suffer, that is, simultaneous access to a database by several users. We propose a priority pricing mechanism that considers the congestion costs suffered by the users due to other users and that prices the access to services accordingly.

The Internet has one important distinction from other service networks: it is a network of computers. Thus the potential computing power could (and perhaps should) be used for development and implementation of a more real-time pricing system. In the next section, we provide the theoretical foundation of our proposed approach. Then we outline the simulation experiments we have developed to evaluate this mechanism. Finally, we present some simulation results and interpret them to assess the performance of a hypothetical network.

THEORETICAL FOUNDATION

Stahl and Whinston (1993) present a priority pricing mechanism for distributed computing. The model presented there is based on general equilibrium theory in economics, but departs from the Arrow-Debreu framework in a manner that makes the results computationally practical. In a pure Arrow-Debreu model (see Debreu 1959), a commodity would be defined for every contingency and every moment in time. Given stochastic demands for computational services, the full state-space model would be much too large for practical purposes. In lieu of state-contingent equilibrium prices, Stahl and Whinston introduce the concept of a stochastic equilibrium in which (i) average flow rates of service requests are optimal for each user given the prices and anticipated delay, and (ii) the anticipated delays are the correct ex-ante expected delays given the average flow rates. Further, an optimal stochastic equilibrium is one that maximizes the net social benefits. The authors derive a formula that characterizes rental prices that support an optimal stochastic equilibrium.

This equilibrium concept with its associated results has significant informational and computational implications. First, it allows the decentralization of the resource allocation process to the user level and reduces the information required for the user's decision problem to current rental prices and current expected delays. The administrative and communication costs of distributing this information pales in comparison to the associated costs of zillions of Arrow-Debreu contingency markets (or even spot auction markets). Second (as presented in more detail later), rental prices can be adjusted in real-time in a manner that pushes them into (and keeps them in) a neighborhood of the theoretically optimal prices, and this process can be decentralized as well. Again the computational and communication cost of this mechanism pales in comparison to that of fixed-point algorithms for Arrow-Debreu equilibrium prices.

Although it might be impossible to achieve exact optimal pricing in practice for a volatile environment such as the Internet, we contend that it is possible to compute near-optimal prices in real time. As a result of this near-optimal pricing, users with different values for the same service will choose different ways or time to obtain the same service. This, in turn, can provide substantial reduction in peak loads and will achieve better distribution of the load over time.

These results are based on an objective function that maximizes collective benefits of the system and its users. The natural question to ask is: why should service providers be concerned about collective benefits of the system? The primary reason is that the market on the Internet can essentially be viewed as a service industry, and customer satisfaction is directly related to the market share in the service industry. However, other objectives might be considered by the service providers, especially under the competitive market environment. Under these different objectives, there might be different pricing strategies, that is, marginal revenue pricing. We will explore these issues in future research.

From the theoretical standpoint these results have significant importance. The rental prices at the servers decentralize the management and accounting problems. They give the users or their clients access to an evaluation mechanism to decide when and what kind of service they want and at what priority.[4] At the server level they will allow the management to assess the queues and delays more accurately and design their systems accordingly. Finally, at the network level the mechanism will allow for a better load distribution because excessively loaded and thus highly priced servers will be avoided by the users.

The price at a particular server for a particular priority class can be represented by the following system of equations (see Stahl and Whinston [1993] for derivation):

$$p_{mk} = \Sigma_l [\partial\Omega_1/\partial z_{mk}]\Sigma_i\Sigma_j\delta_{ij}x_{ijlm} \tag{1}$$

where:

* p_{mk} is the price at server m for priority class k,
* Ω is a continuously differentiable, strictly increasing function of load z_{mk} and capacity v_m, which provides the waiting time at a server m for priority class k,
* δ_{ij} is the delay cost parameter of consumer i for service j, and
* x_{ijkm} is the flow rate of service j for consumer i with priority k at server m.

Let us briefly interpret these equations. The first term on the right side $(\partial\Omega_l/\partial z_{mk})$ is the derivative of waiting time with respect to load. Since the waiting time is a strictly increasing function of load, an increase in load of a certain priority class increases the prices for that priority class. The second term $(\delta_{ij}x_{ijlm})$ can be interpreted as the accumulated delay cost of the system; an increase in this cost increases the price.

The optimal prices can only be computed if the optimal arrival rates are known and true equilibrium waiting times are known. Thus, we still need to find an approach for estimating the rental prices. We propose an iterative approach where the current estimates of the prices are computed given the historical information on flow rates and waiting times. This iterative approach can be implemented and analyzed by using simulation techniques where we estimate the prices using the transient information to guide the system toward a stochastic equilibrium. In the next section we first introduce the conceptual model of the Internet that we are using to evaluate our pricing scheme, and then we present the simulation model which we are using to estimate the prices and calculate the benefits.

ESTIMATION OF PRICES

Figure 3.1 presents a conceptual model of the Internet. Essentially, we model the Internet infrastructure as a black box, that is, we assume that the infrastructure has enough capacity and does not contribute significantly to the delays suffered by the users.[5] The users are connected to the Internet through some access providers (which we can consider as a service in itself). The access providers and the service providers—that is, news, movies, video-conferencing, databases, and so forth—are "directly" connected to the Internet through a data pipeline of a certain capacity. The capacity of the data pipeline is essentially the bottleneck for the service providers. In the absence of any pricing mechanism, as more users demand a service the quality of the service (in terms of data transfer rates) suffers.[6] Furthermore, as the congestion increases at the data pipeline, the backbone experiences more load also, due to the resending of lost packets. Consequently, for our purposes the Internet reduces to a network of servers with various services, where users have direct access to any service. The network service providers are able to monitor the loads at different servers, and they impose prices according to the load imposed by the servers on the backbone due to the congestion at their gateways.

Figure 3.1
A Conceptual Model of the Internet

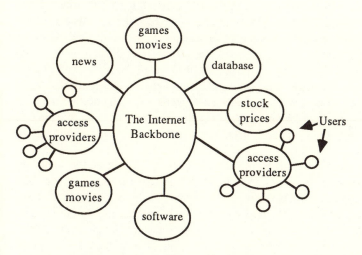

We simulate this model of the Internet and implement our pricing mechanism. The prices are computed based on the system of equations presented in the previous section. However, since these prices are not estimated at the equilibrium conditions, they are approximate at any given time. We implement the following iterative equation to update the prices at any given time (t+1):

$$p_{mk}^{t+1} = \alpha \hat{p}_{mk}^{t+1} + (1 - \alpha)\, p_{mk}^{t} \tag{2}$$

where:

α is a number between 0 and 1

$\hat{p}_{mk}^{t+1}$ is the estimated new price at time (t+1) using equations (1)

p_{mk}^{t} is the implemented price during the time (t, t+1)

The idea behind updating the price this way is to provide a shield against local fluctuations in demand and in the stochastic nature of the process. A lower value of the parameter α means that the price adjustment will be gradual in time, whereas a higher α will result in potentially large changes in the prices from period to period. In our experience with the simulations we have found that smaller values of α, of the order of 0.1, result in reasonably quick convergence and higher stability in prices. However, a number of parameters have to be fine-tuned for a good system design—namely, the time interval for successive updates and the price adjustment parameter α.

Figure 3.2 provides a flow diagram of the simulation model we are using at present. The parameters in this model, that is, update interval, α, simulation length, and so forth, are just example values and provide a good starting point for our exploration; we explore the simulation results for a wide range of these values. In this model the service requests are generated according to a Poisson arrival process with a fixed exogenous arrival rate. Upon the arrival of a service request, the type of service required is identified; a service is characterized by the number of computational cycles required at a server. Then the current estimates of prices and predicted waiting times[7] are obtained for all the servers offering the particular service. The user then evaluates the total expected cost of this service in terms of the delay cost and the service cost against the value of the service. If the total cost of the service is higher than his or her value for the service the user quits the system; otherwise, the user submits the request for obtaining the service.[8]

A user's request is sent to the server that was chosen as the least-cost server. For example, if a service is available at five servers, then the user estimates the total cost of the service by adding his expected delay cost and network services cost at all the five servers and chooses the one where the total cost is expected to be the smallest. If the server queue is empty, the request is immediately processed; however, if some job requests exist in the server queue, then the requests are handled in a FIFO manner. This sequential processing model is the first of the several exploratory models we intend to develop. In future research we will also look at the time-sharing environment, where an additional job in a priority class will slow down the processing of all the current jobs in that class and the jobs in lower-priority classes.

The estimates of waiting times and prices are updated every T units of time. Although we can conceivably update the expectations whenever a request is made, we find three major arguments against frequent updates in stochastic systems: (i) estimating waiting times and prices over a longer time period provides more stable results; (ii) once we are in the vicinity of the stochastic equilibrium, the small fluctuations in prices will not warrant frequent updates; and (iii) the computational effort required in recomputing the prices and waiting times at each request might negate any benefits derived from pricing. However, as other parameters are changed, the update interval also must be changed for any cross-comparison of results.

Figure 3.2
Flow Chart of the Simulation Model

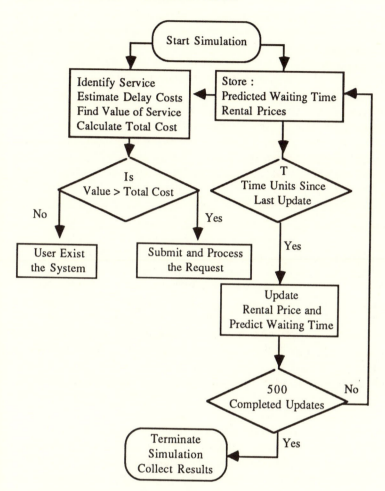

At present we have experimented with a model which has 50 servers and 100 services. The capacity of the servers is randomly generated to be in the range of 1–5 units of work per second. The size of each service is also randomly generated to be in the range 1–20 units of work. The number of servers providing a service is also generated randomly to be in the range 1–30. A server can provide several of the 100 services.

We examine this system under a free-access policy and under our pricing policy for a wide range of arrival rates for service requests. A higher arrival rate induces more load on the system and helps in understanding the behavior of a network with fixed capacity under increasing load. Specifically, we examine this model for an arrival rate of 1–1000; this captures the system behavior under virtually no queues (at the arrival rate of 1) and under extremely long queues (at the arrival rate of 1000). Under these sets of conditions we present results with the following two types of estimation schemes: (i) the perfect waiting-time information scenario: incoming service requests are provided with the exact information on their waiting times; however, the prices are updated every ten units of time for pricing ease; and (ii) periodic update scenario: information on waiting time and prices are both updated every ten units of time. Note that the perfect waiting-time information scenario is the best-case scenario for our implementation of the free access policy, because users first check where can they get the fastest service and the information they get is exact.

In our initial model we have single priority queues only. The results presented here are suggestive of the benefit of applying a single-priority pricing scheme to the Internet services. Essentially, without a pricing mechanism users with zero or low delay cost have nothing to discourage them from over-utilizing the services; however, with a pricing mechanism they are forced to obtain only the services for which their value is higher than the cost.

SIMULATION RESULTS

In this section, we provide some preliminary simulation results from our nonpriority pricing scheme as compared to a free-access policy. The simulations are run on an HP work-station, using the CSIM[9] simulation environment. We present the global or network-wide results in this paper which address the overall performance of the system. However, we also provide some waiting time results at a randomly chosen server.

As discussed earlier, we present results under two conditions, where: i) the information on the waiting time is exact—referred to as the perfect information scenario,[10] and ii) a new prediction about future average waiting times is made every ten units of time. The former case is a best-case scenario for free access policy; however, in practice it will be hard to implement for several reasons: i) the information requirements are intense—a sampling of waiting times has to be done at the arrival of every request; and ii) in a real system several requests may be arriving at the same time and the exact information may never be acquired. We present this scenario solely as a benchmark to compare the benefits due to pricing versus free access. The second case is a more realistic setting; here the predictions about average waiting times are made every ten time units. We use a single-lag autoregressive model to make these predictions; this model was chosen after an empirical analysis of the collected waiting-time data.

Figure 3.3 presents the comparison of benefits[11] accumulated under the free-access and pricing policies using the perfect information scenario. The figure shows net benefits accumulated per unit of time as the exogenous arrival rate is increased. In addition, it also shows the rental benefits and user benefits separately with the pricing policy. The figure clearly indicates that the net benefits are substantially higher under a pricing policy at higher arrival rates (i.e., with higher loads) and are never worse than those under free access. For example, the net benefits are approximately 10,000 units/time-unit with pricing policy and less than 2,500 units/time-unit with free access when the exogenous arrival rate is 40 requests/time-unit; however, at an exogenous arrival rate of 1,000 requests/time-unit, the net benefits with pricing are more than 30,000 units/time-unit, whereas they remain almost the same with free access. The reason for this phenomenon is that under free-access policy a lot of users who have negligible delay costs and low value for services continue to enter the system even when the waiting times are quite high; however, users with higher delay costs (even if they have relatively higher service values) do not enter the system, and eventually the system may be congested with users having low values for the services. When the pricing mechanism is introduced, the users who have low value for the service do not enter the system, and thus the net benefits are higher. Note that when the arrival rates are very small, the prices are negligible and thus the system behaves essentially as it would under free access.

Figure 3.3

A Comparison of Net Benefits under Free-Access Policy and Pricing Policy under the Perfect Information Scenario

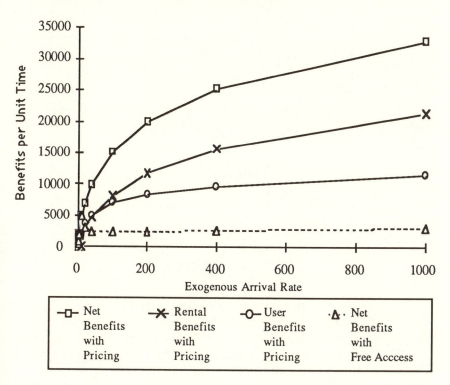

Furthermore, the net benefits under free access are equal to the gross user benefits (since rental revenues, being a cost to users and a benefit to the system, cancel each other in the calculation of net social benefits). However, it is also interesting to compare the net benefits to users (gross benefits less rental revenue). Such a comparison with free-access policy shows that the average net benefits to the users are also higher over the whole range of exogenous arrival rates under the pricing policy even though significant rental revenue is generated at the servers, as indicated by the rental-benefits in Figure 3.3.

Figure 3.4 provides the same comparison when the waiting time information is predicted every ten units of time. The benefits under free access are much smaller and become negative when arrival rates are high. The benefits become negative because the predictions about the waiting times are not accurate, and the decisions to submit the jobs are based on this incorrect information. However, under the pricing policy we still see considerable positive net benefits.

Figure 3.4

A Comparison of Net Benefits under Free Access Policy and Pricing Policy under the Periodic Update Scenario

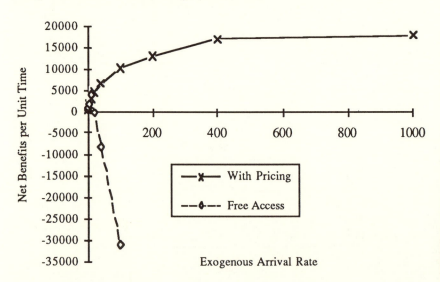

Figure 3.5 provides a comparison of the net benefits with pricing under perfect information versus periodic update. As expected, the net benefits with periodic update are smaller; however, we still obtain a similar trend of increasing benefits with increasing exogenous arrival rate. This result indicates that pricing obtains much better allocation even when relatively inferior information is available.

Figure 3.5

A Comparison of Net Benefits with Pricing under Perfect Information Versus Periodic Updates

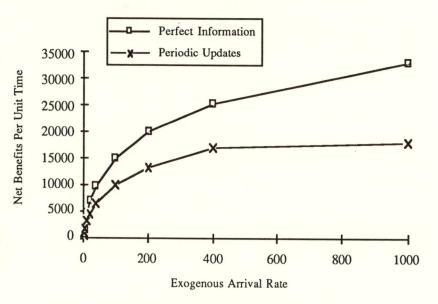

Table 3.1 and Table 3.2 provide the waiting time data for a randomly chosen server under the two scenarios; the behavior of waiting times is similar at other servers. The tables clearly indicate that under free access too many requests may be submitted, resulting in highly inferior performance. As the exogenous arrival rate increases, the waiting times at the servers become several magnitudes larger under the free access policy as compared to our pricing policy, and only users with negligible cost of delay will tend to use the system for most of the time. For example, under the perfect information scenario (Table 3.1), the average waiting time for a service is 4345.79 time-units with free access as compared to 31.28 time-units with pricing when the exogenous arrival rate is 100 requests/time-unit. This difference is further magnified as the exogenous arrival rate increases. Similar trends can be observed with periodic update scenario (Table 3.2).

These preliminary results clearly indicate that even nonpriority-based pricing will result in better system performance at higher congestion levels. Furthermore, the simulation results indicate that an iterative pricing mechanism can be implemented using the approximate prices at any time to achieve significant benefits.

We believe that a priority mechanism can further refine our pricing scheme, and higher net benefits could be realized since users with high value and high delay cost may potentially choose a higher priority class. A further refinement of the pricing mechanism will include the idea of local equilibrium, where users can recompute their expected costs in the queues and switch the server if new estimates make another server seem more attractive at that time. The idea of having smart (software) agents, described later, will be used there. In the next section, we outline some important implementation issues which should be addressed before a successful market can emerge over the Internet.

Table 3.1

Comparison of Waiting Times under the Free Access Policy and Pricing Policy under Perfect Information Scenario

Arrival Rate	Free Access		With Pricing	
	Mean	Std. Deviation	Mean	Std. Deviation
1	0	0	0	0
2	0	0	0	0
4	0.0006	0.0221	0.0001	0.0023
10	0.0805	0.1969	0.1320	0.4527
20	939.9631	244.6980	24.6564	37.5114
40	2175.6600	594.0672	32.2057	46.2508
100	4345.7900	1191.8800	31.2796	41.7017
200	6955.8900	1901.3200	33.6856	45.2784
400	11264.4700	3170.3100	39.2695	52.1729
1000	22852.9500	6705.6600	34.5452	47.1309

Table 3.2

Comparison of Waiting Times under the Free Access Policy and Pricing Policy under the Periodic Update Scenario

Arrival Rate	Free Access		With Pricing	
	Mean	Std. Deviation	Mean	Std. Deviation
1	0.00203225	0.04023404	0.0114375	0.14461355
2	0.05026475	0.26070607	0.45466575	2.44189015
4	7.201656	20.9389782	7.09487125	23.0339496
10	77.824826	137.826614	54.276524	103.459893
20	929.387132	951.561423	61.1874215	117.433725
40	3802.22711	3840.92005	59.0159357	123.636472
100	20334.2348	21809.4396	58.2902245	116.899168

IMPLEMENTATION ISSUES

Several related issues should be explored and developed before a pricing scheme can be successfully implemented on the Internet. Some of these issues are related to the peripheral support for a pricing mechanism, such as client processes which evaluate users' requests, query agents and mechanisms, accounting and billing, and so forth. Others relate to the market structures which could evolve over the Internet. Furthermore, the important issue of supporting the infrastructure costs and investment must be addressed. We plan to explore these issues in detail in future research. However, in the following discussion we pose some relevant questions and provide an outline for the directions of future research in these areas.

Accounting/Billing System

Clearly, a cost-effective accounting/billing scheme is needed to implement a service pricing scheme for the Internet. We will study several schemes. First, each server could meter charges at its location and periodically send an electronic bill to the client-machine, which in turn will process these charges and present the user with a monthly bill. Alternatively, a service request could incorporate a bill portion, and each server would record its charges. When the request returns to the client-machine, it contains a complete bill. The client-machine would process these bills and generate periodic reports (and perhaps execute the appropriate funds transfers to settle the accounts).

It may not be cost-effective to bill for usage below some minimum level. In such cases, nonbillables would become part of the fixed costs. To economize on billing costs, as well as on search costs brokerage services are likely to arise. The brokers would have the volume to justify many accounts with many servers even though individual users may have only a few active accounts.

Cross Subsidization

Since all the Internet services may not be profitable, but may be socially important, we need to incorporate strategies which will allow cross-subsidization of these services through profitable services. To develop a robust approach, both theoretical and empirical ways must be determined to incorporate such services in the present model.

Investment in the Infrastructure

The profitability of each server (based on prices) can be used as a guide for investment and design decisions. The ratio of expected profits to the capital cost of the server can be used as an indicator of rate of return on the investment. This information can be used to decide whether to invest in another server (or increase the capacity of existing server) or to remove the server from the network. However, since the addition/removal of a server may affect the performance of other servers, other considerations must be kept in mind, and proper analysis (possibly using simulation) should be done before making any decisions.

Search Costs and Number of Services

Besides the actual cost of usage (e.g., article retrieval), we must consider the cost associated with the search of the server that can provide the service. Also, the cost of computing the least-cost alternative must be considered when more than one server provides the same service. As mentioned earlier, most of the cost is incurred in searching for the relevant information, and often this cost is difficult to predict. For efficient utilization of the Internet, more effective methodology must be developed for searching as well as for predicting the search pattern. We plan to use the idea of smart agents (possibly using artificial intelligence techniques) to handle the search activities. Etzioni et al. (1993), Moore et al. (1978), and Moore et al. (1992) explore building blocks for designing smart agents.

Even if this search is provided free, as with gopher menus, the user incurs a cost in terms of the time spent in the search. As the number of services of the same type increase, the time spent in searching for the best alternative will also increase. From a network management and investment point of view, management can consider the rate of return on investment (through rental prices) to make a decision on providing more services or eliminating some. Users, on the other hand, can employ their experience or expertise to narrow their search to a limited number of servers.

Smart Agents

Smart agents are the software tools which make appropriate decisions without excessive user input. For example, a user may specify vague guidelines for obtaining some information at lowest cost in the next twenty-four hours. A smart agent will automatically get this information for the user at an appropriate time (possibly by monitoring the prices and analyzing them through an appropriate model) within the next twenty-four hours. Moore, Richmond, and Whinston (1978; 1992) offer decision-theoretic approaches for database search, in which the search strategy optimizes the user's search by incorporating the tradeoff between the cost of search and expected increase in the value of information. This tradeoff is achieved by estimating a user's individual preference function, using the economic and marketing models (for example see Bettman [1979] and Lancaster [1966]). Specifically, a functional representation of a user's preferences can be obtained by using self-explicated weights or various forms of conjoint analysis, as in Hagerty (1986).

We envision that users will either develop or obtain these smart agents by using techniques similar to those mentioned above. These agents will act on behalf of the users and will replicate the users' behavior in terms of their delay sensitivity and information needs—and will obtain and compute the necessary information to fulfill the users' requests. These tools will be essential for users to assimilate and process the information required to make the appropriate decisions. Furthermore, we envision these smart agents computing real-time decisions and dynamically assessing new emerging opportunities for cheaper or better services over time. As mentioned earlier, we plan to explore the possibility of a pricing refinement in which a smart agent can change the chosen server in the future, for example, if another server becomes more attractive at that time.

Competition Among Services

Until now we have discussed the issue of socially optimal prices. However, since potentially thousands of providers of the services will be on-line soon, we will also explore competitive strategies for price setters. The existence of many competitive entities may provide impetus for innovative pricing strategies, narrowly defined services, niche marketing strategies, and so forth, to obtain a better portion of the respective information markets. If, however, a few major entities control the market, queue management for a few highly desired services may be required while other services have to be subsidized. Loch (1991) looks at perfect and imperfect competition in oligopoly. We will draw results from Loch's study, extend these models to competitive markets, analyze the entry/exit incentives for service providers, and explore the competitive equilibrium issues for the Internet in future research.

Furthermore, if the marginal cost of providing a service is negligible, then service providers might implement marginal revenue-pricing for their services. This scheme will completely alter the pricing of congestion—since for larger services the revenues will be larger providing an incentive to subsidize the congestion costs of large users. The result will be the complete opposite of the proposed approach. We will also explore this issue in future research.

CONCLUSIONS

In this chapter we have modeled the Internet as an economy, where the users of the network services are consumers of the economy and the service providers are the producers. We modeled the user-service requests as a stochastic arrival process and proposed that a transaction-based priority price be associated with each server of the network. These prices are a congestion toll in which each service request entering the system pays the incremental delay cost imposed by it on all other users. With these prices, the system reaches a state of stochastic equilibrium in which user expectations are fulfilled on average, and demand is equal to the net benefit-maximizing level.

We presented the results from a simulation model where we compare a nonpriority pricing scheme to a free access scheme. The results conclusively demonstrate that pricing provides much higher net benefits than free access as the exogenous arrival rate of service requests increases. The net benefits decline under free access due to (i) negative externalities and (ii) forecasting errors in the predicted waiting times. Optimal pricing reduces the negative externality and is relatively robust against the forecasting errors in the predicted waiting times. It is conceivable that performance under free access can be improved by developing more sophisticated forecasting models (than the one-lag autoregressive model which we use in this study), and incorporating them in the decision-making process. However, we contend that under those conditions the performance under our pricing mechanism will also improve. Most significantly, we demonstrated that an iterative pricing mechanism can be employed which provides significant improvement in the system performance. The iterative mechanism makes the pricing approach practically attractive when the exogenous arrival rates are changing over time and where exact economic prices cannot be calculated in advance.

This study is a starting point for our exploration of the complex issues involving the pricing of the services at the Internet. The next step in this direction would be the introduction of priority classes with the current objective of maximizing collective benefits of the users. Simultaneously, we will explore the market structure which could evolve over the Internet. For example, the marginal-cost pricing of the product is conveniently assumed for the competitive market assumption. However, the marginal cost of providing services might be negligible over the Internet, especially if fixed access charges for the network backbone are used. How then should the products be priced? One answer could be marginal revenue pricing. However, under this scheme the competition can erode the congestion pricing, that is, service providers will have incentives to subsidize users' network service charges. A subsidy in network charges could, in turn, essentially recreate the current situation with inflated service request rates and could severely affect the load-management capabilities, since prices no longer support the optimal flow rates. We plan to study theoretical issues and provide some potential solutions.

Furthermore, we have considered the Internet backbone as a black box, ignoring questions regarding investment in it and its sustainability. In the future the NSF subsidy for the current Internet backbone, the NSFNET, will be removed, and commercial providers will provide the infrastructure. While the revenues from pricing might achieve better load management, they need not necessarily cover the cost of investment; thus, efficient cost recovering pricing for network infrastructure must be developed. The lack of dedicated links over the Internet makes use of a telephone billing mechanism invalid. The cable pricing model (the current model of charging based on capacity of the pipeline) can easily be implemented, and under sufficient capacity might be the best one to use. However, further research needs to be done to understand and address this issue completely.

In the next phase of our study, we will incorporate priority pricing in our simulation model. We expect to achieve even better system performance with priority pricing. We will also develop alternative strategies for choosing servers using dynamic forecasting, that is, software smart agents to help users monitor the system status continuously and reroute when beneficial.

We believe that our simulation model is an important tool which can be used to address several policy issues and explore important questions. For example, simulation can be used to evaluate the emerging market structures, the effect of monopolistic inefficiencies, and marginal cost versus marginal revenue pricing for services. Furthermore, simulation can be used to test the various approaches that can be used to pay for the infrastructure, that is, how infrastructure providers should recover their fixed costs.

NOTES

This research is funded in part by the National Science Foundation # IRI-9225010 but does not necessarily reflect the views of the NSF. Authors also thank Hewlett Packard Corporation for providing the necessary hardware for the simulation study.

1. TCP/IP, the communication protocol used at the Internet allows a link to be used by several users by probabilistic multiplexing of the packets from different users.

2. We concentrate here on queuing mechanisms; however, much of this argument can be developed for time-sharing mechanisms.

3. This applies to both user and network services.

4. By a priority class we mean that jobs in the highest priority class are processed before all the other jobs. At any time that job of a a higher priority than the rest in the queue arrives, it is put first in the queue. Thus, jobs in the highest priority class impose delays on the jobs in all other priority classes, whereas the jobs in lowest priority classes do not impose any delay on the jobs in other priority classes.

5. This assumption is based on empirical observations made by several researchers and on personal conversations with Smoot Carl-Mitchell, an expert on the Internet at Texas Internet Consulting here in Austin, Texas.

6. Note that some users might decide not to get the service because of the excessive delays; however, users with negligible delay costs will try to obtain the service regardless of the delays. Thus, with no pricing mechanism the services can potentially be accessed by only the users who value it the least.

7. We use a one-lag autoregressive process to predict the future waiting times.

8. Realistically, this work would be done by a smart agent executing on a client on the user's machine. We discuss this and more implementation issues later in the paper.

9. CSIM is a process-based simulation programming environment developed by H. Schwetman, an expert in computer performance evaluation at Mesquite Software, Inc., at Austin, Texas. It provides functions in C/C++ which can be used to control the simulation flow and gather queue statistics at each server. CSIM also has the capability of simulating parallel processing.

10. As mentioned earlier, the price updates are still made after ten units of time, that is, only the waiting time information is exact. Thus, only for free-access policy is this a true perfect information scenario.

11. Net benefits = Total of user values—Total delay costs suffered by the users.

Rental benefits = Rental charges collected at servers.

User benefits = Net benefits - Rental benefits.

REFERENCES

Bettman, J. E. (1979). *An Information Processing Theory of Consumer Choice,* Reading, Mass.: Addison-Wesley.

Cronin, Mary J. (1994). *Doing Business on the Internet: How the Electronic Highway is Transforming American Companies.* NY: Van Nostrand Reinhold.

Debreu, G. (1959). *The Theory of Value,* New Haven, Conn.: Yale University Press.

Etzioni, O., Levy, H. M., Segal R. B., and Thekkath, C. A. (1993). "OS Agents: Using a Technique in the Operating System Environment." *Technical Report 93-04-04.* Seattle: Department of Computer Science and Engineering, University of Washington.

Hagerty, M. R. (1986). "The Cost of Simplifying Preference Models." *Marketing Science,* 5 (4): 298–323.

Lancaster, K. J. (1966). "A New Approach to Consumer Theory." *Journal of Political Economy,* 74 (2): 132–157.

Loch, C. (1991). "Pricing in Markets Sensitive to Delay." Ph.D. dissertation, Stanford University.

Moore, J. C., Richmond, W. B., and Whinston, A. B. (1978). "A Decision Theoretic Approach to Information Retrieval." *ACM Transactions on Database Systems,* 15 (3): 311-340.

Moore, J. C., Richmond, W. B., and Whinston, A. B. (1978). "An Optimal Strategy Based on User Preferences for Choice Oriented Databases." Working paper, Center for Information Systems Management, University of Texas at Austin.

Reinhardt, A. (1994). "Building the Data Highway." *BYTE* (March): 46–74.

Sorenson, J., Tschirhart, J., and Whinston, A. B. (1978). "A Theory of Pricing under Decreasing Costs." *The American Economic Review,* 68 (4): 614–624.

Spigai, Fran (1991). "Information Pricing." In *Annual Review of Information Science and Technology,* vol. 26, ed. M. E. Williams, Learned Information Inc., Medford, N.J. pp. 39–73.

Stahl, Dale (1988). "Queue-Rationing and Price Dynamics." *Scandinavian Journal of Economics.* 89(4): 469–485.

Stahl, D. O., and Whinston, A. B. (1993). "An Economic Approach to Network Computing with Priority Classes." Working Paper, CISM, University of Texas at Austin. A version of this paper is available in postscript form on the World Wide Web server of Center for Information Systems Management, University of Texas at Austin. The URL for linking to this server is "http://cism.

bus.utexas.edu." The paper is under the title of "CISM Working papers." The paper can be viewed with a postscript viewer or can be downloaded and printed on any postscript printer.

4

Needed Innovations in Capital Expenditure Planning

Richard L. Tucker and G. Edward Gibson, Jr.

The construction industry is the country's second largest behind healthcare, representing nearly 8 percent of the GDP. Currently, annual construction volume in the United States is approximately $450 billion. Roughly $150 billion of this total goes for production facilities and infrastructure, which represents a significant source of expenditures for American companies and government. The capital expenditures of most companies are roughly equal to their before-tax profits. Thus, any cost savings created in the capital facility construction process will directly affect their bottom-line profits. Studies have also shown that one-third of all projects fail to meet budget and schedule objectives (Anderson and Tucker 1990). A paradigm shift is necessary to meet the changing global business environment and the challenge of developing world-class manufacturing facilities within budget and on time. A recent research investigation has identified pre-project planning as a process that can provide the vehicle to fuel this change.

The policy implications of the findings of this research investigation are clear. Organizations must invest resources into early planning of facilities, or risk a much higher probability of the facility's not meeting schedule, budget, or operating objectives. Intense global competition and tightened budgets make the assumption of these higher risks untenable for many organizations, and consequently they must improve their pre-project planning process. Several current industry trends are affecting these changes. The team-based, continuous improvement approach that many organizations have adopted focuses on satisfaction of customer expectations. Organizations are also re-engineering their business processes, reducing staff size, and outsourcing services—such as engineering design and construction—that are required to support core business processes. At the center of these changes are engineers and others who are not well prepared to perform in their roles as leaders, team members, communicators, and facilitators. Organizations and universities must provide an environment conducive to success through education in these critical skills.

CURRENT APPROACH

Pre-project planning is at the interface between engineering and business units within companies. The purpose of pre-project planning is to define projects to that point where risks can be adequately assessed in order to increase the likelihood of project success. The deliverable from this process is documentation that enhances the ability of designers and constructors to complete the facility with minimum disruptions. The completion of pre-project planning typically coincides with business representatives' making a decision to proceed with the project. Unfortunately, many companies do not treat this activity as a deliberate process and put little or no emphasis on its completion.

On most projects, a diverse group of participants is involved in the pre-project planning and, subsequently, the design and construction of the capital facility. These parties do not always have the same goals and have different ideas about what will make the project successful. Indeed, many times they represent several different companies. This approach creates a situation where engineers do not understand the strategic objectives of the owner company, and business leaders do not understand the demands of the project environment.

Too often engineers have been unable or unwilling to see the larger picture and have only concentrated on construction budgets and schedules. Project control objectives have a positive effect on the delivery of facilities but many times do not plan for the needs of the customer or measure whey they are being met. Therefore, it is important for engineers to break out of their current mentality and to understand the importance of the requirements of the end user. It is equally important for the owner of a facility to involve engineering, construction, and operations personnel in pre-project planning so that common goals can be created and the expertise of all the parties can be utilized.

Engineering organizations must be able to meet the needs of their clients and realize that their needs are not static (Juran 1988). New technologies create new customer needs that engineers must be ready to understand and meet. Engineers must also be able to forecast how new technologies will affect their customers so they are able to increase the value of the services they provide. An ability to quickly handle problems of customers is one of the most important aspects of customer satisfaction. Juran and Gryna (1993) state that even companies that are perceived as meeting customer needs still lose about one-quarter of their customers. Handling customer problems quickly and correctly is at least as important to customers as meeting their needs. Pre-project planning provides an excellent framework for defining and meeting customer needs, as well as developing a mechanism to respond to customer problems.

An important aspect of pre-project planning involves determining measures of success and incorporating them into the scope of the project. Anecdotal research has shown that pre-project planning can produce cost-benefit ratios as high as fifteen to one (Gibson et al. 1993). Due to the costs of many capital facilities, this is not an insignificant saving. However, for many companies, spending money on pre-project planning is not sanctioned. These companies feel that the expenditures are wastes of money, particularly since many projects are cancelled prior to design and construction.

IMPORTANT CONSIDERATIONS

Is pre-project planning really worth the effort? Can it lead to project and business success? Most experienced project managers believe that it can. However, few data have appeared in the literature supporting this view. As part of a continuing effort to improve the construction industry, the Construction Industry Institute (CII) chartered a research task force consisting of industry and academic representatives to study the effect of pre-project planning on project success.[1]

After a three-year investigation, the task force has determined that pre-project planning prior to project authorization (detailed design and construction) significantly improves the chance for project success. The study involved a detailed questionnaire that measured the level of pre-project planning effort expended and the success of projects. Sixty-two projects submitted by CII owner companies, with a combined total installed cost of $3.4 billion, were extensively studied. The projects ranged in size from $3.3 to $600 million with approximately half of the projects in excess of $25 million. The types (Figure 4.1) and sizes of projects represent significant capital expenditures for these companies.

Figure 4.1
Sample Project Type (N = 62)

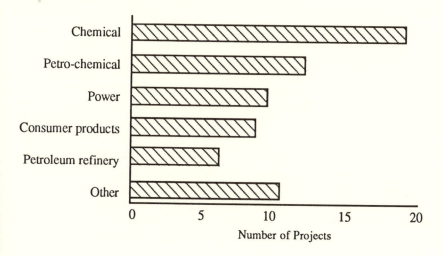

Number of Projects

A statistically correlated pre-project planning curve with 95 percent confidence intervals has been developed from the questionnaire data that demonstrates the positive impact that pre-project planning has on project success (Figure 4.2). The success index represents how the facility performed in terms of budget and schedule, as well as meeting design capacity and utilization targets after startup. The pre-project planning index represents the effort spent on pre-project planning and includes design effort complete at authorization, existence of a corporate charter, number of corporate groups represented in the pre-project planning effort, a project execution approach developed during pre-project planning, pre-project planning plan (process) in place, and the existence of control guidelines prior to authorization (Hamilton 1994).

Figure 4.2
Pre-Project Planning Success Curve with
95 Percent Confidence Intervals

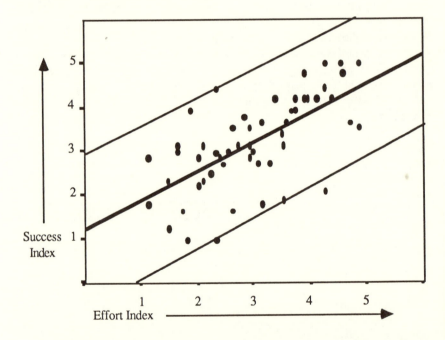

Data analysis of the sample shows that high pre-project planning effort produces a 20 percent average increase in cost predictability for design and construction for well-planned projects as opposed to poorly pre-project planned facilities (Table 4.1). All of these values are normalized versus the original authorization estimates. High, medium, and poor pre-project planning effort corresponds with the upper, middle, and lower third projects in terms of the index. Similar findings relate to schedule, operational, and utilization success.

Table 4.1
Project Outcomes for Pre-Project Planning Effort

Pre-Project Planning Effort	Category	Range	Average	Std. Dev.
High	Cost	-19 to +13%	-4%	7%
	Schedule	-57 to +17%	-13%	17%
	% Attainment	50 to 140%	102%	20%
	% Utilization	52 to 140%	103%	19%
Medium	Cost	-28 to +9%	-2%	10%
	Schedule	-57 to +45%	+8%	24%
	% Attainment	42 to 101%	93%	16%
	% Utilization	42 to 102%	94%	15%
Poor	Cost	-34 to +142%	+16%	45%
	Schedule	-55 to +125%	+26%	44%
	% Attainment	20 to 100%	87%	20%
	% Utilization	46 to 107%	85%	20%

As another part of this study, telephone interviews were conducted with business unit, operations, and project management representatives. A total of 131 telephone interviews were conducted consisting of 40 business unit representatives, 49 project managers, and 42 operations managers from 54 of the surveyed projects. Each was asked to rate his/her project in terms of the success of the project, and to rate the level of effort used in the pre-project planning phase. The results of the telephone interviews demonstrate the diversity of opinion of the different project participants concerning what makes a project successful, as shown in Figure 4.3 for success factors.

Ninety percent of the project managers attributed their perception of the level of success to project controls such as budget and schedule achievement, the number and magnitude of changes and rework, and the extent of the project punchlist. Conversely, only 46 percent of operations representatives perceived that project controls contributed to the success of the project. This is one example of the lack of common goals that exists on most projects. Operations managers, who are in effect the ultimate customers, felt that the success of the project was not determined by the very factors that project managers see as the most important. The individuals interviewed in this survey were all from the same owner corporations. If outside contractors had been surveyed, the lack of common goals would probably have been even more pronounced.

The real value of the success of any project is the success of the product or service that the company uses the facility to produce. Traditionally, project managers have measured the success of construction projects by the construction budget and schedule. However, with increased business competition, another important criterion, quality, is becoming more important. The quality of a finished facility is determined by the increased profitability to the company using the facility and how well it meets the owners' needs. Since design and construction costs are typically only 10–15 percent of the total life-cycle costs, it is more important that the facility meets the needs of the end user.

Figure 4.3
Main Reasons for the Project's Level of Success

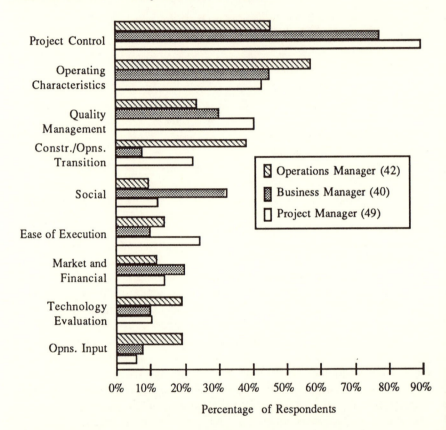

Engineering projects are typically measured by their ability to conform to specifications. This creates a situation where a project can meet the specifications but not meet the needs of the customer. A more rigorous definition of quality requires that the completed facility meet the needs and expectations of the end user (Fergusson and Teicholtz 1994). They studied the differences between perceptions of quality among project managers and strategic (business) and operations personnel. Similar to the results shown above, they found differences between the project managers and strategic and operations personnel concerning the importance of specific project success factors. In key areas such as meeting emission requirements and meeting production requirements, the level of satisfaction between project managers and strategic and operations personnel were significantly different. The results from this study also demonstrate the lack of goal and requirement communication that exists on large industrial projects.

The need to stress pre-project planning is essential to further the economic viability of many companies. The foundation of this change will be customer focus and process understanding. Without this change, we will continue to see the spectacular failures of many ventures that grace the headlines daily.

THE NEW PARADIGM

An evolving paradigm change emphasizing pre-project planning will lead to successful integration of business and engineering disciplines and ultimately to greater business success for many companies. Engineers will no longer be able to assess their performance using only hard measures such as project budget and schedule. Instead, they must understand more abstract concepts such as project quality, team decision making, and financial objectives—many of which are moving targets. Corporate changes will dictate that they be involved in greater detail at an earlier stage of the project than ever before. Team and interpersonal skills will be paramount in meeting this challenging environment. Client objectives and needs will be the cornerstone. Understanding the business process underlying the work will be important. Flexibility and adaptability to change will be a must. The following discussion explores the reasons and important concepts of this paradigm shift in more detail.

Interpersonal Skills

A study conducted by the CII concerning the potential for construction industry improvement points out some of the problems with project managers' managerial skills (Anderson and Tucker 1990). The study found that while 68 percent of owners felt that their project managers had above-average or outstanding technical knowledge, many felt they lacked managerial skills. Fifty-six percent said their project managers had average to poor human-relations skills, and 48 percent had average to poor leadership skills. The study stated that on large projects (over 10 million dollars) these managerial and human-relations skills were more important to the success of the project than technical knowledge. Project managers with high levels of technical knowledge became too involved in the details of projects and failed to manage the projects properly. The study recommended that human-relations and management skills be stressed on all sizes and types of construction projects. These skills are essential to the success of pre-project planning.

Teams

The ability of engineers and managers to work in teams is the goal of the new total quality management (TQM) philosophy inherent in many organizations. An example of this change is evident in the responses given in the telephone interviews discussed earlier concerning perceptions by the interviewees of improvements needed to increase the success of their projects. Thirty-eight percent of the respondents believed that quality management was the most important factor that needed improvement (Figure 4.4). Quality management includes personnel turnover, effective communications, teamwork effort, and guidance from management. However, 45 percent of the project managers, the highest of the three groups, believe that improving quality management is important. Project managers are typically engineers, demonstrating that many engineers know of the need to change their project management approach (Tortora 1993).

Figure   4.4
Factors That Need to be Improved to
Make the Project More Successful

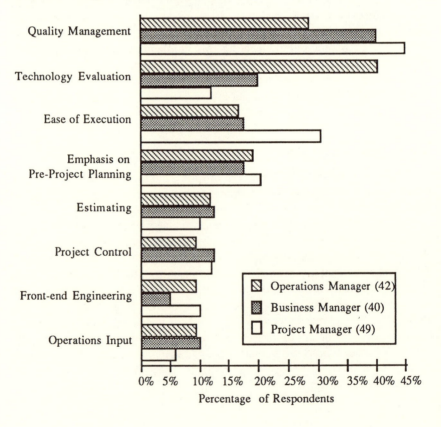

Percentage of Respondents

Technology Development

The evolution of new technologies is another driving force in this new paradigm. When planning for and constructing new facilities, engineers must make sure that they are using the most productive technologies that meet the needs of the customer. In the survey (Figure 4.4), 32 percent of the respondents indicated that better technology evaluation would have made their project more successful. Engineers must be able to evaluate the economic impact of new technologies and understand how these technologies will affect the life-cycle cost and operation of completed facilities. This again requires an engineer to broaden his/her understanding to other disciplines and incorporate their needs and ideas when making decisions. The best time to perform this evaluation is early in the project planning phase.

Corporate Change

The current downsizing of engineering departments by most corporations is another driving factor behind the paradigm shift. As engineering departments decline in size, employees will be forced to work in areas outside their traditional disciplines. Companies will focus on early planning with their scarce engineering resources. More outsourcing will be used for both production and creative activities. Consequently, engineers must be able to understand, interact, and manage people from all areas of the client's business during pre-project planning.

Data from the pre-project planning research investigation indicates that over 90 percent of the projects involved engineering personnel during the pre-project planning phase (Figure 4.5). However, business unit representatives were included on only 60 percent of the pre-project planning teams. Therefore, on approximately 30 percent of the projects, engineering or other discipline personnel had to evaluate project decisions impacting the business objectives of the company. Clearly, a large number of these decisions were made or influenced by engineers, and it is important that they develop some competence in these fields.

Engineers must be able to work with operators and other disciplines to ensure that the projects meet goals. As projects have become more complex, the use of multidisciplinary teams to plan complex projects has become more important. Whereas in the past an engineering staff could design a facility with little or no outside interaction, it now must get input from operations personnel, specialty vendors, environmental consultants, and a wide variety of other interests in order to be successful (Wilson 1994).

Process Re-engineering

Organizations have typically ascribed to a sequential approach when designing facilities which takes time. Cycle time for completion of facilities is extremely important. In *Reengineering the Corporation*, Hammer and Champy (1993) state that task-based thinking has created fragmentation that does not consider the process as a whole. Fragmentation causes companies to look at each element as a separate task and not at all of the tasks as a complete process. The same holds true for pre-project planning. Each of the functional group's inputs is important to pre-project planning but must be viewed as part of the entire process. The new paradigm will require re-engineering.

Figure   4.5
Disciplines   Represented   on   Pre-Project   Planning   Teams

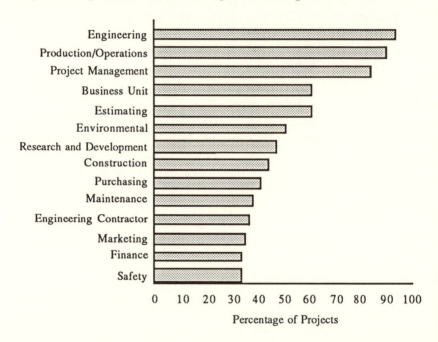

Work in other industries will spill over into the construction industry and influence this paradigm shift. The auto industry is a good example of the importance of teams-based early design. Japanese auto firms have mastered lean production techniques for automobile designs. These teams are largest at the very beginning of the development of the car when large amounts of time are devoted to front end engineering. As the design process continues, the teams are reduced in size. Design teams in the United States work in the exact opposite manner, with the team size peaking just before production as members attempt to fix problems that were not considered during front-end planning. Pre-planning teams allow Japanese car makers to use almost half the engineering hours and reduce the development time by over 30 percent for new car models compared to U.S. manufacturers (Womack et al. 1990).

This same approach is becoming more widespread in the delivery of capital facilities. Interview comments from successful projects during the research investigation such as "created a participative work environment and a team member approach to problem solutions" demonstrate the importance of teamwork on complex projects. Many of the interview respondents indicated that the number of different groups involved in the pre-project planning phase was critical to the success of the project. One of the business representatives surveyed stated, "We had a pie chart organization and everyone was involved up front: safety, project management, construction contractor and design." This project finished under budget and ahead of schedule, indicating that these new techniques have an impact on the traditional engineering measures.

Service Providers

The downsizing of owner-company engineering departments will require Architecture/Engineering/Construction (A/E/C) companies to become better service providers. A/E/C firms will be more involved in the coordination of functions that were previously provided by the client organization. This change will dictate that the services provided by A/E/C companies add more value to the client than just providing a completed facility (Halpin et al. 1993). Engineering and construction firms will have to be aware of emerging technologies that affect their clients, and must be able to advise their clients of the new technologies as part of their design and construction services. This approach will maximize the flow of information between the parties involved in a project and require project managers to become better team players and leaders to ensure that all of the diverse groups involved with the project can work toward a common goal.

Owner companies are also reducing the number of contractors they use. Work that has been traditionally done by the owner organization will now be performed by A/E/C firms that have a vested interest in the success of the company and the facility through alliances. Long-term partnering agreements will become commonplace.

Because of lower cost, American engineering design firms are contracting work overseas for many American projects. Due to this shift, American engineers must be able to adjust to a new role as design managers instead of design creators. Management skills will be as important as engineering skills for these designers because they will have to work with individuals from all over the world.

Education

In the past, the strict hierarchical style of management has allowed engineers to be successful managers because the division of work into simple tasks has created a very logical and fragmented management structure (Hammer and Champy 1993). However, the new management style of worker empowerment and the team process has destroyed the management system to which engineers are most accustomed. Universities must help facilitate their assimilation into this environment.

This new paradigm will also dictate that universities give students new skills in order to stay competitive. Currently, only 30 percent of the skills needed by project managers are taught in the typical four-year B.S. Engineering degree (Dorsey 1992). The remaining 70 percent are obtained through on-the-job training and seminars or through continuing education programs. The percentage of these skills learned in college needs to be increased so that companies receive employees who can quickly become more effective workers. More abstract topics such as team leadership, worker empowerment, and communication skills will be critical in the future. Engineering students will no longer be able to be productive managers with only a technical education, and they will be expected to produce much more quickly when they start their careers.

CONCLUSIONS

The functions of managers in industry will change drastically in the future. Driving this new paradigm will be an emphasis on more extensive early facility planning. As competition increases and technology progresses, engineers will be required to shoulder much of this change. Project managers must become better leaders and team players to successfully complete projects. There are many factors creating this new paradigm including globalization, the downsizing of owner firms, re-engineering, and the new focus on quality. Owners now expect more than a completed capital facility that meets the specifications. They want facilities to add value to their businesses and meet the needs of their operations. These requirements are forcing companies to look at facility construction as a single process that must involve all the participants on a project team. These teams help prevent duplication of effort and facilitate the exchange of ideas between the different project participants. With these changes come new requirements—and new opportunities for engineers.

The authors believe that a change in attitudes and skills is essential for engineers. TQM and re-engineering concepts are driving the integration of business and project objectives during pre-project planning. This new integration requires interpersonal and team skills that most engineers do not have. This new paradigm shift to better pre-project planning is critical to the success of U.S. companies.

In order to be globally competitive in the future, U.S. A/E/C companies must tailor their services so they are adding value to the main business objectives of their clients. This will require technical managers to be knowledgeable in team management and focused on client satisfaction. A/E/C firms must realize that the decisions they make have substantial impacts on the life-cycle costs of facilities and that these costs are significant to the economic welfare of their clients.

Universities must also recognize this change and be sure they are teaching students the skills they will need in the future. Core engineering courses should always be a part of engineering education, but these must be augmented with business and management courses. Universities must also focus on continuing education so they can meet the changing needs of industry.

Universities must realize that they have an opportunity and an obligation to support industry by providing the necessary education and training. They must be sensitive and prepared to adjust their curricula to meet these needs. It is also important that universities continue with research aimed at predicting the future needs of industry.

NOTES

1. CII is a consortium of large owner and engineering firms founded in 1983 to conduct research in the engineering and construction arena. It is headquartered at The University of Texas at Austin in the College of Engineering and currently has approximately ninety members. CII is considered one of the premier research organizations in the world dealing with project issues.

REFERENCES

Anderson, S. and Tucker, R. (1990). "Potential for Construction Industry Improvement. Volume II, Assessment Results, Conclusions and Recommendations," Construction Industry Institute, Source Document 62, November.

Dorsey, R. (1992). "Evaluation of College Curricula Which Prepare Management Personnel for Construction." Construction Industry Institute, Source Document 71, April.

Drucker, Peter. (1992). *Managing for the Future. The 1990's and Beyond.* New York: Truman Talley Books.

Fergusson, K., and Teicholtz, P. (1994). "Industrial Facility Quality Perspectives In Owner Organizations" Accepted for publication, *ASCE Journal of Performance of Constructed Facilities.*

Gibson, G. E., Kaczmarowski, J. H., and Lore, H. E. (1993). "Modeling Pre-Project Planning for the Construction of Capital Facilities," Construction Industry Institute, Source Document 94, July.

Halpin, D., Huang, R., Hastak, M., Dozzi, S., Unkefer, R., and Bopp, P. (1993). "The Future Needs of the Construction Industry's Worldwide Customers." Construction Industry Institute, Source Document 90, April.

Hamilton, Michele R. (1994). "The Relationship Between Pre-Project Planning Effort and Project Success for Capital Construction Facilities." Ph.D. dissertation, Department of Civil Engineering, University of Texas at Austin.

Hammer, Michael, and Champy, James. (1993). *Reengineering The Corporation.* New York: HarperCollins.

Juran, J. M. (1988). *J. M. Juran on Planning for Quality.* New York: Free Press.

Juran, J. M., and Gryna, F. (1993) *Quality Planning and Analysis*. New York: McGraw-Hill.

Tortora, Aniello. (1993). "Perceptions of Project Representatives Concerning Project Success and Pre-Project Planning Efforts." Master of Engineering thesis, Department of Civil Engineering. University of Texas at Austin, December.

Wilson, Charles. (1994). "The Effect of Team Factors on Pre-Project Planning and Project Success." Master of Engineering thesis, Department of Civil Engineering. University of Texas at Austin, August.

Womack, J., Jones, D., and Roos, D. (1990). *The Machine That Changed The World: The Story of Lean Production*. New York: HarperCollins.

5

Interdisciplinary Research in Materials and Devices for Electronics and Photonics

John M. White and Ben G. Streetman

Preparing the next generation of leaders in science and technology requires different, and often collaborative and interdisciplinary, approaches to education and training. In no area is this kind of training more important than in microelectronics. As one part of this enterprise, we describe an interdisciplinary approach to the engineering, chemistry, and physics of materials and devices for electronics and photonics.

INTRODUCTION

The United States was once the unchallenged leader in electronics. Radio, television, transistor circuits, and the early calculators were U.S. products. Unfortunately, in recent years Japan, Europe, and other areas have been able to capture the market for color television, videocassette recording, compact disk systems, and many other drivers of the modern economy. The United States still owns much of the computer business, but our machines increasingly contain components from abroad. Of mounting concern is the fact that Japanese researchers are investing heavily in semiconductor research, including the burgeoning field of optoelectronics and photonics, which will play a major role in computing and communication in the next century. The needed U.S. response to this challenge is a multifaceted problem requiring many solutions. It is clear, however, that the heart of any solution is the strength of advanced research in electronic materials and devices, and the education of the next generation of young people to work on these problems.

Because of the broad nature of the problems involved and the interdisciplinary nature of the possible solutions, it is clear that a collaborative research effort is needed. At the University of Texas at Austin a major thrust in materials and devices for electronics and photonics was initiated in the 1980s, resulting in the addition of faculty specializing in semiconductors and related fields. As a result, the Microelectronics Research Center and the NSF-supported Science and Technology Center are addressing these research issues, involving faculty and students in chemistry and physics, electrical and computer engineering, chemical engineering, and through collaboration with faculty in materials science and engineering, in manufacturing systems engineering. Faculty and graduate students at UT-Austin are working on the materials necessary for the next generation of integrated circuits and optoelectronic systems, advanced crystal growth (with control at the atomic layer dimension) of complex structures for semiconductor lasers, detectors, and modulators for photonic systems, and novel microwave and millimeter wave devices. We are also involved in advanced packaging research, which is of paramount importance to the successful use of devices in systems—an area that has been largely dominated by Japan.

Research in microelectronics and photonics at UT-Austin deals with new ways of making semiconductor materials and new ways of applying them to next-generation systems. We are taking a new look at the chemical precursors used in growing both silicon and compound (e.g., gallium arsenide) crystals, so that they can be made better and more safely. We are growing advanced structures with layer thickness controlled at the atomic-layer scale, allowing us to conceive and develop radically new devices. As an example, we are using multilayer growth to achieve semiconductor lasers that emit light through the top surface of the wafer. It is likely that this type of device will play a role in future optical interconnection schemes for large-scale systems.

One major component of the University of Texas effort is supported by the National Science Foundation under its Science and Technology Centers program. Known as the Center for the Synthesis, Growth and Analysis of Electronic Materials, this center focuses on the critical and intellectually stimulating relationship of chemistry to the physics and engineering of electronic materials crystal growth; it combines the talents of an extremely productive group of researchers selected from excellent academic, industrial, and government laboratories. Through an integrated and collaborative research program that links chemists, physicists, and engineers, we are developing and demonstrating new concepts for electronic materials, structures, and devices—concepts that will lead to smaller, faster, and more densely integrated electronic devices with tailored optical and electronic properties.

Silicon research at UT-Austin includes advanced epitaxial growth techniques involving remote-plasma enhanced growth, laser enhanced growth, and rapid thermal processing applied to chemical vapor deposition. These techniques allow growth at low temperatures and in selective regions of the wafer. New integrated circuit structures are studied, including new approaches to device and process modeling. Research in compound semiconductors involves epitaxial growth of multilayer heterostructures using molecular beam epitaxy (MBE) and organometallic vapor phase epitaxy (OMVPE) techniques. These heterostructures are used in high-speed and microwave devices and in optoelectronic sources, detectors, modulators, and waveguides. The capability of precisely controlling layer dimensions and composition by MBE and OMVPE is used in developing new devices such as resonant tunneling structures, photodetectors, and surface-emitting lasers.

At UT-Austin we have significant research support from the Department of Defense, the National Science Foundation, the Texas Advanced Research and Technology Program, and from industry. We have been designated a SEMATECH Center of Excellence, and we participate with Illinois and Michigan in the Center for Optoelectronics Science and Technology, supported by ARPA. We have one of the largest and most diverse semiconductor research programs at any university in the country, and the faculty involved include several members of the National Academy of Engineering, a Fellow of the Royal Society, and more than six NSF Presidential Young Investigators. Clearly, the investments made by UT-Austin over the past decade in people and facilities have paid off in allowing us to assemble a first-class group of researchers to work on these problems which are so significant to the country's economic development in the twenty-first century.

In 1992 most of the microelectronics group moved into a new facility at the Pickle Research Campus, the Microelectronics and Engineering Research Building. This facility includes cleanrooms, chemical and gas-handling capabilities, testing and evaluation laboratories, and office space for approximately 15 faculty and 120 graduate students in microelectronics and related research. This facility provides an outstanding environment for semiconductor materials and devices research and allows the faculty and students in microelectronics to develop strong interdisciplinary programs in an area of critical importance to the nation and to the state of Texas.

DESCRIPTION OF THE RESEARCH

Chemical Precursors for Semiconductors

The NSF Science and Technology Center brings together faculty from chemistry, physics, and chemical engineering with faculty from electrical and computer engineering to investigate the chemistry involved in semiconductor crystal growth. The subject matter addressed by the center—new routes to electronic materials, structures, and devices—is of fundamental interest and can play an important role in the future strategic and economic competitiveness of the United States. By focusing on chemical issues, our center uniquely complements other university-based centers and industrial laboratories. The rationale for support as a center rests on the complex and naturally interdisciplinary character of the questions being addressed, questions whose timely answers demand close, collaborative interactions between chemists, physicists, and engineers.

The research being undertaken in the center focuses on two types of electronic materials, column IV and column III-V compound semiconductors. The theme of the research is to address the chemical questions that impact the physics and engineering of thin-film electronic materials growth. Moving back and forth between films and molecules, center activities in both thrusts connect molecular precursor synthesis to surface and gas phase reaction chemistry and to precursor chemical and physical properties. In turn, there are strong, mutually reinforcing links of these with thin-film growth science and with electronic and optical characterization. Broadly speaking, the column IV thrust emphasizes the gas phase and surface reaction chemistry and optical and electrical characterization associated with thin-film growth using a broad range of thermal and nonthermal activation methods, for example, remote plasma, photolytic, and rapid thermal processing. While this thrust involves mainly known precursors, both conventional and nonconventional, to Si, Ge, and dopants, chemical synthesis plays a crucial part by preparing isotopically and structurally tailored molecules that are used to test hypotheses related to film growth and reaction mechanisms. In the III-V thrust, known precursors are also heavily investigated, but much more emphasis is given to novel precursors. Thus, chemical synthesis drives many of the center's III-V activities by developing new synthetic strategies and providing a test bed of new molecules for evaluation.

Relying on the across-the-board expertise of its faculty and collaborators, the center gives particular attention to interdisciplinary projects and facilities that address the complex issues associated with our theme. As one example, in the III-V thrust we have successfully synthesized novel single-source precursors, evaluated their properties, and successfully grown thin films from them in bench-scale film growth facilities. The feedback from film growth science to chemistry is built into the day-to-day operation of the center, and new science and engineering is emerging along with heightened awareness of issues that need to be addressed at the boundaries between subdisciplines. Beginning in synthetic chemistry laboratories, instrumentation for first-line pyrolytic screening of new precursor molecules has been developed and connected directly to surface analytical equipment for second-level experiments designed to study the stoichiometry and purity of monolayer films prepared from selected precursors. From among the relatively large number of molecules that are synthesized, we anticipate that several will pass the second level. From among these, only the most promising are studied in the film growers' bench-scale facilities, where thicker films are grown and evaluated electrically and optically, in many cases as model device structures.

Silicon Structures

Fundamental to modern electronics is silicon technology, which accounts for the majority of microelectronics products. Strong research efforts in this area at UT-Austin are focused along two major thrusts: (1) new approaches to scaling of the classical transistors to the farthest limit of miniaturization, resulting in the highest possible levels of integration, reliability, and performance in integrated circuits; and (2) revolutionary new concepts leading to totally new devices which may eventually supplant the classical devices and lead to unprecedented levels of integration and performance in the next century.

Continued Aggressive Scaling of the Classical Devices

This research thrust has major activities in the development of new structural approaches for deep submicron (< 0.35 μm) MOS transistors which provide for not only smaller feature size and improved performance, but high reliability as well. For example, selective silicon epitaxy is being pursued, since it is now recognized that this technological capability is mandatory for deep submicron devices in which structures will be much more three-dimensional in nature. A strong research effort also exists in the development of improved reliability, ultra-thin (< 10 nm) gate dielectrics for deep submicron MOS transistors. The effort is based on a new approach using N_2O for achieving sophisticated oxynitride gate dielectrics and using both conventional furnace processing and rapid thermal processing. The dielectric research is also focused on the development of new alternative capacitor dielectrics for application to 256 Mbit and 1 Gbit DRAMs. Microelectronics Research Center faculty are currently working on ferroelectrics such as alloys of lead-lanthanum zirconate titanate because these materials also hold promise for nonvolatile memory applications. Finally, faculty are developing an understanding of the closely connected microstructure and electrical properties of polysilicon, in view of its increasingly varied use in advanced device structures, in particular for silicon-on-insulator type of approaches to large memories.

Revolutionary New Device Concepts

It is generally believed that the revolutionary new device concepts that replace the classical MOS and bipolar transistors during the next century will be based on materials structures with hyper-abrupt doping and compositional interfaces. Such structures will contain component regions whose dimensions are measured in numbers of atomic layers. Toward this end we have a strong research program in low temperature silicon-based epitaxy and heteroepitaxy. The approaches are focused on the use of substitutes for thermal energy (i.e., low energy photons and particles such as electrons, ions, and neutral atoms). For example, remote plasma-enhanced chemical vapor deposition (RPCVD) has been applied to grow $Si_{1-x}Ge_x/Si$ heterostructures such as quantum wells and strained-layer superlattices. Also, with RPCVD, UT researchers have demonstrated what is believed to be a world record low temperature of 150°C for silicon epitaxy. This effort is also focused on the study of various types of silicon-based structures and heterostructures for optoelectronic applications which would allow easier integration with silicon integrated circuits and devices. Hopes in this research area have recently been strongly boosted by the observation of unusually high efficiency photoluminescence in porous silicon and $Si_{1-x}Ge_x/Si$ heterostructures.

Compound Semiconductor Structures

One of the most exciting and useful developments in modern semiconductor electronics is the capability of engineering band structure, quantum phenomena, optical properties, and other useful effects by the growth of multilayer heterostructures. With the advent of advanced semiconductor growth techniques such as molecular beam epitaxy (MBE) and organometallic chemical vapor deposition (OMCVD), much of modern compound semiconductor device development now involves quite complex and precise multi-heterojunction structures. The availability of high-quality multilayer heterostructures has led to new effects having widespread applications such as two-dimensional transport effects, quantum wells, modulation doping, delta doping, carrier and photon confinement, and so forth. Recently, distributed Bragg reflectors (DBR) have been added to this collection of capabilities. As a result, the future for device invention and development is extremely fertile, combining electronic and photonic effects in new ways for novel applications. Clearly, future computer and communication systems will increasingly depend on high-speed electronic, photonic, and microwave/millimeter-wave devices based on these capabilities. Applications in telecommunications and data transmission are already well underway; new applications such as optical interconnects in VLSI systems are possible and are being pursued aggressively at laboratories around the world.

Photonics, a blending of optics and electronics, has emerged as one of the world's most rapidly developing technologies. It is becoming clear that photonics will become a core technology for telecommunications, information processing, optical storage and display, and sensors. Photonics relies on optoelectronic devices to generate, modulate, switch, and detect optical signals. Among the crucial optoelectronic components for photonic systems are semiconductor lasers, photodetectors, guided-wave devices, and optoelectronic integrated circuits. Experience has shown that significant contributions to this field can be made by university researchers if materials growth studies are coupled intimately with device development. With that goal in mind, we have assembled at UT-Austin a team of research faculty and the requisite equipment and facilities to approach this problem broadly and with the required tools to make significant progress. Crystal growth facilities in MBE and OMCVD enable research on resonant tunneling diodes, waveguides, quantum wells, avalanche photodiodes, photovoltaic devices, vertical cavity surface-emitting lasers (VCSELs), and a variety of other structures.

Photodetectors

Photodetectors perform the essential function of converting optical signals into an electrical format. The thrust of this effort is to develop new photodetector structures capable of enhanced performance relative to conventional photodetectors. In recent years photodetector structures have become more complex in response to more stringent performance demands such as higher bandwidth and lower noise. There are, however, fundamental performance limitations that remain to be addressed. It is clear that these problems call for a major technological breakthrough rather than incremental improvements in conventional structures. As examples, UT faculty have recently demonstrated a novel resonant-cavity photodiode structure that decouples the quantum efficiency from the transit time, and have used Bragg reflectors grown by MBE to tailor mirrors sensitive to more than one wavelength of light.

Semiconductor Lasers

The vertical-cavity surface-emitting laser has recently gained much attention in the research literature because of its unique advantages. This type of structure represents a minimum volume laser, since the Fabry-Perot cavity length is on the order of the lasing wavelength, and thus it has the greatest potential of any semiconductor laser structure for ultra-low threshold current. The device's vertical geometry is tailormade for large scale integration, since light is emitted normal to the epitaxial surface, and thus it is also compatible with large area two-dimensional operation of phased arrays for high power operation. From a manufacturing standpoint, wafer scale testing is possible with the vertical-cavity laser, and it may be a critical component for integrated circuit applications when several lasers are required on a single chip. We have fabricated state-of-the-art vertical-cavity, surface-emitting lasers, and have developed models that reveal new emission phenomena in microcavities.

Optoelectronic Integrated Circuits

Circuits that consist primarily of electronic components and incorporate an optoelectronic device to get an optical signal onto or off of the chip are referred to as optoelectronic integrated circuits (OEIC). The direct benefits of integrating the optoelectronic and electronic devices include higher performance, lower costs, and greater reliability. This has stimulated research on OEICs in industrial and academic laboratories in Japan, Europe, and the United States. Japanese industries, in particular, have already invested heavily in this emerging technology. There is a critical need for parallel research programs in the United States if we are to remain competitive. UT-Austin researchers have begun an effort to fabricate and characterize a receiver OEIC which will consist of a $Si_{1-x}Ge_x$ photodiode and a Si MOSFET preamplifier.

Optical Interconnects

We are beginning to see the emergence of a new technology, optical interconnects, that promises to reduce the interconnect delays that plague high-speed integrated circuits. Optical fibers are already being used to provide high-speed, computer-to-computer communications. Several computer manufacturers are using optical fibers to connect their central processing units with their storage systems. Some manufacturers are already using optical fibers to interconnect modules within their processors. In addition, research is in progress to implement the optical equivalent of printed-circuit interconnects and of optical free-space interconnects.

CONCLUSIONS

The interdisciplinary research outlined here is important not only for the development of new technologies but also for the development of a new type of researcher. To meet future human resource requirements, we are educating a new generation of highly qualified scientists and engineers with multidisciplinary training in the synthesis, growth, and analysis of electronic materials, and the development of new devices for electronics and photonics applications. For graduate students, we provide numerous opportunities for collaborative research projects. For undergraduates, particularly those from underrepresented groups, we operate an undergraduate program of research experience and practice during the academic year and, during the summer, a research apprentice program that includes students from other institutions. For precollege students, we operate a science camp for middle-schoolers and, at the elementary school level, the locally acclaimed "Zavala Young Scientists" program. A number of mechanisms and activities ensure effective knowledge transfer. Most important is the involvement of faculty and students with colleagues in industry and government laboratories. We believe the research described here is an example of the type of collaboration needed among traditional disciplines to address the technological problems of the twenty-first century.

ACKNOWLEDGMENTS

The authors acknowledge the support of the National Science Foundation through the Science and Technology Center program, grant number CHE 8920120. Many of the ideas and much of the text for this article was provided by faculty in the Microelectronics Research Center and the NSF Science and Technology Center at UT-Austin.

Part II
NEW METHODOLOGIES

The Unreasonable Effectiveness of Management Science for Solving Management Problems

Gerald L. Thompson

Several simple examples are described in this chapter that illustrate how management science techniques are used to help make decisions concerning the operation of an organization, so that, without altering the personnel or equipment in the organization, it can be made to operate more efficiently. The management science method starts by deriving a mathematical model of part or all of the organization, applying some kind of mathematical analysis to characterize good operating rules for the model, and then implementing these rules in running the organization. The solution of each example problem involves the application of nontrivial mathematical principles that not only solve the problem at hand but also give additional new, unexpected, and useful information concerning that problem. The added benefits obtained from that extra information justify the phrase "the unreasonable effectiveness of management science."

INTRODUCTION

Traditionally, mathematics has been applied almost exclusively to solving problems in physics and engineering. This tradition held true until about the time of World War II, that is, until about 1940. During that war mathematical ideas were applied to solving entirely different kinds of problems, such as breaking codes used by enemy countries, finding the optimal shape of a convoy, determining optimum search strategies for locating enemy ships at sea, and many other new kinds of problems.

The end of World War II saw the beginning of an explosion of other new applications of mathematical techniques for solving problems—such as optimum operation of organizations, inventory management in a factory, scheduling of work to machines, personnel administration, logistics, and many other areas too numerous to mention. The invention of electronic computers caused this explosion to become even greater. Collectively, these methods have come to be known as both management science and operations research. We shall use the first name in this article.

The title of this paper was inspired by the physicist Eugene Wigner's paper titled, "The Unreasonable Effectiveness of Mathematics Applied to Physics." The point of his fascinating article was that formulating a physics problem as a mathematical model and applying the discipline of mathematics to study the model frequently not only led to the solution of the original physical problem but also gave unexpected new insights into its physics. As we shall see, something quite similar happens when management science is applied to a mathematical model of a management problem.

The number and importance of management science applications is still increasing dramatically. It is safe to say that every organization, large or small, can make use of some of the techniques that appear in the technical journals of the two societies, The Institute for Management Science and The Operations Research Society of America, to which most of the practitioners of these methods belong. In particular it is recommended that readers of the present article who are interested in more details on similar kinds of problems consult with the publication *Interfaces* published jointly by the two societies.

In this article a brief discussion is given of some simple management problems, their solution by management science techniques, and (in some cases) the estimated impact on the companies that used the solutions. A deliberate attempt has been made to keep the models and solution techniques simple enough that any reader can understand them by applying a little effort.

SOLUTIONS OF MODELS OF SMALL MANAGEMENT PROBLEMS

In this section we will discuss, in order of increasing complexity, four problems that will illustrate what a management science method is and how it can help to solve a management problem.

The 3-4-5 Triangle and Pyramid Construction

The ancient Greeks knew that when a triangle is constructed with sides in the proportions 3, 4, and 5, the angle opposite the longest side is a right (90 degree) angle. You can verify that this is so by taking a piece of rope or string, tying two knots in it, and finally tying the two free ends together to form such a triangle. This technique was used by artisans in ancient Egypt who worked on the construction of pyramids and who needed a simple way of checking on the squareness of the building blocks they used. Although it was a simple idea, it had enormous practical significance at that time.

The Snake Heuristic and Parallel Painting of Cars

In the past few years a well known automobile manufacturer has constructed several automated factories having assembly lines with parallel flows of cars under construction, instead of the old assembly line which had only a single flow. In these new factories, a partially completed car is carried from one workstation to another on an automatically guided vehicle (AGV) which is controlled by a central computer. One of these workstations is the paint shop, which has several paint booths that operate in parallel.

In each booth there is a robot painter which can paint a car some color and then either keep the same color to paint the next car or change to a different color, as required. The process of changing colors, called *purging*, involves washing out the old color in a painter with a solvent and then bleeding in the new color. Each time a painter is purged some good paint is wasted, at a cost called the *purge cost*.

Usually there are more colors for vehicles than there are paint booths. As an example, assume that there are four different paint booths, and six different colors are needed to paint the cars. Also assume that sixty cars are to be painted in a given shift and the numbers of vehicles to be painted each of these colors is as shown in Figure 6.1.

Figure 6.1
Data for the Sixty-Car Example

---

12 red, 11 blue, 10 silver, 15 white, 7 grey, 5 orange

If the order in which the cars is scheduled is random, without regard to the colors they are to be painted, then the purge cost may be incurred for nearly every vehicle. In fact, when one of these automated factories first started production in the late 1980s using the random sequencing method, purge rates of 90 percent or more were often observed. In other words, the color was changed after painting nine out of every ten cars produced. Assuming a yearly production of 500,000 cars and a purge cost of $25, this gives an annual purge cost of $11,250,000 for this one factory alone. Besides the purge cost there is also the cost of disposing of the wasted paint.

In about 1988, the author (together with then graduate student Norman Lafond) proposed the following "snake heuristic" rule that reduced the number of purges needed from 90 percent of the number of cars produced in a single shift to one less than the number of different colors being painted in that shift. Thus, if 500 cars are to be painted one of 11 different colors in a given shift, the number of purges can be reduced from (0.9 X 500 =) 4500 to (11 minus 1 =) 10. What this means, in essense, is that the purge cost, which formerly was significantly large, can be essentially eliminated by using this method. As we will see in the next paragraph, the calculations needed to find a good sequence using the snake heuristic are extremely simple.

We illustrate the snake heuristic sequencing method using the problem data given in Figure 6.1. Since there are four paint bays, we arrange the cars in four different rows of fifteen each, by listing in the first row all twelve red cars, followed by three of the blue cars, then snaking down (follow the arrow) to the end of the second row and listing (from right to left) the remaining eight blue cars, followed by seven of the silver cars, then snaking down to the beginning of row three and moving (from left to right) and listing two silver and thirteen white cars, then snaking down to the fourth row and listing (from right to left) three white cars followed by seven green cars followed by five orange cars.

Given the snake diagram in Figure 6.2., in order to get the optimum production sequence we can simply read each column of the snake diagram from top to bottom. Thus the desired production sequence consists of two copies of the group R S S O, followed by three copies of R S W O, followed by three copies of R S W G, followed by five copies of R B W G, and ending with three copies of B B W W. This optimum sequence is given in Figure 6.3. Note that in each group between two and four different colors are required, so that each one of the four paint bays can be dedicated to painting only a single color, changing to a new color only infrequently. In fact, in the above pattern there are only five required color changes, which is one less than six, the number of different colors, as asserted above.

Figure 6.2
Snake Diagram for the Sixty-Car Example

Figure 6.3
Optimum Production Sequence for the Sixty-Car Example

R S S O	R S S O	R S W O	R S W O	R S W O
R S W G	R S W G	R B W G	R B W G	R B W G
R B W G	R B W G	B B W W	B B W W	B B W W

The proof that the minimum number of color changes can always be achieved by using the snake heuristic is not difficult. However, the fact that the optimum sequence can be found so simply by using the snake heuristic is remarkable.

It is a common belief that workers in a factory are likely to sense when there is an inefficiency in a production procedure and will eventually make suggestions which will cause the factory to correct the problem. However, the above paint shop example shows that this is not likely to happen because production sequences are chosen by the central production department, which is located several miles from the paint shop. Communications among the workers who knew about the waste of paint, the accountants who knew the total cost of the wasted paint, and the schedulers who could correct the problem was nonexistent. Hence the identification and solution of the problem depended upon visits by outside consultants.

The Bookbinder's Problem

The production of a book involves two major steps, print and binding, and obviously these steps must be done in that order. Each step involves a different machine, the first a printing press, and the second a binding machine. Suppose a printing company has four books to produce and has estimated the printing and binding times to be as show in Figure 6. 4. How should the printing company schedule these jobs in order to complete all jobs in the shortest possible time?

Figure 6.4
Data for the Bookbinder's Problem

Book	A	B	C	D
Printing Time	5	3	1	3
Binding Time	2	4	4	2

Your first thought might be that it doesn't make any difference, or that it is best to just leave the choice of the order to the printing staff who have had many years of experience in doing this kind of work. Sometimes workmen do have an intuition about how to find good schedules for such a problem. For instance, a workman might say that it is best to start with jobs having short printing times so that they will be free to go on to be bound and give the binding machine some work to do. In fact the rule just stated is a good one, but it does not go far enough to obtain the best possible schedule for the jobs.

In 1954 a mathematician named Selmer Johnson proved that the following procedure would find an optimum sequence for performing the jobs. He first noted that there need not be any idle time on the printing machine regardless of the order in which the jobs are done. Second, he showed that the order of doing the jobs could always be the same on both machines in an optimum schedule. Third, he devised the following simple algorithm (procedure) that would always produce an optimal schedule.

To describe the algorithm we start with an empty list of four jobs as shown in Figure 6.5. What we need to do is to put each of the letters A, B, C, and D in one of the four empty positions, to indicate the order in which each job is to be performed on each machine. We will do this by creating two partial lists: an increasing list which starts at position 1 and moves to the right, and a decreasing list which starts at 4 and moves to the left. The algorithm is then as stated in Figure 6.6.

Figure 6.5
Empty List at the Start of the Algorithm

| --- | --- | --- | --- |
| 1 | 2 | 3 | 4 |

Figure 6.6
Algorithm for the Bookbinder's Problem

---

1. Find the job, X, requiring the shortest time on either machine.
2. If the shortest time is on machine 1 put job X on the right of the increasing list.
3. If the shortest time is on machine 2 put job X on the left of the decreasing list.
4. Cross out the current job from the job list.
5. If any jobs remain on the list got to step 1; otherwise stop.

We illustrate this algorithm with the example in Figure 6.4. On the first step the smallest job time was C's first job requiring 1 time period, which is shown circled in the job list of Figure 6.7. Next to it is the unassigned job list with C put at the right of the increasing list as required in step two of the algorithm, and job C is crossed out of the job list as required in step four of the algorithm. The new job list is shown in Figure 6.8. In that figure we note that the smallest job time is now 2, which occurs twice, once as the second job for A and once as the second job for D. We arbitrarily choose the latter as the job to be removed and circle it as in Figure 6.8. Using rule 3, we put D to the left of the decreasing list, that is, in position 4, as shown in Figure 6.8. Using rule 4, job D is deleted from the job list as shown in Figure 6.9. In the new job list the smallest time is the second job for A shown circled in Figure 6.9. Hence A is put to the left of the decreasing list, as shown in Figure 6.9. After deleting A from the list of unassigned jobs, the only remaining job is B, which has its smallest time on the first machine. Hence we put B to the right of the increasing job list, that is, in position two in the production sequence as shown in Figure 6.10.

Figure 6.7
First Step of the Algorithm

A	B	C	D				
5	3	1	3	C	—		—
2	4	4	2	①	2	3	4

Figure 6.8
Second Step of the Algorithm

A	B	D		C	—	—	D
5	3	3		1	2	3	4
2	4	②					

Figure 6.9
Third Step of the Algorithm

A	B		C	—	A	D
5	3		1	2	3	4
2	4					

Figure 6.10
Fourth Step of the Algorithm.

B		C	B	A	D
3		1	2	3	4
4					

From Figure 6.10 we see that the optimum production sequence found is CBAD. Because A and D each require two hours on the binding machine, the sequence CBDA is another optimum production sequence.

The optimum production sequence CBAD, which requires fourteen hours to complete, can be represented as in Figure 6.11. This way of representing a schedule is called a Gantt chart, after the name of the person who first used it. The number of times a letter is repeated in each row of the chart indicates the number of hours of work that is required by that job on the corresponding machine.

Figure 6.11
Gantt Chart of the Optimum Schedule

Hour	1	2	3	4	5	6	7	8	9	10	11	12	13	14
Mach. 1	C	B	B	B	A	A	A	A	A	D	D	D		
Mach. 2		C	C	C	C	B	B	B	B	A	A		D	D

This algorithm is very easy to use and can be implemented to run very quickly on a personal computer even for problems having tens or hundreds of jobs. Implementing the use of this procedure in a real factory is thus very simple.

It is interesting to note that if we change the above algorithm so that in Step 1 it chooses the longest (instead of the shortest) job time on any machine, then the algorithm will create a schedule having the longest possible completion time, instead of the shortest. By making this change you may verify, if you wish, that the schedule DABC, having the longest completion time of nineteen hours, has the Gantt chart shown in Figure 6.12. Thus the longest schedule requires 36 percent more time to complete than the optimum schedule.

Figure 6.12
Gantt Chart of the Longest Schedule

H:	1	2	3	4	5	6	7	8	9	10	11	12	13	14	15	16	17	18	19
M. 1	D	D	D	A	A	A	A	A	B	B		B	C						
M. 2			D	D		A	A		B	B	B	B	C	C	C	C			

The fact that the longest completion time is considerably longer than the shortest time makes it clear that applying the above algorithm, which requires only a negligible amount of time to solve on a PC, is well worth the effort in terms of increased productivity. This would become even more evident if the problem had forty or four hundred jobs to sequence instead of only four.

Optimal Assignment of Persons to Jobs

At the end of each academic year the U.S. Air Force Academy has the problem of assigning its new graduates to various training schools such as flight training, navigation, logistics, and so forth. These new graduates are given leave of absence to spend some time at their homes before going to their new assignments. Once a decision has been made to assign graduate X to school A, it is easy to calculate the total transportation cost of sending X home and from there on to school A. Assuming that there are 1,000 graduates to be assigned to one of fifty different schools, each of which can accept twenty new students, it follows that there are 50,000 different potential paths that these students can take, and each path has a transportation cost. What is an optimum way of assigning students to schools that minimizes the overall transportation cost?

This kind of problem has been solved both theoretically and practically by using a branch of mathematics called linear programming. We will illustrate it by using a small example consisting of twelve students and four schools, with the requirement that each student should be assigned to exactly one school and each school should accept exactly three students. Figure 6.13 gives a table listing the schools on the left, and the students on the top. The entry in row i and column j of the table is the distance that student j must travel to go home and then go from home to his or her assigned school.

Figure 6.13
Distances for Student j to Go Home and Then to Go to Schools A, B, C, and D, for $j = 1, 2, \ldots, 12$

	1	2	3	4	5	6	7	8	9	10	11	12
A	200	175	(190)	(115)	375	800	(160)	725	450	175	320	170
B	370	225	730	185	(125)	660	555	710	1500	(140)	(235)	295
C	(125)	325	915	295	610	(235)	140	395	205	135	620	(140)
D	175	(115)	350	520	710	240	665	(275)	(185)	105	215	430

The problem just posed is a special kind of linear programming problem, called a transportation problem. This problem can be solved very quickly using a computer, even if it has thousands or millions of variables. Using a computer code, the optimal solution to the stated problem was found to be as follows: school A should accept students 3, 4, and 7; school B should accept students 5, 10, and 11; school C should accept students 1, 6, and 12; and school D should accept students 2, 8, and 9. The entries corresponding to these assignments are shown circled in Figure 6.13. The total transportation cost of this optimum solution is 2040 miles, which can be checked by adding together the circled entries in Figure 6.13.

Examination of the entries in Figure 6.13 shows that in most cases the optimum choice in a column is the minimum number in that column. However, for column 7 the second smallest number was chosen, for column 10 the third smallest entry was chosen, and for column 11 the second smallest entry was chosen. Thus, although one can find three quarters of the optimum solution correctly by inspection, it is not easy to see how to choose the other three column entries. For that reason it is necessary to use a mathematical algorithm to find the complete optimum solution and to prove that it is optimal.

In any case it is obvious that the optimum solution found for the problem in Figure 6.13 probably could not be found by ad hoc methods. Fortunately management science has provided algorithms and very fast computer programs capable of finding solutions quickly to transportation problems having thousands of variables.

CONCLUSIONS

The examples of the previous section were chosen to be as simple as possible so that they could be read by persons having modest mathematical backgrounds. But they were also selected to be examples actually found in some organizations and whose solutions have been applied to improve productivity. Many more such examples can be found in the journal *Interfaces* mentioned in the introduction.

The reason for writing this article was to demonstrate the importance of management science to the science and practice of management. If the reader finds some of the examples described here intriguing and/or informative, then the objective of this article will have been achieved.

NOTE

The author would like to dedicate this article to George Kozmetsky as a recipient of the National Medal of Technology in 1994.

7

Using Computer Intensive Technologies to Aid Insurance Regulators: Early Detection of Insolvency and Fraud

Patrick L. Brockett, Linda L. Golden, and Xiaohua Xia

Insurance insolvency and claims fraud are two of the most vexing problems faced by insurance regulators and insurance firms. Many efforts to construct early warning systems of insurance insolvency have been made. Examples of mainstream approaches to the problem include ratio tests of Insurance Regulators Information System (IRIS), as recommended for many years by the National Association of Insurance Commissioners, A. M. Best's Ratings, and statistical efforts. None of these systems has been wholly satisfactory. Fraud has also been an issue of some importance, but only limited research on the detection of claims fraud has been conducted. In this paper we introduce four computer-intensive technologies as alternatives and discuss their applications in detecting insurance insolvency and claims fraud. These approaches are data envelopment analysis, expert system, feedforward backpropagation neural network and Kohonen's self-organizing feature maps.

THE INSOLVENCY PROBLEM

The insurance industry, specifically either property and liability insurance or life and health insurance, has been vexed by the insolvency problem for a long time. Since 1961, approximately 350 property-liability insurers have failed, more than 249 insurers have voluntarily retired, and over 500 companies have merged into other companies, resulting in more than 1,100 property-liability company retirements (BarNiv and McDonald 1992). This insolvency record dramatically attests that state insurance regulators have been unable to prevent a large number of concurrent insolvencies.

Analysts have also tried to create methods which would provide early and effective warning or detection of insurance insolvency. As early as 1967, Denenberg (1967) created a heuristic analysis of solvency prediction for the insurance industry. Pinches and Trieschmann (Trieschmann and Pinches 1973; Pinches and Trieschmann 1974) considered a wide range of financial ratios in the context of multivariate discriminant analysis. The improvement indicated which financial characteristics were most highly correlated with insolvency and provided a framework in which the statistical validity of the conclusions could be objectively determined (Ambrose and Seward 1988).

The National Association of Insurance Commissioners (NAIC) database and the associated Insurance Regulators Information System (IRIS) ratio tests are among the most widely used insolvency prediction systems. In spite of their wide use, IRIS ratio tests have several problems, which include their pass/fail nature, the fact that the ratios are equally weighted in importance, and their strong dependence on surplus (which is easily manipulated). In addition, the relationship between the number of ratio tests failed and the risk of insolvency is neither specified nor discernible (Barrese 1990).

Multivariate discriminant analysis (MDA), with its many variations, has been suggested as an alternative to the IRIS system. MDA classifies firms according to a linear combination of variables, including any interaction effects and therefore should excel in predicting which firms become insolvent (Harrington and Nelson 1986; Ambrose and Seward 1988). In addition, MDA produces a single measure of financial strength (or distress) based upon the value of the discriminant function (Harrington and Nelson 1986) rather than a binary pass/fail conclusion. The disadvantages of MDA methodology result from its two underlying assumptions, which are often violated, that all sampling variates are drawn independently from a multivariate normal population and that the covariance matrices of the discriminant groups are statistically identical, since classifying an insolvent firm as a solvent one is more dangerous and costly than identifying a solvent firm as an insolvent one.

Many other approaches have been developed or discussed, including the nonparametric discriminant model (NPDM) (BarNiv and Raveh 1986, 1989), the regression approach using surplus premiums as the response variable (Harrington and Nelson 1986), the logit model (Barrese 1990), and so on. Although these alternatives demonstrate a potential to predict insurance insolvency, they also exhibit weaknesses.

THE CLAIMS FRAUD PROBLEM

Claims fraud is another problem which has challenged insurance industries more recently. Individuals and conspiratorial rings of claimants and providers unfortunately can and do manipulate the claim processing system for their own undeserved benefit (Derrig and Ostaszewski 1993). Some 25 percent of all automobile theft claims are fraudulent, costing the insurance industry about $2 billion annually. Automobile bodily injury (BI) insurance is the largest line of property-liability insurance in the United States. Estimates indicate that approximately 40–50 percent of BI claims are under some suspicion, due either to fraud or to intentional cost inflation. The proportion of suspicious BI claims tends to be increasing. According to the National Health Care Association, insurance fraud represented an estimated 10 percent surcharge on the $550 billion annual healthcare bill for the United States in 1988. The total cost of healthcare rose to $604 billion in 1989, with an average cost of $2,354 per person. Many property losses resulting from fire are fraudulent as well. Outside the United States, fraud claims are also increasing. For example, analysts believe that arson cost the United Kingdom £500 million in 1991.

While the research and practice of detecting insurance insolvency has a relatively long history, the use of mathematical models to detect fraudulent or inflated insurance claims started not long ago, and the approaches used are limited. Although some statistical and clustering analyses have been utilized in the automobile bodily injury (BI) claims fraud area (Derrig and Ostaszewski 1993; Weisberg and Derrig 1991, 1992, 1993), those studies were not definitive, and an opening still exists for other models and techniques.

PATTERN RECOGNITION—A PROMISING APPROACH

Although insolvency identification and fraudulent claim detection are two different areas, they share certain common structural characteristics. One of these is that both are intended to separate certain abnormal patterns from normal patterns. More precisely, analysts attempt to separate unhealthy firms from healthy firms in insolvency detection, and suspicious claims from valid claims in claim fraud studies. Both of these areas are within the domain of pattern recognition. In this article, we adopt this unified perspective and briefly introduce four pattern recognition techniques relatively new to the insurance area which have been or can be used in insurance insolvency identification or fraud detection studies and practice. These pattern recognition techniques are data envelopment analysis (DEA), expert systems (ES), feed-forward backpropagation neural networks (NN) and self-organizing feature maps (FM).

Historically, the two major approaches to pattern recognition have been the statistical (or decision-theoretic) and the structural approaches. Recently, the emerging technology of neural networks has provided a third approach (Schalkoff 1992). Specifically, the expert systems technique is related to the structural pattern-recognition approach, because the rule inference process can alternatively be represented by the decision tree or graph and the problem solving thus becomes a structure-matching process. The backpropagation algorithm can be categorized as a neural network approach rather than a statistical approach because of its black-box and adaptive characteristics (as opposed to the statistical convention of adopting an a priori probability distribution and performing parameter estimation). Feature mapping is, to some extent, similar to clustering analysis, which follows the statistical approach; however, feature mapping is also a neural network approach and accordingly, possesses the same characteristics stated previously. DEA, on the other hand, originally developed by Charnes et al. (1978) as a production-efficiency evaluation methodology, is neither a structural approach nor a neural-network approach. Although DEA shares some common features with the neural-network approach—both of them are so-called data-driven approaches—it is sometimes regarded as a statistical approach. We regard DEA as a pattern-recognition technique in a relatively broad sense, since DEA models can be used to identify efficient or inefficient decision-making units (DMUs) from the rest of the DMUs.

In this paper, we will briefly introduce each of the four pattern-recognition techniques and then illustrate its utility using concrete applications in either insurance insolvency identification or fraud claims detection. The following sections discuss, in order, data envelope analysis, expert systems, and feedforward backpropagation algorithm, and Kohonen's self-organizing feature map.

DEA—DATA ENVELOPMENT ANALYSIS FOR INSOLVENCY IDENTIFICATION

The first data envelopment analysis (DEA) model, known as the CCR model (Charnes et al. 1978), was initially applied to evaluate the relative efficiency of not-for-profit institutions such as schools. More recently, DEA approaches have been successfully applied in numerous areas, including the allocation of U.S. Army recruiting efforts (Charnes and Thomas 1990), the efficiency of savings institutions (Charnes et al. 1990a), the efficiency of selling units (Mahajan 1991), and so on. Moreover, the DEA theoretical foundation has been greatly extended, and many other DEA models have been developed. Among these extensions of the original CCR model are the BCC model (Banker et al. 1984), the CCGSS model (Charnes et al. 1985), the FG model (Färe and Grosskopf 1985), the CCWH model (Charnes et al. 1990b), the ST model (Seiford and Thrall 1990), and more recently, the generalized DEA (GDEA) model (Yu et al. 1993). Using different models and based upon different empirical axioms, different production possibility sets and efficient surfaces (relatively efficient frontiers) can be determined.

The DEA methodologies is a nonparametric approach. Rather than determining the average performance curve in evaluating DMUs by regression methodology, DEA models are used to produce different performance surfaces (frontiers), which are either relatively efficient frontiers or inefficient surfaces with regard to the database. With particular DEA models, the conventional economic models of production involving increasing, constant, and decreasing returns to scale can be identified.

DEA is capable of evaluating DMUs with multiple outputs. However, the approach used by DEA models is not simply a linearly weighted summation of multiple outputs, as in traditional goal-programming methods. The DEA method is especially useful for evaluating not-for-profit institutions where different performance outputs cannot be simply mixed with numerical weighting determined in accordance with contribution to profit, and so forth.

The following prototype study (Rousseau 1990) illustrates the role of DEA in detecting financially troubled property-liability insurance companies. The three DEA models used in the study are the ratio (CCR) model, which provides evaluations of both technical and scale efficiency; the modified ratio model, which attempts to distinguish between technical and scale inefficiencies by estimating pure technical efficiency at the given scale of operation; and the additive model, which relates the efficiency results to the economic concept of Pareto optimality.

The data used for this efficiency study came from the NAIC data set on a sample of 111 Texas domestic property and casualty stock companies for the years 1987, 1988, and 1989. These were provided by the staff of the Texas State Board of Insurance (SBI). The DEA analysis was conducted by the Magellan Group, a division of MRCA Information Services.

Although DEA can accommodate both financial and nonfinancial variables, only financial variables were selected in the prototype study. The inputs for the relative efficiency analysis include:

- loss adjustment expenses
- underwriting expenses
- investment expenses
- combined debt and equity, and
- losses paid

In any insurance company, there are many outputs that reflect the firm's survival, return, risk, and other desirable goals. Accordingly, for this study the following outputs were initially selected:

- total surplus
- equity to debt ratio
- net income
- reinsurance risk, and
- combined assets

Difficulties stemming from the tremendous differences in recorded values for reinsurance recoverables, total liabilities, and investment expenses across insurance firms forced analysts to reconsider the input and output variables. By combining the investment expenses and the loss adjustment expenses, and dropping equity to debt ratio and reinsurance risk, four inputs and three outputs were produced for analysis. These inputs and outputs were then analyzed using the additive DEA model.

The results of the DEA analysis study included:

- distribution of overall performance rating across all companies,
- time trends of overall performance ratings for each of the companies,
- potential improvement in each input and output factor, for each company and in total across all companies,
- factor by factor comparison of actual to best-practice performance for each underachieving company,
- distribution of the potential improvement in each input and output factor across all companies, and

• time trends of actual and best-achieving performance for each input and output factor, for each company and in total across all companies.

The efficiency of an insurance company can be assessed from a relative perspective; for example, a performance rating or categorization is relative to all insurance companies. Figure 7.1 provides the overall efficiency ranking of the 111 companies (DMUs) in 1989. Regulators may know which two companies were ranked in the 60–69 percent group relative to the thirty-one fully efficient companies in the data set. Not only are DEA models capable of giving such a rating result or categorization, but they expand the assessment dimensions to time series and factor analysis. By time series, we mean DEA models can provide the time trends for a certain group of companies or an individual company with respect to overall factors or each factor (input or output). Such a capability is very useful in creating an early warning system for the insurance industry. Figure 7.2 illustrates the efficiency trend of company #19984 spanning three years from 1987 to 1989 with respect to its overall performance. Such a consistent downward trend should target the company for immediate closer scrutiny. DEA models can also identify the inefficient inputs or outputs for each company, relative to the most efficient firms. This function can help the regulation department monitor the performance of a particular group of insurance companies, while simultaneously allowing the analysts to attribute the under-performance to specific factors. Figure 7.3 illustrates the efficiency ranking of the underwriting expenses performance in 1989. Clearly, there were two companies that had much room for improvement with respect to their underwriting expenses performance.

In summary, DEA is an evaluation or rating tool which can simultaneously comprehend multiple inputs and multiple outputs. By focusing on its efficiency rating function, DEA can distinguish inefficient or troubled insurance firms from efficiently functioning firms and can focus attention toward specific input or output variables.

EXPERT SYSTEMS

The premise of structural pattern recognition is that the structure of an entity is paramount and that this structure may be used for the purpose of classification and description. Classification may be based upon measures of pattern structural similarity as, for example, when each pattern class is defined in accordance with some common structural representation or description (Schalkoff 1992).

If we insist that there be only two structure-based pattern recognition quantification approaches, namely formal grammars and relational descriptions, then expert systems (as we use the term in this paper) may not be well-defined as a pattern recognition approach. Expert systems technology and pattern-recognition methodologies have previously been considered as two distinct artificial intelligence technologies. Why we treated expert systems technology as a type of pattern recognition will be made clear in the following paragraph.

Figure 7.1
The Overall Efficiency Ranking in 1989

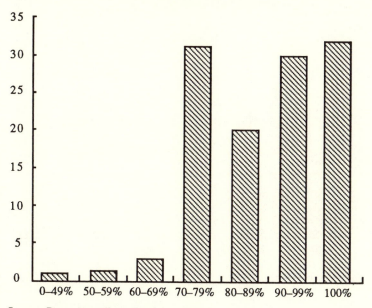

Source: Reproduced from Rousseau 1990

Figure 7.2
Efficiency Trend of Company #19984

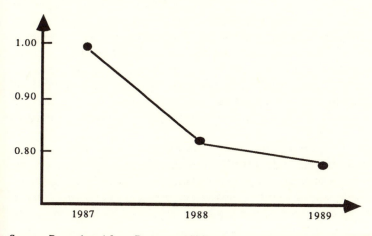

Source: Reproduced from Rousseau 1990.

Figure 7.3
Functional Ranking–Maximum Improvement (%) of Underwriting Expenses in 1989

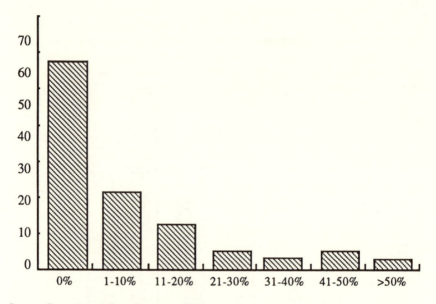

Source: Reproduced from Rousseau 1990.

An expert system usually has two components, a knowledge base (facts and rules) and an inference engine (interpreter and scheduler). Domain knowledge consists of the facts and a set of rules that use those facts as the basis for decision making. The inference engine contains an interpreter that decides how to apply the logical rules to infer new knowledge and a scheduler that decides the order in which the rules should be applied. The features of an expert system include: (1) the knowledge that fuels the expert system is explicitly represented and accessible; (2) the expert system provides the high-level expertise to aid in problem solving; (3) the expert system has predictive modeling power; it provides the output when given a situation as the input; (4) the expert system works over time without discontinuities; and (5) the expert system provides a training environment for personnel and important staff members (Waterman 1986a).

The use of expert systems in the insurance industry is not a new phenomenon. Financial underwriting applications, as well as other life applications, have been developed (Walker and Maurer-Williford 1986). Both life-health and property-casualty insurers also are developing expert systems to aid in the underwriting process. Systems are being developed to assist in claims management and investment planning, while personal financial planning, loss prevention, risk assessment, and product design are all areas where expert system development is under consideration by the insurance industry.

A product of expert systems, called smart systems, is becoming a component in insurers' strategic and competitive underwriting and claim systems. For instance, Connecticut Mutual Life Insurance Company expects to realize a 35 percent productivity gain in underwriting by using image and expert systems. Several companies also use smart systems to assist in the detection of insurance claims fraud. Travelers Insurance Company uses smart systems to detect unusual patterns in health providers' behavior and claims in order to thwart fraud, and the Erie Insurance Group uses smart systems to combat property and casualty fraud.

Firms have often turned to self-insurance in an effort to control healthcare costs. One reason for the lack of success in controlling healthcare costs, however, is that most firms do not have the expertise to properly monitor health-related expenditures (Martin and Harrison 1993). Claims audit is considered a method to monitor the administrator's performance and control costs.

Martin and Harrison (1993) described an expert system used for claim monitoring and fraud detection for such self-insured companies. The expert system monitor's primary task is to review claim payments and identify opportunities for reducing healthcare expenditures. Cost reduction typically results from recovering improper payments and preventing similar mistakes from occurring in the future. The expert system functions as an initial filter, since it reviews claims and identifies potential errors (i.e., unjustified payments) by grouping payments according to likely errors and estimating the value of the total error for each group. The production system consists of a set of if-then rules to determine what (if any) error is made on each payment. The knowledge base comprises approximately fifty rules which are mostly independent of each other, and these rules are used to identify thirty-two different types of errors. For each type of error, there exists a rule that specifies the probability of error, the value of the error, and the time required to further investigate the error (since the data base is too large to investigate every claim). The validation experiments demonstrate that the system is able to screen claims in a manner comparable to human experts in the field.

NEURAL NETWORK APPROACHES

Inspired by the neurophysical structure of the brain, the collection of mathematical models known as neural networks has developed as an approach to provide algorithmic structures that can interact with the environment in much the same manner as does the human brain. The three major ways of interaction are learning from experience, generalizing from examples, and abstracting essence from input data that may contain irrelevant information. Structurally, the neural network model can be represented as a massively parallel interconnection of many simple processing units similar to the interconnection of individual neurons in the brain (Brockett et al. 1993). Mathematically, the neural network functions by constantly adjusting interconnecting weights between individual neural units. The adjustment process, called a learning or training process, attempts to improve performance, recognize patterns and develop generalization. The backpropagation algorithm (Rumelhart et al. 1986) is the milestone of neural network algorithm development based on (multiple) layered feedforward networks.

Supervised learning and unsupervised learning are two distinct learning strategies of neural networks. The difference between the two lies in the input data and associated training approach. In supervised learning, every input pattern includes the values of the explanatory variables and the observed value of the responsive variable as well. Learning adapts the connection weights (strengths) between neural units (cells) in order to minimize the error between the network output values and the observed output values over the training sample. In this situation, the observed values have the same function as teachers or supervisors in the human learning process. In contrast, input patterns in unsupervised learning consist only of values of the explanatory variables. The learning process evolves from chaos to order using training samples, to create categorization, pattern recognition, and other functionalities. Hence, the unsupervised learning process is a self-organizing or competitive process. Feature mapping is one of the main algorithms of unsupervised learning, whereas backpropagation is the most widely used supervised learning algorithm.

To further elaborate on these approaches, we expand on two methods and their applications. First, we present a feedforward backpropagation algorithm, which can be used by insurance regulators to provide early warning of potentially insolvent insurers, and then we present a self-organizing feature map that has been used to detect fraud in automobile bodily injury claims.

The Feedforward Backpropagation Algorithm

Feedforward neural networks are a very gross simplification of human brain architecture and assume that neurons are arranged layer-by-layer. Every neuron in the current layer is connected to each neuron in the layers which directly precede and directly follow the current layer. The input neurons (or sensors) that accept external signals (input information) are located in the first layer, while the processed information (outputs) are produced from the neurons of the last layer. The information flows, layer by layer, from input layer to output layer in the network, thereby providing the name for the feedforward network. The "connection strength" between a neuron in the current layer and each neuron in the directly succeeding layer is represented by a numerical weight. The processing capability of each neuron is accomplished in three successive steps: (1) the neuron accepts the signals from the neurons in the directly previous layer, (2) it sums these signals by multiplying the connection strengths (weights), and

(3) it transform the weighted sum by a monotonically increasing function (activation function). The most widely used activation function is the logistic function. Accordingly, the total computation by a neuron is a logistic aggregation function (see Figure 7.4). See Figure 7.5 for a three-layered feedforward network.

Figure 7.4
A Single Neuron

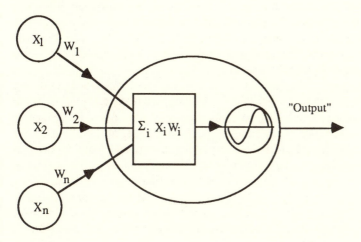

Figure 7.5
A Three-Layered Feedforward Network

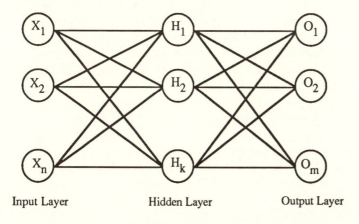

Input Layer   Hidden Layer   Output Layer

Neural networks distinguish themselves from conventional statistical logistic methods by their learning or adaptive capability. By learning we mean that the interconnection strengths (weights) can be changed when networks are fed with examples (patterns). The objective is to minimize the (total) error between the network outputs and the observed values over the training set. The adaptation process, called training, is an iterative and repetitive process until the error reduces to some prespecified level or until training has occurred for some specified time limit (e.g., the desired number of iterations). Weight updating follows the gradient descent updating rule, which assures a better network configuration whenever the training process is terminated. The updating begins with the weights between the last hidden layer and the output layer, and this error is then propagated backward to the previous interconnection until the interconnection between the input and the first hidden layer is updated. The algorithm is thus called the backpropagation algorithm. Obviously, feedforward networks permit multiple inputs and multiple outputs. They are robust because of the passive parallel interconnections.

Neural networks have been extensively used as a black-box modeling approach in process control, stock price forecasting, and many other fields. These networks are useful in modeling complex processes often found in finance or other business industries. For example, Salchenberger et al. (1992) used the feedforward backpropagation model to predict savings and loans failures. A successful study which used the backpropagation algorithm to predict insurance insolvency (Brockett et al. 1993) is presented in the following paragraphs.

The scope of the study was limited to Texas domestic property/casualty insurance companies. Only financial data variables were used, which were available through the National Association of Insurance Commissioners (NAIC) data tapes. For each insolvent insurer, three solvent insurers were randomly selected by NAIC number. Data as of the third year prior to insolvency were collected for all insolvent insurers, and the data for the solvent companies were matched to the data of the insolvent companies by year. For example, if an insurer became insolvent in 1987, this insurer's 1984 annual statement data and also the 1984 annual statement data for three solvent insurers were examined. A subset of variables determined through a stepwise logistic regression procedure was used to predict insurer insolvency propensity. The final set of variables include:

- Policyholder surplus
- Capitalization ratio
- Change in invested assets
- Investment yield based on average invested assets
- Significant receivables from parent, subsidiaries, and affiliates to capital and surplus
- Significant increase in current-year net underwriting loss
- Surplus aid to surplus (IRIS3)
- Liabilities to liquid assets (IRIS7)

Forty-four companies, consisting of eleven companies which became insolvent during the period 1987–1990 and thirty-three companies which remained solvent, were examined. Twenty-six companies were used to train the network, nine were used to determine the termination point of network training, and the remaining nine were used to test to see if the results could be generalized out of the training sample. The network running results, summarized in Table 7.1, may be compared to a correct classification rate of 93.18 percent by multivariate discriminant analysis, and of 54.5 percent by using the NAIC IRIS ratio tests. In contrast, A. M. Best's rating was found to be worthless for predicting insolvencies among the sample.

Table 7.1
Neural Network Training and Predictive Accuracy

Description	Sample Size	Accuracy of Classification(%)
Training Sample	26	96.15
Stopping Rule Sample	9	88.89
Testing Sample	9	91.11
OVERALL	44	95.45

Kohonen's Self-Organizing Feature Map

The rationale behind Kohonen's self-organizing feature map is the research finding that neurons in the brain are spatially distributed, and that a group of neurons in a certain area in the brain adapt to the environment interdependently— that is, not only the activation strengths between neurons but also the topographical location of each of the neurons in the brain is meaningful. Different regions in the brain thereby seem to be dedicated to specific cognitive tasks, and it thus seems as if the internal representations of information in the brain are generally organized spatially (Kohonen 1989, 1990).

Structurally, Kohonen's feature map is a two-layered and fully connected (i.e., every output unit is connected to every input unit) network, with output units arranged in some topographical form such as squares (see Figure 7.6), rectangles, or hexagons. The interconnection strengths are represented by weights, which means that every output unit has a weight vector whose dimensionality is equal to the number of input units or input variables because of the full connection.

The learning process is an iterative process that begins by setting initial weight vectors to small random numbers. Each iteration is comprised of three steps: choosing the next training pattern, selecting the best-matching unit, and updating the weight vectors. These steps are more fully described in the following paragraphs.

Figure 7.6
Kohonen's Self-Organizing Feature Map

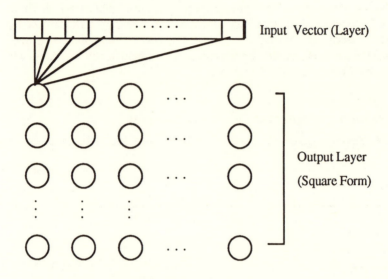

Choosing a training pattern

A training pattern is randomly chosen from the training sample and presented to the feature map as an input vector.

Selecting the best-matching unit

The weight vector of each of the output units is compared with the input vector in order; and the output unit, that is, the best-matching unit, is identified whose weight vector among all weight vectors has the smallest distance to the input vector in a prespecified distance measure—usually the Euclidean geometric measure.

Updapting the weight vectors

The algorithm updates not only the weight vector of the best-matching unit but also those of its neighboring units, that is, the neighborhood set (remember that all output units are arranged spatially). The size of the neighborhood set changes from relatively large initially to usually zero as the algorithm terminates (see Figure 7.7, where $t_1 < t_2 < t_3$ are three time points).

The rationale for using a wide initial N_c, corresponding to a coarse spatial resolution in the learning process, is to first induce a rough global order in the m_i values. After this order is created, a narrowing of the neighborhood N_c improves the spatial resolution of the map. Usually, the final width used is zero, so that $N_c = \{c\}$, that is, the updating occurs only on the best-matching unit. In this case, the process is reduced to simple competitive learning, that is, neurons compete for matching with the current input pattern independently, after the topographical order has been established via sequentially decreasing neighborhood size.

Figure 7.7
Updating Weights in Neighborhood N_c

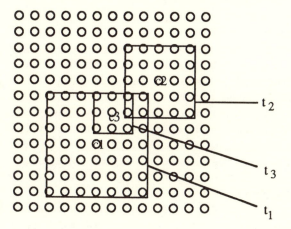

The gradient-descent updating rule is utilized. Let $m_i(t)$ represent the weight vector of output unit i at time t, and $x(t)$ the current input vector. Then the updating rule is: $m_i(t + 1)=m_i(t) + \alpha(t)(x(t) - m_i(t))$, if output unit i is the best-matching unit itself or is inside the neighborhood of the best-matching unit; the weight vectors of any other units remain unchanged.

In the formula, $\alpha(t)$ is a scalar-valued adaptation gain and $0 < \alpha(t) < 1$ (Kohonen 1990). Usually, $\alpha(0)$ is set close to unity and $\alpha(t)$ is decreased over time down to zero at the end of the learning process.

Feature maps have been used in speech recognition, handwriting recognition, control of industrial processes, automatic synthesis of digital systems, image compression, and so on. The feature maps also have applications in human decision making. For instance, an experiment for detecting automobile bodily injury claims fraud may be introduced as follows.

The entire data set of bodily injury fraud claims used in this study contains 127 claims. Of these, 62 claims were deemed apparently fraudulent by at least one of two human experts. The remaining 65 claims were sampled from 325 claims that were considered to be apparently nonfraudulent by the experts. The information available for every claim is a vector consisting of an ID number, 65 objective indicators, and 2 subjective fraud assessments. The 65 objective indicators, which are binary coded, are grouped into six categories: accident characteristics, claim characteristics, insured characteristics, injury characteristics, treatment characteristics, and lost wage characteristics. The subjective assessments include an assessment by an insurance adjuster, and an assessment by an insurance investigator. The adjuster's and investigator's assessments reflect the suspicion level for the particular claim and range between 0 and 10, with 10 representing a certainly fraudulent claim, and 0 representing an apparently valid claim. Four suspicion level categories are then defined by grouping the subjective assessment scores: not suspicious (0), slightly suspicious (1–3), moderately suspicious (4–6), and strongly suspicious (7–10).

A sample of 77 claims was used for training, and the remaining 50 claims were reserved as a testing data set.

The purpose of the study is to investigate how well human experts perform in assessing suspicion of bodily injury claims and, mainly, to construct a more consistent and reliable approach to reassessing bodily injury claim fraud.

In order to use feature map analysis for fraud detection, it is assumed that if two claims have common or similar objective characteristics they should result in approximately equivalent suspicion levels. Euclidean geometric distance is proposed to measure the similarity of two vectors. Consequently, the two input vectors with a sufficiently short distance should be assigned similar output values (suspicion levels). We further assume that every objective indicator is of equal importance in explaininging suspicion levels of claims.

After the feature maps had been obtained, a layered feedforward neural network and backpropagation algorithm by the universal approximator property (Hornik and Stinchcombe 1989; Hornik et al. 1990) were used to compare the performance of the feature map approach with those of the adjusters' and investigators' subjective assessments. A three-layered feedforward network was used, comprised of 65 input units (65 objective indicators), 4 output units (4 suspicion categories) and 40 hidden units. The comparative results are summarized in Tables 7.2 and 7.3. In both tables, the first number in each cell is the number of patterns classified correctly by the feedforward network with respect to the corresponding assessing approach; and the second number is the correctly classified rate. An epoch is completed when each of the training patterns in the training sample has been chosen and presented to the network as input vector once and only once.

The tables provide a comparison between the feature map approach and the subjective assessments, by the average number of correct classifications (the first number in each cell) and classification rates (the second number) over every five runs. As shown in both tables, the performance of the proposed categorization, either on the training data set or on the testing data set, dominates those of the adjusters and investigators. Another feedforward network, other parameters being equal but containing 20 hidden units, provides similar results, which is not illustrated here.

Table 7.2
Classification on the Training Data

Epoch	Adjuster	Investigator	Feature Map
5	48.4 / 62.9	36.8 / 47.8	48.8 / 63.4
10	54.8 / 71.2	46.4 / 60.3	68.2 / 88.6
15	66.0 / 85.7	61.6 / 80.0	75.2 / 97.7
20	75.2 / 97.7	69.4 / 90.1	76.8 / 99.7
25	75.4 / 97.9	71.8 / 93.2	77.0 / 100
30	75.8 / 98.4	72.0 / 93.5	77.0 / 100
35	75.8 / 98.4	73.2 / 95.1	77.0 / 100
40	75.8 / 98.4	73.4 / 95.3	77.0 / 100

Table 7.3
Classification on the Testing Data

Epoch	Adjuster	Investigator	Feature Map
5	14.4 / 28.8	16.0 / 32.0	16.0 / 32.0
10	13.4 / 26.8	13.2 / 26.4	19.8 / 39.6
15	14.0 / 28.0	12.8 / 25.6	21.6 / 43.2
20	13.2 / 26.4	14.8 / 29.6	22.2 / 44.4
25	13.8 / 27.6	13.8 / 27.6	22.6 / 45.2
30	13.4 / 26.8	14.4 / 28.8	23.0 / 46.0
35	13.4 / 26.8	14.4 / 28.8	23.0 / 46.0
40	13.4 / 26.8	13.8 / 27.6	23.0 / 46.0

SUMMARY

We have introduced four approaches and studied them for their applications in insurance insolvency prediction or claims fraud detection. The four techniques are DEA, expert systems, and two neural network models—the backpropagation and self-organized feature map.

DEA is a multiple-objective programming methodology that is capable of incorporating multiple outputs and qualitative variables. It is also a data-driven approach, by which we mean that it uses minimal assumptions when applied to data for evaluating the performance of entities. We have examined DEA models, which have often been used to produce efficient or inefficient frontiers for not-for-profit institutions, for their use in evaluating the performance of insurance companies as part of the activities of a state regulatory agency.

Expert systems, an important branch of artificial intelligence, express the problem domain, such as cancer diagnosis, geological detection, and so forth, by a knowledge base explicitly as facts and rules. The knowledge base supports the inference process such that the whole system is capable of doing "intelligent" jobs in the domain.

Neural networks, either feedforward networks or feature maps, are a black-box modeling technique. The connections are realized by numerical weights that represent the magnitude of interactions between neurons. After they have been trained properly and sufficiently, the neural network models can offer predicted results as given input information.

These seemingly different approaches have been found to have similar features from the perspective of pattern recognition when they are applied to identifying unhealthy insurance companies and detecting suspicious insurance claims.

With respect to the significance of insurance insolvency and the severity of insurance fraud, any improvement, such as that achieved by the methodologies discussed above, in practice will lead to great benefit.

REFERENCES

Ambrose, J. M., and Seward, J. A. (1988). "Best's Rating, Financial Ratios and Prior Probabilities in Insolvency Prediction." *Journal of Risk and Insurance*, 55(2): 228–244.

Banker, R. D., Charnes, A. and Cooper, W. W. (1984). "Some Models for Estimating Technical and Scale Inefficiencies in Data Envelopment Analysis." *Management Science*, 30(9): 1078–1092.

BarNiv, R., and McDonald, J. B. (1992). "Identifying Financial Distress in the Insurance Industry: A Synthesis of Methodological and Empirical Issues." *Journal of Risk and Insurance*, 59(4): 543–574.

BarNiv, R., and Raveh, A. (1986). "A Nonmetric Approach for Predicting Financial Distress." Discussion Paper #86-8, Monster Center of Economic Research, Ben Gurion University.

BarNiv, R., and Raveh, A. (1989). "Identifying Financial Distress: A New Nonparametric Approach." *Journal of Business Finance and Accounting*, 16(3): 361–384.

Barrese, J. (1990). "Assessing the Financial Condition of Insurers." *Journal of CPCU* (Society of Chartered Property and Casualty Underwriters) 43(1): 37–46.

Brockett, P. L., Pitaktong, U., Golden, L. L., and Cooper, W. W. (1993). "A Comparison of Neural Network and Alternative Approaches to Predicting Insolvency for Texas Domestic Property and Casualty Insurers." CCS Research Report 707, Center for Cybernetic Studies, the University of Texas at Austin.

Brockett, P. L., Xia, X., and Derrig, R. (1994). "Using Neural Networks to Uncover Automobile Bodily Injury Claims Fraud." CCS Research Report 727, Center for Cybernetic Studies, the University of Texas at Austin.

Charnes, A., Cooper, W. W., Golany, B., Seiford, L., and Stutz, J. (1985). "Foundations of Data Envelopment Analysis for Pareto-Koopmans Efficient Empirical Production Functions." *Journal of Econometrics*, 150(1): 54–78.

Charnes, A., Cooper, W. W., Huang, Z., and Sun, D. B. (1990a). "Polyhedral Cone Ratio DEA Models with an Illustrative Application to Large Commercial Banks." *Journal of Econometrics*, 46: 73–91.

Charnes, A., Cooper, W. W., and Rhodes, E. (1978). "Measuring the Efficiency of Decision Making Units." *European Journal of Operational Research*, 2(6): 429–444.

Charnes, A., Cooper, W. W., Wei, C., and Huang, Z. (1990b). "Fundamental Theorems of Nondominated Solutions Associated with Cones in Normal Linear Space." *Journal of Mathematical Analysis and Applications*, 150: 54–78.

Charnes, A., and Thomas, D. (1990). "Measuring the Impact of Advertising on Army Recruiting: DEA and Advertising Effectiveness." CCS Research Report 656, Center for Cybernetic Studies, the University of Texas at Austin.

Denenberg, H. (1967). "Is A-Plus Really a Passing Grade?" *Journal of Risk and Insurance*, 34(3): 371–384.

Derrig, R. A., and Ostaszewski, K. M. (1993). "Fuzzy Techniques of Pattern Recognition in Risk and Claim Classification."

Färe, R., and Grosskopf, S. (1985). "A Nonparametric Cost Approach to Scale Efficiency." *Scandinavian Journal of Economics*, 87(4): 594–604.

Harrington, S. E., and Nelson, J. M. (1986). "A Regression-Based Methodology for Solvency Surveillance in the Property-Liability Insurance Industry." *Journal of Risk and Insurance*, 53(4): 583–605.

Hornik, K., and Stinchcombe, M. (1989). "Multilayer Feedforward Networks are Universal Approximators." *Neural Networks*, 2: 359–366.

Hornik, K., Stinchcombe, M., and White, H. (1990). "Universal Approximation of Unknown Mapping and Its Derivatives Using Multilayer Feedforward Networks." *Neural Networks*, 3: 551–560.

Kohonen, T. (1989). *Self-Organizing and Associative Memory*, 3rd ed. Berlin: Springer-Verlag.

Kohonen, T. (1990). "The Self-Organizing Map." *Proceedings of the IEEE*, 78(9): 1464–1480.

Mahajan, J. (1991). "A Data Envelopment Analytic Model for Assessing the Relative Efficiency of the Selling Functions." *European Journal of Operational Research*, 53(2): 189–205.

Martin, J. L., and Harrison, T. P. (1993). "Design and Implementation of an Expert System for Controlling Health Care Costs." *Operations Research*, 41(5): 819–834.

Pinches, G. E., and Trieschmann, J. S. (1974). "The Efficiency of Alternative Models for Solvency Surveillance in the Insurance Industry." *Journal of Risk and Insurance*, 43(4): 563–577.

Rousseau, John J. (1990). "The Role of DEA in the Development of an Early Warning System for Detecting Troubled Insurance Companies: Report on a Feasibility Study." Working Report, The Magellan Group, Division of MRCA Information Services, Austin, Texas.

Rumelhart, D. E., Hinton, G. E., and Williams, R. J. (1986). "Learning Internal Representations by Error Back Propagation." In D. E. Rumelhart and J. L.

McClelland (eds), *Parallel Distributed Processing: Explorations in the Microstructure of Cognition*, Chap. 8. Cambridge, Mass.: MIT Press.

Salchenberger, L. M., Cinar, E. M., and Lash, N. A. (1992). "Neural Networks: A New Tool for Predicting Thrift Failures." *Decision Sciences*, 23(4): 899–916.

Schalkoff, R. (1992). *Pattern Recognition: Statistical, Structural and Neural Approaches*. New York: John Wiley.

Seiford, L. M. and R. M. Thrall. (1990). "Recent Development in DEA, The Mathematical Programming Approach to Frontier Analysis." *Journal of Econometrics*, 46: 7–38.

Trieschmann, J. S., and Pinches, G. E. (1973). "A Multivariate Model for Predicting Financially Distressed P-L Insurers." *Journal of Risk and Insurance*, 289–298.

Walker, S. A., and Maurer-Williford, M. (1986). "Emulating the Expert." *Best's Review*.

Waterman, Donald A. (1986a). *A Guide To Expert Systems*. Reading, Mass.: Addison-Wesley.

Waterman, Donald A. (1986b). *Expert Systems: Techniques, Tools, and Applications*. Reading, Mass.: Addison-Wesley.

Weisberg, H. I., and Derrig, R. A. (1991). "Fraud and Automobile Insurance: A Report on the Baseline Study of Bodily Injury Claims in Massachusetts." *Journal of Insurance Regulation*, 9(4): 497-541.

Weisberg, H. I., and Derrig, R. A. (1992). "Massachusetts Automobile Bodily Injury Tort Reform." *Journal of Insurance Regulation*, 10: 384–440.

Weisberg, H. I., and Derrig, R. A. (1993). "Quantitative Methods for Detecting Fraudulent Automobile Bodily Injury Claims." *AIB 1994 Fraudulent Claims Payment Filing*, D.O.I. Docket G93–24.

Yu, G., Wei, C., and Brockett, P. L. (1993). "A Generalized Data Envelopment Analysis Model: A Unification and Extension of Existing Methods for Efficiency Analysis of Decision Making Units." Working paper, 93/94-3-1, Department of Management Science and Information, the University of Texas at Austin.

8

A Two-Stage DEA Approach for Identifying and Rewarding Efficiency in Texas Secondary Schools

Victor L. Arnold, Indranil R. Bardhan, and William W. Cooper

Results are reported from a two-stage use of DEA (data envelopment analysis) to evaluate the performance of over six hundred secondary schools in Texas. Stage One identifies a subset of schools that performed with full (100%) DEA efficiency but did not meet standards of excellence mandated by the State of Texas. Stage Two introduces an extension of DEA so that it can be used to obtain estimates of future resource requirements as well as to evaluate past performance. Modifications are made in the usual treatment of nondiscretionary variables which are here reversed in order to (a) eliminate nonzero slack possibilities which would represent reductions in the exogenously fixed values for low English proficiency or other disadvantaged students, and (b) ensure that efficiency evaluations are effected from points on the efficiency frontier that do not have smaller proportions of these inputs. Other modifications include a use of constraints to ensure that the excellence standards are met. A new measure called CREA (coefficient of resources for excellence achievement) is also introduced which, along with the nonzero slacks, provide multidimensional estimates of the resources that are then required. Such resource increments are allowed only for the efficient subset of schools, and resource increments to achieve excellence are estimated for each such efficient school. This paper proposes a new use of DEA in budgeting resources for future performance and extends previous uses of DEA that were restricted to evaluating past performance. In addition, a new approach is provided for recognizing and rewarding efficiency in public school performance by taking account of resources used as well as outputs produced. This is in contrast to the existing (common) practice of recognizing only output accomplishments by reference to excellence standards without considering the inputs utilized.

INTRODUCTION

The performance and cost of elementary and secondary public school education have, justifiably, occupied a prominent place as issues for consideration in recent presidential (and other) elections. These topics have been the subject of scholarly studies[1] as well as policy reports[2] and they have received extensive attention in the journalistic literature. Even more specialized outlets, such as the business literature, have provided front-page coverage and extensive articles and editorial pronouncements on this topic, because the outputs from public schools hold great importance for the future wellbeing of business as well as the country. See, for instance, "Saving Our Schools," the cover story and the featured article and editorial in the September 14, 1992, issue of *Business Week*, pages 70–80.

At the state and local levels, the subject of public school education is of major fiscal importance, constituting some 25 percent of all state and local direct expenditures in 1992–1993 and totaling approximately $228 billion.[3] Not surprisingly, these expenditures, their relative allocations, and how they relate to school performance have also been the subject of legal action and political activity by various groups with resulting political fallout that has also led to court cases and judicial opinions that have now begun to produce constitutional crises—as exemplified in Texas, where a deadline has now been mandated by the courts for instituting a new system of school financing.[4]

One approach to improving school performance that needs to be explored is improved accountability. With this in mind the Texas Legislative Education Board initiated a coordinated study by the Universities of Texas, Texas A&M, and Houston. The part of the effort to be covered in this paper represents one part of a series of experiments with DEA for its possible use in evaluating efficiency and excellence in the performance of public schools in the state of Texas. See Arnold et al. (1993, 1994a, 1994b) for other papers in this series.

BACKGROUND

The topic of efficiency of school performance is of special interest in Texas where, as described in Cooper et al. (1991), the state's constitution prescribes its use as a criterion of educational performance. Efficiency is a topic of general interest, of course, and so is effectiveness, where we distinguish between the two as follows:

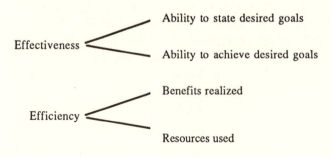

Differences and relations between effectiveness and efficiency have, from the start, entered into the DEA literature. See, for example, Charnes et al. (1978). Hence we do not discuss them further, but, instead, simply summarize with the words of Peter Drucker: "Effectiveness consists of doing the right things, while Efficiency consists of doing things right [and at the right levels]."

Issues of efficiency and effectiveness are not restricted to school performance. They are common to all public-sector activities and, hence, have been accorded prominence in a recent report prepared by the staff of the Urban Institute for the Government Accounting Standards Board (GASB). Entitled *Service Efforts and Accomplishments* (SEA) *Reporting: Its Time Has Come* (1990), this report is prefaced as follows: "SEA information is needed for setting goals and objectives (effectiveness), planning program activities to accomplish these goals and objectives, allocating resources to these programs (efficiency), monitoring and evaluating the results to determine if they are making progress in achieving the established goals (effectiveness), and modifying program plans to enhance performance (efficiency and effectiveness)." The report continues, "Information on SEA indicators is . . . useful to management and to elected officials in making resource allocation decisions, and in assessing governmental performances."

SEA reporting includes issues involved in the selection of variables and the way they are measured as well as the manner in which both plans and results are reported. In usages that are now customary, DEA is generally pointed toward efficiency evaluations—after effectiveness has been decided upon by choices of the inputs and outputs and the ways in which they are to be measured. However, in Texas, as in other states, there are also legislatively mandated levels of performance which need to be brought to bear if issues of relevance and potential use by elected officials are a consideration. To accommodate these additional criteria, standard uses of DEA will be modified later in this chapter—and then, as might be expected, new interpretations of DEA and its results will also be required.

The plan of development in the rest of this chapter is as follows. The next section provides a statement of the problems to be addressed, after which the types of DEA models we use are described and discussed. The models we use take the form of what are now called the CCR Ratio Models as introduced in Charnes et al. (1978).[5] Next the choice of DMUs (decision making units), as selected from the list of Texas secondary schools maintained by the Texas Education Agency (TEA), will be discussed, along with the data on inputs and outputs that are also obtained from the databases maintained by TEA. Applications of our CCR models to these data yield results on performance efficiency which will then be examined en route to the further developments that will be used to extend these DEA models and results.

As noted above, we are introducing new elements and new interpretations into DEA. The model developments needed to do this will therefore form a separate topic of discussion. Their uses will then be described and interpreted relative to the results that were secured from the usual type of DEA analysis, as described in the preceding paragraph. Proceeding in a two-stage manner we will (1) start with a use of DEA for efficiency evaluations, and then (2) go on to effect extensions to these models that will make it possible to accommodate excellence in performance as an added feature of DEA. Concrete results will be supplied in numerical form for individual schools with both types of DEA approaches. A final section will suggest further developments from and possible uses of these analyses and modeling efforts.

STATEMENT OF THE PROBLEM AND PROPOSED APPROACH

As noted in Charnes et al. (1978), DEA had its origin in an attempt to overcome limitations of the results obtained from customary statistical approaches when applied to the evaluation of Program Follow Through (PFT) which represented a huge federally sponsored effort at an experimental design (statistical) approach that attempted to evaluate public school performances with data from matching schools grouped into what are called PFT and NFT (non-follow through) sets in Charnes et al. (1981). The efficient and inefficient performances in both the PFT and NFT data were intermingled, however, and this clouded the inferences and led to questionable statistical results. This was one origin for DEA modeling which can now be used to distinguish between program inefficiencies (across programs) after managerial inefficiencies (within programs) are allowed for.

Subsequent studies, as in Ahn (1987), Ahn et al. (1989), and Cooper et al. (1991) have continued to extend and use DEA in a variety of additional applications directed to evaluating educational activities. In the present study we confront a somewhat different problem because state-mandated excellence standards need to be brought into consideration explicitly. Note, for instance, that allowance needs to be made for the possibility that a school may be performing efficiently with the resources at its command while falling short in the mandated excellence standards. The reverse result is also possible: a school may achieve excellence while performing inefficiently. See the distinction drawn earlier between effectiveness and efficiency.

Our approach to these issues will be as follows. First we conduct a DEA efficiency analysis, which is of interest in its own right, since it enables us to identify efficient and inefficient performances in individual schools with further possibilities for reductions in resource usage and/or output augmentation. Then we restrict attention to the subset of schools which were found to be efficient (in the first stage) and introduce constraints in second-stage analyses which ensure attainment of the prescribed excellence standards. Finally, proceeding on an assumed continuation of efficient performance by these schools, we obtain estimates of the resource increments (including mix changes) needed to eliminate the excellence shortfalls which were obtained during the first-stage treatment of these schools.

MODEL DEVELOPMENT

As noted in Cooper et al. (1992), DEA has now evolved into a body of concepts and related methods of implementation in its own right. The mathematical programming formulations we use here represent only one mode of implementation. However implemented, the orientation in DEA is toward evaluating the performance for each of a collection of decision making units (DMUs) each identified as an entity responsible for converting inputs into outputs. Choices of DMUs and the inputs and outputs are fundamental in evaluating either efficiency or effectiveness. The choice of individual schools to serve as DMUs is a very natural one for this study and that is how we will proceed, while leaving statistical extensions in the uses of DEA and aggregation into school districts, etc., to be undertaken in separate studies. See, e.g., Arnold et al. (1994b).

The input and output choices are discussed in more detail below. We also introduce another set of input variables identified as "nondiscretionary inputs."[6] These nondiscretionary inputs represent demographic characteristics of the student population of each school in the form of the proportion (or percentage) of minorities, economically disadvantaged, and low English proficient (LEP) students. In keeping with other uses of DEA we note here that we will (i) require all observed inputs, outputs, and nondiscretionary variables to be positive,[7] and (ii) require these same inputs and outputs to be common to all DMUs. We will also require that the DMUs be numerous enough to obtain a sufficient number of degrees of freedom.

The results secured from DEA are intended to make it possible (i) to judge each school's performance relative to the entire set of schools (= DMUs) to be examined, (ii) to provide measures of efficiency for this performance relative to a subset of schools that are efficient in converting inputs into outputs, and (iii) to identify sources and amounts of inefficiency in the inputs utilized and outputs produced by each DMU.

Mathematically, the CCR model we use in our DEA analyses can be represented in linear programming form as follows,

$$\text{Maximize} \quad \phi_0 + \varepsilon[\sum_{i \in D} s_i^- - \sum_{r=1}^{s} s_r^+]$$

subject to $\hspace{8cm}$ (1)

$$\phi_0 y_{ro} - \sum_{j=1}^{n} y_{rj}\lambda_j + s_r^+ = 0 \qquad r \in \{1, \ldots, s\}$$

$$\sum_{j=1}^{n} x_{ij}\lambda_j + s_i^- \;=\; x_{io} \qquad i \in D$$

$$\sum_{j=1}^{n} z_{kj}\lambda_j + s_k^+ \;=\; z_{ko} \qquad k \in ND$$

$$\lambda_j, \, s_i^-, \, s_k^+, \, s_r^+ \;\geq\; 0$$

The symbols employed in (1) are defined as follows,

y_{ro} = observed amount of the rth output of the $DMU_j = DMU_o$ being evaluated,

y_{rj} = observed amount of rth output for DMU_j, j = 1, 2, ..., n,

x_{ij} = observed amount of ith input for DMU_j, j = 1, 2, ..., n,

x_{io} = observed amount of the ith input for the $DMU_j = DMU_o$ being evaluated,

z_{kj} = observed amount of kth nondiscretionary input for DMU_j, j = 1, 2, ..., n,

z_{ko} = observed amount of the kth nondiscretionary input for the $DMU_j = DMU_o$ being evaluated.

The first expression in the constraints refers to the outputs and the second to those inputs which are discretionary, for example, inputs that can be controlled and varied by school administration officials. Using the notation in Banker and Morey (1986), we let i ∈ D index the discretionary inputs. Then we let k ∈ ND index the nondiscretionary inputs that are not under the control of individual school administrative officials. It is also possible to identify the latter with floors and ceilings or ranges which are discretionary (or nondiscretionary), as discussed in Banker et al. (1989); but this is not done here because the information needed to do this is not available.

The s_i^-, s_k^+, and s_r^+, all constrained to be nonnegative, represent slack variables which are introduced to convert inequalities into corresponding equations. Hence, $s_r^+ \geq 0$ means that every solution must satisfy $y_{ro} \leq \sum y_{rj}\lambda_j$, so that efficiency comparisons and evaluations will be effected only from solutions with outputs at least as great as the outputs achieved by DMU_o in every case. Similarly, $s_i^- \geq 0$ means the solutions must satisfy $x_{io} \geq \sum x_{ij}\lambda_j$ for each of i ∈ D discretionary inputs utilized by DMU_o. Therefore, efficiency evaluations are effected only by reference to a comparison set which utilizes no more of the discretionary inputs than the DMU_o being evaluated. Finally, $s_k^+ \geq 0$ for each of k ∈ ND nondiscretionary inputs means that efficiency comparisons of DMU_o will be effected only from solutions with nondiscretionary input values at least as great as the level of nondiscretionary input associated with DMU_o for every k ∈ ND.

We are making an unusual use of these nondiscretionary inputs in the above formulation, and so we elucidate further after introducing the conditions for efficiency as follows: DMU_0 (the DMU being evaluated) is fully (100%) efficient if and only if the following conditions are both met,

(i)   The Farrell efficiency measure is unity, i.e., $\phi_0^* = 1$, and   (2)

(ii) All slacks associated with the discretionary constraints are equal to zero in an optimum solution of (1), that is, $s_i^{-*} = 0$ for all inputs $i \in D$ and $s_r^{+*} = 0$ for all outputs,

where "*" refers to an optimum value. This means, of course, that nonzero slacks, or $\phi_0^* > 1$, identify inefficiencies that may be present by reference to shortfalls in the outputs or excesses in the discretionary inputs.

It should be noted that the slacks associated with z_{ko}, $k \in ND$, do not enter directly into these evaluations. Their effects, if any, are reflected only indirectly by reference to the value of the variables listed in (i) and (ii) above. As discussed in Cooper et al. (1994), this usually reflects the status of these excesses as free goods with an opportunity cost of zero in the constraints for any $s_k^{+*} > 0$.[8] It also reflects the fact that they have zero coefficients in the functional which corresponds to the treatment that is usually accorded to the slacks in ordinary linear programming but is sometimes identified in the DEA literature[9] with the assumption of free disposal, a term introduced by T. C. Koopmans (1957) to deal with what he referred to as disposal activities in his economic models.[10]

These interpretations correspond to an assumption that none of these nondiscretionary inputs have negative (or detrimental) effects on outputs. Here, however, the nondiscretionary inputs are all associated with disadvantaged students and, in fact, were found to have such negative effects on the outputs (or school outcomes) in statistical analyses conducted in other parts of the present study. For instance, as noted in Arnold et al. (1993), the regression coefficients associated with these variables were found to be negative and statistically significant in their effects on outputs in estimated regression relations obtained, both from classical ordinary least squares and the more recent stochastic frontier regression approaches—and in fact, it was these results that caused consortium members to turn to DEA as a possible route to follow.

With this in mind, we altered the standard formulations, as given in Banker and Morey (1986), by reorienting the inequality to $\sum z_{kj}\lambda_j \geq z_{ko}$, $k \in ND$. We do not use the reverse of this inequality, as in the customary treatment of nondiscretionary variables, because this would admit possibilities for reducing these inputs and this is not allowed. Use of an equality condition would be too tight, but if we had the necessary information we might have further restricted this to $Z_{k0} \geq \sum z_{kj} \lambda_j \geq \underline{z}_{k0}$ for $k \in ND$, where Z_{k0} and $\underline{z}_{k0}$ represent ceilings (upper bounds) and floors (lower bounds), respectively, on the allowable ranges for improvements. However, we do not do this here. The role of these constraints is to restrict evaluations to combinations of schools with at least as much of these nondiscretionary inputs as the DMU_0 to be evaluated, and this is the route taken in this study.

We can express these considerations by using the following versions of the CCR projections introduced in Charnes et al. (1978):

$$\hat{y}_{ro} = \phi_o^* y_{ro} + s_r^{+*}, \qquad r = 1, 2, \ldots, s$$

$$\hat{x}_{io} = x_{io} - s_i^{-*} \leq x_{io}, \qquad i \in D \qquad\qquad (3)$$

$$\hat{z}_{ko} = z_{ko} + s_k^{+*} \geq z_{ko}, \qquad k \in ND$$

Then we note that the point with coordinates represented by $(\hat{y}_{ro}, \hat{x}_{io}, \hat{z}_{ko})$ is the point on the efficiency frontier from which DMU_0 is evaluated. The first pair of expressions in (3) are the ordinary CCR projection operators.[11] The third expression refers to the coordinates formed from the expression $\sum z_{kj}\lambda_j^*$ in (1), and the constraints ensure that the evaluation of DMU_0 will be effected from a point with at least as much in each disadvantaged student category. This is seen by reference to $\hat{z}_{ko} \geq z_{ko}$ for each $k \in ND$ in the third expression of (3).

This brings us to the non-Archimedean element $\varepsilon > 0$ which Charnes et al. (1978) introduced into the CCR models to insure that all of the discretionary slacks are maximized without worsening the value of ϕ_o^* in the resulting optimum. This avoids the possibility of being misled by achieving a value of $\phi_o^* = 1$ with zero slacks while an alternate optimum with the same value of ϕ_o^* would have some nonzero slack as part of its solution. The use of ε in (1) has been operationalized by implementing a two-stage optimization in several of the DEA computer codes now available, and this is only a way of giving effect to the pre-emptions associated with the properties of ε relative to ϕ which, together, form parts of a two-component number as explained in Arnold et al. (1994).[12]

To see how the discretionary and nondiscretionary variables are evaluated, we write the dual to (1) in the following form:

$$\text{Minimize} \qquad \sum_{i=1}^{m} v_i x_{io} - \sum_{k \in ND} \rho_k z_{ko}$$

$$\text{subject to} \qquad\qquad\qquad\qquad\qquad\qquad\qquad (4)$$

$$\sum_{r=1}^{s} \mu_r y_{ro} = 1$$

$$-\sum_{r=1}^{s} \mu_r y_{rj} + \sum_{i \in D} v_i x_{ij} - \sum_{k \in ND} \rho_k z_{kj} \geq 0$$

$$\mu_r \geq \varepsilon$$

$$v_i \geq \varepsilon$$

$$\rho_k \geq 0$$

We now note that μ_r, $v_i \geq \varepsilon > 0$ so that an increment in any of the discretionary inputs must necessarily involve an increment to the value of the objective in the primal with $\mu_r^* = \varepsilon$ or $v_i^* = \varepsilon$ associated with nonzero slacks that worsen the performance score for DMU_o.[13] This follows from the dual theorem of linear programming. However, a value of $\rho_k^* > 0$ for any $k \in ND$ means that an increment in this nondiscretionary input will lower the value of the functional in the primal and thereby improve its efficiency score. This could only occur, however, if the nondiscretionary inputs z_{ko} were in short supply relative to the other inputs, and this was not found to occur in any of the DMUs. In fact, even in those DMUs which exhibited zero slack(s) on the nondiscretionary input(s) the corresponding dual variables ρ_k^* were found to be equal to zero. Thus the only cases of interest here are those associated with $s_k^{+*} > 0$ for some $k \in ND$ in (1), in which case variations in the value of this variable will have no effect on the value of the objective in (1). This follows from the fact that $\rho_k^* = 0$ is allowed to occur in (4) for all $k \in ND$, but such a zero value is not available for any other dual variable. Thus, our approach allows us to treat the appearance of nonzero slacks for the nondiscretionary variables in a manner that differs from our treatment of the other variables. Variations in the latter do effect the efficiency scores and hence we add or subtract them to the observed values when they occur in order to achieve the improvements with which they are associated in the performance scores. We do not make such additions or subtractions for nonzero slacks in the nondiscretionary variables, however, but simply regard them as providing information on the points on the efficiency frontier from which DMU_o's evaluation was made. In this way we also use our nondiscretionary constraints as categorizing the conditions that are allowed for these comparisons.

Finally, we conclude our discussion of the formal aspects of DEA and come to our choice of the DEA model. The model in (1), known as the CCR model, was selected to avoid the need for adding a discussion of returns to scale that would further lengthen this article and divert attention from other very important issues that we want to address. There is a certain amount of confusion on this topic caused by relabeling (1) as the CRS (constant returns-to-scale) model in DEA.[14] This is correct but misleading since, as shown in Banker et al. (1984), the CCR model evaluates performance with respect to *both* technical *and* returns-to-scale efficiencies. A separation of the two is possible in the CCR model by reference to the $\sum \lambda_j^*$, as noted in Banker and Thrall (1992), and as elaborated in Banker et al. (1994b), but we content ourselves with these references and do not address these issues further in the present paper except to note that Bardhan (1995) subsequently found the savings from returns to scale to be relatively unimportant compared to technical inefficiency savings in these schools.

Selection of Input and Output Variables

In consultation with legislators and education officials involved in this study, it was decided to use individual schools for the DMUs in these DEA experiments. Results could then be validated (as was done) either from familiarity of state officials with individual schools or by field visits to selected schools, as was also done by other members of the consortium in this study.[15] With help and advice from officials at the Texas Education Agency (TEA) and the Texas Legislative Education Board (LEB), a set of 638 public secondary schools was selected from a total of about 1,030 such schools in Texas.

Having settled on the individual schools to serve as our DMUs, we next turn to the important task of selecting the inputs, outputs, and nondiscretionary variables that we will use. Here the orientation is toward evaluating the educational activities of the schools we are considering. Numerous problems exist in the selection of suitable inputs and outputs, which here included considerations of data availability and acceptability to state education officials and others; thus, these selections were made in consultation with others involved in this study. Non-cognitive aspects of learning, such as self-esteem, work habits, and citizenship qualities are not included at this stage of the study, partly because they are difficult to deal with and partly because these kinds of data are absent or subject to widely varying interpretations.[16] State-level measures of student outcomes are often not comparable across states, and they also change from time to time in ways that affect the comparability of educational achievement across time even within a state. Standardized tests designed for across-state comparability such as ACT (American Collegiate Tests) and SAT (Scholastic Aptitude Tests) are also subject to challenge, and so on.

For this study, the data on inputs and outputs were all collected from the Public Education Information Management System (PEIMS) database of the TEA with help and advice from TEA officials and others involved in the consortium study noted in the opening section of this paper. PEIMS data have the advantage of availability, and they have the further advantage of the error detection and correction treatments accorded them by TEA. They also have the advantage of reflecting judgments and the experience of the many educators and others involved in planning and administering their collection.[17] The subset of six outputs, six discretionary inputs, and three nondiscretionary inputs we use are shown in Table 8.1.

We have already indicated some of the reasons for selecting these variables by reference to their availability and the advice we received from education officials in TEA and elsewhere. These variables were also selected because they form a part of the SEA indicators for use in evaluating secondary school education activities recommended by GASB in the report we cited earlier, GASB (1990: 106-109). It must also be noted that the data we use for this study pertain to the 1990–1991 school year.[18] Starting at the top of Table 8.1, we note that the output variable Attend represents the average annual attendance rate in Grades

Nine through Twelve. This is calculated as the average annual attendance divided by the average annual student enrollment. This variable is included as an output indicator for two reasons. First, it provides a measure of student participation in classes, and it provides an indication of their interest or at least their opportunities for learning. Second, it is part of a state-of-Texas mandate which requires 97 percent attendance for a school to achieve the academic excellence rating which is of interest in this study.

Table 8.1
Input and Output Variables Used in DEA Evaluations

Outputs

1. **Attend**   Attendance in Grades Nine through Twelve expressed as a percentage of total student enrollment.

2. **Notdrop**   Proportion of students who do not drop out of school (in Grades Nine through Twelve) expressed as a percentage of total student enrollment.

3. **Math**   Average Student Score on Standardized Math test in Grades Nine and Eleven.

4. **Reading**   Average Student Score on Standardized Reading test in Grades Nine and Eleven.

5. **Writing**   Average Student Score on Standardized Writing test in Grades Nine and Eleven.

6. **Criterion**   Proportion of students scoring above the criterion score on the ACT or SAT expressed as a percentage of the number of graduates.

Inputs

1. **Teachers**   Total Number of Full-Time Equivalent (FTE) Teachers.
2. **Salary**   Average Annual Teacher Salary (in dollars).
3. **Avgexpn**   Average Teacher Experience (in years).
4. **Reged**   Total Number of Teachers Employed in Regular Education.
5. **Speced**   Total Number of Teachers Employed in Special Education.
6. **Instexp**   Average Instructional Expenditure per Student (in dollars).

Non-discretionary Inputs

1. **Minority**   Number of Minority Students expressed as a percentage of student enrollment.

2. **Disadv**   Number of Economically Disadvantaged Students expressed as a percentage of student enrollment.

3. **LEP**   Number of Limited English Proficiency (LEP) Students expressed as a percentage of student enrollment.

Notdrop, the next variable in Table 8.1, represents the proportion of the students (in Grades Nine through Twelve) who do not drop out of school. It is calculated as the difference between the total number of students enrolled and the number of students who drop out of school during the academic year, expressed as a percentage of the average annual student enrollment. In this way we account for the total number of dropouts—an undesirable output—and we also continue to point our analysis in the direction of the net outputs which are considered to be desirable.

The variables Math, Reading, and Writing represent average student scores on the standardized math, reading, and writing tests, respectively. These variables have been included in our analysis because they provide widely used measures of student achievement in academic subjects and they also allow comparisons with established achievement norms which are discussed below.

The variable Criterion represents the number of students scoring above the criterion score[19] on one or both college entrance tests—the ACT and the SAT—expressed as a percentage of the number of graduates. This variable has been included because it represents one of the indicators of academic excellence as defined by the Texas State Board of Education. Another, possibly more relevant, variable that could have been used in this situation is the number of graduates gainfully employed or continuing their education two years after graduation. However, these data are not available on a uniform statewide basis and, in particular, the TEA database system we used does not collect this statistic.

Next we turn to a discussion of the discretionary input variables. The input variable Teachers represents the number of full-time equivalent (FTE) teachers reported as being employed in 1990–1991. This is an important input in its own right and it also provides a measure of the size of the teaching staff. Finally, it offers a possible advantage in its conformance to standard practices such as one-output-to-one-input accounting approaches which take such forms as the teacher-to-student ratios which are frequently used as measures of the provision of educational services and their results. See Ahn et al. (1989).

We also use input variables in the form of Salary (average annual teacher salary) and Avgexpn (average teacher experience in years). These variables can be regarded as surrogates for teacher quality. The average teacher salary also provides an obvious measure of resource cost, and the same is true of Avgexpn, at least indirectly. Moreover, these variables have been used extensively in the education literature in almost every study dealing with educational performance and efficiency of schools. See the survey by Hanushek (1986) for an extensive review of 147 education production-function studies dealing with these variables.

The input variables Reged and Speced refer to the number of teachers employed in regular education and special education, respectively. These variables represent different components of instruction, with the latter supposedly reflecting special needs and concerns associated with the student body. For instance, schools in poor districts may have a high percentage of teachers employed in special education to guide disadvantaged students with special requirements, and they may also help with the counseling of troubled students.

Instexp, the last discretionary input variable represents the instructional expenditure per student in each school. This is also an extensively used measure in educational studies; see Ahn et al. (1989). We also use it here as an aggregate measure of cost per outcome in each attribute of interest or in terms of average grade-level score gains, partly because the latter could not be obtained.

Finally, we turn to a discussion of the nondiscretionary inputs. The variables Minority, Disadv, and LEP represent the proportion of minority students, economically disadvantaged students, and limited English proficiency students, respectively, expressed as a percentage of the total student enrollment. These variables can be regarded as providing information on demographic factors that are likely to affect school achievement records. Information on these variables is also required to determine how well schools perform with large minority and economically disadvantaged student populations—and, in fact, they all constituted variables of central interest in the statistical and other analyses in this study, as discussed in Arnold et al. (1994b). See also Cooper et al. (1991) for a discussion of their importance in recent court decisions.

We now turn to a discussion of the outcome indicator variables (as distinct from outputs) on which excellence standards are mandated by the State of Texas.[20] The Texas State Board of Education sets a standard for excellence in five outcome categories. These outputs (on which the excellence standards are mandated), as listed in Table 8.2, are regarded as outcome indicators, and we thus distinguish them from other outputs in a manner that corresponds to what is prescribed in the GASB report.

Table 8.2
State-mandated Excellence Standards on Student Outcomes

Outcome Indicator	State-mandated Excellence Standard
1. Texas Assessment of Academic Skills (TAAS) Test	90% of students passing on all standardized tests
2. Attendance	97% of total enrollment in the school
3. Dropout Rate	Less than or equal to 1% of total enrollment
4. Graduation Rate	99% of graduating class
5. College Admission Tests	• 35% of graduates scoring above the criterion score which is equal to 25 on the ACT and 1000 on the SAT • 70% of graduates taking either the ACT or the SAT

Cross-comparing the list of variables in Table 8.2 with the variables in Table 8.1, it is observed that data were not available for all of the five outcome indicators. Only three of the excellence indicators listed in Table 8.2 were used—attendance rate (Attend), dropout rate (Notdrop), and percentage of graduates scoring above the criterion score (Criterion) as shown in rows 2, 3, and 5 of Table 8.2—in order to show what might be accomplished with more complete information.

FIRST-STAGE DEA EVALUATION: USES OF RESULTS

In this section we use the DEA model proposed in (1) to evaluate the performance of the 638 public secondary schools in Texas that were included in the present study. As discussed above, in the first-stage evaluation we use DEA efficiency analysis to identify efficient and inefficient performances of individual schools, and to obtain estimates of the reductions in resource usage and/or output augmentation that are possible. Since the emphasis here is on efficiency, the first-stage analysis will serve as a first cut to identify those schools that were rated as efficient under the conditions stated earlier in (2). The summaries provided in Table 8.3 show that 111 out of these 638 schools were rated as efficient by the Farrell measure given in (2), above. Table 8.3 also provides a summary of the range of Farrell inefficiency ratings for the inefficient schools. As observed from Table 8.3, about 197 schools (or 30%) fall in the category 1.001–1.10, while 235 schools (or 37%) were in the range 1.101–1.20, and about 95 schools (or 15%) exceeded 1.20 in their Farrell measure of inefficiency values.[21]

As can be seen from (2) above, the Farrell efficiency measure forms only one component for the attainment of full (100%) efficiency in DEA. In this case, however, the nonzero slack condition was also satisfied for the n = 111 schools in this category. On the other hand, a failure to attain full Farrell efficiency means that no further analysis is required prior to classifying a school (= DMU) as inefficient, as was done in Table 8.3. Finally, sensitivity tests conducted by removing and adding one or more variables did not substantially affect the efficiency status of the schools in the efficient category, which is the center of our interest.

Proceeding to further analysis, we note that Table 8.4 provides a comparison of the mean values of inputs and outputs as calculated from their observed values for the n=111 efficient and n = 527 inefficient schools. As can be seen, the efficient school averages are better in every category—viz., greater outputs[22] and lower inputs—except for the nondiscretionary inputs. However, from what was said earlier we can interpret this to mean that the efficient schools performed better even in these categories, which all involve disadvantaged students. Thus, using this as a justification we extend the concepts of efficiency dominance as given in Bardhan et al. (1994), and also relate these results to the classical economic concept of a representative firm in the following way: On average, the efficient DMUs dominate the inefficient DMUs in this study in every input and output category.

Table 8.3
Results from First-stage DEA Evaluations of 638 Schools

Range of Efficiency Scores (ϕ)	Number of Units in Each Category
1.0	111
1.001 – 1.10	197
1.101 – 1.20	235
> 1.20	95

Table 8.4
Mean Output and Input Values for the Technically Efficient and Inefficient Categories of Schools

	Efficient Schools (n = 111)	Inefficient Schools (n = 527)
Outputs		
Attend	94%	94%
Notdrop	95%	94.5%
Math	1525	1513
Reading	1586	1578
Writing	1576	1579
Criterion	14.3%	11.5%
Discretionary Inputs		
Teachers	53	65
Salary	$ 26,197	$ 27,530
Avgexpn	11.2 Years	12.8 Years
Reged	36	44
Speced	3	5
Instexp	$ 2,302	$ 2,485
Non-Discretionary Inputs		
Minority	41%	40%
Disadv	28.5%	24%
Lep	7%	3%

Table 8.5 is illustrative of some of the further detail that can be supplied from these DEA results—perhaps en route to a detailed audit of each school,

which might be necessary to identify the sources and cost drivers associated with these inefficiencies. Here we have used Crockett H.S. (High School) in Austin I.S.D. (Independent School District) to illustrate the possibilities for input reductions and output augmentations obtainable from DEA evaluations by applying the CCR model of (1). The efficiency rating provided as the "Phi" value at the top is the Farrell efficiency rating for Crockett H.S. This provides a measure of the school's output capabilities with the resources at its disposal. Thus this Phi value of 1.075 at the top of Table 8.5, as obtained from our DEA analysis, means that Crockett H.S. should have been able to achieve about 7.5 percent more than it did in all of its outputs without increasing any of its inputs.

Table 8.5
An Example of DEA Results from the First-stage:
Crockett H.S., Austin I.S.D.

Efficiency (Phi): = 1.075					
DEA Model: CCR Model of (1)					
REFERENCE SET (PEER GROUP):					
FACET:	51	150	193	478	503
LAMBDA:	0.02	0.49	0.02	0.74	0.03

	Current Level (1)	Value if Efficient (2)	Slack (3)
Outputs			
Attend	89	100	4.30
Notdrop	93	100	—
Math	1504	1623	6
Reading	1578	1697	—
Writing	1525	1682	42
Criterion	16	17.2	—
Discretionary Inputs			
Teachers	102	39	63
Salary	30956	28298	2658
Avgexpn	15.6	11.5	4.1
Reged	70	29	41
Speced	10	3	7
Instexp	2579	2579	—
Non-Discretionary Inputs			
Minority	47	47	—
Disadv	14	14	15
Lep	3.3	3.3	—

This does not end the matter, however, since the nonzero values under the column labeled Slack show where further augmentation is needed in the outputs if full (100%) efficiency is to be attained. Thus, starting with the Outputs we apply the first part of formula (3), the CCR projection formula, and find that the observed value (= Current Level) for Writing would need to be augmented to $1525\phi_0^* + s_r^{+*} = 1525 \times 1.075 + 42 = 1682$, where 42 represents the slack that needs to be added to $1525 \times 1.075 = 1640$ for this purpose. Similar remarks apply to the other output values listed in the column labeled Value if Efficient. Hence the values in this column represent the efficiency-adjusted levels of output obtained by using the projection formulas in (3) to correct for the presence of inefficiency, both in the Farrell measures and nonzero slacks.

Turning next to the discretionary inputs in Table 8.5, we observe (from the CCR projection formulas introduced earlier in (3)) that the Phi rating of 1.075 is not applied to any input. This identifies (1) as an output-oriented model and means that input inefficiencies, as identified by DEA, are all to be found under the column headed as Slack. For instance, the slack value 2658 reported for Salary (average annual teacher salary in dollars) is an inefficiency. Subtracting this slack from the Current level for Salary (= $30,956) yields the efficiency-adjusted value of $28,298 located in the column labeled Value if Efficient. Hence the observed values of the discretionary inputs are reduced by their respective slacks, if any, to obtain the efficiency-adjusted input values reported under the column labeled Value if Efficient.

Similar adjustments are not made for any of the three nondiscretionary inputs—Minority, Disadv and LEP—because, as noted earlier, we want to use these variables in a different manner. Hence, the values under Current Level are the same as in the column Value if Efficient to reflect the fact that the values of these variables are fixed exogenously. The slack values are then treated as having informational content, as noted in our discussion of (4), which we now bring to the fore more concretely by reference to the 15 percent value located in column 3 for the category Disadv (economically disadvantaged students).

In this case the DEA results indicate that Crockett H.S. in Austin I.S.D. should have been able to do better in the amounts already indicated for the values of its discretionary variables, as determined from a comparison point (on the efficiency frontier) which had the same percent enrollment of Minority and LEP students but did have 15 percent more of Disadv students. The evidence for this is obtained from the row labeled Facet at the top of Table 8.5, where the DMUs used to effect these evaluations are identified as the relevant efficient reference set (= peer group).

The DMUs identified as facet members are designated by DEA as the best subset of efficient DMUs for evaluating Crockett H.S. where the term best means that this combination of efficient DMUs locates a point on the efficiency frontier which is closest (or most similar) to Crockett H.S. In fact, the values of the coefficients used to form this combination (and generate this reference point on the efficiency frontier) are displayed in the row labeled Lambda and can be used as follows: 0.02 is applicable to DMU #51 (Ben Bolt H.S. in the Palo

Blanco I.S.D), 0.49 is applicable to DMU #150 (Van Horn H.S. in the Culberson I.S.D), 0.02 is applicable to DMU #193 (Westlake H.S. in the Eanes I.S.D), 0.74 is applicable to DMU #478 (Pleasant Grove H.S. in the Pleasant Grove I.S.D) and 0.03 is applicable to DMU #503 (Robstown H.S. in the Robstown I.S.D.).[23] The thus-identified sources provide additional advantages that are also obtainable from DEA. Their identification in the DEA printout of Table 8.5 makes it possible to consider the estimates and the efficiency ratings in more detail. The indicated comparison sources for improving Crockett's performance are also thereby identified for scrutiny via performance audits or otherwise. See Charnes et al. (1989) for a description of the way the Texas Public Utility Commission uses DEA to identify reference units as bases for comparisons in the efficiency audits that they are required to perform.[24]

EXCELLENCE AND EFFICIENCY: A TWO-STAGE STRATEGY

Results like those we have been discussing are evidently of interest for possible use in efficiency evaluations. They can also be used in additional ways that are described in the literature dealing with DEA, but here we turn our attention to a still further use which involves an extension of DEA to deal with the excellence standards mandated by the State of Texas.[25]

To effect this extension we employ a two-stage strategy as follows. In the first stage, which at this writing has just been completed, we focus on the efficiency of individual schools as a subject of interest in its own right. In these evaluations we have included the outputs which the state of Texas mandates for use in the excellence evaluations that are listed in Table 8.2. As already noted, a school may be efficient in its performance but may fail, nonetheless, to achieve one or more of the state-mandated levels of excellence.[26] We can nevertheless credit each school for efficiency (or failure to achieve it) in the manner that we have described in the immediately preceding section. After this has been done we can then proceed to a second-stage in which the customary DEA models (and interpretations) are extended to identify the added resources, if any, that may be needed to achieve excellence as well as efficiency.

In going to this second stage, it seems natural to change from an output orientation, in which phi and the slacks are maximized (subject to resource constraints), and to go over to an input orientation which can be used to determine the resource increments that are minimally needed to achieve excellence. This follows from our interpretation of stage one in our two-stage strategy as dealing with already budgeted resources, so the orientation is toward maximizing the outputs from these given budgets. On the other hand, in stage two we try to ascertain the minimal resources needed to attain the increases in performance needed to achieve excellence.[27]

There are other choices to be made, of course, among which we choose the following. First we confine the schools that are candidates for resource augmentations to those which were determined to be 100 percent efficient in the preceding stage. This eliminates any problem in changing from an output to an input orientation, as we now do, since the projection operators in (3) will give the same result in either case for the efficient schools.[28] We also further restrict our choices to the DMU subsets which proved to be robustly efficient as defined and operationalized in Thomas (1990). This means that we restrict our choice of efficient schools to those which are frequently used in the efficient reference sets to evaluate other schools and eliminate those which are mainly self evaluators.[29] See the above discussion of the Facet and Lambda rows of Table 8.5.

Proceeding in this manner reduces our original list from 111 to 79 robustly efficient schools. These are the DMUs we use in our extensions from efficiency (only) to excellence (as well) in going from stage one to stage two in our study strategy. Thus, after designating these robustly efficient DMUs, we introduce excellence constraints into our DEA model. This is done in the next section; but before proceeding to this task, we stop to note that all but one of these schools failed to achieve the state-mandated levels of excellence. Stated differently, we can note that only one of the schools recognized as excellent was also a member of this efficient set. This suggests that excessive resources had been used by the schools that had achieved excellence but were inefficient. We have therefore helped to identify a need to accord recognition to efficiently-performing schools and, perhaps, to supply them with added resources for the achievement of excellence. DEA has helped us perform the former task, and in the next section we begin to examine how it might be extended to accomplish the latter task as well.

SECOND-STAGE DEA EVALUATION: THE EXCELLENCE-ORIENTED MODEL

In this section, we extend our DEA model by adjoining constraints, where necessary, to ensure that excellence is also achieved. Indeed, except for Highland Park H.S. in the Highland Park I.S.D., this adjunction of constraints is needed for all of the schools identified as efficient in the preceding analysis. This can be seen in Table 8.6 which shows the shortfalls in the required level of attainment for each of the mandated outcomes—Attend, Notdrop and Criterion (= percentage of graduates scoring above the requisite level on the SAT or ACT).[30]

The model we use in this second stage analysis can be written as follows;

Minimize $\quad \theta_0 - \varepsilon[\sum_{i \in D} s_i^- + \sum_{r=1}^{s} s_r^+]$

subject to   (5)

$$y_{ro} = \sum_{j=1}^{n} y_{rj}\lambda_j - s_r^+ \qquad r \in \{1, \ldots, s\}$$

$$\theta_0 x_{io} = \sum_{j=1}^{n} x_{ij}\lambda_j + s_i^- \qquad i \in D$$

$$z_{ko} = \sum_{j=1}^{n} z_{kj}\lambda_j - s_k^+ \qquad k \in ND$$

$$b_{ro} \leq s_r^+ \qquad r \in \{Attend, Notdrop, Criterion\}$$

$$\lambda_j, s_i^-, s_r^+, s_k^+ \geq 0$$

where the representations in these expressions have the same meanings as before. Comparison with (1), however, shows that the objective has been altered from maximizing ϕ_0 in (1) to the minimization objective shown for θ_0 in (5), while maximization of the slacks associated with ε remains the same with preemptive priority now assigned to θ_0 instead of ϕ_0.[31] Finally, a new set of constraints is adjoined in the following form,

$$b_{ro} \leq s_r^+ ; \qquad r \in \{Attend, Notdrop, Criterion\} \qquad (6)$$

Here $b_{ro} = \text{Max}\{0, MS_{ro} - y_{ro}\}$ is the shortfall experienced by DMU_0 with regard to the excellence requirement on output r, with MS_{ro} representing the mandated excellence standard requirement on output r for DMU_0. It should be noted that b_{ro} can only assume nonnegative values and hence it is a lower bound on the output slacks (s_r^+). By constraining s_r^+ to be greater than or equal to b_{ro}, we ensure that we will attain a level of $z_{ko} + b_{ro} \leq z_{ko} + s_k^+$ for the three excellence standards—Attend, Notdrop, and Criterion.

For illustration, we use Davis H.S. located in the Houston I.S.D (Obs. #29 in Table 8.6) as an example. This school has a relatively high proportion of students in minority enrollment of approximately 96 percent. It has been rated technically efficient in the first-stage DEA evaluation, but has failed to attain the state-mandated excellence standards in every one of the three excellence indicators we have used. In particular, as Table 8.6 shows, Davis H.S. has a shortfall of 7 percent (= 98 students) with regard to the excellence requirement on Attend, a shortfall of 12 percent (= 179 students) with regard to Notdrop and a shortfall of 32 percent (= 59 students) with regard to Criterion.

To ensure that the desired levels for excellence in these outputs will be attained we need something more than the usual DEA models for efficiency evaluation. We accomplish this by introducing the additional constraints shown in (5) and (6). For instance, the average daily attendance rate of 90 percent (= 1292 students) at Davis H.S. needs to be adjusted to 97 percent (= 1390 students) to achieve a level of 1433 students who are enrolled (on average) during the school year to meet the state-mandated level of excellence for this output. Formally then we require $7 \leq s_r^+$ if the average daily attendance rate is to be raised by at least 7 percent per year at Davis H.S.

Similar constraints are introduced on other outputs where shortfalls from the state-mandated excellence standards were experienced. This is done for all 79 schools in Table 8.6 where, as explained earlier, we focus our attention on only the three excellence indicators—Attend, Notdrop and Criterion—for which excellence standards have been mandated.[32]

Finally, we turn to the behavior of θ_0 which is to be optimized (preemptively) along with the slack values that are represented in the objective of (5). Mathematically, we have $\theta_0^* = 1/\phi_0^*$, for the CCR model,[33] so the two would simply be reciprocals if the b_{ro} constraints (and the new slacks they occasion) were omitted from (5). Since our 79 schools were all efficient, we would therefore have $\theta_0^* = 1$ from (5) applied to these same data without the added constraints. Instead, with (5) as altered, we must expect $\theta_0^* \geq 1$ and $\theta_0^* > 1$ when an optimum solution indicates that additional resources are required.[34]

We now depart from the customary interpretations of these results in terms of Farrell measures and refer to θ_0^* as the coefficient of resources for excellence achievement (CREA). Other possibilities such as the coefficient of resource utilization were ruled out because of earlier uses by persons such as Debreu (1951) and point in a direction that conforms to DEA usage in which $\theta_0^* \leq 1$ designates the shrinkage in resources needed for full (radial) efficiency in the DMU being evaluated.

RESULTS FROM THE EXCELLENCE-ORIENTED MODEL

Our models evidently introduce extensions to the ordinary efficiency frontiers of DEA to deal with what is required to attain state-mandated excellence standards. The results of this analysis are provided in Table 8.7. The first two columns identify the school district and the school. The third column identifies the CREA value, which is a measure of the increase in resource inputs minimally required by each efficient school to obtain excellence with respect to all three of the excellence outcome indicators. For instance, observation #2 in Table 8.7, which is Belton H.S. in Belton I.S.D., has a CREA rating of 1.137. This means that Belton H.S. is estimated to need 13.7 percent more in all its discretionary inputs to attain excellence on all three academic excellence indicators.

Further insights into the results obtained using the proposed excellence-oriented DEA model in (5) can be gained by analyzing the individual results of each DMU. As an example, the DEA results for Belton H.S. are provided in Table 8.8, where the 1.137 value for the coefficient of resources for excellence achievement is shown opposite CREA at the top. This rating is obtained from DEA in the following manner.

Table 8.6
Shortfalls from Excellence on Three Academic Excellence Indicators for 79 Efficient Schools

OBS.	DISTRICT (ISD)	SCHOOL (HS)	ATTEND	NOTDROP	CRITERION	OBS.	DISTRICT (ISD)	SCHOOL (HS)	ATTEND	NOTDROP	CRITERION
1	Bartlett ISD	Bartlett HS	2	1	30	41	Littlefield ISD	Litlefield HS	3	0	30
2	Belton ISD	Belton HS	2	5	23	42	Lorena ISD	Lorena HS	0	0	25
3	Ben Bolt-Palito Blanco	Ben Bolt-Palito Blanco HS	2	2	29	43	Lytle ISD	Lytle HS	2	1	23
4	Blanket ISD	Blanket HS	2	1	25	44	Marfa ISD	Marfa HS	3	2	32
5	Blum ISD	Blum HS	0	1	22	45	Mart ISD	Mart HS	0	2	16
6	Burnet Consolidated ISD	Burnet HS	3	2	27	46	Merkel ISD	Merkel HS	1	0	30
7	Canadian ISD	Canadian HS	0	1	2	47	New Diana ISD	New Diana HS	2	2	30
8	Carrizo Springs Cons. ISD	Carrizo Springs HS	2	7	34	48	Nocona ISD	Nocona HS	3	4	16
9	Celeste ISD	Celeste HS	0	1	31	49	Odem-Edroy ISD	Odem-Edroy HS	1	2	23
10	China Spring ISD	China Spring HS	2	4	30	50	Ore City ISD	Ore City HS	4	2	29
11	Clifton ISD	Clifton HS	3	3	24	51	Palmer ISD	Palmer HS	1	0	27
12	Corpus Christi ISD	King HS	3	1	15	52	Paris ISD	Paris HS	5	4	24
13	Crandall ISD	Crandall HS	4	4	26	53	Pearsall ISD	Pearsall HS	5	3	33
14	Culberson County ISD	Van Horn HS	3	1	29	54	Pleasant Grove ISD	Pleasant Grove HS	2	0	12
15	Dallas ISD	Hillcrest HS	6	15	16	55	Port Aransas ISD	Port Aransas HS	2	1	6
16	Dallas ISD	Jeffereson HS	8	21	26	56	Quitman ISD	Quitman HS	3	0	17
17	Eanes ISD	Westlake HS	2	0	0	57	Rio Grande City ISD	Rio Grande City HS	3	18	34
18	Fannindel ISD	Fannindel HS	0	0	21	58	Rio Hondo ISD	Rio Hondo HS	0	0	34
19	Forney ISD	Forney HS	1	0	30	59	Rio Vista ISD	Rio Vista HS	1	1	23
20	Fort Bend ISD	Clements HS	3	2	0	60	Robinson ISD	Robinson HS	1	2	21

152

OBS.	DISTRICT (ISD)	SCHOOL (HS)	ATTEND	NOTDROP	CRITERION	OBS.	DISTRICT (ISD)	SCHOOL (HS)	ATTEND	NOTDROP	CRITERION
21	Fort Bend ISD	Kempner HS	4	2	10	61	Robstown ISD	Robstown HS	5	4	34
22	Fort Bend ISD	Willowridge HS	5	9	28	62	Rosebud-Lott ISD	Rosebud-Lott HS	3	1	26
23	Fort Worth ISD	Dunbar HS	4	3	0	63	Round Top-Carmine ISD	Carmine HS	0	0	27
24	Fort Worth ISD	Northside HS	11	7	23	64	Royse City ISD	Royse City HS	3	5	25
25	Gorman ISD	Gorman HS	0	0	29	65	Runge ISD	Runge HS	1	1	30
26	Highland Park ISD	Highland Park HS	0	0	0*	66	Sherman ISD	Sherman HS	3	10	12
27	Houston ISD	Austin HS	10	18	34	67	Spring Branch ISD	Memorial HS	1	4	0
28	Houston ISD	Bellaire HS	2	4	0	68	Spring Branch ISD	Stratford HS	1	1	0
29	Houston ISD	Davis HS	7	12	32	69	Stockdale ISD	Stockdale HS	1	4	25
30	Houston ISD	Lamar HS	4	8	0	70	Troy ISD	Troy HS	3	2	15
31	Houston ISD	Madison HS	5	4	33	71	West ISD	West HS	1	0	31
32	Houston ISD	Milby HS	9	11	30	72	Wimberly ISD	Danforth HS	16	1	2
33	Houston ISD	Scarborough HS	5	8	25	73	Winnsboro ISD	Winnsboro HS	3	6	20
34	Houston ISD	Sharpstown HS	8	14	14	74	Woden ISD	Woden HS	3	1	27
35	Humble ISD	Kingwood HS	1	2	0	75	Woodsboro ISD	Woodsboro HS	2	1	31
36	Iola ISD	Iola HS	2	5	30	76	Wylie ISD	Wylie HS	1	3	6
37	Kennedy ISD	Kennedy HS	2	4	33	77	Ysleta ISD	Del Valle HS	5	7	32
38	La Joya ISD	La Joya HS	3	15	33	78	Ysleta ISD	J. M. Hanks HS	2	5	20
39	Lago Vista ISD	Lago Vista HS	3	4	10	79	Ysleta ISD	Riverside HS	5	7	30
40	Laredo ISD	Dr. Leo Cigarroa HS	2	7	33						

The asterisk * represents an efficient school that has also achieved excellence on all three excellence indicators.

Table 8.7
Second Stage DEA Evaluation of 79 Efficient Schools Using the Excellence-Oriented Model (3 Academic Excellence Indicators —ATTEND, NOTDROP, and CRITERION)

Obs.	DISTRICT (ISD)	SCHOOL (HS)	CREA	Obs.	DISTRICT (ISD)	SCHOOL (HS)	CREA
1	Bartlett ISD	Bartlett HS	2.194	41	Littlefield ISD	Littlefield HS	1.402
2	Belton ISD	Belton HS	1.137	42	Lorena ISD	Lorena HS	2.179
3	Ben Bolt-Palito Blanco ISD	Ben Bolt-Palito Blanco HS	2.240	43	Lytle ISD	Lytle HS	1.928
4	Blanket ISD	Blanket HS	3.500	44	Marfa ISD	Marfa HS	2.142
5	Blum ISD	Blum HS	1.893	45	Mart ISD	Mart HS	1.842
6	Burnet Consolidated ISD	Burnet HS	1.220	46	Merkel ISD	Merkel HS	1.233
7	Canadian ISD	Canadian HS	1.061	47	New Diana ISD	New Diana HS	1.862
8	Carrizo Springs Cons. ISD	Carrizo Springs HS	1.795	48	Nocona ISD	Nocona HS	1.724
9	Celeste ISD	Celeste HS	1.734	49	Odem-Edroy ISD	Odem-Edroy HS	1.826
10	China Spring ISD	China Spring HS	2.584	50	Ore City ISD	Ore City HS	1.909
11	Clifton ISD	Clifton HS	1.783	51	Palmer ISD	Palmer HS	1.894
12	Corpus Christi ISD	King HS	1.074	52	Paris ISD	Paris HS	1.312
13	Crandall ISD	Crandall HS	1.742	53	Pearsall ISD	Pearsall HS	1.984
14	Culberson County ISD	Van Horn HS	2.877	54	Pleasant Grove ISD	Pleasant Grove HS	1.224
15	Dallas ISD	Hillcrest HS	1.551	55	Port Aransas ISD	Port Aransas HS	1.207
16	Dallas ISD	Jefferson HS	1.481	56	Quitman ISD	Quitman HS	1.189
17	Eanes ISD	Westlake HS	1.014	57	Rio Grande City ISD	Rio Grande City HS	1.695
18	Farmindel ISD	Farmindel HS	1.962	58	Rio Hondo ISD	Rio Hondo HS	2.364
19	Forney ISD	Forney HS	1.365	59	Rio Vista ISD	Rio Vista HS	1.957
20	Fort Bend ISD	Clements HS	1.028	60	Robinson ISD	Robinson HS	2.500
21	Fort Bend ISD	Kempner HS	1.113	61	Robstown ISD	Robstown HS	1.656

Obs.	DISTRICT (ISD)	SCHOOL (HS)	CREA	Obs.	DISTRICT (ISD)	SCHOOL (HS)	CREA
22	Fort Bend ISD	Willowridge HS	1.416	62	Rosebud-Lott ISD	Rosebud-Lott HS	1.524
23	Fort Worth ISD	Dunbar HS	1.029	63	Round Top-Carmine ISD	Carmine HS	2.357
24	Fort Worth ISD	Northside HS	1.675	64	Royse City ISD	Royse City HS	1.698
25	Gorman ISD	Gorman HS	1.975	65	Runge ISD	Runge HS	2.044
26	Highland Park ISD	Highland Park HS	1.000 *	66	Sherman ISD	Sherman HS	1.295
27	Houston ISD	Austin HS	1.481	67	Spring Branch ISD	Memorial HS	1.028
28	Houston ISD	Bellaire HS	1.034	68	Spring Branch ISD	Stratford HS	1.008
29	Houston ISD	Davis HS	1.695	69	Stockdale ISD	Stockdale HS	1.907
30	Houston ISD	Lamar HS	1.073	70	Troy ISD	Troy HS	1.655
31	Houston ISD	Madison HS	1.443	71	West ISD	West HS	2.533
32	Houston ISD	Milby HS	1.368	72	Wimberly ISD	Danforth HS	1.144
33	Houston ISD	Scarborough HS	1.410	73	Winnsboro ISD	Winnsboro HS	1.560
34	Houston ISD	Sharpstown HS	1.363	74	Woden ISD	Woden HS	1.749
35	Humble ISD	Kingwood HS	1.016	75	Woodsboro ISD	Woodsboro HS	1.548
36	Iola ISD	Iola HS	1.837	76	Wylie ISD	Wylie HS	1.207
37	Kennedy ISD	Kennedy HS	2.112	77	Ysleta ISD	Del Valle HS	1.546
38	La Joya ISD	La Joya HS	1.934	78	Ysleta ISD	J. M. Hanks HS	1.135
39	Lago Vista ISD	Lago Vista HS	1.400	79	Ysleta ISD	Riverside HS	1.475
40	Laredo ISD	Dr. Leo Cigarroa HS	1.649				

The asterisk * represents an efficient school that has also achieved excellence on all 3 excellence indicators.

Belton H.S. is part of the set of 79 public secondary schools in Texas that had been evaluated as efficient by the CCR model in (1). From this set DEA selects a subset of DMUs to effect its evaluation of Belton H.S. The thus-selected DMUs are explicitly identified in the row labeled Facet at the top of Table 8.8. These form the efficient subset of schools selected by DEA for evaluating Belton H.S. Also provided are the coefficients from which a best comparison DMU is synthesized as follows: 0.48 is applicable to the discretionary inputs and outputs of DMU #28 (Bellaire H.S. in Houston I.S.D), 0.42 is applicable to DMU #70 (Troy H.S. in Troy I.S.D), 0.08 is applicable to DMU #72 (Danforth H.S. in Wimberly I.S.D), and 0.03 is applicable to DMU #66 (Sherman H.S. in Sherman I.S.D).

From Table 8.8 we find also that this increase due to a CREA value of 1.137 (= 13.7%) is not all that is involved. Modification is needed to take account of the slacks and the corresponding changes in mix to attain efficiency at this new level of operations. This can be seen as follows. Column 1 of Table 8.8 lists the measured (i.e., reported) values of all outputs produced and inputs used by Belton H.S. Column 2, labeled Value if Excellent, lists the inputs required by Belton H.S. to attain excellence on the three excellence indicators. Also provided are other outputs which would have resulted from an increase in input resources. For instance, all outputs except for Writing increase by amounts equal to the values reported in column 3, labeled Slack. We observe that Attend, Notdrop and Criterion are all augmented by additional amounts equal to 2 percent, 5.5 percent and 23 percent, respectively. These values are exactly equal to the shortfalls from excellence for Belton H.S. as observed from Table 8.6. However, it is projected that the increased availability of resource inputs should also improve the average Math and Reading scores by 146 and 95 points, respectively. That is, because of the increase in available resources, such as more teachers per student and higher instructional expenditures per student, there should be improvements in other outcomes as well, including the graduation rates which are reflected in the category Notdrop.

Next, we turn to a discussion of the additional resources (monetary and human) required by Belton H.S. to achieve excellence. For instance, Belton H.S. would require 77 (= 1.137 X 68) Teachers as reported under the column labeled "Value if Excellent." Hence an additional 9 (= 77 − 68) teachers would be needed to improve the quality of instruction at Belton H.S. to achieve the state-mandated excellence standards. Moreover, both Salary (teacher salary) and Instexp (instructional expenditure per student) would require some augmentation to attain excellence in the three indicated categories, with additional augmentation in other input categories as well. Note therefore that our DEA analysis is supplying more than just an estimated dollar increment of resources. It is supplying details on each (discretionary) input and also on each output that is to be augmented.

Thus more is being supplied than just the CREA rating applied to all inputs. The results suggest that teachers with more experience do make a difference in student outcomes for these efficient schools. However, more emphasis needs to be placed on regular instruction compared to special education, as reflected by the need for an increase in the number of teachers in regular education (Reged) from 47 to 59 as compared to a corresponding increment of only 2 teachers in special education (Speced).[35]

Table 8.8
An Example of DEA Results from the Excellence-oriented Model (Second-stage Evaluation): Belton H.S., Belton I.S.D.

Coefficient of Resources for Excellence Achievement (CREA): = 1.137
DEA Model: Excellence-oriented DEA Model of (4)
REFERENCE SET (PEER GROUP):

FACET:	28	70	70	66
LAMBDA:	0.48	0.42	0.08	0.04

	Current Level (1)	Value if Excellent (2)	Slack (3)
Outputs			
Attend	95	97	2
Notdrop	94	99.5	5.5
Math	1527	1673	146
Reading	1620	1715	95
Writing	1673	1673	-
Criterion	12	35	23
Discretionary Inputs			
Teachers	68	77	—
Salary	24,903	28,307	—
Avgexpn	12.7	16	1.5
Reged	47	59	6
Speced	4	6	1
Instexp	1640	1865	—
Non-Discretionary Inputs			
Minority	22	22	5
Disadv	13	13	—
Lep	0	0	3

Based on the results of the model proposed in (5), it is estimated that the seventy-nine efficient schools would require an average increase of 64 percent over their current available resource level to achieve the state-mandated excellence standards. This increase in resources may be funded entirely or partially by reducing inefficiencies within the 527 inefficient schools and reallocating the excess resources from the inefficient schools among the efficient schools.[36]

Table 8.9
Second Stage DEA Evaluation of 79 Efficient Schools Using the Excellence-Oriented Model (2 Academic Excellence Indicators —ATTEND and NOTDROP)

Obs.	DISTRICT (ISD)	SCHOOL (HS)	CREA	Obs.	DISTRICT (ISD)	SCHOOL (HS)	CREA
1	Bartlett ISD	Bartlett HS	1.020	41	Littlefield ISD	Littlefield HS	1.006
2	Belton ISD	Belton HS	1.034	42	Lorena ISD	Lorena HS	1.000*
3	Ben Bolt-Palito Blanco ISD	Ben Bolt-Palito Blanco HS	1.021	43	Lytle ISD	Lytle HS	1.016
4	Blanket ISD	Blanket HS	1.021	44	Marfa ISD	Marfa HS	1.026
5	Blum ISD	Blum HS	1.010	45	Mart ISD	Mart HS	1.021
6	Burnet Consolidated ISD	Burnet HS	1.020	46	Merkel ISD	Merkel HS	1.006
7	Canadian ISD	Canadian HS	1.005	47	New Diana ISD	New Diana HS	1.020
8	Carrizo Springs Cons. ISD	Carrizo Springs HS	1.048	48	Nocona ISD	Nocona HS	1.034
9	Celeste ISD	Celeste HS	1.010	49	Odem-Edroy ISD	Odem-Edroy HS	1.012
10	China Spring ISD	China Spring HS	1.042	50	Ore City ISD	Ore City HS	1.027
11	Clifton ISD	Clifton HS	1.029	51	Palmer ISD	Palmer HS	1.010
12	Corpus Christi ISD	King HS	1.013	52	Paris ISD	Paris HS	1.042
13	Crandall ISD	Crandall HS	1.043	53	Pearsall ISD	Pearsall HS	1.047
14	Culberson County ISD	Van Horn HS	1.032	54	Pleasant Grove ISD	Pleasant Grove HS	1.020
15	Dallas ISD	Hillcrest HS	1.132	55	Port Aransas ISD	Port Aransas HS	1.016
16	Dallas ISD	Jefferson HS	1.033	56	Quitman ISD	Quitman HS	1.009
17	Eanes ISD	Westlake HS	1.014	57	Rio Grande City ISD	Rio Grande City HS	1.138
18	Fannindel ISD	Fannindel HS	1.000 *	58	Rio Hondo ISD	Rio Hondo HS	1.000*
19	Forney ISD	Forney HS	1.010 *	59	Rio Vista ISD	Rio Vista HS	1.010
20	Fort Bend ISD	Clements HS	1.028	60	Robinson ISD	Robinson HS	1.021
21	Fort Bend ISD	Kempner HS	1.042	61	Robstown ISD	Robstown HS	1.050

Obs.	DISTRICT (ISD)	SCHOOL (HS)	CREA	Obs.	DISTRICT (ISD)	SCHOOL (HS)	CREA
22	Fort Bend ISD	Willowridge HS	1.078	62	Rosebud-Lott ISD	Rosebud-Lott HS	1.004
23	Fort Worth ISD	Dunbar HS	1.029	63	Round Top-Carmine ISD	Carmine HS	1.000 *
24	Fort Worth ISD	Northside HS	1.084	64	Royse City ISD	Royse City HS	1.025
25	Gorman ISD	Gorman HS	1.000 *	65	Runge ISD	Runge HS	1.009
26	Highland Park ISD	Highland Park HS	1.000 *	66	Sherman ISD	Sherman HS	1.112
27	Houston ISD	Austin HS	1.178	67	Spring Branch ISD	Memorial HS	1.028
28	Houston ISD	Bellaire HS	1.034	68	Spring Branch ISD	Stratford HS	1.008
29	Houston ISD	Davis HS	1.115	69	Stockdale ISD	Stockdale HS	1.025
30	Houston ISD	Lamar HS	1.073	70	Troy ISD	Troy HS	1.026
31	Houston ISD	Madison HS	1.041	71	West ISD	West HS	1.010
32	Houston ISD	Milby HS	1.112	72	Wimberly ISD	Danforth HS	1.121
33	Houston ISD	Scarborough HS	1.076	73	Winnsboro ISD	Winnsboro HS	1.021
34	Houston ISD	Sharpstown HS	1.120	74	Woden ISD	Woden HS	1.024
35	Humble ISD	Kingwood HS	1.016	75	Woodsboro ISD	Woodsboro HS	1.014
36	Iola ISD	Iola HS	1.053	76	Wylie ISD	Wylie HS	1.024
37	Kennedy ISD	Kennedy HS	1.036	77	Ysleta ISD	Del Valle HS	1.068
38	La Joya ISD	La Joya HS	1.141	78	Ysleta ISD	J. M. Hanks HS	1.042
39	Lago Vista ISD	Lago Vista HS	1.038	79	Ysleta ISD	Riverside HS	1.051
40	Laredo ISD	Dr. Leo Cigarroa HS	1.063				

The asterisk * represents an efficient school that has also achieved excellence on both excellence indicators.

Sensitivity analyses and other tests need to be applied, of course, in order to ascertain whether the results obtained are sensitive to variation in the variables used in the analysis. As a case in point Table 8.9 presents results from DEA evaluations using only two excellence indicators—Attend and Notdrop. The results suggest only a 4 percent increase in input resources would be required (on average) by the seventy-nine efficient schools to improve their attendance and dropout rates to excellence levels. This is a significant reduction compared to the estimates of a 64 percent increment for resource increases found for Table 8.7 and, hence, raises questions as to whether Criterion should be dropped or its state-mandated levels of attainment modified.

The results obtained even in this experimental use of DEA provide other insights as well. Specifically, the inputs that play a significant role in attaining improvements in student outcomes are the number of teachers (or teacher-to-student ratios), teacher salary, and the instructional expenditures per student. These findings are corroborated by the conclusions of Hanushek's (1986) survey paper "The Economics of Schooling," in which he has summarized the results from 147 studies of education production functions. Hanushek concludes (see page 1161) from his survey of numerous econometric studies that the variables which had a significant positive impact on student outcomes were teacher experience, teacher salary, and expenditures per pupil. Hence it is quite reasonable to expect that a better quality of instruction and, consequently, excellence in student outcomes can be achieved by increasing teacher-per-student ratios and teacher salaries in the efficient schools. Note that this restriction to efficient schools contrasts with Hanushek's application to *all* schools. Indeed, our own further statistical studies—which were combined with DEA in a new and innovative way, as reported in Arnold et al. (1994b)—raise serious questions as to the wisdom of making inferences or applying policies uniformly to a mixture that involves both efficient and inefficient schools.

SUMMARY AND CONCLUSIONS

Evidently, these DEA results lead to additional interpretations which provide insights that can lead to new approaches to the problems of public secondary school performance in other states as well as Texas. Our two-stage approach also makes it possible to distinguish between efficiency and excellence, with several consequences. First we can distinguish between schools that are excellent and schools that are efficient, and then we can identify in detail the resources needed to move the latter to excellence frontiers without sacrificing efficiency; and, as noted in Arnold et al. (1993), this does not preclude also using the results from our efficiency evaluations to improve the performance in schools that are not fully efficient.

There is, of course, more to be done. Attention must be devoted to the need for qualifying these CREA, estimates since these involve linear extrapolations outside the set of observations. This can lead to extremely high CREA estimates as, for example, in Table 8.7, where Barlett H.S. (Obs. #1) in Bartlett I.S.D., Blanket H.S. (Obs. #4) in Blanket I.S.D., China Spring H.S. (Obs. #10) in China Spring I.S.D., and Van Horn H.S. (Obs. #14) in Culberson County I.S.D. all exhibit very high CREA values.

Extensions to the present study are needed and new methods and concepts developed but, provisionally at least, we can take these CREA values as pointing to situations where more detailed studies (including field studies) are warranted. We can also note that the results of the study reported in this paper can be interpreted as raising new questions of concern on current approaches to education. Using "excellence only" as a criterion of performance is not in itself enough and may lead to using excessive amounts of inputs. Shortcomings in public education policy like these that are revealed in the present study suggest that state-mandated standards applied uniformly across the state of Texas do not provide adequate allowance for the wide variations and diversity in conditions confronted by different schools. Such uniformly mandated (excellence only) standards are, of course, even more questionable when applied across the entire nation, as in the proposals for education reform by ex-President Bush and ex-Secretary Alexander, or in the proposed "Clinton 2000" plan.[37] At a minimum, some method of taking account of inputs used, as well as outputs produced, needs to be considered, and recognition needs to be accorded to schools that are then found to be performing efficiently. Additionally, some kind of flexible plan for recognizing incremental attainment is needed, with accompanying mechanisms for allocating (and reallocating) resources. A school with a high percentage of LEP or other disadvantaged classes of students might then be allocated resources directed to helping it attain reasonable increments in specified output categories over time.

As noted in our opening section, the study reported in this paper forms one part of a legislatively supported effort devoted to improved accountability for public school performance. Although experimental in character, even these preliminary results from DEA point to an urgent need for improved methods for evaluating public school performance. The models and methods used here (including our extensions of DEA) should be regarded as a start for exploring some of the further possibilities that might be developed.

NOTES

Support from the Texas Legislative Education Board and the IC^2 Institute of the University of Texas at Austin is gratefully acknowledged.

1. These reports include *Why Johnny Can't Read* by R. Flesch (1955) and *A Nation at Risk* published by the United States National Commission on Excellence in Education (1983).

2. Including sharp criticism such as Jonathan Kozol's *Savage Inequalities* (1991).

3. See the *Digest of Education Statistics* (1993) published by the National Center for Education Statistics.

4. A summary discussion may be found in Cooper et al. (1991), which also provides a map showing the many other states where the same situation is receiving urgent attention.

5. Other types of DEA models and their relations to each other are covered in Ahn et al. (1988).

6. Banker and Morey (1986) introduced this approach to deal with variables which they refer to as exogenously fixed.

7. This requirement may be relaxed, as described in Charnes et al. (1991).

8. As noted in Cooper et al. (1994), only the nondiscretionary variables can have a zero opportunity cost since all other dual variables are constrained to be positive. See Arnold et al. (1994a) for a fuller discussion.

9. See, for example, Färe et al. (1985).

10. As a matter of historical interest relative to managerial uses of linear programming, it may be worth noting that the term "disposal activities" is a reversion to earlier uses in economic (theory) analyses. The term slack was introduced to avoid having to explain to managers what was meant by a disposal activity. See Charnes et al. (1952).

11. For further discussion see Banker et al. (1994).

12. The analogy is to complex numbers which also require two components in their representation and which therefore cannot be replaced by a single real number. See Arnold et al. (1994).

13. See the discussion of the principle of "complementary slackness" in Arnold et al. (1994) and its extension to the treatment for μ_r, $v_i \geq \varepsilon > 0$.

14. This misleading characterization occurs even in some of the computer codes. See, for instance, the manual accompanying the computer code IDEAS (Integrated Data Envelopment Analysis System) devised by Ali (1989).

15. These field studies subsequently led to recommendations for capping the ratio of overhead and auxiliary expenditures to instructional expenses by the Texas State Comptroller's Office. See Arnold et al. (1993).

16. See the discussion of the Coopersmith self-esteem score in Charnes et al. (1981).

17. Including legislators and legislative committees concerned with education policies and problems.

18. As data from the following years become available to us, we plan to use them to study the performance of these schools over time in terms of efficiency and excellence—for example, via the window analyses that are available for use in DEA. See Charnes et al. (1993).

19. See Table 8.2 for the definition of the criterion score as defined by the Texas Education Agency.

20. For further discussion of the importance of distinguishing between outcomes and outputs in evaluating educational activities. See Lovell et al. (1994).

21. It should be noted that these numbers are somewhat sensitive to the input and output measures used in the DEA evaluation. However, our interest in this study centered on the efficient schools, most of which continued to be rated efficient even when one or more variables were added or removed during additional sensitivity analyses.

22. A minor exception is Writing where the average for the inefficient schools exceeds the average for the efficient schools by less than 0.2 percent.

23. A complete listing of the 638 schools and the data used in the analysis can be obtained from the authors.

24. A similar precedent is apparently also being established by the performance audits of school districts now being conducted by the office of the State Auditor of Texas. See the reference to the Texas State Auditor's report.

25. Efficiency, we may note, is mandated by the state constitution. See Cooper et al. (1991).

26. See the distinction drawn earlier between effectiveness and efficiency.

27. We are allowing the solutions to go outside the production possibility set generated by past behavior.

28. In other words, all schools which are rated 100 percent efficient by the output-oriented CCR model will maintain their 100% efficiency rating when we switch to an input-oriented CCR model.

29. See Charnes et al. (1989a) for further discussion, including the topic of inefficient self evaluators.

30. These tests are allowed as alternate possibilities to establish excellence by reference to the same level of achievement.

31. Note: These ε values are not to be interpreted as real numbers since all real numbers, however small, are Archimedean. See Arnold et al. (1994a) for further discussion of the pre-emptions associated with ε and their ordering properties and interpretations.

32. Other models and possibilities for the nonexistence of solutions are discussed in Arnold et al. (1993).

33. See Cooper et al. (1994).

34. A complementary approach which also allows $\Theta_0^* > 1$ may be found in Golany and Roll (1994). Their approach differs from the one used here in that the added constraints in their case are applied directly to the λ_j and thus yield different interpretations.

35. An analysis of the DEA results showed that almost all schools required more teachers for regular instruction compared to special education activities.

36. See the paper by Bessent et al. (1982) which describes a similar reallocation of resources from inefficient to efficient schools effected in the Houston I.S.D. by the school superintendent on the basis of a DEA analysis (augmented, of course, by other information and past experience with the schools involved).

37. This is a matter of some urgency since education expenditures are now rising at a faster rate than expenditures for healthcare services. See Hanushek (1993).

REFERENCES

Ahn, T. (1987). "Efficiency and Related Issues in Higher Education: A Data Envelopment Analysis Approach." Ph.D. thesis, University of Texas at Austin.

Ahn, T., Arnold, V., Charnes, A., and Cooper, W. W. (1989). "DEA and Ratio Efficiency Analyses for Public Institutions of Higher Learning in Texas." *Research in Governmental and Nonprofit Accounting*, 5:165–185.

Ahn, T., Charnes, A., and Cooper, W. W. (1988). "Efficiency Characterizations in Different DEA Models." *Socio-Economic Planning Sciences*, 22, 6: 253–257.

Ali, A. I. (1989). "Computational Aspects of Data Envelopment Analysis." CCS Research Report 640. Center for Cybernetic Studies, University of Texas at Austin.

Arnold, V., Bardhan, I. R., and Cooper, W. W. (1993). "DEA Models for Evaluating Efficiency and Excellence in Texas Public Schools." Research Report. Austin: IC^2 Institute, University of Texas.

Arnold, V., Bardhan, I. R., Cooper, W. W. and Gallegos, A. (1994a). "Primal and Dual Optimality in Computer Codes Using Two-Stage Solution Procedures in DEA." In J. Aronson and S. Zionts, eds., *Operations Research: Methods, Models and Applications, Proceedings of a Conference in Honor of G. L. Thompson.* New York: Kluwer Academic Publishers, forthcoming.

Arnold, V., Bardhan, I. R., Cooper, W. W. and Kumbhakar, S. C. (1994b). "DEA Extensions to Statistical Regressions for Efficiency Evaluations—With Illustrative Applications to Secondary Schools in Texas." *The Annals of Operations Research* (to appear).

Banker, R. D., Bardhan, I. R., Cooper, W. W. and Thrall, R. M. (1994). "Projection Operators in DEA." *The Annals of Operations Research* (forthcoming).

Banker, R. D., Chang, H., and Cooper, W. W. (1994). "Returns to Scale Equivalences and Methods of Implementation in DEA Models." *European Journal of Operational Research* (to appear).

Banker, R. D., Charnes, A. and Cooper, W. W. (1984). "Models for Estimating Technical and Returns to Scale Efficiencies in DEA." *Management Science*, 30: 1078–1092.

Banker, R. D., Charnes, A., Cooper, W. W., Swarts, J., and Thomas, D. A. (1989). "An Introduction to Data Envelopment Analysis with Some of its Models and their Uses." *Research in Governmental and Nonprofit Accounting*, 5: 125–163.

Banker, R. D., and Morey, R. (1986). "Efficiency Analysis for Exogenously Fixed Inputs and Outputs." *Operations Research*, 34, 4: 513–521.

Banker, R. D., and Thrall, R. M. (1992). "Estimation of Returns to Scale using Data Envelopment Analysis." *European Journal of Operational Research*, 62: 74–84.

Bardhan, I. (1995). "DEA and Stochastic Frontier Regression Approaches Applied to Evaluating the Performances of Public Secondary Schools in Texas." Ph.D. thesis, Austin: the University of Texas.

Bardhan, I., Bowlin, W. F., Cooper, W. W., and Sueyoshi, T. (1994). "Models for Measuring Efficiency Dominance in DEA." *Journal of the Operations Research Society of Japan* (forthcoming).

Bessent, A., Bessent, W., Kennington, J., and Regan, B. (1982). "An Application of Mathematical Programming to Assess Productivity in the Houston Independent School District." *Management Science*, 28 12: 1355–1367.

Business Week, September 14, 1992. "Cover Story: Saving Our Schools." pp. 70–80.

Charnes, A., Clarke, R. L., and Cooper, W. W. (1989). "An Approach to Test for Organizational Slack Via Banker's Game Theoretic DEA Formulations." *Research in Governmental and Nonprofit Accounting*, 5: 211–229.

Charnes, A., and Cooper, W. W. (1985). "Preface to Topics in Data Envelopment Analysis." *Annals of Operations Research*, 2: 59–95.

Charnes, A., Cooper, W. W., Divine, D., Ruefli, T. W., and Thomas, D. (1989). "Comparisons of DEA and Existing Ratio and Regression Systems for Effecting

Efficiency Evaluations of Regulated Electric Cooperatives In Texas." *Research in Governmental and Nonprofit Accounting*, 5: 187–210.

Charnes, A., Cooper, W. W., Lewin, A., and Seiford, L. (1994). *Data Envelopment Analysis: Theory, Methodology and Applications*. New York: Kluwer Academic Publishers.

Charnes, A., Cooper, W. W., and Mellon, B. (1952). "Blending Aviation Gasolines: A study in Programming Interdependent Activities." *Econometrica*, 20: 135–159.

Charnes, A., Cooper, W. W., and Rhodes, E. (1978). "Measuring the Efficiency of Decision Making Units." *European Journal of Operational Research*, 3: 429–444.

Charnes, A., Cooper, W. W., and Rhodes, E. (1981). "Evaluating Program and Managerial Efficiency: An Application of DEA to Program Follow Through." *Management Science*, 27: 668–697.

Charnes, A., Cooper, W. W., and Thrall, R. M. (1991). "A Structure for Classifying and Characterizing Efficiency and Inefficiency in Data Envelopment Analysis." *The Journal of Productivity Analysis*, 2: 197–237.

Cooper, W. W., Kumbhakar, S., Thrall, R. M., and Yu, X. (1992). "DEA and Stochastic Frontier Evaluations of the Effects of the 1978 Chinese Economic Reforms." Research Report, Austin: IC^2 Institute, The University of Texas.

Cooper, W. W., Messer, K. H., and Yu, X. (1991). "A DEA study of Public School District Performance and Financing in Texas." Working Paper, Austin: IC^2 Institute, the University of Texas.

Cooper, W. W., Tone, K., Takamori, H., and Sueyoshi, T. (1994). "Data Envelopment Analysis: Survey and Interpretations." *Communications of the Operations Research Society of Japan*, (August, September and October, 1994) In Japanese–English translations available from authors on request.

Debreu, G. (1951). "The Coefficient of Resource Utilization." *Econometrica*, 19: 273–292.

Färe, R., Grosskopf, S., and Lovell, C.A.K. (1985). *The Measurement of the Efficiency of Production*. Boston: Kluwer-Nijhoff.

Flesch, R. F. (1955). *Why Johnny Can't Read*. New York: Harper Brothers.

Golany, B., and Roll, Y. (1994). "Incorporating Standards in DEA." in Charnes, A., Cooper, W. W., A. Lewin and L. Seiford, Editors, *Data Envelopment Analysis: Theory, Methodology and Applications*. New York: Kluwer Academic Publishers.

Governmental Accounting Standards Board (1990). *Service Efforts and Accomplishments Reporting: Its Time Has Come—An Overview*, H. P. Hatry, J. M. Sullivan., J. M. Fountain., and L. Kremer, eds., Norwalk, Conn.: GASB.

Hanushek, E. (1986). "The Economics of Schooling: Production and Efficiency in Public Schools." *Journal of Economic Literature*, XXIV: 1141–1177.

Hanushek, E. (1993). "School Finance and Educational Reform." Testimony before the Subcommittee on Education, Arts and Humanities, Committee on Labor and Human Resources, U.S. Senate, July.

Koopmans, T. C. (1957). *Three Essays on the State of Economic Science*. New York: McGraw-Hill.

Kozol, J. (1991). *Savage Inequalities: Children in America's Schools*, first edition. New York: Crown Publishers.

Lovell, C.A.K., Walters, L. and Wood, L. (1994). "Stratified Models of Education Production Using Modified DEA and Regression Analysis" in Charnes, A., Cooper, W. W., Lewin, A., and Seiford, L., eds., *Data Envelopment Analysis: Theory, Methodology and Applications*. New York: Kluwer Academic Publishers.

National Center for Education Statistics. (1993). *Digest of Education Statistics*, NCES 93-292. Washington D.C.: U.S. Government Printing Office.

The Texas State Auditor's Office, November 1992, *Making the Most of Our Education Dollars: Details from the Management Audit of Public Schools*, SAO Report No. 3–010. Austin: Office of the State Auditor.

Thomas, D. A. (1990). *Data Envelopment Analysis Methods in the Management of Personnel Recruitment Under Competition in the Context of U. S. Army Recruiting*. Ph.D. thesis. Austin: the University of Texas.

United States National Commission on Excellence in Education, 1983, *A Nation at Risk: The Imperative for Educational Reform—A Report to the Nation and the Secretary of Education*. Washington D.C.: U.S. Government Printing Office.

A Management System for Monitoring and Analyzing the Productivity of Armed Forces Recruiting

David B. Learner, Fred Young Phillips, and John J. Rousseau

This chapter is an edited version of a concept paper that the authors submitted to the Office of the Assistant Secretary of the Army on behalf of MRCA Information Services. Two conditions that existed in the late 1980s led us to see an opportunity and submit the paper:

*   The U.S. Army was experiencing difficulty in attracting qualified recruits; and
*   The various offices of Department of Defense and the Army—that is, the Office of the Assistant Secretary, the Deputy Secretary for Personnel (DESPER), and the Army Recruiting Command—needed to utilize separate management information systems in order to avoid the appearance of overlap of responsibilities or command.

The submission was motivated by our desire to apply and promote Rosetta™, a decision-support system developed and marketed by MRCA. Rosetta is based on MRCA research and on university research in data envelopment analysis (DEA) and decision-support systems (DSS), some of which was performed by us in collaboration with A. Charnes, W. W. Cooper, B. Golany, and others in activities supported in part by the IC² Institute.

The results of this work were trebly gratifying. First, the Office of the Assistant Secretary of the Army (OASA) remarked that our analysis of recruiting and readiness issues was "the most accurate and concise statement of our problem we have ever seen." Second, following a more formal proposal from MRCA, OASA purchased a Rosetta installation.

The third gratifying result had to do with actual changes in the composition and performance of the fighting forces. Whereas the Viet Nam-era Army suffered from drug use and some untrainable enlisted ranks, troops at the time of Desert Storm were the most highly educated in recent history, and disciplinary problems, according to the press, were minimal. General Norman Schwartzkopf publicly remarked on his satisfaction with the quality of the troops. It seems clear that to some extent the quick conclusion of the operations in Kuwait and Iraq were due to the improved aptitude of Army recruits, and hence to the Army

Recruiting Command—which made extensive use of modern management methods and analytical techniques as exemplified by some of the concepts and methods used in this chapter. It is therefore reasonable to infer that this was partially attributable to improved use of the Army's limited recruiting resources, and we would like to believe the research reported here played a contributory role.

INTRODUCTION

The Armed Forces must attract sufficient numbers of qualified recruits to the All-Volunteer Force (AVF). Given the magnitude and complexity of the recruiting task, the most advanced information and decision technologies must be used. To accommodate the ever-changing realities of the situation, it is essential that an adaptive system be in place employing appropriate technologies and modeling procedures for measuring and monitoring recruiting efforts and providing timely access to needed information. Recruiting management should be supported by tools and methods that are comprehensive, systematic, and flexible. Only then can the recruitment process be both efficient in its use of scarce resources and effective in terms of attaining the prescribed goals.

In this chapter, we outline an improved way to deal with these issues. The central concept is a continually updated database of recruiting-related and other information, integrated with leading-edge mathematical technologies to provide the meaningful evaluation and detailed guidance needed by the Department of Defense (DoD) for recruitment efficiency, effective advertising planning, and other purposes. Existing mathematical models and variations can be used for improved decision making in current activities aimed at meeting accession targets, desired quality of recruits, and military occupational specialties (MOS) goals. They can also be used in such future or potential activities as testing the impact of changes in various goals or programs. The models are linked with novel data displays, user interfaces, and reporting procedures to enable comprehensive, detailed, and interactive analysis. The system and models do not disrupt the recruiting process; there is no need to restrict recruiting efforts or procedures in order to satisfy the requirements of the model.

Such an information system provides significant benefits to all parties jointly responsible for success of the recruiting effort: DoD, the armed services, congressional offices, and federal agencies. The DoD has increased control over its own activities, leading to better resource allocation and continuity of effort. The existing autonomous activities and decisions of the individual services are maintained, as is both required and desirable; but the system allows greater flexibility in guiding, assisting, and monitoring service responsibilities—leading to improved cooperation, understanding, and mutual support. It further enables DoD to establish better working relations with congressional offices and federal agencies, since the output of this new capability leads to objective evaluation of recruiting efficiency and improved understanding of the complex issues involved in recruiting. It allows DoD and the services to jointly assess alternatives for the best employment of such additional resources as may become available and permits individual services to reallocate resources among more-efficient and less-efficient units and activities. As such, it serves as a comprehensive and an easily comprehended rationale for decisions on budgets, programs, and other matters.

PROBLEM DEFINITION

Following the formal end of the military draft in 1973 and the creation of the AVF, DoD has been beset with problems in its attempt to recruit sufficient numbers of adequately qualified enlisted personnel. These problems have not been of DoD's making. Rather, they stem from the particular circumstances leading up to and surrounding the decision to move to an AVF, the inadequately analyzed implications of such a move, budgetary considerations, and other factors beyond DoD's control. See Binkin (1986); Hadley (1986); Hart (1986).

In February 1970, the Gates Commission, appointed by then-President Nixon and headed by former Secretary of Defense Thomas S. Gates, issued its favorable report on the prospects for an all-volunteer force and the end of the military draft. Undoubtedly, creation of the AVF involved political considerations, but there were also other factors that led to the recommendations in the final report. In particular, in 1965 the pool of young men aged 17 to 20 numbered 6.5 million, whereas in 1980 the same age group would contain 8.5 million men. The commission calculated that, with appropriate financial compensation, the nation could comfortably maintain armed forces of 2.5 million men for the foreseeable future, with no problems of quality or representativeness. This force level was the midrange of their projected two to three million man force. Ironically, 1980, the end of the unusually short (ten-year) time horizon adopted by the commission, was also the point at which the pool of eligible recruits would begin to decline.

The analysis (using econometric models) and recommendations of the Gates Commission were based on the methodological and ideological assumptions of free-market economics, and were strongly influenced by liberal thought. The commission proceeded from the premise that a volunteer force was the most desirable one, and that the only proper manpower question was whether sufficient numbers of capable men and women could be attracted by voluntary means.

Major concerns with the all-volunteer force are representativeness, numerical strength, quality, and overall war readiness. Important as the issue of representation is, the problems of numbers, quality, and organizational effectiveness are far more severe. The Gates Commission did not adequately describe the magnitude of the recruiting task it was thrusting upon the armed services. Rather, it suggested that the experience of other countries (notably, Great Britain) indicated that the transition would be a fairly easy one. This was misleading in that the report failed to examine the implications for Britain of its move to an all-volunteer force.

After 1960 the American armed forces suffered a considerable reduction in strength, and in 1984 the AVF barely met the low-range projection of the Gates Commission, the two-million manpower level that the commissioners had assumed an AVF would easily achieve. Curiously enough, the problem is not yet a demographic one. The year 1979 was the peak year for the pool of 18–21 year old men (with over 8,800,000 of them), and the decade's low would not be reached until 1988, when the pool totaled slightly over 7,500,000. (The pool has continued to shrink, however, to near six million in 1995.)

In spite of an expanding pool of eligible men through the 1970s, the quality of recruits to both the active and the reserve forces had deteriorated sharply by the end of the decade. Of concern here are the time, money, and effort required for training substandard recruits, and the difficulty such recruits have in learning new skills or in improvising. A more serious problem has to do with combat readiness and the ability of recruits to plug the gaps when key personnel have been incapacitated. One indicator of the quality of the AVF is the attrition rate of nearly one third; that is, one-third of first term enlistees did not complete a three-year term.

In the early 1980s, an economy in recession and substantial pay increases to the armed forces made possible recovery of some lost ground. Increased recruiting of women also improved the figures. Nonetheless, the services did not have the manpower required by their force structure.

Shortfalls in manpower have led defense planners to two other measures beyond acceptance of low quality recruits: the large scale recruitment of women, and the Total Force concept. Although female recruits are usually more intelligent than male recruits, it was feared the increasing use of women in the general-purpose military could create numerous morale and disciplinary problems. In addition, there were questions of combat exclusion and the possible detraction from military effectiveness by the influx of women into nontraditional areas of service.

The total force concept mandated the interweaving of active and reserve units. However, since two-thirds of the tactical support the total force would require comes from the reserves, no major military operation could be undertaken without a reserve mobilization and all of its attendant delays and political problems. Moreover, it is unreasonable to think that reserve units, particularly those composed of nonveteran soldiers, are likely to be at the same level of readiness and fitness or be nearly as proficient as their active duty counterparts.

Most of the quantitative and qualitative recruiting shortfalls are in those areas of military service for which no civilian counterpart exists, the all-important realm of combat arms—armor, artillery, and infantry. Substandard recruits raise problems in maintaining complicated equipment, and they fail to provide line units with resourceful and intelligent soldiers. Retention is also a problem, especially after two or three terms and in selected categories, since valuable experience with sophisticated technologies is lost and additional resources must be allocated to train new personnel. There are shortcomings in the Selective Service System and reserve components, also. But the main problem for the Department of Defense continues to be the inability of the AVF to attract and maintain the required numbers of qualified enlisted personnel, in particular the college-educated—or even the college-bound—soldier.

Recruiting is a complex and difficult task involving a variety of related and interrelated variables. They must all be considered simultaneously if the recruiting process is to be both efficient in its use of scarce resources and effective in terms of attaining the prescribed goals. Historically, recruiting studies have typically suffered from several or all of the following drawbacks: misplaced emphasis on advertising as the sole causal variable in the recruitment process, overreliance on econometric models based on the price system of free market economics, use of out-of-date or obsolete data, long time lapses between study initiation and the results needed for current and future decisions, and use of static, time-invariant models that fail to capture the everchanging realities of the situation.

Given the magnitude of the recruiting task set by the Gates Commission, a much more comprehensive, systematic, yet flexible approach needs to be developed.

THE NEW DEA SYSTEM

Requirements for an Improved System

Clearly, what is needed is a systems approach to the entire recruitment process that integrates the following features:

(i)   A continually updated and well maintained database to support all recruiting and other modeling activities

(ii) State-of-the-art mathematical and statistical models and techniques for evaluating efficiency, enhancing effectiveness, and a variety of other potential applications

(iii) Capability for simultaneous consideration of all of the relevant variables for a given application

(iv) Timely access to information for supporting decisions

(v)   Adaptive methods and procedures that will accommodate the inevitable changes that occur over time

Within such a system, for example, efficient advertising levels and mixes would be determined as part of the total recruitment effort so that all resources would be considered simultaneously and balanced with each other. Moreover, this systems approach would contain a monitoring element installed in DoD which would make it possible to utilize up-to-date information in order to detect when one or more of the mix of resources is not being utilized with full efficiency.

Existing mathematical models, and variations as may be developed, can be used for improved decision making in current activities such as attempting to meet accession targets and quality and MOS goals. They can also be used in such future or potential activities as testing the impact of changes in various goals or in the age/quality definition of the target market, or reducing attrition in the delayed-entry program pool.

In a dynamic and uncertain world there is a fundamental need to be able to respond quickly and appropriately as changing conditions dictate. Computer hardware and software are needed that will make possible fast and easy access to detailed information, thus providing that capability. Moreover, the availability of such information will in turn suggest other possible projects and uses perhaps not yet envisioned.

Such an information system provides DoD increased control over its own activities and also allows greater flexibility in monitoring the individual services or other units. It further provides DoD with ample support in its dealings with the services and congressional or other agencies, since the output of this new capability will serve as a comprehensive and easily comprehended rationale or justification for decisions on budgets, programs, and other matters.

Concept for a New System

System Overview

We believe the improved system just described is implementable. Its purpose is to monitor, support, and optimize current recruiting goals and activities and to provide for future department plans and for unexpected contingencies. The key to its success is the integration of flexible analytic tools (models) with a continually updated database. The resulting unified computer-based information system would be accessible as appropriate to DoD and to all the services.

The system's major design features would include innovative and productivity-oriented reports, displays, and communication facilities; efficiency and media-allocation analyses as principal parts of the modeling component; provision for the anticipated large size of the models and database; and minimal requirements for training and organizational disruption, leading to early DoD control over the operation of the system. The maximum appropriate use of existing MRCA software and off-the-shelf commercially available (non-MRCA) software will speed completion of the system.

This concept may best be summed up as a pragmatic balance of theory, data, methods and practice (see Learner and Phillips 1993). We believe that immutable universal laws of management are beyond the foreseeable reach of marketing science. A statistical relationship between advertising and sales, for example, will not hold true for all time—no matter how well it fits current data. Computer-based stores of carefully collected data, with flexible retrieval modes, are therefore needed to monitor the changing state of the world. Models of current conditions may have to be quite large to capture the pertinent factors, and must be recalibrated or reformulated continually. Such systems can offer a better way, but never the ultimate answer.

The computer system must be able to support this modeling process—and support, as well, management responses to new and unforeseen events. The latter response must involve data gathering and inspection, specification of alternative actions, and, if necessary, adoption or invention of new analytic methodologies.

Models must employ a mature conception of the systems approach. Far from being a simple-minded reduction of all human motivation to price responses, the systems approach means simultaneously considering as many pertinent factors as is feasible, examining their impact as they vary jointly in an all-things-considered manner—rather than singly in an all-other-things-remaining-the-same manner. All other things never remain the same. Good models let the data speak. They do not impose arbitrary or simplistic structures on the data.

Suppose that over the course of a calendar quarter the efficiency rating of a recruiting office in Des Moines has dropped from 75 percent to 60 percent. The proposed system may include this unusual occurrence as part of DoD's topline report. The DCS or recruiting command for the particular armed service, having access to the database, may combine database access with a phone call to the recruiting office in question. The answer: this quarter, at that office, two recruiters fell ill and a mission statement did not arrive on time. Superior officers may consider these to be good reasons or bad reasons; in any event something has been learned, namely that two recruiters plus a late mission has led to drop of fifteen efficiency points.

Procedural changes can then prevent similar occurrences at other recruiting offices if the matter is judged to be of sufficient importance. This outcome is of immediate administrative value, and it also can be used to further calibrate the model's "what if?" inquiry capabilities.

It is our practice to implement models that make maximum use of the client executive's knowledge and show maximum conformance with his style and patterns of operation and communication. In this way the models aid operating decisions in a constant, ongoing basis. Beyond being useful, they are *used*.

This perspective is different because it is somewhat at odds with the main trends in academic marketing studies today and with many current approaches to marketing consulting. It is important because it recognizes the fact of change; it balances methodology, data, and practice; and it allows rapid, interactive question-and-answer, best supporting the human process of problem solving. These features bring maximum benefit to the client-user.

The understanding-for-use concept means that models and data systems must focus on the marketing variables that are managerially controllable. Although the recruiting process can be addressed with well-known marketing principles, its controllable variables (other than advertising and the "salesforce" of recruiters) do differ from most other consumer marketing situations. Programs such as the delayed-entry option (DEP) and the Army College Fund, and recruiting "events" and recruiter aid expenditures, are examples. Word-of-mouth campaigns seem to play an important role in military recruiting. Pay does not differ across services and so will not differentiate the services to the prospective recruit, although it will be compared to civilian alternatives. These are all controllable. The decision support system (DSS) should, of course, be positioned to gather evidence on the effects of changes in these factors (see Phillips 1986).

The DSS should be positioned for response to uncontrollable factors as well. The most certain uncontrollable factor in the recruiting situation is demographics. Others with a much greater degree of uncertainty are budget limitations, the economy, and the possibility of active military engagements.

The Database

The database, structured after careful planning and consultation with DoD and the services, will contain information by time period on the inputs to and outputs from the recruiting process. These include advertising expenditures by medium, recruiter manning, and the other controllable and uncontrollable variables, and contracts and accessions. Census and registration data will be linked or integrated, as well as special surveys as needed, and other data as required or desired. The reconciliation of recruiting data structures and formats across services, as well as the compatibility of computer hardware and communications protocols, are very important considerations. The application of ingenuity, administrative skill, and modern technology can prevent this task from becoming an obstacle.

There are several commercially available databases on media costs and audience sizes. The DoD system should utilize some of these. Together with the well-known media decision models that MRCA has authored or is familiar with, the DSS can aid allocation decisions and measure and control the cost-per-impression. The quantitative medium for accomplishing this would be the frequency-of-impression distribution, which we have found to be much more useful than the customary measure in terms of gross rating points.

The first step in constructing the recruiting database is to compile a catalog of data available from the services, its formats, and the hardware and software used to process it. Much of this catalog already exists. At this point it will be necessary to specify the inputs and outputs of the recruiting process with precision—although this will be an ongoing, evolving process. The database components must be specified and selected in conformance to DoD needs and U.S. government procurement regulations. Finally, record and file structures must be decided upon, and the first data loaded.

Maintenance, updating, and administration of the database are, of course, central to the smooth functioning of an information/decision support system. Personnel and procedures for collecting, checking, and entering data updates must be arranged with the branches of service. Database administration procedures are now well-known and widespread; qualified personnel must be assigned. Existing data-handling procedures may need review in order to make them more reliable. Facilities must also be in place to control access to and use of selected features and data within the system; to manage the description and organization of the data used and maintained; to aid in detecting, locating, and correcting errors; and to manage data files within the system. The functions of the system should also be integrated in such a way as to make the transfer of data between functions transparent to the user.

Analytical Models

With the recruiting database installed, a variety of analytical models can then be employed to provide the meaningful evaluation and detailed guidance needed by DoD for recruitment efficiency and other purposes.

The centerpiece of such software will be industry's most sophisticated models and supporting procedures for evaluating efficiency and improving managerial effectiveness. (We elaborate on these concepts in the next subsection.) We emphasize that although they are continually improved and enhanced, the basic techniques are not the subject of research and development. Rather, they are already established, with a proven record of performance in a variety of applications.

The models are linked with novel data displays, user interfaces, and reporting procedures to enable comprehensive, detailed, and interactive analysis. Later we present samples of these displays and reports, with discussion. It is anticipated that the particular needs of DoD may require that additional special-purpose output or reporting procedures be developed to supplement those already in place.

In addition to efficiency and effectiveness analysis, software can be installed to support improved decision making in other important areas such as advertising media mix questions and managing the delayed-entry and incentive programs. Indeed, the concept provides considerable scope for ad hoc analysis at the user's discretion.

Efficiency and Effectiveness

Efficiency refers to a measure of performance in conducting a given activity or set of activities, expressed as a ratio of the outputs achieved to the inputs or resources utilized. Effectiveness may be viewed as the extent to which the activities undertaken contribute to the attainment of stated objectives. The combination of efficiency and effectiveness is then called productivity (see Golany et al. 1990b).

Marketing efforts produce a number of desirable outputs such as satisfied customers, sales revenues, market share, and brand awareness. Marketers use various inputs to produce these outputs. Among them are salespersons, advertising, pricing, promotion, packaging, and so on.

In most marketing situations, many units utilize similar inputs to produce similar outputs. These units might be brands, departments, recruiting battalions or the like. The units may be independent or may be in situations of cooperation or competition (MRCA's efficiency analysis treats these three cases separately and differently).

In any system, output is less than input. For example, the output of an automobile engine is less than the energy in the gasoline it consumes. The engine produces heat as well as useful work. In general,

Input = Useful Output + Waste   (1)

Efficiency is the rate at which an output is produced by an input.

Efficiency = Output / Input (times 100%)   (2)

Efficiency cannot exceed 100 percent for any system or business. Comparing many brands or markets allows the most efficient units to be labeled 100 percent efficient. Other units are defined relative to the most efficient units; a brand half as efficient as the most efficient brand is labeled 50 percent efficient. Unlike the case of the car engine, the laws of physics do not limit the efficiencies of marketing processes—so this relative-efficiency formulation is indeed the most appropriate.

Figure 9.1 shows that a marketing process has many inputs and many outputs. How can its efficiency be measured? The simple output/input ratio no longer applies, because we cannot add all the outputs and divide by all the inputs:

$$\frac{\text{Sales Revenue} + \text{Market Share} + \text{Loyal Consumers}}{\text{Ad Budget} + \text{Promotion Budget}} \qquad (3)$$

Inputs and outputs are not expressed in the same units. The ratio above is meaningless.

How can loyal customers be equated with share points and revenue? Often this is attempted by seeking a consensus of informed but subjective judgments. Sometimes it works. Even then, the subjective method is wasteful of management time and may have to be repeated every quarter. Because it is arbitrary, it is contestable.

Data envelopment analysis (DEA) efficiency analysis, which we will apply to the question of recruiting efficiency, solves this problem in an objective, consistent, and meaningful way. A number of operating units are observed and the values of their inputs and outputs recorded. Using proprietary mathematical methods that relate each input and output within each unit, DEA finds that relationship which optimizes the efficiency ratio for each unit. This approach to measuring relative efficiency yields an objective and fair efficiency measure for each unit.

Figure 9.1
The Input-Output Process of Market Management and Response

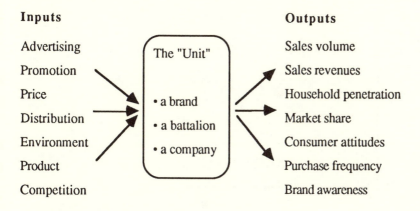

Inputs		Outputs
Advertising	The "Unit"	Sales volume
Promotion		Sales revenues
Price	• a brand	Household penetration
Distribution	• a battalion	Market share
Environment	• a company	Consumer attitudes
Product		Purchase frequency
Competition		Brand awareness

It does so even when multiple inputs and outputs are measured in different units. Additional benefits of DEA are:

- Diagnosis of inefficiencies and prescriptions for improving the efficiency of each unit
- Management guidance for setting goals and evaluating achievement
- Real time, real world examination and evaluation, making best use of managers' time.

Figure 9.2 illustrates these ideas by plotting a single marketing unit according to the value of its advertising (an input) and its sales (an output). The location of the dot shows the amount of sales output and advertising input for unit #1. In Figure 9.3, dots show the observed inputs and outputs of all units being evaluated. One of the boxed units produces more output from the same amount of input. It is the more efficient of the boxed units. One of the circled units produces the same output from less input. It is the more efficient of the circled units.

The entire collection of units may be a product category, a recruiting command, or an industry. Efficiency analysis proceeds to summarize the productivity pattern of the whole and provide a basis for comparing the efficiency of individual units.

The traditional way to do this is to find a regression line such as the one shown in Figure 9.4. The regression line shows the average performance of all units at a given advertising (input) level. But every manager wants to be better than average! Although popular, this method is hardly a useful or satisfactory guide for action, or for setting standards and objectives.

Figure 9.2
Plotting of a Single Marketing Unit

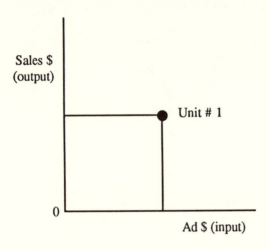

Figure 9.3
Observed Inputs and Outputs

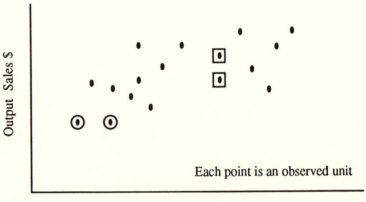

In contrast, DEA draws a cap over the points, highlighting an efficient production frontier. This is the solid line in Figure 9.5. The units on or near this curve are the efficiency leaders. They are the best within a range of inputs and provide examples which are worthy of emulation by their less efficient neighbors.

Figure 9.4
Fitting a Regression Line

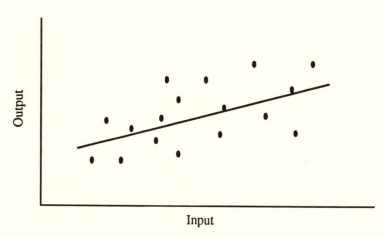

Figure 9.5
Drawing a Piece-wise Linear Frontier

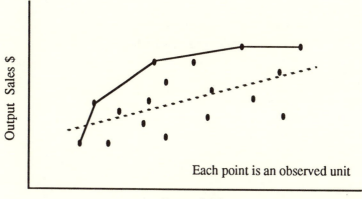

The DEA efficient production frontier (solid line) contrasts with the regression line (broken line). In an example based on actual observed data (Charnes et al. 1994) (Figure 9.6), the existence of the efficient production frontier is readily apparent. In this case at this time, this figure provides the long-sought relationship between advertising and sales when performed efficiently.

In Figure 9.7 one unit is enclosed by a square. It is more efficient than the average because it lies above the broken line which represents the regression relation for this collection of points. Yet the boxed unit is not an efficiency leader, because it lies below the solid line. Two other units (circled) are efficiency leaders, much like unit #1 in their input/output mix. They serve as guides for new policies and plans for the boxed unit.

Figure 9.6
Scatter of Observations, Reproduced from Charnes et al. (1994)

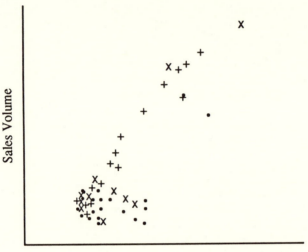

Advertising Expenditure

Figure 9.7
Efficient and Inefficient Observations

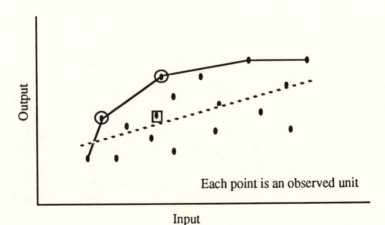

Each point is an observed unit

Input

DEA shows, for each unit, a path to a point on the efficiency frontier that represents improvement over its current position. Notice that the unit boxed in Figure 9.8 could possibly get more output for less input by following the indicated path. Other units, much like it, already occupy efficient positions close by. These are attainable goals.

Figure 9.8
Moving   Toward   Efficiency

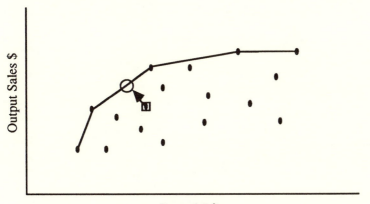

Input Ad $

The efficiency frontier levels off on the right. This is because of diminishing returns from advertising expenditures. The circled unit and the boxed unit in the interior of the diagram are both initially inefficient. They may move to efficiency as shown by the arrows in Figure 9.9. After both achieve efficiency, the circled unit will be on a flatter, higher section of the efficiency frontier than the boxed unit. The circled unit's new position is highly desirable, because management wants to maximize sales. Both units' new positions are equally efficient. But because high sales are a management goal, the circled unit's new position is more effective than any position to the left of it on the efficient frontier. Other management goals may be more complex than high sales. MRCA's effectiveness analysis handles complex objectives accordingly, showing their relationship to efficiency and illuminating the tradeoffs involved.

Figure 9.10 shows the dynamic aspect of the analysis. The boxed recruiting district (let us say it is Des Moines) has, following last quarter's analysis, followed the indication to increase efficiency by reducing advertising expenditure. As a part of the economy move, a new local agency was retained. The agency aired a new creative campaign in Des Moines that was very successful. This quarter's analysis, shown in Figure 9.10, reveals that the Des Moines district improved to the efficiency frontier—and in addition improved and repositioned the frontier, as a result of a new commercial. The adaptive model now shows Des Moines as a leader to be followed by districts with similar characteristics.

Figure   9.9
From   Efficiency   to   Effectiveness

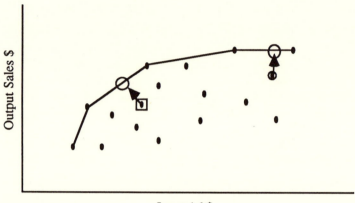

Figure   9.10
Efficiency   Dynamics

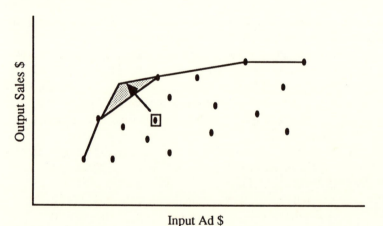

To summarize, DEA efficiency analysis provides resource leverage and real time management control. It helps define attainable goals and targets. Its results can be used to assess current goals, and identify and assess alternative marketing goals. In addition, it aids in resource allocation decisions (Golany et al. 1990a).

Although the concepts are simple, the tasks of computing the efficiency scores, the efficient production frontier, the indications for action, and the effectiveness goals are complex. They have become do-able only as a result of recent advances in theory and in computing technology.

Potential Displays and Reports: Samples and Discussion

Table 9.1 is typical of the summary reports generated by DEA efficiency analysis. In this example, taken from a consumer marketing application (Charnes et al. 1994), the marketing tactics of different brands of insect-control products are being evaluated. This detailed numerical example taken from a familiar marketing arena will help make clear what is possible when analyzing recruiting efficiency.

Table 9.1
Response Unit Summary Table

Product Category: Insect Control Products
Brand: Ortho
Efficiency = 76.6%
Reference Brands (100% Efficient) :   Rid-a-Bug; D-Con

	Actual	Efficient	D-Con	Rid-A-Bug
Inputs				
Price (¢/Oz.)	16.7	20.1	32.8	10.7
Deal Value (¢/Oz.)	3	3	3	2
Advertising Expenditures	$2,790,900	$1,054,920	$2,264,500	$80,100
Brand Share Prior Quarter	3.3%	3.3%	3.8%	2.9%
Outputs				
Volume (Tons)	215	363.5	468.5	279
Brand Share	2.6%	5.4%	5.5%	3.3%
Purchases Per Quarter	1	1.33	1.25	1.4
Deal Volume (Tons)	116(54%)	189.5(52%)	228(49%)	158(57%)
Deal Purchases Per Quarter	.35	.58	.5	.65
Buying Households	259,600	501,600	935,500	151,800
Buying Rate (Lbs./Hh)	1.66	1.45	1.0	3.68

A brand within an area of dominant influence (ADI)—or a brand considered regionally or nationally, depending on the particular application—is called a market response unit. Our efficiency analysis calculates an efficiency rating and generates a summary table for each response unit, and they may be expected to change from one time period to the next. To determine this rating, there must be agreement on a set of measures to be regarded as the inputs and outputs of the marketing process. These appear as the leftmost column of the summary table.

Actual input and output values for the particular response unit being analyzed are given in column two. In the present example, Ortho has an efficiency rating of 76.6 percent. This rating of Ortho's performance is relative to the achievements of those other response units (in this case, Rid-a-Bug and D-Con) which have been determined as appropriate reference units for Ortho. That is, the analysis has determined that, out of all response units, these latter two brands operate in the same general input/output range as Ortho but more efficiently; accordingly, they are given an efficiency rating of 100 percent. The input/output values for the reference brands are given in columns four and five of the summary table, and, of course, the reference units will generally differ in their values for the different inputs and outputs.

Ortho might interpret this summary table information in the following ways. Rid-a-Bug has lower input values across the board than Ortho, with considerably less advertising, yet sells more and increases its market share, partially at the expense of Ortho. Perhaps this is due to the effectiveness of its advertising or its lower price. On the other hand, in spite of selling for almost twice the price of Ortho, spending less on advertising, and selling less on deal, D-Con sells twice Ortho's volume and also increases its brand share. Again, perhaps advertising effectiveness is involved, or perhaps the higher price signals consumers that D-Con is a superior product. At any rate, the suggestion is that Ortho look carefully at the methods employed by its reference brands to see how it might make changes in its own tactics and improve its efficiency.

To aid in this endeavor, the input/output profile of a response unit in the region of Ortho's current position but operating at 100 percent efficiency is constructed from a combination of the efficient input and efficient output levels of the reference brands. This profile appears in the Efficient column of the summary table and can be thought of as describing a position toward which Ortho should move. The extent to which Ortho then adjusts along any of these input/output dimensions is a matter of managerial policy and choice. Targets may be set in different directions and reviewed periodically as circumstances dictate.

This and other informative tables are generated for each analysis unit. In a DoD installation, the analysis units will be recruiting districts and recruiting battalions.

Advancing technology has made possible computer-based systems leading to management insights and actions that would not be possible using models alone (e.g. of the regression variety). MRCA's system combines visual exploration with quantitative analysis, as this example shows.

Figure 9.11 shows Army contracts (on the vertical axis) plotted against stated intentions to enlist, SITE (on the horizontal axis). Each plotted point is a recruiting battalion—those marked "x" are efficient producers of contracts, according to MRCA's efficiency criterion. Inspection of the graph shows no discernible relationship between SITEs and contracts—either at efficient units or at inefficient battalions. Furthermore, it shows that SITE is not an important variable for determining the efficiency of a battalion; see the high density of x's that lie far from the efficiency frontier (the solid line at top left).

Figure 9.11
Army Contracts Plotted Against Stated Intentions to Enlist (SITE)

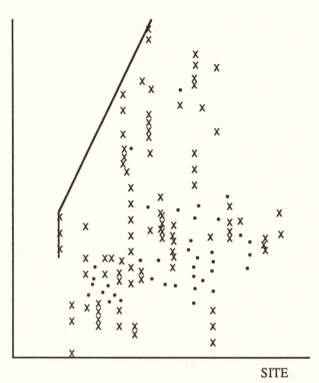

The benefits of using such a charting program for recruiting analysis are:

- Management insights emerge visually rather than from text or numeric tables.
- Some of these insights are impossible to obtain in any other manner.
- Many data relationships can be explored quickly.
- The computer output is the display medium for briefings and presentations.

These benefits are available only because of very recent advances in computer hardware, software, and data structures. This method of analysis and presentation improves management efficiency because

- Chart generation is fast—trains of thought are not lost while analyses are being run.

- The program is self-explanatory—efficiency cannot be impaired by lost manuals or personnel turnover.
- No plotters, color devices, or additional artwork are needed. Charts may be quickly modified and printed directly to transparencies, with titles. Thus the method is appropriate when briefings are frequent or unexpected.

The ability to produce dynamic displays of information has other important ramifications. For example, in an analysis of army contracts versus local unemployment level for each battalion, the displays can be used as an exploratory inspection device prior to any quantitative analysis. It is then possible to identify those battalions where local conditions have resulted in unusually low response rates, and (literally!) to temporarily eliminate such outliers from the picture in order to get a better understanding of the underlying relationship.

Moreover, it is possible to see whether more than one relationship might be present. Response rate may change according to the range of values for the variables, and quantitative analysis alone could easily fail to reveal such market segmentation.

Subsequent to an efficiency analysis, eliminating the less responsive battalions from the graphical display will reveal the behavior of a subset of units and suggest a possible functional relationship. We can expect the hypothesized relationship to become even sharper and more certain when the inefficient battalions are also eliminated from the picture. This is an exciting and important implication of MRCA's research on efficiency—that much of the noise in standard statistical curve fitting is a result of operating inefficiencies in the units evaluated. When these inefficiencies are eliminated, curve fitting is tighter and more reliable. MRCA has found that this theoretical advance is well in accord with the intuition of managers. Efficiency analysis thus allows DoD greater certainty in setting performance standards.

As all this suggests, improved human-factors design of computer inquiry systems has been a principal benefit of the new technology. Another advance in human factors is the use of maps as direct system outputs and inputs. For instance, a map of ADIs serves equally as

- an *input*. The operator points at a number of ADIs on a screen display. The selected ADIs are automatically shaded. The computer displays the efficiency ratings for districts in these ADIs, or any other requested measure.
- an *output*. The operator requests identification of ADIs satisfying a criterion such as efficiency below 75 percent. The computer shades the appropriate ADIs.
- a *crosswalk*. A visual display of the relationships among ADIs, recruiting districts, and recruiting battalion boundaries, and the command medium for performing numerical conversions among these entities.

This use of maps increases ease of interpretation and decreases training requirements.

The types of displays we have suggested allow insights that would have been obscured by standard statistical techniques when such techniques are used alone. Moreover, we stress that with MRCA's new capability such analyses require only minutes to conceive, set up, and execute.

SUMMARY

In this paper we have described a new data-oriented approach which can be used to coordinate and guide recruiting activities.

The managerial implications of the DSS we have described are many and pervasive. Since DoD will have physical and operating control of the system, it can be used to satisfy a variety of ongoing needs.

Improved information flow will lead to better resource allocation, and enhanced continuity of effort, and will provide DoD greater flexibility in monitoring the services.

The effects of all kinds of advertising (media, modes, and messages) may be evaluated separately and jointly, we believe for the first time. On the output side the benefits are similar. Numbers of contracts, numbers of accessions, percent of high school graduates, percent eligible for training or occupational slots, and percent satisfying various aptitude grades may all be controlled. This is in contrast to the usual causal analyses in which one of these measures (usually contracts) must stand as a surrogate for all the others.

In addition to having increased control over its own activities, DoD will be able to establish better working relations with the services and congressional and other agencies. The powerful analytic capability of this system will lead to improved understanding of the complex issues involved in recruiting. Hence, consensus may more easily be reached on crucial issues such as determining equitable performance criteria for recruiters. For example, newer recruiters will tend to have smaller DEP pools than will their more tenured counterparts, unduly biasing their efficiency ratings. Including some measure of "time spent as a recruiter" as an input would eliminate this unfair bias, setting appropriate (realistic and realizable) goals, advertising planning, and recruiting programs, and on budgetary matters. In this way all parties concerned can be assured of a uniform and fair analysis of performance.

REFERENCES

Binkin, M. (1986). *Military Technology and Defense Manpower*. Washington, D.C.: The Brookings Institution.

Charnes, A., Cooper, W. W., Eechambadi, B., Golany, B., Learner, D. B., Phillips, F. Y., and Rousseau, J. H. (1994). "A Data Envelopment Analysis of High-Turnover Consumer Products in Competitive Markets." In A. Charnes, W. W. Cooper, A. Y. Lewin, and L. M. Seiford, eds., *Data Envelopment Analysis: Theory, Methodology, and Application*. Westport, Conn.: Quorum Books.

Golany, B., Learner, D. B., Phillips, F. Y., and Rousseau, J. J. (1990a). "Efficiency and Effectiveness in Marketing Management." In B.-H. Ahn, ed. *Asian-Pacific Operations Research: APORS '88*. Amsterdam: Elsevier Science Publishers.

Golany, B., Learner, D. B., Phillips, F. Y., and Rousseau, J. J. (1990b). "Managing Service Productivity." *Computers, Environment & Urban Systems*, 14 (2).

Hadley, A. T. (1986). *The Straw Giant: Triumph and Failure of America's Armed Forces*. New York: Random House.

Hart, G. (1986). *America Can Win: The Case for Military Reform*. Bethesda, MD: Adler & Adler.

Learner, D. B., and Phillips, F. Y. (1993). "Method and Progress in Management Science." *Socio-Economic Planning Sciences*, 27 (1): 9–24.

Phillips, F. Y. (1986). "Advanced DSS Design in Consumer and Marketing Research." Presented at the *DSS'85: Fifth International Conference on Decision Support Systems*, and published in R. Sprague and H. Watson, eds., *Decision Support Systems: Putting Theory into Practice*. Englewood Cliffs, N. J.: Prentice-Hall.

10

The Competitiveness of Nations

Boaz Golany and Sten Thore

In the current economic debate, it is often argued that a prime concern of the United States should be to improve its competitiveness. What, precisely, is the competitiveness of a nation, and how can it be measured? There exists no consensus among economists on this matter. In contrast to terms like productivity, or terms of trade, which have relatively clear and accepted definitions, the term competitiveness has many dimensions and is invoked in many different economic contexts. But one idea seems to be common to these various interpretations: the idea of a "race" in the international marketplace, where some nations are forging ahead, pushing forward a frontier of maximal performance, while others are falling behind.

The mathematical technique of data envelopment analysis (DEA) was developed precisely to effect a comparison and ranking of the performance of entities or decision making units when (1) their performance is measured by several criteria rather than a single criterion, and (2) it is desired to rank their actual performance (their competitiveness) in relation to the envelope spanned by the most efficient units.

Using data published by the U.S. Council for Competitiveness, we use DEA to measure the competitiveness of seven advanced industrialized nations (the so-called G-7 nations) during a twenty-one-year period (1972–1992), from which we obtain the following findings: (i) Italy and Japan systematically outperform the other countries; the United States belongs to a second tier also comprised of France, Germany, and the United Kingdom; Canada obtains the lowest scores. Furthermore, all countries tend to maintain their relative rankings over time, so that no significant gains or losses in relative competitiveness positions can be identified. (ii) The competitiveness ratings of all seven nations have been systematically falling over time, that is, their performance has been systematically declining over the said twenty-one-year period.

One school of economic thought that recently has gained some prominence states that the very concept of the competitiveness of a nation is meaningless and should be accorded no attention for the formulation of national policy. This unfortunate idea was able to gain some ground since there are many dimensions to the concept of competitiveness. We hope that our work will dispel these notions and return the concept of competitiveness to the academic respectability that it deserves—and that, for the policy maker, competitiveness policy becomes once again a viable enterprise.

Routine DEA calculations such as those reported below are suggested to monitor the development of U.S. competitiveness.

MOTIVATION

Few terms in the economic vocabulary seem to cause such heated discussion and dissent as the international competitiveness of a nation. On the one hand, there are economists who declare the term meaningless at best, and inherently misleading and dangerous to boot. On the other hand, powerful groupings of economic policy makers in the United States and elsewhere have pronounced competitiveness to be the lodestar of forward-looking national policy.

In his widely read book *The Competitive Advantage of Nations*, Porter (1990) cites some of the reasons why some nations are commonly viewed as competitive and others are not. Many economists see national competitiveness as a macroeconomic phenomenon, as evidenced by a nation's GNP or its standard of living. Others argue that competitiveness is a function of cheap and abundant labor, or that it depends on possessing bountiful natural resources. More recently, many have argued that the competitiveness of a nation depends on successful government industrial policy promoting infrastructure or high technology. And yet, Porter argues, these arguments are all misplaced, because, although each of these measures—and others—may say something about a nation's industry, none relates clearly and uniquely to national economic prosperity. Therefore, "we must abandon the whole notion of a 'competitive nation' as a term having much meaning for economic prosperity" (ibid. 6).

In a recent article entitled "Competitiveness: A Dangerous Obsession," Krugman (1994) goes even further, claiming that "the growing obsession in most advanced nations with international competitiveness should be seen, not as a well-founded concern, but as a view held in the face of overwhelming contrary evidence." (p. 30). "Every few months," Krugman complains, "a new best-seller warns the American public of the dire consequences of losing the 'race' for the 21st century" (ibid.). He lists some of these dark prophets: L. D'Andrea Tyson (1992), head of the President's Council of Economic Advisors, L. N. Luttwak (1993), C. V. Prestowitz, Jr. (1988), and L. C. Thurow (1992).

The aim of the present chapter is to try to pour oil on these troubled waters by insisting that some mathematical precision be lent to concepts that have been used indiscriminately on both sides of the debate. In particular, we define competitiveness as a multidimensional rather than a single-dimensional concept. Much of Krugman's objection seem to rest with the fact that no single criterion of competitiveness will do. But in this day and age, the theory of international trade should be ready to take on the mathematics of vector calculus. Drawing on the recent technique of data envelopment analysis (the original contribution is Charnes et al. 1978), we shall

- define the competitiveness of a nation as a vector of attributes, such as its standard of living, its exports, and its productivity
- rank the competitiveness of a nation, as measured by this vector of attributes, in relation to an empirical efficiency frontier made up by the top competitive nations
- calculate numerically a rating of competitiveness of seven leading industrial nations since 1972
- comment on the competitiveness ratings of the individual countries, comparing their performance with that at the efficiency frontier

The particular dimensions of competitiveness to be used in the numerical calculations are those of the Council for Competitiveness, Washington, D.C. Wisely, the council measures the competitiveness of nations as a multidimensional concept, listing data on six key indicators. Our present purpose is to demonstrate how raw data such as these can be employed to calculate a single efficiency ranking of each country, using the technique of DEA.

Is there a race of competitiveness between nations? We shall leave it up to the reader to answer that question, but this much is certain: there is a frontier or envelope spanned by the most competitive nations, and the performance of each nation relative to the envelope can be expressed by a single scalar, the nation's efficiency rating.

Our interest in ranking the economic performance of nations employing data envelopment analysis goes back to Golany and Thore (1996), where we estimated a cross-country production frontier for seventy-four countries, featuring not just conventional economic input and output variables but also more general socioeconomic indicators. Earlier, Land, Lovell, and Thore (1994) had estimated a cross-country macroeconomic production frontier for seventeen western European market economies and seven eastern European state-socialist countries, using a chance-constrained version of DEA.

There are in principle two different ways that frontier analysis may be employed to study the changing competitiveness of nations. The approach to be employed below aims at determining a global competitiveness frontier spanning the entire time period analyzed. By design, then, the frontier remains static and unchanged over time. Any single nation will in a given year either be located at the frontier (efficiency) or below it (subefficiency). An alternative approach is to estimate a global frontier for every single year, and to permit this frontier to shift over time. This is the approach of Färe et al. (1994), who analyzed productivity growth in seventeen OECD countries over the period 1979–1988, enveloping data on GNP, capital, and labor. They attributed the changes in productivity occurring in each country to two components: a change in relative efficiency (that is, whether production is getting closer to or farther from the frontier) and technical change (a movement of the frontier itself). The advantage of a single static frontier is that it permits the analyst to compare the competitiveness of nations over an entire time span rather than just between two consecutive years. As we shall see, it invites analysis of the performance of a single country over a longer time period—not only the current rate of change but also the long-term trends.

The following section describes the data. In the present study, we were limited to data from the seven countries; for each such country the desired information was available for the twenty-one years 1972–1992. Next is the review of the basic mathematics of data envelopment analysis. The resulting rankings are presented and commented on. A new nonparametric rank statistics technique developed by Brockett and Golany (1996) for DEA is then used to demonstrate that the competitiveness of the countries in our study systematically declined over the twenty-one year period, while the relative rank positions of the individual countries tended to be maintained (rather than interchanged). The final section sums up the policy implications of our work.

THE DATA

Founded in 1986, the Council for Competitiveness in Washington, D.C., is a nonprofit, nonpartisan organization of chief executives from U.S. industry, organized labor, and higher education. The council is governed by a twenty-seven-member executive committee and draws on the resources of its national affiliates—forty research organizations, professional societies, and trade associations. The council is privately supported.

Since 1987, the council has published an annual assessment of the economic competitiveness of the group of advanced industrialized nations known as the G-7, which in addition to the United States includes Canada, France, Germany, Italy, Japan, and the United Kingdom. The publication is the *Competitiveness Index* (1993), providing annual statistics on the following six indicators:

the standard of living	investment in plant and equipment
exports	investment in civilian R&D
manufacturing productivity	investment in education

The statistical series extend back to 1972. All monetary terms are calculated in 1985 prices and exchange rates (real 1985 dollars).

The six competitiveness indicators listed are all variables of macroeconomic analysis. More specifically, they are readily identified as the variables of a one-sector growth model built around a macroeconomic production function, say y = f(N,K), displaying how the gross national product of a country (the dependent variable y) is related to the use of labor (N) and capital (K). The first of the six indicators listed, the standard of living, is GDP per capita. In national accounting, GDP arises as domestic consumption, investment in plant and equipment, and exports. Increase of productivity appears as shifts of the function $f(\ )$; often such changes occur as improvements of the quality of labor (investment in education) and as improvements of the quality of capital (investment in civilian R&D).

Equally conspicuous are the variables *not* listed by the Council. Some readers may have thought that competitiveness somehow would be related to the ability of the producers of a country to compete in markets—both in domestic markets (where the competition is with imports) and in export markets—and that this ability somehow had to do with the quality of the product offered and its price. In other words, that competitiveness is related to a market-oriented paradigm for assessing competitiveness rather than a macroeconomic one.

There are no doubt weighty reasons for the council to avoid these microeconomic associations. One of the difficulties is the special connotations of competition and competitive markets employed in mainstream neoclassical economics, defining a competitive market as one where a uniform and standardized product is being exchanged. That definition has rapidly become obsolete in the world of high technology and customized sales efforts. Competition these days is mainly in terms of quality of a product rather than price. Prices of individual goods and services, as well as price indices and indices of relative prices such as the terms-of-trade of a nation, are becoming less and less indicative of the competitiveness of a nation. It is the quality of workmanship, engineering, design, and the array of novel technological features that count. How does one measure the rate of improvement of the quality of goods and services of a nation?

One of the main accomplishments of DEA in the present application might be to bring into focus what might be the most helpful theme for future research: not what *the* competitiveness of a nation is, but rather, which of the many possible dimensions of competitiveness should be included in the analysis. Our own belief is that the definition provided by the Council for Competitiveness is too heavily tilted toward macroeconomic growth concepts, and that it would be beneficial to supplement that definition with attributes reflecting the strength of a country in its particular export markets.

A Preliminary Look at the Data

In absolute terms, the United States still enjoys a leading position in its real standard of living compared to the other G-7 countries. The nearest challengers in 1992 were Germany, Canada, and Japan. But the rate of growth of the living standard has for some time been much lower in the United States than in the other nations, and the gaps seem to be closing. In particular, Japan and Italy have made large gains over the past two decades.

The living standard in the United States increased by only slightly more than 1 percent in 1992, after negative performances in 1990 and 1991. Its best performance during the past two decades was in 1984, with a 5.25 percent gain.

U.S. exports rose briskly in 1992, growing by over 7 percent. Partly due to a depreciation in the dollar, U.S. exports have grown rapidly in real terms since 1987. But the largest exporter of manufactured goods among the G-7 countries is Germany, with the United States. coming in second and Japan third.

The United States made strong manufacturing productivity gains during the 1980s, often attributed to plant closings and restructurings. But the pace of advance slackened in 1989, the most recent year for which data are available. Several of the G-7 nations are catching up, with the French worker reaching 96 percent of U.S. productivity levels.

A strong case can be made for the proposition that the growth rate of living standards is determined by the growth of productivity. National living standards are overwhelmingly determined by domestic factors (see Krugman 1994: 34).

Turning to investments in plant and equipment, Japan is the clear leader, investing about 20 percent of its GDP in 1992. The United States is at the bottom of the league, with an investment rate about half of that of Japan. The Japanese dominance is just as pronounced in investments in civilian research and development. But Japan is lagging badly in investment in education, spending only 3.2 percent of its GDP on public education in 1990. Here, France is the leader (close to 5 percent during the 1980s), with Italy close on its heels.

THE BASIC CONCEPTS OF DATA ENVELOPMENT ANALYSIS REVIEWED

The first step of the analysis is to identify a list of indicators of the performance of a country, to be called "outputs." The Council for Competitiveness provides data on three outputs, which we will represent as y_r, r = 1, 2, 3, as follows

y_1 = percentage change in real standard of living
y_2 = percentage change in real exports, manufactured goods
y_3 = percentage change in real manufacturing productivity

While data on outputs give an idea of the absolute performance of a country, the purpose of the competitiveness rankings is somehow to measure the industry and economic wellbeing of a nation relative to its resources. For this purpose, a second list of indicators is needed, to be called inputs. Among the data listed by the Council for Competitiveness, we identify three inputs with x_i, i = 1, 2, 3 as follows:

x_1 = percent change in real non-residential investment
x_2 = non-defense research and development as a share of GDP
x_3 = public expenditure on education as a share of GDP

The relation between inputs and outputs may be formalized as a generalized production correspondence

$$F(y_1, y_2, y_3, x_1, x_2, x_3) = 0$$

In simple words, the three investment variables represent the prime resources utilized by each of the seven countries to produce the three output variables. Refer also to Figure 10.1, which uses a black-box representation to portray the relationship between inputs and outputs.

Figure 10.1
Inputs and Outputs in Data Envelopment Analysis

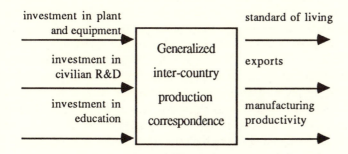

The purpose of the envelopment calculations is to use empirical observations to estimate a correspondence like (1) without having to prescribe a form of F explicitly. We have data for seven countries, and for each country there are observations available for the twenty-one years 1972–1992. An obvious method of analysis is to use DEA by treating each country and each year as a separate DMU (decision-making unit). Treating each of our seven countries as a different DMU in each year gives 21 times 7 = 147 DMUs in all. For each of these $j = 1, 2, \ldots, 147$ DMUs we have individual observations in the following form:

y_{rj} = amount of output r obtained by country j
x_{ij} = amount of input i used by country j
with $r = 1, 2, 3$ and $i = 1, 2, 3$ as defined in (1) and (2) for each DMU$_j$,
    $j = 1, 2, \ldots, 147$.

Conventional studies of production relationships postulate some given functional form (like a Cobb Douglas function) and then estimate the parameters of the function by some standard econometric method like least squares regression. Such methods are usually two-sided in that errors on both sides of the postulated relationship are permitted.

By contrast, data envelopment analysis is a one-sided or frontier estimation method. Deviations from the postulated relationship are permitted in only one direction. Furthermore, data envelopment is nonparametric, in that it postulates no a priori functional form but just traces a piecewise linear frontier relationship, enveloping all points on one side. This is referred to as an envelope. A subset of data points will be located on the envelope itself; these data points span the envelope. Furthermore, a subset of these frontier points are said to be efficient, or more precisely, they are regarded as relatively efficient (compared to all other DMUs) and are assigned an efficiency rating equal to 100 percent. All other points are subefficient, and they are assigned an efficiency rating less than 100 percent.

For the detailed mathematics of data envelopment analysis, the reader is referred to surveys like Seiford and Thrall (1990) or summary characterizations like Cooper (1994). For an undergraduate textbook presentation, see Thompson and Thore (1992) (which also contains suitable software for the numerical solution of envelopment problems). Formally speaking, a linear programming problem is formulated to determine the efficiency rating of each individual observation relative to the envelope. The rating is defined as the greatest possible equiproportional contraction of all inputs, while still obtaining the same outputs, or more. If no such contraction is possible, the observation lies on the frontier; otherwise, the observation falls behind the frontier.

To prepare for the mathematical treatment, the raw data needed some preliminary manipulation. Missing inputs were replaced by an arbitrary large positive number; missing outputs were replaced by an arbitrary small positive number. On balance, we prefer imputing the missing data in this manner rather than dropping the incomplete observations entirely. But such data repair can by itself introduce errors. The repaired observation is likely to obtain a lower efficiency rating than the complete one, had it been available. We shall have reason to return to this point later, when we discuss the results for Canada. (Every single observation for Canada had to be repaired, since no data on expenditures on R&D and on education were available for that country. Yet, as seen in Table 10.1, Canada 1983 obtained an efficiency score of 1.00.)

Next, the figure 100 was added to each percentage change; the resulting variable is then no longer a percentage change but rather an index of the *level* of the variable. That is, we prefer to stick to an interpretation of the causal scheme indicated in Figure 10.1 in terms of a conventional static production correspondence (rather than its time differential). At the same time, this stratagem happens to dispose of an intriguing problem in DEA confronting us, the presence of negative outputs. Percentage changes are often negative, but 100 plus the percentage change is always positive! (For a detailed study of various ways of handling negative outputs in DEA, see Golany and Thore [1994].)

Several variants of DEA have been discussed in the literature; we prefer here to use the so-called CCR model (see Charnes et al. 1978), which is applicable when points on the frontier are required to exhibit constant returns to scale (but points off the frontier may show increasing or decreasing returns to scale).

Table 10.1

Efficiency Ratings of the G-7 Nations, 1972–1992, Top 24 Entries

Observation	Efficiency rating
Canada 1983	1.
Germany 1973-74	1.
Italy 1972-76,1978,1981-82	1.
Japan 1972-1974, 1976	1.
UK 1981	1.
US 1975	1.
Italy 1983	0.999
Italy 1979	0.996
US 1983	0.989
Germany 1972	0.988
Japan 1990	0.988
Japan 1987	0.985
Italy 1980	0.98

Note: See Table 10.3 for details on all years.

EFFICIENCY RATINGS

It turns out that seventeen observations span the efficiency frontier; please refer to the entries in Table 10.1 listed with an efficiency rating equal to 1.000. All other observations, 147 − 17 = 130 observations in all, are inefficient, located under the frontier.

The top ratings were scored by six nations: Canada, Germany, Italy, Japan, the United Kingdom, and the United States. Germany and Japan scored their top results in the early 1970s. Italy was on a prolonged winning streak during the 1970s and early 1980s (note the close-to-the top scores for Italy in 1979–80).

Each country in each year of the twenty-one-year period participates in the competitiveness rankings in Table 10.1 as an individual competitor. Italy did very well during the early part of this time span, but it fell seriously behind in the late 1980s and in the early 1990s. (A complete listing of the efficiency ratings for all G-7 nations, 1972–1992, is provided in Table 10.3.)

Canada, the United Kingdom and the United States hit the efficiency frontier only once, in 1983, 1981, and 1975, respectively. Actually, the performance of the United States in the three years 1974–1976 was quite good (see Table 10.3). The United States chalked up another series of good scores in 1980–1983 and 1986–1991.

The results of the efficiency calculations for the U.S. and for Japan are exhibited graphically in Figure 10.2. In the early 1970s, Japan was located at—

or close to—the efficiency frontier, but the Japanese ratings display a falling trend which accelerates toward the end of this twenty-one-year period. The results for the United States are more erratic, with 100 percent efficiency recorded only once, in 1975. Since 1987, the U.S. experience has been disappointing, the efficiency score falling in every year except for a brief improvement in 1991.

Figure 10.2
Efficiency Ratings for Japan and for the United States, 1972–1992

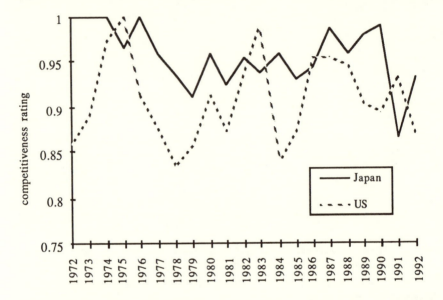

To further illustrate the power of the envelopment analysis, we present in Table 10.2 a detailed study of the U.S. performance in 1989 (this is the last year for the United States with complete data). The efficiency rating of the United States that year was 0.902. In other words, this observation was located off the frontier. In addition, DEA forms the *projection* of the observed point onto the frontier. This projection or hypothetical frontier performance (sometimes called best practice) is formed as a weighted average of other observations on the frontier—the reference points. The hypothetical frontier performance is the performance that the United States would have scored had it been able to move up to the frontier. Table 10.2 lists actual performance, and frontier performance.

There were three reference observations for the United States. in 1989: Germany 1974 with the weight 0.578, Italy 1975 with the weight 0.311, and Japan 1974 with the weight 0.139 (using the CCR model, the weights need not add up to unity). The frontier inputs and outputs recorded in Table 10.2 are obtained as nonnegative combinations of the inputs and outputs of these reference observations, using the weights mentioned. That is, the frontier performance is a linear combination of these reference DMUs, and we need to emphasize that these are a "best set" of weights for United States 1989 as determined by DEA. Hence, the weights may differ from one DMU to another, including the United States treated as a DMU in other years.

Table 10.2
DEA Results for the United States 1989—Efficiency Rating 0.902

	Actual Performance	Frontier Performance
outputs:		
standard of living	101.57	101.57
exports, manufactured goods	112.04	112.04
manufacturing productivity	99.71	101.21
inputs:		
non-residential investment	101.75	91.74
R&D as a share of GDP	1.9	1.71
education as a share of GDP	4.5	3.79

The efficiency ranking 0.902 has the following meaning: Creating the projection on the DEA frontier, it would involve (at least) an equiproportional contraction of all three resource variables by 90.2 percent and yet deliver the same performance in terms of the output variables (or more).

Indeed, inspecting the frontier performance listed in Table 10.2, we see that both nonresidential investment and R&D as a share of GDP at the frontier equals 90.2 percent of actual performance; education as a share of GDP is even smaller. At the same time, the same performance is obtained in terms of the standard of living and of exports of manufactured goods. And the frontier manufacturing productivity is even better.

In the manner now demonstrated, it is possible to interpret all observations. In the case of points located below the efficiency frontier (efficiency ratings less than 1.00), the DEA calculations provide detailed information about the hypothetical improvement in performance that would be available at the frontier.

A NON-PARAMETRIC RANK STATISTICS ANALYSIS

In this section, we discuss two important areas of investigation that were undertaken with the outcomes of the DEA evaluation of the competitiveness data. First, we attempted to detect efficiency trends in the performance of the DMUs (countries) over time. Since such trends may develop slowly, sometimes unevenly across different units, they might not be noticed by the individual DMUs. Intertemporal analysis offering early detection of such global trends may be crucial to the understanding of the data and its implications. Second, we investigated whether the DMUs tended to maintain their relative competitive position over the twenty-one-year period. Both tasks were performed using rank statistics techniques which were recently developed for these purposes by Brockett and Golany (1995).

Analysis of Overall Trend

A complete tabulation of the efficiency ratings for the G-7 nations, 1972–1992, is provided in Table 10.3. When analyzing each country, we are interested to see whether the later years in our study are associated with higher, smaller, or about the same efficiency values as the early years in the study.

Here we no longer focus on the actual efficiency ratings; instead, for the purpose of identifying trends, we prefer to measure the relative ranks of the efficiency ratings for each DMU across time. Thus, we replace the actual efficiency ratings in each column of the efficiency matrix with the corresponding rank statistic obtained by ordering within the column. In this manner, we obtain the rank value matrix displayed in Table 10.4. When efficiency ties are present (this is very likely to occur due to the upper bound of 1.00 on the efficiency scores), we replace the relevant ranks with their midrank.

We shall use the index $k = 1, 2, \ldots, K$ to identify the years, and the index $n = 1, 2, \ldots, N$ to identify the countries (here, $K = 21$, $N = 7$) and use the notation $C = [C_{kn}]$ for the matrix of ranks displayed in Table 10.4. The null hypothesis to be tested is that the vector of 21 ranks for each country n is independent over time; that is, that the observed rankings $C_{1,n}, C_{2,n}, \ldots, C_{21,n}$ are exchangeable, so that any rearrangement of the elements of such a vector is equally likely to occur. That is, under the null hypothesis, the rank vector is uniformly distributed over the set of all 21! possible arrangements of 1, 2, \ldots, 21; that is, each possible arrangement has the same probability ($^1/21!$) of occurring.

The test statistic we compute is:

$$S = \Sigma_k \, \Sigma_n \, kC_{kn} = 19{,}322$$

As shown in Brockett and Golany (1996), the distribution of S is approximately normal with the mean and variance parameters derived as follows:

$$\mu = E(S) = 0.25 NK(K + 1)^2 = 17{,}787$$

$$\sigma^2 = Var(S) = (1/144)K^2(K^2 - 1)(K + 1) = 206{,}137$$

where $N = 7$ and $K = 21$.

Table 10.3
Efficiency Scores of the G-7 Nations, 1972–1992

Year	Canada	France	Germany	Italy	Japan	UK	US
1972	0.905	0.978	0.988	1	1	0.938	0.86
1973	0.839	0.907	1	1	1	0.913	0.893
1974	0.846	0.955	1	1	1	0.881	0.974
1975	0.813	0.975	0.911	1	0.966	0.891	1
1976	0.917	0.879	0.956	1	1	0.919	0.913
1977	0.892	0.915	0.898	0.963	0.959	0.896	0.875
1978	0.918	0.921	0.9	1	0.936	0.896	0.835
1979	0.796	0.901	0.893	0.996	0.911	0.914	0.858
1980	0.773	0.874	0.88	0.98	0.959	0.908	0.913
1981	0.805	0.948	0.919	1	0.925	1	0.874
1982	0.96	0.928	0.921	1	0.952	0.897	0.937
1983	1	0.951	0.925	0.999	0.937	0.973	0.989
1984	0.976	0.925	0.93	0.934	0.958	0.885	0.84
1985	0.852	0.878	0.891	0.959	0.93	0.92	0.874
1986	0.869	0.856	0.903	0.905	0.943	0.948	0.952
1987	0.83	0.854	0.902	0.887	0.985	0.889	0.952
1988	0.796	0.866	0.918	0.868	0.96	0.855	0.944
1989	0.842	0.862	0.918	0.902	0.979	0.912	0.902
1990	0.912	0.868	0.828	0.888	0.988	0.951	0.895
1991	0.873	0.913	0.839	0.887	0.868	0.958	0.932
1992	0.925	0.933	0.894	0.906	0.931	0.897	0.869

The next step is to transform the test statistic S to another test statistic Z which has an approximately standard normal distribution:

$$Z = (S - \mu)/\sigma = 3.38$$

Reference to a normal table then shows that the value of $Z = 3.38$ is statistically significant at a level of $\alpha = 0.001$. The null hypothesis that there is no trend in the observed efficiencies is therefore rejected. The direction of the trend is evident from Figure 10.3, which presents the average rank positions for each year (given in the last column on the right of Table 10.4). This trend means then the efficiency ratings have consistently deteriorated over time. In other words, the relative competitiveness of the G-7 nations, taken as a group, has deteriorated with respect to their own performance in earlier years.

Table   10.4
Ranks C_{kn} of   Efficiency   Scores,   by   Country,   1972–1992

Year	Canada	France	Germany	Italy	Japan	UK	US	Average
1972	8	1	3	4.5	2.5	6	18	6.143
1973	15	12	1.5	4.5	2.5	10	13	8.357
1974	13	3	1.5	4.5	2.5	20	3	6.786
1975	17	2	11	4.5	8	17	1	8.643
1976	6	14	4	4.5	2.5	8	9.5	6.929
1977	9	10	15	12	10.5	15.5	14	12.29
1978	5	9	14	4.5	16	15.5	21	12.14
1979	19.5	13	17	10	20	9	19	15.36
1980	21	16	19	11	10.5	12	9.5	14.14
1981	18	5	8	4.5	19	1	15.5	10.14
1982	3	7	7	4.5	13	13.5	7	7.857
1983	1	4	6	9	15	2	2	5.571
1984	2	8	5	14	12	19	20	11.43
1985	12	15	18	13	18	7	15.5	14.07
1986	11	20	12	16	14	5	4.5	11.79
1987	16	21	13	19.5	6	18	4.5	14
1988	19.5	18	9.5	21	9	21	6	14.86
1989	14	19	9.5	17	7	11	11	12.64
1990	7	17	21	18	5	4	12	12
1991	10	11	20	19.5	21	3	8	13.21
1992	4	6	16	15	17	13.5	17	12.64

Analysis of Trend for 1985–1992

Looking at the graph in Figure 10.3 we see some leveling of the curve during the last eight years (1985–1992). We therefore form a new null hypothesis similar to the one employed earlier but this time pertaining to the last eight years of data only. Calculations carried as before then result in the following statistics:

$S = 1117$, $\mu = 1134$, $\sigma^2 = 1759$, $Z = -0.405$

This value is far below what is usually required to achieve statistical significance, so we cannot reject the null hypothesis. When the last eight years are isolated from the rest of the data, one cannot establish any significant trend in the overall competitiveness positions.

Figure   10.3
Average   Rank   across   Time

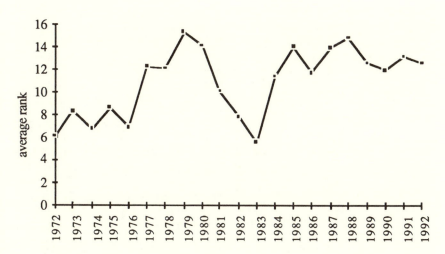

Analysis of the Stability in the Relative
Position of the DMUs

The information gathered in Table 10.1 can be used for another important aspect of the intertemporal analysis. Ranking the set of NK = 147 efficiency ratings and collecting the sum of ranks associated with each DMU provides an indication of the relative position of the DMUs vis-à-vis each other in any given time. Whereas we have previously analyzed whether the performance of the entire group deteriorates, improves, or stays the same over time, here we investigated whether it can be said, with statistical confidence, that the DMUs maintained their relative position in the group over time. A cursory look at Figure 10.4 shows that it is quite difficult to come up with intuitive observations on the stability of the rank positions, since all countries experienced some ups and downs in their relative rankings.

To provide an analytical answer to the stability question, we applied here the Kruskal-Wallis nonparametric ANOVA test (see, again, Brockett and Golany 1996). There are seven "populations" in this case, and the null hypothesis is that all N = 7 populations have the same distribution of ratings. Rank ordering the set of 147 scores in an ascending order and letting R_j denote the sum of the ranks corresponding to DMU$_j$, we obtain:

	Canada	France	Germany	Italy	Japan	UK	US
R_j	908	1345	1454	2133	2229	1467	1342

Figure 10.4
Relative Rank Positions of Countries across Time

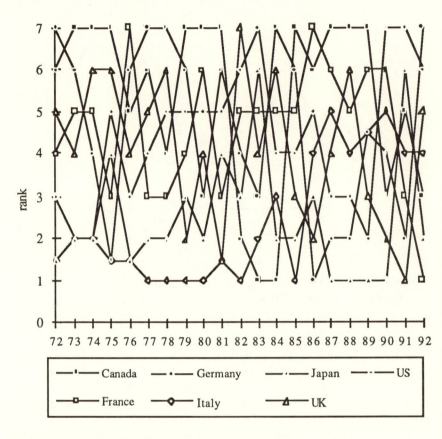

Then, we compute the Kruskal-Wallis test statistic as:

$$H = (12/(NK(NK+1)))\ \{\ R_1^2/K + R_2^2/K + ... + R_7^2/K\} - 3(NK + 1) = 34.52$$

This test statistic is distributed according to a χ^2 distribution with $n - 1$ degrees of freedom. In this case, $H > 12.6 = \chi^2$ ($\alpha = 0.05$ with six degrees of freedom) will allow us to reject the null hypothesis that the distribution of the ranks for the seven countries is the same. In other words, there are significant differences in the relative rank positions that these countries have achieved over the twenty-one-year period.

Pairwise Analysis of Stability in the Efficiency Results

    To further strengthen the outcome of the analysis reported above, we undertook the task of testing a similar null hypothesis related only to pairs of countries. Starting with the United States and Japan, we tested the null hypothesis that the distribution of the relative rankings for these two countries was the same across the study period. The parameters computed for this case were:

$H = 9.036$	Japan	United States
R_j	571	332

Again, the null hypothesis is easily rejected (χ^2 with $\alpha = 0.05$ and one degree of freedom = 3.84), meaning that the efficiency ratings clearly indicate a significantly higher position for Japan than for the United States. The same exercise repeated for the pair Japan-Italy revealed no significant change in the relative position of these two countries. However, testing pairs composed of Japan or Italy with any one of the remaining four countries revealed again the existence of a significant difference in the relative rankings. The conclusion is that the group of seven countries could be segregated into clusters in which Japan and Italy form the top group followed by the rest of the countries.

To sharpen this result even more we ran a four-way analysis of the relative rankings of Germany, France, United Kingdom. and the United States. The parameters computed for this case were:

$H = 0.593$	France	Germany	United Kingdom	United States
R_j	859	931	939	841

The low value of H does not allow us to reject the null hypothesis of identical distributions for these four countries, suggesting that all four can be grouped into a second cluster (after that of Japan and Italy).

Finally, when running a pairwise analysis of Canada with each of the four countries in the second cluster, the results indicate a significant difference in the distributions that are involved. This leads us to conclude that Canada forms a third group containing only itself at the bottom of the list of the G-7 countries.

However, this assignment of Canada to a third group that is lowest is subject to qualification. As already pointed out, missing data for Canada may have introduced a systematic downward bias in the efficiency calculations for that country. Therefore, we cannot be certain whether the low ranking for Canada truly reflects a weak competitive position or whether it is due to bias resulting from our assignment of large input values for data that were missing in the case of Canada.

CONCLUSION

The preceding development is intended to illustrate how recent developments in management science and operations research can be drawn upon not only to provide new and powerful insights into economic questions but also to assist in the formulation of economic policy.

Here we have focused on the issue of international competitiveness, using the dimensions of competitiveness from reports of the Council for Competitiveness. We analyzed the relative competitiveness of the G-7 nations over a recent twenty-one-year period, and established the following results:

(i)   Italy and Japan systematically outperformed the other countries; the United States belongs to a second tier also comprising France, Germany, and the United Kingdom. Canada obtained the lowest scores. Furthermore, although all countries displayed considerable erratic variation in their rankings, they tended to maintain their relative positions over time. No single country gained or lost in its competitiveness relative to the others.

(ii)   The competitiveness ratings of all seven nations have been systematically declining over the last twenty years. But, looking at developments since 1985 alone, no significant trend is evident.

Thus, without alternating the multiple dimensions of competitiveness suggested by the council, it proved possible to use DEA to show that U.S. competitiveness has not changed relative to other members of the G-7 nations. U.S. competitiveness has not deteriorated. On the other hand, it is true that for a long time the United States has ranked behind world leaders in its international competitiveness. To monitor this situation, data envelopment analysis provides a tool that can assist in examining annual developments and in assessing the nation's progress and shortcomings.

Rather than sounding alarms over the deterioration of U.S. competitiveness (at least relative to these countries), a greater concern is our finding that the performance of the entire group of G-7 nations has deteriorated over time. We suspect that if we had extended our rankings to include other countries as well— in particular, the Far Eastern countries now known as the Asian Tigers—the results would have been different. Additional research expanding the list of countries under analysis is therefore called for.

NOTES

    The authors indebted to Mr. Daniel Burton Jr., president of the Council for Competitiveness, Washington, D.C., who made available the data used for the numerical calculations.

REFERENCES:

Brockett, P. L., and Golany, B. (1996). "Using Rank Statistics for Determining Programmatic Efficiency Differences in Data Envelopment Analysis." *Management Science*, 42 (3): 466–472.

Charnes, A., Cooper, W. W., and Rhodes, E. (1978). "Measuring the Efficiency of Decision Making Units." *European Journal of Operational Research*, 2 (6): 429–443.

Cooper, W. W. (1994). "Data Envelopment Analysis." In *Encyclopedia of Operations Research and Management Science*, S. I. Gass and C. M. Harris, eds., New York: Kluwer Academic Publishers, forthcoming.

Council on Competitiveness, *Competitiveness Index*. Annual publication 1987–1993, Washington, D.C.

Färe, R., Grosskopf, S., Norris, M., and Zhang, Z. (1994). "Productivity Growth, Technical Progress, and Efficiency Change in Industrialized Countries." *The American Economic Review*, 84 (1): 66–83.

Golany, B., and Thore, S. (1996). "Restricted Best Practice Selection in DEA: An Overview with a Case Study Evaluating the Socio-Economic Performance of Nations." *The Annals of Operations Research*, special issue on Data Envelopment Analysis edited by L. M. Seiford and A. Y. Lewin, forthcoming.

Golany, B., and Thore, S. (1994). "On the Treatment of Negative Output Values in DEA," Austin: IC^2 Working paper, the University of Texas.

Krugman, P. (1994). "Competitiveness: A Dangerous Obsession." *Foreign Affairs*, 7 (2): 28–44.

Krugman, P. R., and Lawrence, R. Z. (1994). "Trade, Jobs, and Wages." *Scientific American*, 270 (4): 44–49.

Land, K. C., Lovell, C.A.K., and Thore, S. (1994). "Productive Efficiency under Capitalism and State Socialism: An Empirical Inquiry Using Chance-Constrained Data Envelopment Analysis." *Technological Forecasting and Social Change*, 46: 139–152.

Luttwak, E. N. (1993). *The Endangered American Dream: How to Stop the United States from Becoming a Third World Country and How to Win the Geo-economic Struggle for Industrial Supremacy*. New York: Simon and Schuster.

Porter, M. E. (1990). *The Competitive Advantage of Nations*. New York: The Free Press-McMillan Inc.

Prestowitz, C. V., Jr. (1988). *Trading Places: How We Allowed Japan to Take the Lead*. New York: Basic Books.

Seiford, L., and Thrall, R. M. (1990). "Recent Developments in DEA: The Mathematical Programming Approach to Frontier Analysis." *Journal of Econometrics*, (46): 7–38.

Thompson, G. L., and Thore, S. (1992). *Computational Economics: Economic Modeling with Optimization Software*. South San Francisco: The Scientific Press.

Thurow, L. C. (1992). *Head to Head: The Coming Economic Battle among Japan, Europe, and America*. New York: William Morrow.

Tyson, L. D. (1992). *Who's Bashing Whom: Trade Conflict in High-Technology Industries*. Washington, D.C.: Institute for International Economics.

11

Instability, Complexity, and Bounded Rationality in Economic Change

Ilya Prigogine, Ping Chen, and Kehong Wen

Economic order and structural change can be better understood from the perspective of self-organization under nonequilibrium constraints. The constructive role of instability, prevalence of complexity, and source of bounded rationality are demonstrated by examples of traffic flow, complex business cycles, economic crises, the division of labor, and economic development. The socioeconomic order can only be maintained by self-organization processes.

INTRODUCTION

A central theme in equilibrium economics is the mechanism of stability and simplicity in the market economy. It is believed that optimal solutions can be achieved by rational behavior, including utility/profit maximization, risk aversion, and rational expectations. A fundamental problem in economics is how to understand the origin of diversity and complexity of economic systems. Increasing numbers of economists are seeking solutions of many economic puzzles, such as irregular and recurrent business cycles, diverse patterns in economic growth, hysteresis and path-dependence in innovation, and structural changes.

The equilibrium view of neoclassical economics is parallel to the ideas of mechanical stability and thermodynamic equilibrium in classical physics. According to this perspective, economic order is characterized by self-convergence or a tendency toward equilibrium. Economic problems such as unemployment and crises are in the nature of temporary disequilibrium caused by external shocks. Various economic policies are designed on the basis of returning to equilibrium. Therefore, negative feedback is considered as the "good" mechanism of economic stability while positive feedback is regarded as the "bad" source of market instability. Equilibrium economics does help us understand one side of the story in economic movements—the self-correction mechanism and the tendency of convergence—but falls short of another side of the story, the self-organization mechanism and the origin of diversity.

It is true that order and difference will disappear in isolated systems according to the second law of thermodynamics when they approach equilibrium. However, economies, like organisms, are open systems under nonequilibrium conditions. In nonequilibrium situations, fluctuations play an essential role. Bifurcations appear, and we have to go from a deterministic to a probabilistic description.

Sciences dealing with human behavior have always been influenced by the dominating paradigms in physical sciences. Now these paradigms are shifting, and that will likely have a lasting influence on economic sciences (Prigogine and Stengers 1984; Prigogine 1993).

In this chapter, we will discuss several examples from the point of view of instability and complexity. The constructive role of instability sheds new light on the origin of economic complexity. Bounded rationality in human behavior is not only caused by external limitations of imperfect information, but is also constrained by the internal limitations of unstable dynamics.

MICRO IRREGULARITY AND MACRO REGULARITY: THE CASE OF TRAFFIC FLOW

Let us make a preliminary remark related to the description of complex systems. There are conflicting views in economic studies. One popular approach is to use a representative agent in characterizing average behavior, an equivalent of the one-body problem. Another extreme is system dynamics in terms of a large number of variables. The complexity of human interaction may not be fully grounded on individual optimization. Can we understand complex systems in terms of relatively few variables?

An interesting example of the reduction of a complex problem to few variables is traffic flow. In the case of single-lane traffic flow without passing, observational data of vehicle-following behavior can be described by a stimulus-response equation with a time delay, T. We have the following continuous-time difference-differential equation (Herman et al. 1959; Herman 1993):

$$d^2X_n(t + T)/dt^2 = \lambda \ (dX_{n-1}(t)/dt - dX_n(t)/dt) \qquad (1)$$

where X_n denotes the coordinates of the nth vehicle.

In the case of a multiple-lane traffic flow, the Boltzmann-type kinetic equation is introduced to describe the evolution of a speed distribution (Prigogine and Herman 1971).

$$df(x, v, t) \ / \ dt = \partial f \ / \ \partial t + v \ df/dx = - \ (f - f_0)/T + (1 - P) \ c(x, t) \ (\bar{v} - v)f \qquad (2)$$

where v is velocity, $f(x,v,t)$ is the velocity distribution function, f_0 is the desired speed distribution, $c(x, t)$ is vehicle concentration, T is the relaxation time, P is the probability of passing, and $\bar{v} = \int vf\, dv/c$, the average speed. We need to solve a nonlinear continuous-time integral-differential equation. At low concentration, the driver's desired speed can be realized. But as the concentration increases, the driver's speed will deviate from the desired speed more and more.

To explain the observed patterns of moving and stopping cars in town traffic, a two-fluid model has been developed (Herman and Prigogine 1979).

These models can be verified quantitatively with empirical data. Unlike linear econometric models, more sophisticated mathematical models are used in traffic flow. The nature of the local interacting mechanism is an essential part of the aggregate problem.

Comparing traffic models with econometric models, several considerations may arise for economic modeling. First, the popular assumption of i.i.d. (independent identical distribution) in econometrics is not relevant under the changing environment of concentration and speed. Second, the expectation distribution is subject to change due to people's interactions. There is little chance for rational expectations with perfect foresight in the traffic situation. Third, a difference-differential equation can be approximated by large systems of differential equations but cannot be approximated by low-order difference equations.

LONG CORRELATIONS AND COMPLEX CYCLES: STRANGE ATTRACTORS IN ECONOMIC MOVEMENTS

In neoclassical economics, economic order is described by a fixed point or periodic cycles. In most econometric models, economic dynamics is characterized by linear stable systems driven by external noise.

From a wide range of empirical data of economic aggregates, we have found clear evidence of *nonlinear* mechanisms including complex patterns of phase portraits, long serial correlations, stable fundamental frequencies, and low correlation dimensions (Barnett and Chen 1988; Chen 1993a; Wen 1993). It is widely believed that monetary movements are the main sources of external shocks and that stock price changes follow a random walk. We have identified substantial evidence of continuous-time chaos from monetary and stock price movements (Chen 1988; Wen 1993, 1995). The role of time scale and observational reference is critical to recover deterministic dynamics from noisy data with growing trends. Complex business cycles can be better described by strange attractors than by harmonic cycles or random walks.

In physics, the role of chaos came as a surprise, as chaos leads to a probabilistic behavior, while the basic equations are deterministic. This does not apply to human behavior as there are no Newtonian equations on the level of individual behavior. Human decisions depend on the memory of the past and anticipation of the future. Moreover, a condition associated with chaos—

sensitivity to initial conditions—is obviously satisfied in most human activities. As a result, we expect a chaos type of behavior to be prevalent in human sciences, including economics.

BUSINESS CYCLES AND RULE-INDUCED EXPECTATIONS: FREEWAY MODELS AND SOFT-BOUNCING OSCILLATORS

In economics, the harmonic oscillator and exponential growth represent two polar linear models. Nonlinearity is introduced by resource limitations in the logistic model. In economic theory, various nonlinear limitations are considered. Examples are floors and ceilings in investments, monetary control, and exchange rate targets. The problem of the quadratic or piecewise linear model is the rigidity of its boundary specification. Hard boundaries are rarely observed in human behavior. A typical case is the upper and lower speed limits for American freeways: no one exactly follows the rule, but few drivers can ignore the rule without the risk of punishment. The theory of rational expectations in equilibrium economics asserts that people on the average make no mistakes in economic forecasting, so that rational behavior based on perfect information is the very foundation of market stability. The model of rule-induced expectations is based on empirical observations that people's expectations are shaped by mass psychology as well as by institutional arrangement. Changes of collective expectations can be a major source of market instability and economic innovation.

In studies of monetary cycles and stock price movements, we have developed a family of freeway models (Wen 1993; Wen et al. 1994; Wen 1995), based on the following simple model of a soft-bouncing oscillator (Chen 1988):

$$dX(t)/dt = aX(t) - b\, F(\, X(t-T)\,) \tag{3}$$

$$F(X) = X \exp{(-X^2/\sigma^2)} \tag{4}$$

$$G(X) = X[1 - (X/\sigma)^\mu] \tag{5}$$

where X is the deviation from the desired (equilibrium) state (of the price level, say) and T is the time delay. $F(X)$ is the control function with soft boundaries. By contrast, $G(X)$ has a hard boundary; it is the logistic model. This equation is compared to equation (1) for traffic flow. Both equations predict instabilities. In particular, equations (3)–(4) may have chaotic solutions characterized by positive Liapunov exponents.

The observed low-dimensional attractors and long-term correlations can be well described by these models. The soft-bouncing oscillator can be used as a building block in economic modeling, an intermediate model between periodic motion and random walk. For example, the stock market prices can be well simulated by the two-variable freeway model, as shown in Figure 11.1 (Wen 1995).

Figure 11.1
The Chaotic Time Path of the 2D Freeway Model (Wen 1995)

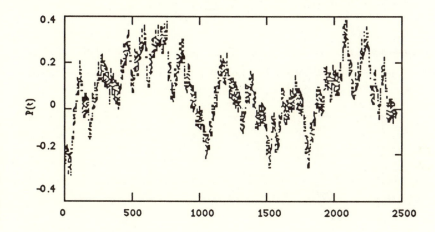

LOCAL INSTABILITY AND GLOBAL STABILITY: THE CASE OF OIL PRICE SHOCK AND STOCK MARKET CRASH

A fundamental difficulty in analyzing economic time series is the nonstationary nature of economic aggregate data. Conventional tools of correlation analysis and spectral analysis are not capable of detecting structural changes, because they are based on the assumption of stationarity. The recent progress in time-frequency analysis provides a powerful tool in analyzing nonstationary time series (Qian and Chen 1994; Chen 1994, 1995).

Under the time-frequency representation, most economic indicators have stable characteristic frequencies like oscillating chemical reactions or living organisms. The evolution pattern of these characteristic frequencies reveals new information about the sources of economic instability and structural changes. Impacts of economic policies and historical events such as war and crises can be quantitatively observed from the changes in the economic pulse.

A notable example is the oil price shock. It is speculated by econometricians that a major trend break in real GDP in the United States was caused by the oil price shock (Perron 1989). This conjecture is directly confirmed by our time-frequency analysis, since the breaking point coincides with the date of the oil price shock in October 1973. (See the top panel in Figure 11.2.).

However, the stock market crash tells another story of endogenous changes (bottom panel of Figure 11.2). From the time-frequency analysis, we can see that the market instability emerged as a small bump in the characteristic frequency from early 1987 to the end of 1987. The stock market crash in October 1987 happened near the end of the twelve-month frequency shift. The frequency recovered two-months after the crash. This suggests that the stock market crash was the result of internal instability instead of external shocks.

Figure 11.2
Frequency Stability and Time Evolution in History (1947–1992)

The Time Series were Detrended by a Hodrick-Prescott Filter (Hodrick And Prescott 1981)

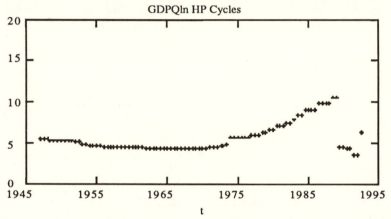

(a). Time evolution of characteristic period P_c of GDPQ (Real Gross Domestic Product Quarterly) HP cycles. N=184.

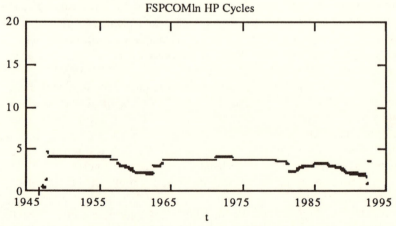

(b). Time evolution of characteristic period P_c of FSPCOM (Standard & Poor Stock Price Monthly) HP cycles. N=552.

The market resilience is quite remarkable since most characteristic frequencies are very stable against external shocks and internal instabilities (Chen 1994, 1995).

INNOVATION, DIFFERENTIATION, AND ORDER THROUGH FLUCTUATION: THE ORIGIN OF DIVISION OF LABOR

Pattern formation, as it occurs in chemical reactions, is the result of bifurcations. Fluctuations play a dominant role. We may also consider innovation and creativity as the result of "hopeful" fluctuations that correspond to deviations from the average behavior. Pattern formation occurs on a macroscale as well (Nicolis and Prigogine 1977, 1989; Prigogine 1980).

Notable examples are the auto industry in Detroit and the computer industry in the Silicon Valley. Increasing returns to scale and path-dependence are economic terms of nonlinearity and irreversibility in economics (David 1985; Arthur et al. 1987; Krugman 1991).

The equilibrium outcome of price competition is formulated as a static optimization model in neoclassical economics. Nonprice competition, such as competition for natural resources or market share, can be explicitly described by the dynamic competition model in theoretical biology (Nicolis and Prigogine 1977; Chen 1987). Geographical patterns of urban development are a vivid example of self-organizing processes (Allen and Sanglier 1981). The origin of division of labor and the trade-off between stability and prosperity can be understood by learning and competition under a changing environment such as technology revolution and resource expansion (Chen 1987, 1991).

BOUNDED RATIONALITY AND DECENTRALIZED EXPERIMENT: THE CASE OF CHINA'S ECONOMIC REFORM

The rise of the Japanese economy has puzzled many economists analyzing the role of its unorthodox economic policy. China's successful economic reform is another anomaly of the conventional economic wisdom (Singh 1991). Why is it that a decentralized, bottom-up, experimentally based approach to reform brought China institutional change at a much lower social cost than reforms elsewhere?

Big-bang proponents like to argue that "you cannot leap over a chasm in two steps." Chinese reformers counsel instead that "you can only walk across a river by feeling first for the stones." This clash of metaphors reflects a difference in the underlying paradigms. The former approach, based on the Newtonian paradigm of classical mechanics, believes that after the shock therapy knocks the economic system out of the orbit provided by central planning, the forces that move individual markets toward an equilibrium position can and will steer the entire economic system into a new, stable regime. This approach reflects the underlying paradigm of modern economics—an equilibrium-oriented approach that says, "Get the prices right, and the rest will follow." But, in reality, social change is a complex, path-dependent, and unpredictable process. Great uncertainty exists during the bifurcation and transition stage. This uncertainty translates to a high risk of expensive errors when coupled with the high cost of any social restructuring. Therefore, decentralized experiments will have less uncertainty in social changes and more opportunity of institutional innovations (Chen 1993b).

Equilibrium economics mainly focuses on the stabilization policy in a market economy. The nonequilibrium perspective gives more weight to growth and development as a self-organizational process. The discovery of limited predictability in the time path and bounded rationality caused by unstable dynamics is further improving our understanding of the real world (Prigogine 1993).

In a recent report to the European Communities, C. K. Biebracher, G. Nicolis, and P. Schuster wrote (private communication): "The maintenance of the organization in nature is not—and cannot be—achieved by central management; order can only be maintained by self-organization. Self-organizing systems allow to adapt to the prevailing environment, i.e. they react to changes in the environment . . . which makes the systems robust against perturbations." We believe that this conclusion is of importance in economic sciences.

SUMMARY

The design of economic policy is based on our understanding of economic dynamics. From the perspective of equilibrium economics, the ideal state of an economy is perceived as the steady state with Gaussian deviations. There is no place for innovation, creativity, or structural change, since they are anomalies under the equilibrium perspective. The shortcomings of equilibrium economics are visible in the difficulties in the understanding of the causes of business cycles, the origins of division of labor, and so on.

The new perspectives of self-organizing economics under nonequilibrium constraints emphasize the constructive role of instability and complexity in economic dynamics and economic evolution that leads to new methods of analytic analysis and theoretical modeling that provide better tools of economic analysis and forecasting.

NOTES

It is a great privilege to dedicate this chapter to an eminent colleague and to a friend. It gives us the opportunity to express our admiration for his pioneering work combining foresight and practical applications (Kozmetsky 1985).

REFERENCES

Allen, P. M., and Sanglier, M. (1981). "Urban Evolution, Self-Organization, and Decision Market." *Environment and Planning A*, 167-183.

Arthur, W. B., Ermoliev, Y. M., and Kaniovski, Y. M. (1987). "Path-Dependent Processes and the Emergence of Macro-Structure." *European Journal of Operational Research*, 30, 294–303.

Barnett, W. A. and Chen, P. (1988). "The Aggregation-Theoretic Monetary Aggregates are Chaotic and Have Strange Attractors: An Econometric Application of Mathematical Chaos." In W. A. Barnett, E. Berndt, and H. White eds., *Dynamic Economic Modeling*, Cambridge: Cambridge University Press.

Chen, P. (1987). "Origin of Division of Labor and a Stochastic Mechanism of Differentiability." *European Journal of Operation Research*, 30: 246–250.

Chen, P. (1988). "Empirical and Theoretical Evidence of Monetary Chaos." *System Dynamics Review*, 4: 81–108.

Chen, P. (1991). "Needham's Question and China's Evolution: Cases of Nonequilibrium Social Transition." in G. P. Scott ed., *Time, Rhythms, and Chaos in the New Dialogue with Nature*. Ames: Iowa State University Press.

Chen, P. (1993a). "Searching for Economic Chaos: A Challenge to Econometric Practice and Nonlinear Tests." In R. Day and P. Chen eds., *Nonlinear Dynamics and Evolutionary Economics*. Oxford: Oxford University Press.

Chen, P. (1993b). "China's Challenge to Economic Orthodoxy: Asian Reform as an Evolutionary, Self-Organizing Process." *China Economic Review.*, 4: 137–142.

Chen, P. (1994). "Deterministic Cycles in Evolving Economy: Time-Frequency Analysis of Business Cycles." *Proceedings of International Conference on Dynamical Systems and Chaos*. Tokyo.

Chen, P. (1995). "Trends, Shocks, Persistent Cycles in Evolving Economy: Business Cycle Measurement in Time-Frequency Representation." In W. A. Barnett, M. Salmon, and A. Kirman eds., *Nonlinear Dynamics in Economics*. Cambridge: Cambridge University Press.

David, P. A. (1985). "Clio and the Economics of QWERTY." *American Economic Review*, 75: 332–337.

Herman, R. (1993). "From Micro Behavior to Macro Dynamics: The Case of Vehicular Traffic." In R. Day and P. Chen eds., *Nonlinear Dynamics and Evolutionary Economics*, Oxford: Oxford University Press.

Herman, R., Montroll, E. W., Potts, R. B., and Rothery, R. W. (1959). "Traffic Dynamics: Analysis of Stability in Car Following." *Operational Research*, 7: 86.

Herman, R., and Prigogine, I. (1979). "A Two-Fluid Approach to Town Traffic." *Science*, 204: 148.

Hodrick, R. J., and Prescott, E. C. (1981). Post-War U.S. Business Cycles: An Empirical Investigation, Discussion Paper No. 451, Carnegie Mellon University.

Kozmetsky, G. (1985). *Transformational Management*. Cambridge, Mass.: Ballinger.

Krugman, P. (1991). *Geography and Trade*. Cambridge: MIT Press.

Nicolis G., and Prigogine, I. (1977). *Self-Organization in Nonequilibrium Systems, From Dissipative Structure to Order through Fluctuations*. New York: Wiley.

Nicolis, G., and Prigogine, I. (1989). *Exploring Complexity*. New York: Freeman.

Perron, P. (1989). "The Great Crash, the Oil Price Shock and the Unit Root Hypothesis." *Econometrica*, 57: 1361–1401.

Prigogine, I. (1980). *From Being to Becoming: Time and Complexity in the Physical Sciences*. San Francisco: Freeman.

Prigogine, I. (1993). "Bounded Rationality: From Dynamic Systems to Socio-economic Models." In R. Day and P. Chen, eds., *Nonlinear Dynamics and Evolutionary Economics*. Oxford: Oxford University Press.

Prigogine, I., and Herman, R. (1971). *Kinetic Theory of Vehicular Traffic*. New York: Elsevier.

Prigogine, I., and Stengers, I. (1984). *Order Out of Chaos: Man's New Dialogue with Nature*. New York: Bantam Books.

Qian, S., and Chen, D. (1994). "Time-Frequency Distribution Series." *Proceedings of IEEE, ICASSP* (Australia) 3: 29–32.

Singh, I. (1991). "Is There Schizophrenia about Socialist Reform Theory? Some Thoughts about the Two-Track Approach." *Transition* (The World Bank), 2(7): 1–4.

Wen, K. H. (1993). "Complex Dynamics in Nonequilibrium Economics and Chemistry." Ph. D. dissertation, University of Texas at Austin (May).

Wen, K. H. (1995). "Continuous-Time Chaos in Stock Market Dynamics." In W. A. Barnett, M. Salmon, and A. Kirman eds., *Nonlinear Dynamics in Economics*. Cambridge: Cambridge University Press.

Wen, K. H., Chen, P., and Turner, J. S. (1994). "Bifurcation and Chaos in a Lienard Equation with Two Delays." In G. S. Ladde and M. Sambandham eds., *The Proceedings of Dynamic Systems and Applications–1*. Atlanta: Dynamic Publishers.

Diversification Strategy, Strategy Change, Performance and State-Defined Risk: Some Longitudinal Evidence

Timothy W. Ruefli, Donde P. Ashmos, and James M. Collins

The general consensus in the strategic management literature is that change of strategy is motivated by poor performance, and the implication is that commensurate benefits do not follow. While the strategic management literature contains a number of empirical studies that have considered the relation between corporate strategy and economic performance, these studies have, for the most part, treated only those firms that have maintained the same strategy over a period of time. This limitation has restricted the range of findings and has distanced formulations for research from situations faced by corporate strategists. Further, with a few exceptions, studies of diversi. ation strategy and performance have ignored the notion of risk, and with no exceptions have ignored the relation between strategy change and risk. The study reported here examined the economic performance and risk levels of groups of firms that changed diversification strategies during the period 1949–1969 and compared them to firms that maintained the same strategy over time. Utilizing data on a sample of 239 *Fortune* 500 U.S. manufacturing firms classified by diversification strategy at three points in two decades, performance based on annual data in terms of return on assets and return on sales for the period 1954–1985 was examined. Employing a new measure of state-defined risk, the risk levels of various strategies and strategy changes were generated. Specifically, this study found that while strategy change in general was associated with relatively poorer performance and somewhat higher risk, particular changes in strategy were associated with subsequent economic performance that was superior to maintaining any one of a number of diversification strategies over time. Findings support the hypothesis that troubled firms were the most likely to change strategy, but also indicate that at least one out of four high-performing firms changed strategy in a given decade.

The material in this chapter is not directed primarily at policymakers at either the national or regional level of government. The primary audiences are the top management teams of large corporations, the researchers who study such corporations, and the analysts who evaluate such corporations. Even to this audience, given that the data here are two decades old, the relevance of any directly derived policy recommendations may be, on the surface, of dubious value. However, there are policy implications for both practicing managers and researchers at all levels of policy-making systems.

The research here is built on a foundation of over three decades of investigation by numerous researchers into one of the greatest organizational transformations in history—the movement of the largest corporations in the economy from single-business to multiple business enterprises. Yet in spite of its basis in change, research in this area and derived policy recommendations to practicing managers have been dominated by approaches that are static in concept, design, and methodology. In an environment characterized by giant firms changing strategy and structure, researchers have traditionally chosen samples of firms that maintained their strategies and structures over time; and writers for the popular business press have generally followed suit (e.g., Peters and Waterman 1982). Results, then, have been framed in terms of comparisons of static situations—without discussion of how to shift from one to the other, or even if such movement was possible. This ignoring of change has resulted in ignorance of change and an implied message that change is nonexistent, foolish, and perhaps downright bad.

Even when change has been made an explicit subject of investigation, the presumption, carried over from studies ignoring change, has been that change results in inferior performance. When the first author presented results of this and allied studies of structural change and noted that there were some changes that resulted in superior performance, he was met not only with outright skepticism but also with emphatic denial of that possibility. "Change," he was told numerous times, "simply could not have those results—for change is too costly." It leads one to wonder how individuals holding those perceptions reconcile them with the positive dynamics of private and public sector organizations over time—and the answer lies in a static paradigm that has become entrenched. Historical as the data employed in this study may be, they and the analysis they support are relevant today because they are contemporaneous with the foundation of the received wisdom that "sticking to one's knitting" is good—and by implication, change is bad. The analysis in this chapter qualifies and calls into question the general wisdom of this assertion and militates in favor of a broad program of research on change in large organizations.

Research on change is by its very nature research over time—longitudinal research. And while it is true that such research requires conceptualizations, methodologies, and data that are more complicated, more demanding, and more problematic to assemble than those employed in static formulations, such difficulties can no longer be justified as supporting an adequate rationale for ignoring the investigation of change. As we enter a period in national and international competition in which change becomes not just something to be dealt with as it arises but, rather, something to be sought as a tool of positive competitive advancement, it is ignorance of change that will become at best foolish and at least undesirable—if not downright hazardous.

INTRODUCTION

Diversification through acquisitions or internal growth continues to be a major strategic activity, having steadily increased in recent years to levels near or above those prevalent in the late 1960s. A significant number of empirical studies reported in the strategic management literature have evaluated types of diversification strategy in terms of their associated economic performance (for a recent review, see Ramanujam and Varadarajan 1989). For the most part, these studies have examined strategy and performance in a single period of time (limited to five or ten years or so), by a single aggregated measure of performance, with contemporaneous measures of strategy classification and performance, and with a uniform length of time for holding a strategy. As a result of these self-imposed constraints, our knowledge of the relationships between diversification strategies, especially change of diversification strategy, and performance has been circumscribed. In his review article on changes in strategy, Ginsberg (1988) noted that, "The empirical literature does not appear to support any generalizable conclusions regarding the effects of changes in strategy on performance." An extensive review of the strategic management research literature revealed few instances of empirical studies of change of strategy and economic performance in general (for exceptions, see Rumelt 1974; Schendel and Patton 1976; Miller and Friesen 1980; Oster 1982; Fombrun and Ginsberg 1986; Smith and Grimm 1987; Boeker 1989; Zajac and Shortell 1989; Mascarenhas and Aaker 1989; and Zajac and Kraatz 1993) and fewer instances of empirical studies evaluating change of diversification strategy in terms of economic performance (Rumelt 1974 discussed this just briefly; Hill and Hansen 1991, more directly).

In contrast to the more common approach of examining only firms with the same strategy over time, this research attempts to increase our understanding of diversification strategy by also examining the economic performance of firms that have changed their strategy. We will first review the literature on strategy change as a preliminary to the development of a set of hypotheses. These latter will be examined via an empirical study of the performance over 32 years of a sample of 239 manufacturing firms classified by their diversification strategies. From this we will develop preliminary evidence on the nature of change of diversification strategy. In passing, we will demonstrate the worth of revisiting a well-constructed database by accomplishing the foregoing via data that have been widely available for some time.

LITERATURE UPDATE

Strategy/Performance

While the primary concern of this research is examining the impact of strategy change on economic performance, the context for this research is the more traditional research on the relationship between maintained strategies and performance. In this regard, Rumelt's seminal work (1974) on diversification strategy is significant not only for the comprehensiveness and importance of its findings, but also for the numerous replications and partial replications which it spawned. These include Pitts (1976, 1977), Salter and Weinhold (1979), Montgomery (1979, 1982), Beard and Dess (1981), Christensen and Montgomery (1981), Bettis (1981), Bettis and Hall (1982), Rumelt (1982), Chandrasekaran (1982), Bettis and Mahajan (1985), Wernerfelt and Montgomery (1986), Palepu (1985), Ruefli and Ashmos (1990), Chang and Thomas (1987), and Grant, Jammine, and Thomas (1988). Since Rumelt's work is extensively reviewed in the abovementioned works, it will not be further reviewed here. Also, since much of the wider research on maintained strategies and performance through 1989 is summarized in Ramanujam and Varadarajan (1989), a re-review will not be essayed here. Suffice it to say that while Rumelt's 1974 results have been qualified in terms of industry effect (see, e.g., Christensen and Montgomery 1981; Bettis and Hall 1982; Rumelt 1982), they have been generally supported by most successor studies. Therefore, in the rest of this chapter, reference to Rumelt's results should be understood to pertain to the aggregate of the set of works mentioned above.

Strategy Change Literature

Much of the strategic management literature dealing with strategy change focuses on the process of change. Of those works, one of the most frequently cited is that by Quinn (1978), who describes strategy as an evolving process in which strategic changes are made incrementally, proceeding logically from broad concepts to specific commitments. Along with Quinn (1978, 1980a, 1980b), others offer prescriptions for how managers can effectively bring about strategic change. Aaker and Mascarenhas (1984) argue for flexibility in adapting to environmental changes; Carnall (1986) offers an integrated approach to change, and Edstrom (1986) observed the importance of leadership in bringing about strategic change. Kay (1982: 115–119) argued that technological change was a driving force behind change of strategy.

A related area of the literature deals with the process of strategic change and the variables that affect that process. In this stream of research, variables such as issue diagnosis and strategic planning (Dutton and Duncan 1987), politics (Gray and Ariss 1985), the demography of the top management team (Wiersema and Bantel 1992) and organizational culture (Lorsch 1986; Conner, Piman, and Clements 1987) have been related to the process of bringing about strategic change. Another major area of research on strategic change has focused on the causes of strategic change, in particular the influence of environmental changes, performances outcomes, and changing internal conditions on strategic change. A review of this work is presented in Ginsberg (1988) and will not be repeated here except to note that the findings from much of the work are equivocal.

A third major area of concern in the strategy change literature has been the examination of the content of strategic change, and it is this literature that is most relevant in the present study. One difficulty that arises in this regard is the problem of defining strategic change. Snow and Hambrick (1980) argue the importance of distinguishing between a strategic adjustment and a change, yet empirically this presents measurement difficulties. The determination of when a strategic change has occurred is not obvious and can prove difficult to measure. Ginsberg (1988) defines strategic change as either a change in position or a change in perspective, each of which may differ in magnitude or in pattern. In this research we will define a change of diversification strategy to be a change in a firm's specialization, related and/or vertical ratio (Rumelt 1974: Ch. 1) such that a change in diversification category (see Appendix) occurs (Rumelt 1974: 29–32).

As was mentioned earlier, the literature on strategic change includes little in the way of empirical work that explores the changes in financial performance that accompany changing from one diversification strategy to another, for example, Ginsberg's Link V (1988: 563). Rumelt's study did discuss changes in diversification strategy in terms of the types and frequencies of the transitions (Rumelt 1974: Ch. 2). These strategy changes were not, however, linked to performance, with the exception of a brief analysis of the performance of firms that maintained a dominant constrained strategy through two decades (2.5% of his sample) versus those that changed to another strategy in the second decade (ibid.: 129). He showed that the former group had a significantly higher return on equity in the ensuing decade than did the latter. Smith and Grimm (1987) studied Canadian railroad companies before and after deregulation and found that companies that changed their strategy (strategy was conceptualized as service quality, marketing focus, pricing, innovativeness, or product dependability) performed better than those that did not change their strategy. Tushman and Anderson (1986) related technological changes to growth, while Hambrick and Schecter (1983) related turn-around strategies to performance. Zajac and Shortell (1989) investigated strategy change and associated economic performance in the light of changes in the environment. Fombrun and Ginsberg (1986) also considered environmental impacts on strategies defined in terms of resource deployments. They found that high and low performers were less likely to change their strategies in the ensuing period. Hill and Hansen (1991), in a study of the pharmaceutical industry, found that diversification was associated with lower performance.

CONCEPTUAL MODEL

Figure 12.1 depicts the conceptual model employed in structuring this research. The model has four key factors, and the research will examine the three binary relationships indicated by the arrows.

Figure 12.1
Relationship of Performance and Diversification Strategy and Strategy Change

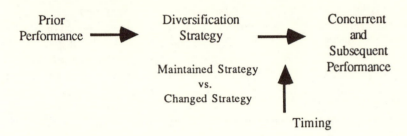

The first area of the model to be investigated is the relationship between maintained strategy and concurrent and subsequent performance; strategy here will be taken to mean diversification strategy as realized by a corporation. With the maintained strategy-performance relationship as a benchmark, the relationship between strategy change and concurrent and subsequent performance will be maintained. The focus will then shift to the antecedent relationship between prior economic performance and strategy change, and will conclude with an examination of the role of timing of strategy change in the strategy change–performance relationship. Each of these areas will first be examined in terms of the relevant literature.

Frequency of Change

The first issue to be addressed in this chapter concerns the relative importance of change in the scheme of corporate strategic behavior. It is generally accepted that the middle decades of this century were a period of diversification for large domestic corporations, as single business firms diversified into multiple businesses and as already-diversified firms expanded their range of business even further. Chandler (1962), Wrigley (1970), and Rumelt (1974) all acknowledge these changes; but the latter two, in their empirical work, concentrate on firms whose strategies were maintained over time. Thus it can be argued that while strategy change motivated their studies, it was not given equivalent treatment in those studies. Miller and Friesen (1980), for example, examined the frequency of strategy changes and found that strategic changes of great magnitude occurred infrequently. In studies of strategic groups, Oster

(1982) concluded that the average rate of strategy change in eighteen industries (= average mobility rate) was only 0.07 in seven years, while Mascarenhas and Aaker (1989), in studying mobility barriers between strategic groups, observed even lower mobility rates (less than 0.02 in nine years), suggesting that strategy change is quite rare. Individual researchers appear to vary in their opinion from time to time. Porter (1980) in his first book implied, via the vehicle of generic strategies, that change was not necessary. However, in his second book (Porter 1985), he acknowledged that changes in an industry's structure, which may be caused by technological evolution, may create a need for changes in a firm's generic strategy. The original formulation of evolutionary economics (Nelson and Winter 1982) postulated that firms could not easily change their strategies. More recently, however, Nelson (1991) has moderated this position by noting that, "However, within this theory [i.e., evolutionary theory] of the firm structure is far more difficult to change effectively than is strategy" (p. 67), and "Structure and core capabilities are far more difficult to change than management and articulated strategies" (p. 70), implying that strategy change is at least less difficult than other major changes. The majority of the literature suggests the hypothesis:

H1: Change of diversification strategy is an infrequent event for mature firms.

Obviously, if the empirical evidence strongly supported this hypothesis, the relative importance of the rest of this study might be called into question. Without prejudging here results to be presented subsequently, however, the general issue to be treated in this research is whether there is any economic value associated with changing strategies. Given that firms start their existence with a single product diversification strategy, there is obviously an ontological pattern of strategy change as a firm matures. There is also, clearly, historical evidence that many firms have changed their diversification strategies in a significant manner during the middle years of this century (Chandler 1962; Wrigley 1970; Channon 1971; Rumelt 1974; Kay 1982). Forces militating in favor of diversification have, in the literature, occasionally assumed the proportions of historical inevitability (Leavitt 1975). Presumably, at least some of these changes would not have taken place if there was not some concomitant economic benefit. Smith and Grimm's (1987) study of Canadian railroad companies found that companies that changed their strategy performed better than those that did not change their strategy. Organization adaptation views of the firm (Burns and Stalker 1961; Thompson 1967; Galbraith 1977; Zajac and Shortell 1989) argue that the firm should adapt its strategy as the environment changes, and Zajac and Kraatz (1993) found that strategic change was performance-enhancing. Kelly and Amburgey (1991), in a study of airlines, did not find that changes in strategy were associated with failure of the firm.

Be that as it may, the preponderance of opinion in the more recent literature seems to be that for mature firms, change of strategy is to be avoided because it has negative consequences. Hill and Hansen (1991), for example, found that pharmaceutical firms that diversified during the 1977–1986 period suffered in terms of their financial performance. On a pragmatic level, managers have been urged to take a conservative approach with respect to change (see, e.g., Peters and Waterman 1982), while some mainstream theorists see strategy change as highly dysfunctional. For example, adherents of population ecology views of strategic management (e.g., Hannan and Freeman 1977), with their emphasis on birth and death events, have argued that a fundamental change, such as a change of strategy, "robs an organization's history of survival value" (Hannan and Freeman 1984: 60). Evolutionary economics (Nelson and Winter 1982) posited that change of strategy would be infrequent and costly. This leads us to the next hypothesis:

H2: Mature firms that change strategy have lower associated concurrent and subsequent performance in comparison with firms that maintain strategies.

Another, equally important, issue in addition to that of the consequences of change addresses the performance antecedents of change of strategy. Oster (1982), citing Cyert and March (1963), Simon (1957), and Nelson and Winter (1982), maintains that, "In particular, one might expect that, as long as profit performance is satisfactory, firms will continue to allocate internal resources using whatever rules of thumb they have used in the past" (p. 376). She goes on to state (p. 377) that, "The central feature of firm strategies is that they persist over time." Nelson (1991) agrees, "Firms that systematically lose money will have to change their strategy and structure and develop new core capabilities, or operate the ones they have more effectively, or drop out of the contest" (p. 69). These statements suggest support for H2, that firms that hold strategies for longer periods of time are those with higher performance, and suggest that only firms with poor performance will change strategies.

The foregoing is in agreement with Bowman (1982), who, following prospect theory (Kahneman and Tversky 1979), proposed that troubled firms are risk-takers, while average and above-average performance would evidence risk-averse behavior. Hambrick and Schechter (1983) and Tushman and Romanelli (1985) support the idea that strategic change is initiated by poor performance. However, Wiersema and Bantel (1992) found that there was no relation between prior performance and strategic change. In their study of strategy change, Fombrun and Ginsberg (1986) proposed a variant on the foregoing, and held that firms that maintained a strategy over time were more likely to be those with performance that was either higher or lower than the performance of those that changed strategies. The preponderance of arguments in the literature suggest the third hypothesis:

H3: Firms with poor antecedent performance are more likely to change diversification strategies than firms with significantly better antecedent performance.

However the issue of the value and performance antecedents of change in diversification strategy is settled, a subsidiary question involves the timing of change of strategy. Ginsberg (1988) does not raise the issue of timing with respect to change of strategy; and while there has been much research on the effects of order of market entry (Lieberman and Montgomery 1988; Lambkin 1988), no comparable research exists with respect to timing of changes in diversification strategy. The studies of diversification trends in large mining and manufacturing firms that dominated the domestic economy in the middle of this century carry the implicit assumption that this change was positive at least for those firms that, folowing a change, held certain diversification strategies. Rumelt (1974), in treating as equivalent the two decades he studied, implied the invariance of relative performance over time. Absence of expressed concern in the literature is interpreted here to mean that timing of strategy change is not perceived to be a significant factor in evaluating the strategy change–performance association. This gives rise to the following hypothesis:

H4: The diversity-performance relationship is invariant to the timing of a strategic change.

Wernerfeldt and Karnani (1987) observed that, "Since strategy is concerned with the future, the strategic context of the firm is always uncertain, . . ." (p. 187). While uncertainty is a prominent aspect of the practice of strategic management, only a few of the studies of diversification strategy and performance have included risk as one of the factors to be examined (Bettis and Hall 1982; Bettis and Mahajan 1985; Montgomery and Singh 1984). Further, since these studies were crosssectional in nature, they yield little direction in developing hypotheses about the nature of the relationship between strategy change and risk. Hill and Hansen (1991), in one of the few studies to employ pooled time-series methods, found a negative relation between diversification and risk. Their logic for hypothesizing such a relationship was based on financial economic theory that diversification spreads risk over the portfolio of businesses. Since, during the period of time covered by this study, diversification was on the increase, our last hypothesis is:

H5: Firms changing diversification strategies will have lower associated subsequent risk than those maintaining their strategies.

The next sections will outline an empirical study designed to investigate the five hypotheses just presented.

DATA AND METHODOLOGY

Data and Measures

Rumelt's sample of 246 *Fortune* 500 firms (Rumelt 1974: Appendix C) classified by diversification strategy in the years 1949, 1959, and 1969 served as the basis for the sample used in this study. (See the appendix for strategy definitions.) Data in the period 1954 to 1985 could not be found for seven of those firms, giving this study a base of 239 firms. However, the omission of the seven firms should not affect the comparability of this study to Rumelt's, since these firms dropped out of the *Fortune* 500 before 1959 and, hence, would not have figured in his analysis. Since the *Fortune* data series begins in 1954, the first "decade" of this study in terms of performance covers the period 1954 to 1959, giving a first "decade" of six years, compared to Rumelt's (1974: 88) nine-year first "decade." Following Rumelt, firms that had the same diversification strategy at the beginning and end of a period were assumed to have held that strategy for the entire period. Strategy change in this study is therefore defined as a change from one of Rumelt's diversification categories to another at some point in the period studied. Chatterjee and Blocher (1992) have recently tested Rumelt's categories vis-à-vis continuous measures and found that the latter discriminate satisfactorily among the former.

Performance data for this study are from a data base on the *Fortune* 500 manufacturing companies for the years 1954–1985. Three measures of performance, two return and one risk measure, were selected for the complementarity of their attributes and for their ability to provide a diverse perspective on performance. Return on assets (ROA, defined as net income after taxes and extraordinary items, divided by total assets net of depreciation and depletion) and return on sales (ROS, defined as net income after taxes and extraordinary items, divided by net sales) were the measures chosen. These are two of the three measures of performance used by *Fortune* in evaluating the performance of its rated firms. ROS has been criticized because it varies so highly across industries; on the other hand, it is not affected directly by the debt/equity mix (Palepu 1985: 244) and net sales is a relatively precisely measured quantity. A limitation of ROA is that it is sensitive to depreciation schedules; on the positive side, it is viewed as more stable across industries than is ROS. Both measures represent two commonly used measures of profitability in the literature (Chakravarthy 1986: 441; Christensen and Montgomery 1981: 341; Bettis 1981; Woo and Willard 1983). In the section presenting results, ROA results will be reported and augmented with ROS results when appropriate.

In previous studies of the relationship between diversification strategy and performance, the role of risk has only infrequently been addressed. When it has, the mean and variance of returns have been the most commonly selected measures to represent return and risk, respectively, (Bettis and Hall 1982; Bettis and Mahajan 1985; Chang and Thomas 1987; Grant et al. 1988; Hoskisson 1987). The use of mean and variance in this respect has recently been questioned

(Ruefli 1990b, 1991; Bromiley 1991; Ruefli and Wiggins 1994). Moreover, the other most commonly used measure, β from the capital asset pricing model (Amit and Livnat 1988a; Montgomery and Singh 1984), has recently been called into question (Fama and French 1992; Roll and Ross 1994), leaving a gap in our knowledge in this area.

This study will employ a state-defined measure of risk (Collins and Ruefli 1995) that is based on ordinal risk (Collins 1991; Collins and Ruefli 1992). To implement this methodology, the returns of the *Fortune* 500 firms were ranked in each year and then for each year mapped into twenty-five ordered categories (Argresti 1984) each containing twenty firms (a dummy twenty-sixth category was employed to account for firms not in the *Fortune* 500 that year). Transitions between categories in subsequent years in an eleven-year period generated an incidence matrix of transitions (Collins and Ruefli 1992: 1711), which was then transformed into a conditional probability matrix. For each cell in this latter matrix, a weighted entropy measure was calculated from the formula:

$$h_{ij} = -w_{ij}\, p_{ij} \ln (p_{ij})$$

where p_{ij} is the probability of moving from rank i to rank j at the next step, w_{ij} is the weight measuring the relative importance assigned to the shift from category i to category j, and ln means natural logarithm.

This weighted entropy was then partitioned across the sample of firms in proportion to their participation in the transition (Collins and Ruefli 1992: 1715). Summing an individual firm's contribution to the weighted entropy across those cells for which there was a loss in category rank (i.e., for which $i >$ j) yielded the state-defined risk level for that firm in that period. The eleven-year period was then rolled through the longitudinal sample to generate a time sequence of risk levels for each firm. The risk levels for the firms in Rumelt's sample were employed in this study.

Operational Methodology

Two methodologies were employed to estimate the diversity-performance-risk relationships. Ordinal time series analysis (Ruefli and Wilson 1987; Ruefli 1990) was employed to serve as a basis for computing state-defined risk levels (Collins and Ruefli 1995); it also served as a control on the ensuing cardinal ratio analysis. The latter was employed to maintain comparability with previous studies of the relationship between diversification strategy and performance. In each case, three cross-sectional periods were employed. The first two cover the sequential periods 1994–1959 and 1959–1969, thus giving a longitudinal flavor to the analysis. The third period studied was the entire period 1954–1969, which permitted the investigation of longer-term sequences of strategy changes. Comparisons of performance associated with various strategies and strategy changes were accomplished with t-tests and ANOVAs. The results of the ordinal and cardinal analyses were equivalent; but since the latter analysis is most comparable with antecedent studies, it will be reported here, along with the ordinal risk results.

Attributes of the Sample

Table 12.1, Part A—Maintained Strategy, shows the number of firms that maintained each strategy category in each period, the total number that maintained strategies, and the total number that changed strategies during each period—plus an additional category of firms that entered or left the sample during the period. The latter two categories formed Rumelt's miscellaneous category (Rumelt 1974: 89) and were not used by Rumelt in discussing financial performance. Table 12.1, Part B—Strategic Change, shows the numbers of firms in each of the strategy change categories represented by three or more firms in a period. These are small numbers. However, in the sequential crosssectional analyses to follow, three firms in a category represents eighteen and thirty data points in the first and second periods, respectively, and forty-eight points in the two periods combined. Part A of Table 12.1 also contains information pertinent to the first of the hypotheses posed earlier in the chapter. In the first decade studied, 30 percent of the firms changed diversification strategy; in the second period this increased to 42 percent, and over the two-decade period 55 percent of the firms changed strategy. If these rates are converted to rates for periods comparable to those used by Oster (1982) and Mascarenhas and Aaker (1989), this study finds strategy change to be much more prevalent than in either of the earlier studies, and yet still an event that occurs for a firm less than once a decade on average. With this evidence in hand the next section will provide the context for the findings on strategy and performance and strategy change and performance.

MAINTAINED STRATEGY FINDINGS

While the research reported here focuses on the nature of the relationship between strategy change and performance, to provide a benchmark for comparison it was necessary to replicate Rumelt's study in terms of unchanged strategies. The empirical results for ROA for this replication are given in summary form in Tables 12.2 through 12.5.

It should be noted in passing that the relative performance findings here differed in some important aspects from those of Rumelt (1974). In his original study, Rumelt had data for the period 1951 to 1969 but reported performance levels for strategies only for the decade 1959–1969. He stated that performance for the strategy groups for the first decade (as measured by his rather complex formula) differed by only a constant from performance for the second decade; therefore he did not report the earlier decade's financial performance values (Rumelt 1974: 90). A comparison of Tables 12.2 and 12.3 reveals that this

Table 12.1
Numbers of Firms in Each Category

A. MAINTAINED STRATEGY

	49–59	59–69	49–59–69
SINGLE BUSINESS (SB)	39	12	12
DOMINANT CONSTRAINED (DC)	20	12	7
DOMINANT VERTICAL (DV)	29	25	25
DOMINANT LINKED (DL)	1	4	1
DOMINANT UNRELATED (DU)	3	1	0
RELATED CONSTRAINED (RC)	43	35	26
RELATED LINKED (RL)	15	16	10
UNRELATED PASSIVE (UP)	5	7	3
ACQUISITIVE CONGLOMERATE (AC)	0	14*	0
TOTAL MAINTAINING STRATEGY	155	112	83
CHANGE OF STRATEGY	67	80	102
MISCELLANEOUS**	17	47	54

* by 1969 strategy, Rumelt (1974; p. 89).
** firms that entered sample after start date or left before end date

B. STRATEGY CHANGE

	49–59	59–69	49–59–69
SB to DC	13		
SB to DL	6		
SB to DV		7	
SB to DU	3		
SB to RC	6	3	
SB to RL	4		
DC to RL	12	6	
DL to RL		4	
DV to RC	4		
RC to RL	3	17	
RC to UP		5	
UP to AC		5	
SB to SB to DV			6
SB to SB to RC			3
SB to DC to DC			3
SB to DL to DL			3
SB to RL to RL			3
DC to DC to RC			3
DC to RC to RC			4
DC to RC to RL			3
DC to RL to RL			3
RC to RC to RL			11

study found some differences in performance by strategy category from one decade to the next—for the most part, pairwise permutations of rankings. More dramatic differences were found when this study's results were compared with those obtained by Rumelt (1974). See Table 12.3. Specifically, Rumelt's best and worst performing categories were dominant-constrained and unrelated-passive firms, while here related-constrained and acquisitive-conglomerate firms held those positions at significant levels. Results here indicate that single-business firms outperformed those with dominant-constrained strategies in the period 1960–1969. A preliminary assessment suggests that the most likely reasons our findings differed from those in prior studies with regard to performance of strategies are related to the different performance measures employed and different samples used. The findings of Chatterjee and Blocher (1992) support this conjecture in terms of the performance measures; however, while studies that followed Rumelt's (1974) employed differing samples, the sample used here was effectively the same as Rumelt's and the variables we used are well-accepted indicators of financial performance and are from a reliable public source. If differing but standard measures of financial performance yield alternative evaluations of diversification strategies from those found by previous studies employing the same sample, then the relation of strategy to economic performance is a strong candidate for further research.

Table 12.2
Performance by Diversification Strategy—Return on Assets Same Strategy 1949 and 1959

	Number	54–59	60–69	70–79	60–85
S B	39	0.0760	0.0739	0.0626	0.0679
DC	20	0.0858	0.0731	0.0648	0.0661
D V	29	0.0671	0.0476	0.0483	0.0432
D U	3	0.0336	0.0381	0.0225	0.0050
RC	43	0.0861	0.0866	0.0775	0.0781
RL	15	0.0787	0.0690	0.0595	0.0594
UP	5	0.0590	0.0658	0.0435	0.0563

Ramanujam and Varadarajan (1989) cited the need for research on the measures of diversification as one of the most important issues facing the field (p. 538–540). While acknowledged as an archetypal study in the area of diversification research, Rumelt's diversification strategy categorizations have been called into question on one hand (Christensen and Montgomery 1981; Nathanson 1985), and partially validated on the other (Chatterjee and Blocher 1992). For example, using a subsample of Rumelt's sample, Christensen and

Montgomery (1981) found that there were no significant differences in performance by strategy category in the period 1972–1977. Table 12.4 presents analysis of variance results for Rumelt's full sample and shows that in most periods there were significant differences—even in periods subsequent to the categorization and even when low-performing strategies were omitted. The results when ROS was employed were similar and hence are not given.

Table 12.3
Performance by Diversification Strategy—Return on Assets Same Strategy 1959 and 1969

	Number	60–69	Ranking	Rumelt's Rankings	70–79	60–85
SB	12	0.0766	3	4	0.0687	0.0742
DC	12	0.0743	4	1	0.0677	0.0672
DV	25	0.0496	7	6	0.0488	0.0443
DL	4	0.0804	2	–	0.0558	0.0671
RC	35	0.0899	1	2	0.0754	0.0788
RL	16	0.0743	5	3	0.0623	0.0623
UP	7	0.0596	6	7	0.0489	0.0508
AC	14	0.0424	8	5	0.0353	0.0415

Table 12.4
Analysis of Variance—Same Strategies 1959 and 1969

Period	All Strategies F-Value	Except DV F-Value	Except UP, & AC F-Value	Except UP, AC & DV F-Value
1955–59	7.306***	7.254***	2.281**	1.445
1960–64	11.859***	7.648***	12.089***	2.528**
1965–69	12.409***	11.604***	12.585***	3.045**
1970–74	10.505***	10.725***	6.207***	2.686**
1975–79	5.046***	3.325**	6.207***	1.329
1980–84	4.142***	1.196	6.184***	1.583

* significant at .1 or better
** significant at .05 or better
*** significant at .01 or better

Finally, most studies of maintained strategies have been limited to ten years or less. However, although he did not take advantage of it in his book, Rumelt's data permit examination of twenty years of the strategy-performance association. Results for such an analysis are shown in Table 12.5 and indicate that, in general, those firms that maintained a diversification strategy for two decades had an associated performance that was higher in all cases than firms that held the same strategy for shorter periods of time. This is preliminary evidence in support of H2.

Table   12.5
Return   on   Assets   Performance   by   Diversification   Strategy—Same Strategy   1949,   1959,   and   1969

	Number	54–59	60–69	70–79	60–85
S B	12	0.0787	0.0755	0.0652	0.0713
D C	7	0.1000	0.0803	0.0693	0.0720
D V	25	0.0704	0.0492	0.0482	0.0438
R C	26	0.0945	0.0947	0.0820	0.0851
R L	10	0.0942	0.0768	0.0635	0.0639
U P	3	0.0771	0.0681	0.0473	0.0610

STRATEGY CHANGE RESULTS

Operational Methodology

The performance of groups of firms that made a change of strategy in the periods 1954–1959 and 1960–1969 will be reported first. The results of this effort can then be compared to the respective one decade constant strategy categories results developed above. Following that, the results of a two-decade format that allowed for multiple changes in strategy will be outlined. The results of this model can be compared to the results of both the two-decade maintained strategies developed above and the one-period strategy change results to be reported below.

As a first step in this process, strategy changes in the two periods 1949 to 1959 and 1959 to 1969 were identified. Not all of the possible strategy changes occurred, and as Table 12.1, Part B indicates, fewer still had sufficient instances to permit meaningful statements about the transition. In the first decade, eight transitions were accomplished by three or more firms, and in the second decade there were seven such transitions. As stated above, three was chosen as the minimum number of firms making a transition to be analyzed.

One point to be made from Table 12.1 is that, as observed by Rumelt (1974: Ch. 2), the nature of the strategy transitions differed from decade to decade. In the period 1949 to 1959, transitions away from the single-business strategy to dominant and related strategies and movements from dominant business strategies to related strategies predominated. In the period 1959 to 1969, only two categories of transitions away from single-business strategies had more than three participants, while the bulk of the transitions were from dominant to related strategies and away from related-constrained strategies. This is consistent with Rumelt's findings. In both decades the most common strategic transitions were toward more loosely coupled systems, but otherwise the differing nature of the changes in strategy represents a reason for treating changes in the two decades separately. The results for strategy changes during 1949–1959 will be presented first, followed by the results for strategy changes in the period 1959–1969.

Implications of Change 1949–1959 for Performance

Part A of Table 12.6 shows the average ROA figures for each of three decades and for the period 1960–1985 for those firms that maintained their diversification strategies from 1949 to 1959 as compared to those that changed strategies. As can be seen, in all periods firms that held their strategy did better on average (significant at $\alpha = 0.05$) than those that changed. This result lends general support to H2 and to the arguments of the evolutionary and population ecology approaches to strategy.

This general result, however, does not particularize to specific strategy categories or pairs of categories. For example, if the results in Part A of Table 12.6 are compared with the data in Table 12.2, Part A, it can be seen that in the period 1954–1959, any change of strategy was superior in terms of returns to staying with a dominant-vertical, dominant-unrelated, or unrelated-passive strategy. In the next decade this advantage held with respect to firms that maintained a dominant-vertical or dominant-unrelated strategy in the first decade.

To evaluate the relative effects of specific strategic change on performance, the average ROA for each set of firms making one of the transitions listed in Table 12.1, Part B, in the first decade was computed for the periods 1954–1959, 1960–1969, 1970–1979, and 1960–1985. The results are reported in Table 12.6, Part B. As can be seen, the transition in the first period with the highest average ROA in the first period was single-business to related-linked at 10.13 percent, while dominant-vertical to related-constrained firms were second at 8.87 percent. Both of these performance levels are superior (the former significantly so) to any maintained strategy in the period 1949–1959 (Table 12.2). Transitions from single-business to dominant-unrelated yielded the poorest ROA performance. This latter result suggests that, in terms of performance, there may be performance limits on the magnitude of change of diversification strategy (Jones and Hill 1988)—that is, too much diversification all at once may result in inferior performance.

Table 12.6
Effect of Strategy Change on ROA Performance
Strategy Transition 1949-1959

A. EFFECTS OF CHANGE IN GENERAL

	Number	54–59	60–69	70–79	60–85
Strategy Change	67	0.0710	0.0622	0.0498	0.0534
Maintained Strategy	155	0.0772	0.0706	0.0630	0.0633

B. EFFECTS OF SPECIFIC CHANGES

	Number	54–59	60–69	70–79	60–85
SB to DC	13	0.0583	0.0490	0.0339	0.0456
SB to DL	6	0.0730	0.0549	0.0291	–
SB to DU	3	0.0472	0.0531	–	–
SB to RC	6	0.0669	0.0743	0.0718	0.0660
SB to RL	4	0.1013	0.0783	0.0608	0.0711
DC to RC	12	0.0795	0.0607	0.0502	0.0426
DC to RL	3	0.0697	0.0567	0.0474	0.0482
DV to RC	4	0.0887	0.0916	0.1060	0.1016

C. IMPACT OF CHANGE IN STRATEGY RELATIVE TO MAINTAINING SAME
STRATEGY 1949–59

PERIOD: RANK	1954–59	1960–69
1	SB to RL**	DV to RC**
2	DV to RC	RC**
3	RC	SB to RL
4	DC**	SB to RC
5	DC to RC	SB
6	RL	DC**
7	SB	RL
8	SB to DL	UP**
9	DC to RL	DC to RC
10	DV	DC to RL
11	SB to RC**	SB to DL
12	UP	SB to DU**
13	SB to DC**	SB to DC
14	SB to DU	DV*
15	DU	DU

** = significant (.05) difference between mean return and next lowest mean return.

To provide some perspective on the performance figures for strategic change, they can be ranked by performance against firms that maintained the same strategy through the decade 1949–1959 (see Table 12.6, Part C). It should be noted that not all of the differences between adjacent categories were significant. To provide a rough way of grouping categories by performance, t-tests assuming unequal variances were performed between the means of categories that were adjacent in the rankings by performance. The double asterisks in Table 12.6, Part C, indicate when the differences between a given rank and the next lower rank were significant. On average, firms that changed from single-business to related-linked in the first period had a significantly higher ROA in the first period than the averages for any of the other changed or maintained strategy categories. Note that this is in spite of the advantage held by the overrepresentation of firms from the high-performing pharmaceutical industry in the related-constrained category (Bettis 1981). Dominant-vertical to related-constrained firms had about the same performance levels on average as did related-constrained and dominant-constrained firms in the first period, and had a significantly higher average return in the second period. In all, those transitions that were selected by three or more firms in 1949 to 1959 did better than at least one of the constant-strategy categories in the first decade. This provides evidence that support for H2 must be qualified, since some strategy changes outperformed maintaining any strategy.

ROS results differed somewhat from ROA results when strategy change was involved. dominant-vertical to related-constrained firms, however, were also the best performers in terms of ROS, indicating that this was a generally robust strategy change for this period.

Implications of Change 1959–1969 for Performance

Table 12.7, Part A, reports the average ROA performance for firms that held their strategies from 1959 to 1969 versus those firms that changed strategy in this period. Again, change in general was associated with lower average returns than were obtained by maintaining any strategy, providing further general support to evolutionary economics and population-ecology views of strategy change. But, by comparison with maintained-strategy categories in Table 12.3, Part A, firms that made any change at all had higher average ROA than unrelated-passive, dominant-vertical, and acquisitive-conglomerate. Thus, on average, any change of strategy would have been better in terms of returns than any of several maintained strategies. Only nine specific transitions had three or more participants in the period 1959 to 1969, as shown in Table 12.1, Part B. Table 12.7, Part B, shows the average performance of the strategy groups of firms making a specific change of diversification strategy in that period. Single-business to related-constrained firms outperformed any other change by a significant amount.

Table 12.7, Part C, compares the ROA performances of specific categories of strategy changes in the period 1959–1969 to maintained strategy firms in that decade and the next. In terms of ROA performance, those firms that changed from single-business to related-constrained also performed better than all of the maintained strategy categories in the decade of the change—but not significantly better than related-constrained firms. Firms that went from dominant-linked to

Table   12.7
Effect of Strategy Change on Performance—Strategy
Transition   1959–1969

A. EFFECTS OF CHANGE IN GENERAL

	Number	60–69	70–79	60–85
Strategy Change	80	0.0670	0.0521	0.0559
Maintained Strategy	112	0.0721	0.0635	0.0640

B. EFFECTS OF SPECIFIC CHANGES

	Number	54–59	60–69	70–79	60–85
SB to DV	7		0.0557	0.0581	0.0528
SB to RC	3		0.0932	0.0778	0.0795
DC to RC	6		0.0488	0.0519	0.0446
DC to RL	3		0.0468	0.0605	0.0462
DC to UP	3		0.0393	0.0547	0.0444
DC to RL	4		0.0669	0.0576	0.0750
RC to RL	17		0.0515	0.0310	0.0348
RC to UP	5		0.0585	0.0517	0.0376
UP to AC	5		0.0378	0.0521	–

C. IMPACT OF CHANGE IN STRATEGY RELATIVE TO MAINTAINING SAME
STRATEGY 1959–69

PERIOD: RANK	1960–69	1970–79
1	SB to RC	SB to RC
2	RC**	RC**
3	DL	SB
4	SB	DC**
5	RL	RL
6	DC**	DC to RL
7	DL to RL	SB to DV
8	UP	DL to RL
9	RC to UP	DL
10	SB to DV**	DC to UP
11	RC to RL	UP to AC
12	DV	DC to RC
13	DC to RC	RC to UP
14	DC to RL**	UP
15	AC	DV**
16	DC to UP	AC
17	UP to AC	RC to RL

** = significant (.05) difference between mean return and next lowest mean return.

related-linked and those that changed from related-constrained to unrelated-passive
strategies performed at middle levels. Similar results were found when ROS was

the measure of performance, but no strategy change performed in the top group on both dimensions.

In the decade following the strategy changes, performance of several of the lower-ranked change categories improved relative to unrelated-passive, dominant-vertical, and acquisitive-conglomerate strategies. The group of single-business firms that vertically integrated in 1959–1969 was an average performer in terms of ROA but stands out as an excellent performer in terms of ROS. These firms most likely picked up value-added in their industry's chain of production, giving them a higher return on sales. Similarly, those firms that made the transition from related-constrained to related-linked in the later period were good midlevel performers by both measures.

Category Discrimination Under Change

While questions of the adequacy of Rumelt's diversification strategy when change of diversification strategy is involved have not been raised in the literature, an analysis of variance indicated that strategy-change categories accounted for variance in performance at a significant level for the sample here. F-ratios for five year-periods 1955 to 1984 were significant at the .01 level for both ROA and ROS in all periods for strategy changes in either period, 1949–1959 or 1959–1969. Student's t-tests revealed that strategy-change categories also produced levels of performance that were significantly different from the rest of the sample. This indicates that not only did Rumelt's strategy categories account for differences in performance among many maintained-strategy categories (Rumelt 1974; Ruefli and Ashmos 1990), but, more significantly, changes in those categories also accounted for differences in performance.

RESULTS FOR THE TWO PERIOD MODEL

Nature of Strategy Sequences

The results reported above for the two single-period models imply a stages-of-growth model and suggest that diversification strategy might be thought of in terms of a sequence of timed changes on a longitudinal basis. To investigate this concept more thoroughly, sequences of strategy-category changes over the two-decade period 1949 to 1969 were examined. Those sequences of diversification with three or more representatives from the sample of firms are shown in Part B of Table 12.1. As can be seen, only one of these sequences (dominant-constrained to related-constrained to related-linked) had two changes of strategy in the two decades. This implies that diversification strategy is not a matter of a sequence of moves, since, on average, a single change is made in a two-decade period.

ROA Performance

Table 12.8, Part A, compares the performance associated with maintaining a strategy for two decades with any change in strategy over that period. In contrast to the single period models, more firms changed diversification strategy over two periods than maintained it. The general results from the single-decade analyses that indicated that changing strategy in general was associated with poorer performance than holding a strategy also obtained when the period was raised to two decades. Thus support for H2 at the general level is reinforced and extended to longer time periods. Table 12.8, Part B, reports the ROA performance statistics of the strategy-sequence categories. Part C of the same table shows the relative ROA positions of the strategy sequences in the context of the two-decade maintained strategies. Strategy-change sequences were well-mixed in performance with the maintained strategies. The single-business to single-business to related-constrained (SB to SB to RC) category improved its position in each decade to finish just below those firms that maintained a related-constrained strategy for two decades, while the strategy sequence dominant-constrained to related-linked to related-linked was only slightly inferior.

The relation of timing of a strategy change to the associated returns can be illustrated by noting that since the DC to DC to RC sequence (i.e., those firms that made the change from DC to RC in 1960–1969) performed at a consistently higher level than the DC to RC to RC sequence (i.e., those firms that made the same change in the earlier 1950–1959 period), the implication is that early movers from a dominant-constrained to a related-constrained strategy did not do as well in general as those who changed later. Thus H4 is not supported. The statistics also indicate that the initial point for a change may also be important, since firms that had a single-business strategy in 1949 but then changed to related-linked and held it can be compared to firms that were dominant-constrained in 1949 and changed to related-linked by 1959 and held this strategy through 1969. The SB-RL-RL sequence was the higher performer in the first decade, but the DC-RL-RL sequence was superior by a wide margin in the second and ensuing periods. Thus the antecedents of a strategy may be a significant factor in the performance of a strategy in a subsequent period. For example, to say that related-linked firms in the period 1959–1969 performed in such and such a way obscures the fact that those related-linked firms that were single businesses in the period 1949–1959 were substantially better performers than those which were dominant-constrained in that prior period.

ROS Performance

Table 12.9 presents the two-period results in terms of ROS. A comparative examination of the performance of strategy sequences across the two measures (ROA and ROS) indicates that the performance measure makes a difference in the evaluation of strategy change as well as maintained strategies. Single-business to

Table 12.8
Performance by Diversification Strategy—Return on Assets
Strategy Sequence Compared to Same Strategy
1949, 1959, and 1969

A. EFFECTS OF CHANGE IN GENERAL

	Number	54–59	60–69	70–79	60–85
Strategy Change	102	0.0745	0.0675	0.0549	0.0577
Maintained Strategy	83	0.0852	0.0736	0.0653	0.0657

B. STRATEGY SEQUENCE

	Number	54–59	60–69	70–79	60–85
SB to SB to DV	6	0.0756	0.0687	0.0598	0.0634
SB to SB to RC	3	0.0768	0.0846	0.0818	0.0787
SB to DC to DC	3	0.1040	0.0750	0.0732	0.0666
SB to DL to DL	3	0.0789	0.0746	—	—
SB to RL to RL	3	0.0766	0.0476	—	—
DC to DC to RC	3	0.0575	0.0640	0.0596	0.0588
DC to RC to RC	4	0.0384	0.0336	0.0277	0.0308
DC to RC to RL	3	0.0780	0.0608	0.0486	0.0563
DC to RL to RL	3	0.0687	0.0903	0.0795	0.0726
RC to RC to RL	11	0.0756	0.0723	0.0632	0.0613

C. RANKINGS: Sequence and Two-Decade Maintained Strategies

RANK	54–59	60–69	70–79	60–85
1	SB to DC to DC	RC**	RC	RC**
2	DC	DC to RL to RL	SB to SB to RC	SB to SB to RC**
3	RC	SB to SB to RC	DC to RL to RL	DC to RL to RL
4	RL**	DC	SB to DC to DC	DC
5	SB to DL to DL	RL	DC	SB
6	SB	SB	SB	SB to DC to DC
7	DC to RC to RL	SB to DC to DC	RL	RL
8	UP	SB to DL to DL	RC to RC to RL	SB to SB to DV
9	SB to SB to RC	RC to RC to RL	SB to SB to DV	RC to RC to RL
10	SB to RL to RL	SB to SB to DV	DC to DC to RC**	UP
11	SB to SB to DV	UP	DC to RC to RL	DC to DC to RC
12	RC to RC to RL**	DC to DC to RC	DV	DC to RC to RL**
13	DV	DC to RC to RL**	UP	DV
14	DC to RL to RL	DV	DC to RC to RC	DC to RC to RC
15	DC to DC to RC**	SB to RL to RL		
16	DC to RC to RC	DC to RC to RC		

** = significant (.05) difference between mean return and next lowest mean return.

single-business to related-constrained was the best change sequence in terms of ROA, while single-business to single-business to dominant-vertical was best in terms of ROS. In fact, this sequence was a better performer than any of the two-decade maintained strategies in terms of ROS. As in the case of the one-period model, it can be surmised that the superior performance of this sequence was due to the addition of value-added in the vertical integration. Unlike the case for maintained strategies, there is no good compromise change candidate that performed well on both measures.

Table 12.9
Performance by Diversification Strategy—Return on Sales Strategy Sequence Compared to Same Strategy 1949, 1959, and 1969

A. EFFECTS OF CHANGE IN GENERAL

	Number	54–59	60–69	70–79	60–85
Strategy Change	102	0.0555	0.0549	0.0438	0.0460
Maintained Strategy	83	0.0658	0.0605	0.0522	0.0528

B. STRATEGY SEQUENCE

	Number	54–59	60–69	70–79	60–85
SB to SB to DV	6	0.0930	0.0922	0.0612	0.0721
SB to SB to RC	3	0.0612	0.0595	0.0501	0.0517
SB to DC to DC	3	0.0772	0.0595	0.0567	0.0523
SB to DL to DL	3	0.0618	0.0607	—	—
SB to RL to RL	3	0.0418	0.0580	—	—
DC to DC to RC	3	0.0357	0.0409	0.0359	0.0364
DC to RC to RC	4	0.0217	0.0213	0.0201	0.0213
DC to RC to RL	3	0.0491	0.0443	0.0351	0.0411
DC to RL to RL	3	0.0438	0.0592	0.0512	0.0467
RC to RC to RL	11	0.0595	0.0604	0.0538	0.0515

C. RANKINGS: Sequences and Two-Decade Maintained Strategies

RANK	54–59	60–69	70–79	60–85
1	SB to SB to DV**	SB to SB to DV**	RC**	SB to SB to DV
2	RL	RC**	SB to SB to DV	RC**
3	SB to DC to DC	RL	RL	SB to DC to DC
4	RC**	SB to DL to DL	RC to RC to RL	RL
5	DV	RC to RC to RL	SB to SB to RC	SB to SB to RC
6	SB to DL to DL	SB to SB to RC	SB to DC to DC	RC to RC to RL
7	SB to SB to RC	SB to DC to DC	DC to RL to RL	DC to RL to RL
8	RC to RC to RL	DC to RL to RL	DV	SB
9	DC**	SB to RL to RL**	SB	DC
10	DC to RC to RL	DV	DC	DV
11	SB	SB	DC to RC to RL**	DC to RC to RL
12	DC to RL to RL	DC	DC to DC to RC	UP
13	SB to RL to RL	DC to RC to RL	UP	DC to DC to RC**
14	UP	DC to DC to RC	DC to RC to RC	DC to RC to RC
15	DC to DC to RC**	UP**		
16	DC to RC to RC	DC to RC to RC		

** = significant (.05) difference between mean return and next lowest mean return.

Antecedent Performance and Strategy Change

Preliminary evidence regarding antecedent performance and strategic change can be found by comparing strategy sequence performance in Table 12.8 with the performance of first-period maintained strategies in Table 12.2. All single-business firms that maintained their strategy in the first period averaged ROA of 0.076, as did the subset of single-business firms that changed to dominant-vertical in the second period—as did the subset of single-business firms that subsequently changed to related-constrained. Thus, there was no difference in prior performance of those that changed diversification strategy. However, all dominant-constrained firms in the first period averaged 0.086, while the subset that changed to related-constrained in the second period averaged only 0.058 in the first period. Also all related-constrained firms average 0.086 in the first period, while the subset that changed to related-linked averaged 0.076 in the first period. This provides evidence that change of diversification strategy was associated with poor antecedent performance.

This evidence is obviously mixed. To more fully investigate the issue of antecedent performance and strategy change, average returns for each strategy category at the beginning two years of each period were computed and divided into quartiles. The fraction of firms maintaining and changing strategy in a period were then computed for each quartile. The results in Table 12.10 indicate that Bowman's troubled-firm hypothesis (i.e., firms with low performance will take greater risks and make changes) was supported for both periods insofar as firms in the bottom quartile of returns were twice as likely to change strategies as were firms in the top quartile. On the other hand, Oster's assertion (1982: 376) that firms with satisfactory performance would not change their strategy was shown not to hold for a significant fraction of the high-performing firms. More than one-fourth of the top quartile firms changed their strategy, indicating that persistence of strategy was overcome—even in the face of high returns. The overall results are in general agreement with Schendel and Patton's (1976) findings but in disagreement with the findings of Fombrun and Ginsberg (1986), who found that strategy change was more likely for firms with average performance. The findings were also consistent across ROA and ROS dimensions. This evidence suggests that there are likely to be multiple motivations for change of strategy, and it further indicates that high-performing firms that change strategy might make interesting subjects for further research.

Strategy Change and State-Defined Risk

As noted earlier, we use a concept called state-defined risk measured by a weighted entropy measure of transferring from one rank (or state) to another. Because we use an eleven-year period to calculate this state-defined risk level, the first year for which risk levels were available was 1964. Thus only the association between strategy change and risk in the period 1964–1969 could be tested. Employing a finer-grained set of data on strategy classification (Rumelt 1978), strategies for the firms in the sample were identified for 1964. To identify before-and-after risk, the risk levels for each firm in the sample were computed by averaging the state-defined risk levels for 1964–1965 and for 1969–1970. Average risk levels for firms that changed their diversification strategies and for firms that maintained their strategies were computed. The results are shown in Table 12.11.

Table 12.10
Fraction of Firms Holding or Changing Strategy by Antecedent Performance Quartile

PERIOD:	1949–59		1959–69	
PERFORMANCE QUARTILE	HOLD	CHANGE	HOLD	CHANGE
1	0.74	0.26	0.68	0.32
2	0.67	0.33	0.57	0.43
3	0.65	0.35	0.59	0.41
4	0.40	0.60	0.39	0.61

Table 12.11
Average State-Defined Risk Levels

	1964–65		1969–70	N=
Strategy Change	0.169	t = −1.241 Pr(T ≤ t) = 0.221	0.194	48
	t = 1.053 Pr(T ≤ t) = 0.293		t = 2.267 Pr(T ≤ t) =0.025	
Maintained Strategy	0.146	t = −0.557 Pr(T ≤ t) = 0.578	0.151	142

A two-tailed t-test was employed and indicated no significant difference between the means of the risk levels of the two groups in the period preceding the change of strategy, and a t-test with paired values indicated no differences between the means of the risk levels of either group from the 1964–1965 to the 1969–1970 periods. The nature of the results are contrary to the findings of Hill and Hansen (1991); moreover, in 1969–1970 the mean of the risk level for the set of firms that changed strategy was significantly higher ($\alpha = 0.05$) than the mean risk level for those firms that maintained their strategy. Since the set of firms that changed strategy included a few firms that retrenched rather than diversified, these firms were removed from the sample and the analysis was re-run—yielding the same results. Risk for those firms that diversified from 1965 to 1969 went from 0.155 in 1964–1965 to 0.185 in 1969–1970. Contrary to Hill and Hansen (1991: 194), while the former level was not significantly higher than that of nondiversifying firms, the latter was significantly higher than the risk level for firms that had not diversified. Thus, for the period investigated, change of diversification strategy was associated with a significantly higher risk level following the change—contradicting H5. Since there was no significant difference between the means of the two groups before the change, there was no support for an analogue to H3 in the realm of risk. That is, higher risk levels do not appear to be significant antecedents to change of strategy.

Summary of Results

The results of this study in terms of the hypotheses set out earlier are summarized in Table 12.12.

Table 12.12
Summary of Results

Hypothesis	Findings
H1: Strategy change infrequent.	Diversification strategy changed less than once a decade on average.
H2: Strategy change associated with lower performance.	Supported in general, but not supported for particular strategy changes.
H3: Poor antecedent performance associated with strategy change.	Supported in general, but a significant number of high performing firms changed strategy.
H4: Timing of change not significant.	Not supported.
H5: Strategy change is associated with lower risk.	Not supported for antecedent risk levels, contradicted for subsequent risk levels.

DISCUSSION

Overview

Using established strategy classifications for a set of 239 large manufacturing companies, generally available performance data, and generally accepted performance measures, this study has attempted to refine our knowledge about the relationship between strategy change and economic performance. Limitations of previous evaluations were addressed in this study through the use of longitudinal data, analyzed via three performance measures—including risk, applied over a time span of thirty-two years, and focused on categories of firms that changed strategy. The specific results presented to this point can be summarized and examined in terms of their implications; but to place these results in context, some of the limitations of the study should first be stated.

Limitations

The most evident limitation of this study is with respect to the age of the data employed. The use of historical data in a world where the environment is subject to substantial change makes extrapolation of the findings to current practice problematic. However, the extrapolation to current and future research is more direct and all the more meaningful, given the paucity of empirical research of any age on change of strategy. By studying a period that immediately predates that in which many of the concepts and assertions regarding strategy change to be found in the current literature were developed, new information on some of those concepts was generated from established data—and this, in turn, forms a foundation for further studies of strategy change in a more recent context.

This study also shared a number of limitations, both conceptual and empirical, with other studies in the area. The restriction of the sample to large manufacturing and mining firms limits the generalizability of results of this and like studies; for example, firms that have as their core the provision of services may have entirely different strategy-change–performance relationships (Nayyar 1992). In common with the vast majority of studies, this research studied only survivors, so the possibility of a bias in that regard exists. In addition, time and resource limitations precluded the inclusion of information on external environmental conditions that provided the context for change. In this regard, data on changes in the top management team would have been most desirable.

Potentially more serious was the limitation of data and time that precluded analysis of industry effects on the relation between strategy and performance on any meaningful basis. While Rumelt (1991) has recently presented an analysis that indicates that industry effect is not significant, Christensen and Montgomery (1981) and Bettis (1981) reported such effects in subsamples of Rumelt's firms in periods subsequent to those he studied. An examination of the sample of Rumelt's firms that changed strategies indicated that, unlike maintained-strategy categories, change categories were distributed across industries in a fashion that understates the results here. For example, firms in the pharmaceutical industry did not change strategies, so that industry's known high levels of profitability (Bettis 1981) did not influence the performance of firms that changed strategies. Potential bias from industry effects was therefore restricted to bias against firms that changed strategies in comparison with firms that held related diversification strategies, making the results presented here conservative.

Implications

With respect to the strategy-change–performance relationship, some general conclusions can be derived. One such conclusion is that, for this sample, change in general was associated with performance that was, in general, inferior to holding a strategy. This lends support to prescriptions of a conservative attitude on the part of managers with respect to the status quo (Rumelt 1974; Peters and Waterman 1982) and supports evolutionary-economics and population-ecology views of strategy. Countering this is the finding that some specific changes in diversification strategy with particular timing outperformed all maintained strategies. This suggests that (just as Newtonian mechanics is limited to macroscopic phenomena) population-ecology and evolutionary-economics views of strategic behavior may be appropriate only to a general level of strategy analysis and may be misleading at more detailed levels of analysis. What is needed in the strategy area, therefore, are theories at the more detailed level of change of strategies to explain why specific strategy changes are high performers.

The research reported here also indicates that there is most likely not a simple answer to the question of the performance antecedents of strategy change. Even the troubled-firm hypothesis, which held in that the lowest performers were the most likely to change, did not account for the majority of firms that made a change in any period. The finding that a substantial fraction of higher-performing firms changed diversification strategy suggests that this is a possible fertile area for further research.

Studies of strategies maintained over time, in identifying better-performing strategies, have neglected the problem of the effects of moving from here to there. In agreement with broader findings of effects of corporate history (Boeker 1989), this study illustrates the importance of initial position on the worth of a strategy. Given the evidence here, the knowledge (even the prescient knowledge) that a related-constrained strategy is a high performer, is of little use to a firm with a dominant-constrained strategy—given that the evidence shows that firms that changed from dominant-constrained to related-constrained are among the worst performers. In fact, it can be argued that information regarding the performance of related-constrained strategies in general would have been dysfunctional to the dominant-constrained firm, if acted upon, since the firm could have done better on average by maintaining that strategy. Further, the results showed that the effects of a particular strategy or change of strategy lasted even through two decades beyond the classificatory period, lending support to the notion of diversification strategy (and change of strategy) as a factor in the persistence of profit (Rumelt, Schendel and Teece 1991).

For the sample of firms investigated, the rankings of strategies by performance were dependent, in part, on the measure selected. For example, with ROA as the measure of performance, vertical integration yielded among the worst performance, while this strategy was at least an average performer in terms of ROS. Differences in results between performance measures were even more pronounced when change of strategy was involved. This implies that investigations of the diversification strategy-strategy change-performance relationship should employ multiple measures of performance to insure the robustness of results. On both measures, ROA and ROS, this study found that Rumelt's (1974) contention that his strategy categories did account for differences in performance was supported for most of the subperiods throughout the period of his study for both of the performance measures herein employed. This property of Rumelt's strategy classifications was extended by this study to strategy-change categories on one- and two-decade bases.

The results of this study do not support an image of a manager engaged in a series of major diversification maneuvers to position a firm ahead of its peers. Rather, the evidence presented here suggests that good performance was associated with a very limited number of changes involving both timing and choice of strategy. Previous researchers, by confining themselves to firms that maintained strategies in one relatively short period of time, asserted that the key to obtaining successful performance from a diversification strategy was having the appropriate type of strategy and, by implication, holding it. This research, however, indicated that the key involves a quadruple contingency that includes (1) the type of diversification strategy held initially, (2) the timing of adoption of a new strategy, (3) the type of strategy adopted, and (4) the measure of performance that is selected.

Directions for Further Research

Based on the results here, a number of implications for further research can be drawn. While the relationship of maintained strategies and performance was not the focus of this research, the presentation of results in this area indicated that there may be grounds to question descriptions of this relationship that have appeared in the literature. The opportunity to simultaneously explore the relationships between performance and maintained and changed strategies should mitigate the burdens of so ambitious an undertaking.

Although it was not raised as an issue at the outset of the chapter, the issue of the timing of the measurement of performance relative to that of categorization was revealed in the tables of results. But while it was apparent that lagging performance with respect to strategy classification yielded different evaluations of strategy categories, no preferred lag interval could be determined.

The only clear implication that can be drawn was that commonly-used contemporaneous classification and measurement of performance was only one of several alternatives. This is clearly an issue that would benefit from some additional investigation.

In addition, the complexity of relationships between strategy change and performance revealed in this research presents a strong argument against investigations with time frames shorter than two decades. Further, the measures of strategic change employed here were based solely on diversification strategy. The results obtained here need to be compared to those obtained from studies using different measures of strategic change.

Finally, the focus here has been on strategy and strategy change. A companion issue, not addressed here, is that of structure and structure change. The relations among structure, structure change, risk, and performance is treated in a separate research effort by Carlin and Ruefli (1995), while the combination and sequencing of strategy and structure changes is examined by Harris and Ruefli (1993). Both of these studies rely on databases that overlap with that employed in this research.

CONCLUSION

The findings from this analysis demonstrate that the strategic issue of the relationships of diversification strategy and change of diversification strategy and corporate performance has levels of complexity beyond that heretofore addressed in the literature. The parameters of a research effort designed to further investigate these issues can also be inferred from the design of this study. A study employing a five- or even ten-year time frame will probably not be adequate to the task; two or more decades of performance and classification data will likely be required. Fortunately for strategic management researchers, longitudinal data on multidecade bases are becoming more available; unfortunately, the task of supplementing these data with categorizations, and so on, is a most formidable undertaking. This places a premium on studies such as Rumelt's (1974), which shouldered much of that burden for ensuing studies, and makes a case for the critical value of such studies in the future.

Clearly, the assembling and analysis of prodigious amounts of data over decades of time to provide the basis for more refined conclusions than those presented here will require motivation and substantial ingenuity on the part of strategy researchers undertaking the effort. A prerequisite to all of this, however, is that the researchers have a dynamic view of strategy and performance and implement this view in their research design. After all, the key classification data for this study were available in the appendix of what is probably the best-known book in the area for seventeen years without receiving the attention that they merited.

The authors would like to thank Richard Rumelt for his efforts in compiling the data on categorization of the sample by diversification strategy, and W. W. Cooper and Sten Thore for their comments and suggestions.

APPENDIX

Rumelt's Strategic Types

Definitions

A—Single Business (SB)—firms which are basically committed to a single line of business.

B—Dominant Businesses—firms which have diversified to some extent, but still obtain most of their revenues from a single business. Four types of dominant businesses include:

1—Dominant-Vertical (DV)—vertically integrated firms.

2—Dominant-Constrained (DC)—nonvertical dominant business firms which have diversified by building on some particular strength, skill, or resource associated with the original dominant activity.

3—Dominant-Linked (DL)—nonvertical dominant business firms where most diversified activities are not linked to the dominant business but each is somehow related to some other of the firm's activities.

4—Dominant-Unrelated (DU)—nonvertical dominant business firms in which most diversified activities are not related to the dominant business.

C—Related Businesses—nonvertically integrated firms that are diversified but without a dominant line of business and in which diversification has been accomplished primarily by relating new activities to old activities. Two types of related businesses are:

1—Related-Constrained (RC)—related business firms which have diversified chiefly by relating new businesses to a specific central skill or resource and in which each activity is somehow related to almost all of the other of the firm's activities.

2—Related-Linked (RL)—related business firms which have diversified by relating new businesses to some strength or skill already possessed, but not always to the same strength or skill.

D—Unrelated Businesses—nonvertical firms that have diversified without regard to relationships between new businesses and current activities. Two types of related businesses are:

1—Unrelated-Passive (UP)—unrelated business firms that do not qualify as Acquisitive Conglomerates.

2—Acquisitive Conglomerates (AC)—unrelated businesses firms which have aggressive programs for the acquisition of new unrelated businesses.

REFERENCES AND FURTHER READINGS

Aaker, D. A., and Mascarenhas, B. (1984). "The Need for Strategic Flexibility." *Journal of Business Strategy*, 6: 74–82.

Amit, R., and Livnat, J. (1988a). "Diversification, Capital Structure, and Systematic Risk: An Empirical Investigation." *Journal of Accounting, Auditing, and Finance*, 3: 19–48.

Amit, R., and Livnat, J. (1988b). "Diversification and the Risk-Return Trade-off." *Academy of Management Journal*, 31 (1): 154–166.

Amit, R., and Livnat, J. (1988c). "Diversification Strategies, Business Cycles and Economic Performance." *Strategic Management Journal*, 9: 99–110.

Ansoff, H. I. (1965). *Corporate Strategy*. New York: McGraw-Hill.

Argresti, A. (1984). *Analysis of Ordinal Categorical Data*. New York: John Wiley and Sons.

Balakrishnan, S., and Wernerfelt, B. (1986). "Technical Change, Competition and Vertical Integration." *Strategic Management Journal*, 7: 347–359.

Beard, D. W., and Dess, G. G. (1981). "Corporate-level Strategy, Business-level Strategy, and Firm Performance." *Academy of Management Journal*, 24: 663–688.

Bettis, R. A. (1981). "Performance Differences in Related and Unrelated Diversified Firms." *Strategic Management Journal*, 2: 379–393.

Bettis, R. A., and Hall, W. K. (1982). "Diversification Strategy, Accounting Determined Risk and Accounting Determined Return." *Academy of Management Journal*, 25 (June).

Bettis, R. A., and Mahajan, V. (1985). "Risk/Return Performance of Diversified Firms." *Management Science*, 31 (7): 785–799.

Boeker, W. (1989). "Strategic Change: The Effects of Founding and History." *Academy of Management Journal*, 32 (3): 489–515.

Bowman, E. H. (1982) "Risk Seeking by Troubled Firms." *Sloan Management Review* (Summer): 33–40.

Bromiley, P. (1991). "Paradox, or at Least Variance Found: A Comment on 'Mean-Variance Approaches to Risk-Return Relationships in Strategy: Paradox Lost' by Timothy W. Ruefli," *Management Science*, 37 (9): 1206–1210.

Burns, T., and Stalker, G. M. (1961). *The Management of Innovation*. London, Tavistock.

Capon, N., Hulbert, J. M., Farley, J. U., and Martin, L. E. (1988). "Corporate Diversity and Economic Performance: The Impact of Market Specialization." *Strategic Management Journal*, 9: 61–74.

Carnall, C. A. (1986). "Toward a Theory for the Evaluation of Organizational Change." *Human Relations*, 39: 745–766.

Chakravarthy, B. S. (1986). "Measuring Strategic Performance." *Strategic Management Journal*, 7: 437–458.

Chandler, A., Jr. (1962). *Strategy and Structure: Chapters in the History of the American Industrial Enterprise*. Cambridge, Mass.: MIT Press.

Chandrasekaran, G. (1982). "Strategy, Structure, Market Concentration and Organization Performance," doctoral dissertation, State University of New York at Buffalo.

Chang, Y., and Thomas, H. (1971). "The Impact of Diversification Strategy on Risk-Return Performance." *Academy of Management Proceedings*, pp. 2–6.

Channon, D. F. (1971). "Strategy and Structure of British Enterprise." DBA dissertation, Cambridge: Harvard Business School.

Chatterjee, S., and Blocher, J. D. (1992). "Measurement of Firm Diversification: Is It Robust?" *Academy of Management Journal*, 35 (4): 874–888.

Christensen, H. K., and Montgomery, C. A. (1981). "Corporate Economic Performance: Diversification Strategy versus Market Structure." *Strategic Management Journal*, 2: 327–343.

Ciscel, D. H., and Evans, D. (1984). "Returns to Corporate Diversification in the 1970's." *Managerial and Decision Economics*, 5 (2): 67–71.

Collins, J. M. (1991). "Strategic Risk: An Ordinal Approach." Ph.D, dissertation. Austin: the University of Texas (December).

Collins, J. M., and Ruefli, T. W. (1992). "Strategic Risk: An Ordinal Approach." *Management Science*, 38 (12): 1707–1731.

Collins, J. M., and Ruefli, T. W. (1995) *Strategic Risk: A State-Defined Approach.* Boston: Kluwer Academic Press.

Conner, D. R., Piman, B. G., and Clements, E. E. (1987). "Corporate Culture and Its Impact on Strategic Change in Banking." *Journal of Retail Banking*, 9 (2): 16–24.

Cool, K., and Schendel, D. (1988). "Performance Differences Among Strategic Group Members." *Strategic Management Journal*, 9: 207–223.

Cyert, R., and March, J. (1963). *A Behavioral Theory of the Firm.* Englewood Cliffs, N.J.: Prentice-Hall.

Dutton, J., and Duncan, R. B. (1987). "The Influence of the Strategic Planning Process on Strategic Change." *Strategic Management Journal*, 8: 103–116.

Edstrom, A. (1986). "Leadership and Strategic Change." *Human Resource Management*, 25 (4): 581–606.

Fama, E. F., and French, K. R. (1992). "The Cross-Section of Expect Stock Returns." *Journal of Finance*, XLVII (2): 427–465.

Fombrun, C. J., and Ginsberg, A. (1986). "Enabling and Disabling Forces on Resource Deployment." *Proceedings of the Decision Sciences Institute Annual Meeting*, Hawaii, pp. 1249–1241.

Galbraith, C., and Schendel, D. (1983). "An Empirical Analysis of Strategy Types." *Strategic Management Journal*, 4: 153–173.

Galbraith, J. R. (1977). *Organization Design.* Reading, Mass.: Addison-Wesley Publishing Company.

Ginsberg, A. (1988). "Measuring and Modeling Changes in Strategy." *Strategic Management Journal*, 9 (6): 559–575.

Goodstein, J., K. Gautam, and Boeker, W. (1994). "The Effects of Board Size and Diversity on Strategic Change." *Strategic Management Journal*, 15: pp. 241–250.

Grant, R. M., and Jammine, A. P. (1988). "Performance Differences Between the Wrigley/Rumelt Strategy Categories." *Strategic Management Journal*, 9: 333–346.

Grant, R. M., Jammine, A. P., and Thomas, H. (1988). "Diversity, Diversification, and Profitability among British Manufacturing Companies, 1972–84." *Academy of Management Journal,* 31 (4): 771–801.

Gray, B., and Ariss, S. S. (1985). "Politics and Strategic Change Across Organizational Life Cycles." *Academy of Management Review,* 10: 707–723.

Greenwood, R., and Hinings, C. R. (1993). "Understanding Strategic Change: The Contribution of Archetypes." *Academy of Management Journal,* 36 (5): 1052–1081.

Hambrick, D. and Schecter, S. M. (1983). "Turnaround Strategies for Mature Industrial-Product Business Units." *Academy of Management Journal,* 26: 231–248.

Hannan, M., and Freeman, J. (1977). "The Population Ecology of Organizations." *American Journal of Sociology,* 32: 929–964.

Hannan, M., and Freeman, J. (1984). "Structural Inertia and Organizational Change." *American Sociological Review,* 2: 149–164.

Harris, I. C. and Ruefli, T. W. (1993). "The Strategy/Structure Debate: Through An Historical Empirical Lens." IC^2 working paper, the University of Texas at Austin; presented at the Academy of Management National Meeting, Atlanta, Georgia, August 1993.

Hill, C.W.L., and Hansen, G. S. (1991). "A Longitudinal Study of the Cause and Consequences of Changes in Diversification in the U.S. Pharmaceutical Industry 1977–86." *Strategic Management Journal,* 12: 187–199.

Hill, C.W.L., and Hoskisson, R. E. (1983). "Conglomerate Performance over the Economic Cycle." *Journal of Industrial Economics,* 32 (12): 197–211.

Hinings, C., and Greenwood, R. (1988). *The Dynamics of Strategic Change.* Oxford: Basil Blackwood.

Hoskisson, R. E. (1987). "Multidivisional Structure and Performance: The Contingency of Diversification Strategy." *Academy of Management Journal,* 30 (4): 625–644.

Hoskisson, R. E., and Johnson, R. A. (1992). "Corporate Restructuring and Strategic Change: The Effect on Diversification Strategy and R & D Intensity." *Strategic Management Journal,* 13: 625–634.

Johnson, G., and Thomas, H. (1987). "The Industry Context of Strategy, Structure and Performance: The U.K. Brewing Industry." *Strategic Management Journal,* 8: 343–361.

Jones, G. R., and Hill, C. W. (1988). "Transaction Cost Analysis of Strategy-Structure Choice." *Strategic Management Journal,* 9: 159–172.

Kay, N. M. (1982). *The Evolving Firm: Strategy and Structure in Industrial Organization.* New York: St. Martin's Press.

Kelly, D., and Amburgey, T. L. (1991). "Organizational Inertia and Momentum: A Dynamic Model of Strategic Change." *Academy of Management Journal,* 34 (3): 591–612.

Kimberly, J. R. (1976). "Issues in the Design of Longitudinal Organizational Research." *Sociological Methods and Research,* 4: 321–347.

Lambkin, M. (1988). "Order of Entry and Performance in New Markets." *Strategic Management Journal,* 9: 127–140.

Leavitt, T. (1975). "Dinosaurs Among the Bears and Bulls." *Harvard Business Review,* 53 (1): 41–53.

Leontiades, M. (1980). *Strategies for Diversification and Change*. Boston, Mass.: Little, Brown and Company.

Lieberman, M. B., and Montgomery, D. B. (1988). "First-Mover Advantages." *Strategic Management Journal*, 9: 41–58.

Lorsch, J. (1986). "Managing Culture: The Invisible Barrier to Strategic Change." *California Management Review*, 28 (2): 95–109.

MacDonald, J. M. (1984). "Diversification, Market Growth, and Concentration in U.S. Manufacturing." *Southern Economic Journal*, 50 (4): 1098–1111.

Markham, J. W. (1973). *Conglomerate Enterprise and Corporate Performance*. Cambridge, Mass.: Harvard University Press.

Mascarenhas, B. (1989). "Strategic Group Dynamics." *Academy of Management Journal*, 32 (2): 333–352.

Mascarenhas, B., and Aaker, D. A. (1989). "Mobility Barriers and Strategic Groups." *Strategic Management Journal*, 10: 475–485.

Michel, A., and Shaked, I. (1984). "Does Business Diversification Affect Performance?" *Financial Management*, 13 (4): 18–25.

Miller, D., and Friesen, P. (1980). "Momentum and Revolution in Organizational Adaptation." *Academy of Management Journal*, 23: 591–614.

Miller, D., and Friesen, P. (1982). "The Longitudinal Analysis of Organizations." *Management Science*, 28 (9): 1013–1034.

Montgomery, C. A. (1979). "Diversification, Market Structure, and Firm Performance: An Extension of Rumelt's Work." Ph.D. dissertation, Purdue University.

Montgomery, C. A., and Singh, H. (1984). "Diversification Strategy and Systematic Risk." *Strategic Management Journal*, 5: 181–191.

Montgomery, C. A. (1982). "The Measurement of Firm Diversification: Some New Empirical Evidence." *Academy of Management Journal*, 25 (2): 299–307.

Nathanson, D. A. (1985). "The Strategic Diversity Classification System: A Framework for Decision Making." In W. D. Guth, ed., *Handbook of Business Strategy*. New York: Warren, Groman, and Lamont.

Nayyar, P. R. (1992). "On the Measurement of Corporate Diversification Strategy: Evidence from Large U.S. Service Firms." *Strategic Management Journal*, 13: 219–235.

Nelson, R. R. (1991). "Why Do Firms Differ, and How Does it Matter?" *Strategic Management Journal*, 12: 61–74.

Nelson, R. R., and Winter, S. (1982). *An Evolutionary Theory of Economic Change*. Cambridge, Mass.: Belknap Press.

Oster, S. (1982). "Interindustry Structure and the Ease of Strategic Change." *Review of Economics and Statistics*, 64: 376–384.

Palepu, K. (1985). "Diversification Strategy, Profit Performance and the Entropy Measure." *Strategic Management Journal*, 6: 239–255.

Peters, T. J., and Waterman, R. H., Jr. (1982). *In Search of Excellence*. New York: Harper and Row.

Pitts, R. A. (1976). "Diversification Strategies and Policies of Large Diversified Firms." *Journal of Economics and Business*, 28 (2): 181–188.

Pitts, R. A. (1977). "Strategies and Structures for Diversification." *Academy of Management Journal*, 20 (2): 197–208.

Porter, M. E. (1980). *Competitive Strategy: Techniques for Analyzing Industries and Competitors.* New York: The Free Press.

Porter, M. E. (1985). *Competitive Advantage: Creating and Sustaining Superior Performance.* New York: The Free Press.

Quinn, J. B. (1977). "Strategic Goals: Process and Politics." *Sloan Management Review*, 18: 21–37.

Quinn, J. B. (1978). "Strategic Change: 'Logical Incrementalism.'" *Sloan Management Review*, 19: 7–21.

Quinn J. B. (1980a). *Strategies for Change: Logical Incrementalism.* Homewood, IL: Irwin.

Quinn, J. B. (1980b). "Managing Strategic Change." *Sloan Management Review*, 21: 3–20.

Ramanujam, V., and Varadarajan, P. (1989). "Research on Corporate Diversification: A Synthesis." *Strategic Management Journal*, 10: 523–551

Roll, R., and Ross, S. (1994). "On the Cross-sectional Relation between Expected Returns and Betas." *Journal of Finance*, 49 (1): 101–121.

Ruefli, T. W., ed. (1990a). *Ordinal Time Series Analysis: Methodology and Applications in Management Strategy and Policy.* Westport, Conn.: Quorum Books.

Ruefli, T. W. (1990b). "Mean Variance Approaches to Risk-Return Relationships in Strategy: Paradox Lost." *Management Science*, 36 (3): 368–380.

Ruefli, T. W. (1991). "Reply to Bromiley's Comment and Further Results: Paradox Lost Becomes Dilemma Found." *Management Science*, 37 (9): 1210–1215.

Ruefli, T. W., and Ashmos, D. (1990). "Strategy, Structure and Corporate Performance." Chapter 6 in Timothy W. Ruefli, ed., *Ordinal Time Series Analysis: Methodology and Applications in Management Strategy and Policy.* Westport, Conn.: Quorum Books.

Ruefli, T. W., and Wiggins, R. R. (1994). "When Mean Square Error Becomes Variance: A Comment on 'Business Risk and Return: A Test of Simultaneous Relationships.'" *Management Science*, 40 (6): 750–759.

Ruefli, T. W. and Wilson, C. L. (1987). "Ordinal Time Series Methodology for Industry and Competitive Analysis." *Management Science*, 33 (5): 640–662.

Rumelt, Richard P. (1974). *Strategy, Structure and Economic Performance.* Boston, Mass.: Graduate School of Business Administration, Harvard University.

Rumelt, R. P. (1982). "Diversification Strategy and Profitability." *Strategic Management Journal*, 3: 359–369.

Rumelt, R. P. (1978). "Data Bank on Diversification Strategy and Corporate Structure." Working paper MGL-55, University of California at Los Angeles.

Rumelt, R. P. (1991). "How Much Does Industry Matter?" *Strategic Management Journal*, 12: 67–185.

Rumelt, R. P., Schendel, D., and Teece, D. J. (1991). "Strategic Management and Economics." *Strategic Management Journal*, 12: 5–29.

Salter, M. S., and Weinhold, W. A. (1979). *Diversification through Acquisitions: Strategies for Creating Economic Value.* New York: The Free Press.

Schendel, D. E., and Patton, G. R. (1976). "Corporate Turn-around Strategies: A Study of Profit Decline and Recovery." *Journal of General Management*, Spring: 3–11.

Scherer, Frederick M. (1980). *Industrial Market Structure and Economic Performance.* Chicago, Ill.: Rand McNally.

Simon, H. A. (1957). *Models of Man.* New York: John Wiley.

Singh, H., and Montgomery, C. A. (1987). "Corporate Acquisition Strategies and Economic Performance." *Strategic Management Journal,* 8: 377–386.

Smith, K., and Grimm, C. M. (1987). "Environmental Variation, Strategic Change, and Firm Performance: A Study of Railroad Deregulation." *Strategic Management Journal,* 8: 363–376.

Snow, C., and Hambrick, D. (1980). "Measuring Organizational Strategies: Some Theoretical and Methodological Problems." *Academy of Management Review,* 5: 363–376.

Thompson, J. (1967). *Organizations in Action.* New York: McGraw-Hill.

Tushman, M. L., and Anderson, P. (1986). "Technological Discontinuities and Organizational Environments." *Administrative Science Quarterly,* 31: 439–465.

Tushman, M. L., and Romanelli, E. (1985). "Organizational Evolution: A Metamorphosis Model of Convergence and Reorientation." In L. L. Cummings and B. Staw, eds, *Research in Organizational Behavior.* Greenwich, Conn.: JAI Press, 7: 171–222.

Varadarajan, P., and Ramanujam, V. (1987). "Diversification and Performance: A Reexamination Using a New Two-dimensional Conceptualization of Diversity in Firms." *Academy of Management Journal,* 30: 380–397.

Wernerfeldt, B., and Karnani, A. (1987). "Competitive Strategy Under Uncertainty." *Strategic Management Journal,* 8: 187–194.

Wernerfeldt, B., and Montgomery, C. A. (1986). "What is an Attractive Industry?" *Management Science,* 32: 1223–1230.

Wiersema, M. F., and Bantel, K. A. (1992). "Top Management Team Demography and Corporate Strategic Change." *Academy of Management Journal,* 35 (1): 91–121.

Williamson, O. E. (1975). *Markets and Hierarchies.* New York: The Free Press.

Woo, C. Y., and Willard, G. (1993). "Performance Representation in Business Policy Research: Discussion and Recommendation." Paper presented at 23rd Annual National Meeting of the Academy of Management, Dallas.

Wrigley, L. (1970). "Divisional Autonomy and Diversification." DBA dissertation Harvard University.

Zajac, E. J., and Kraatz, M. S. (1993). "A Diametric Forces Model of Strategic Change: Assessing the Antecedents and Consequences of Restructuring in the Higher Education Industry." *Strategic Management Journal,* 14: 83–102.

Zajac, E. J., and Shortell, S. M. (1989). "Changing Generic Strategies: Likelihood, Direction, and Performance Implications." *Strategic Management Journal,* 10: 413–430.

Part III
NEW SCIENCE

13

The Role of Basic Research in Developing New Treatments for Parkinson's Disease

Creed W. Abell and Sau-Wah Kwan

In the late 1970s, a major effort in the psychiatric community began to focus on attempting to identify biological markers for behavioral disorders such as schizophrenia and depression. Although definitive identification of defective components in the central nervous system (CNS) has been frustratingly elusive, a few hypotheses have emerged that promise to increase our understanding of these disorders. For example, the catecholamine hypothesis, which proposes that elements of certain neurotransmitter systems malfunction (e.g., the dopamine system), is supported by considerable experimental evidence.

Neurotransmitters such as dopamine are a group of messengers that are responsible for relaying signals between individual neurons. The dopamine system is made up of different but related subsystems of nerve cells or neuronal pathways that make and use dopamine as a neurotransmitter. One of these pathways is responsible for the control of movement and has been shown to be defective in Parkinson's disease. Alteration of this pathway is also responsible for the movement disorders commonly observed in schizophrenic patients who have been treated with high levels of neuroleptic drugs. Another neuronal pathway in the dopamine system has been linked to brain functions that control emotion.

Many of the drugs that can cause psychotic behavior and several major classes of drugs used to treat psychoses have known effects on the dopamine system. Although in most cases the precise role of dopamine in behavior is still undetermined, direct or indirect evidence has linked one or more components of the dopamine system to schizophrenia, depression, alcoholism, Parkinson's disease, Alzheimer's disease, Tourette's syndrome, migraine, and essential hypertension.

To function properly, the dopamine system must perform three critical processes. First, the synthesis, storage, and release of dopamine at appropriate levels is required for communication between neurons. Second, when it is no longer needed or when excess amounts are present, dopamine is broken down into an inactive substance by the enzyme monoamine oxidase (MAO), in order to maintain proper control of communication between brain cells. Third, dopamine released from one neuron (the presynaptic neuron) must bind to receptors located on the membrane surface of the target neuron (the postsynaptic neuron). Malfunctions at any one of these steps could result in the sending of inappropriate or distorted messages within the brain. Long-term recurrence of such errors could also cause cumulative damage to brain cells and progressive mental deterioration with age. Since the second of these processes, the breakdown of neurotransmitters by MAO, has been implicated in schizophrenia and depression, we decided to characterize the molecular properties of this important neurotransmitter-degrading enzyme.

PRODUCTION OF ANTIBODIES THAT RECOGNIZE TWO ENZYME FORMS (MAO A AND B)

MAO, which is located in the outer membrane of organelles in the cell called mitochondria, catalyzes the breakdown of the major amine neurotransmitters, dopamine, norepinephrine, and serotonin. Two forms of the enzyme (A and B) have been distinguished by their different response to various inhibitors and substrates (White and Tansik 1979; Johnston 1968), and it is reasonable to suggest that these enzymes could be located in different tissues and subsets of neurons. Consequently, we decided to examine the distribution of MAO A and B by using hybridoma technology to produce monoclonal antibodies that recognize either MAO A or B and that exhibit undetectable cross-reactivity for the alternate form of the enzyme. A preparation in which MAO represented 20–30 percent of the total protein was used to immunize BALB/c mice. One clone produced an antibody, MAO B-1C2, which recognized both inactive and catalytically active MAO B (Denney et al. 1982). To verify the specificity of the proteins recognized, MAO B-1C2 was used in immunoaffinity chromatography to resolve MAO B from MAO A in crude mitochondrial preparations of human liver (which contains both forms of the enzyme).

Using a similar strategy, several monoclonal antibodies that recognize purified human placental MAO A were produced and characterized (Kochersperger et al. 1985; Westlund et al. 1993). MAO A- or B-specific antibodies were then used to visualize the location of these enzymes in peripheral tissues and selected regions of monkey and human brain (Westlund et al. 1985, 1988) and to measure the concentration of MAO B in blood platelets.

STUDIES OF MAO B CONCENTRATION AND ACTIVITY IN SCHIZOPHRENIC PATIENTS

Human blood platelets provide a convenient source to study MAO B in patients with neurological and psychiatric disorders because MAO A is not expressed in platelets. Platelet MAO B has been investigated extensively in psychiatric patients in attempts to establish this enzyme as a biological marker for schizophrenia. Many but not all studies found decreases in MAO activity, but the results are difficult to interpret because of numerous potential sources of variability, both in diagnostic classification of subjects and in preparation of biological materials. Rigorously defined diagnostic criteria are essential for the creation of relatively homogeneous subject groups. The development by psychiatrists of objective and operationally defined diagnostic classification systems has given rise to improved criteria for research diagnosis of schizophrenia and more reliable instruments for systematic gathering of data. For example, the Schedule for Affective Disorders and Schizophrenia (SADS) was developed by Endicott and Spitzer (1978) to allow accurate and uniform data collection for determination of diagnoses. The SADS is a semistructured interview that attempts to reduce information variance by providing a standardized format of specific questions. The SADS uses scaled scores which allow assessment of symptom severity and provides for a detailed description of current episode and past history.

Given that relatively homogeneous subject groups can be obtained for study, further confounding issues that influence platelet MAO B activity include age, sex, race, hormonal status, drug treatment (particularly neuroleptics), and dietary factors (Robinson et al. 1971; DeLisi et al. 1981; Sullivan et al. 1980). Furthermore, platelet MAO B activity assays in clinical studies are sensitive to changes in platelet preparation and assay procedures (Wyatt et al. 1980).

Using the monoclonal antibody (MAO B-1C2) elicited to human platelet MAO B, a novel radioimmunoassay was used to compare MAO B concentrations in schizophrenics and age- and sex-matched controls (Fritz et al. 1986). Female schizophrenics showed no differences from female normal subjects in platelet MAO B activities and concentration, but male schizophrenics treated with neuroleptics expressed significantly reduced platelet MAO activity compared to untreated male patients (Rose et al. 1986). Compared with normal males, male schizophrenics showed significantly lowered enzyme activities along with elevated specific concentrations, which did not appear to be explained solely by neuroleptic drug usage. These results suggest that diminished enzyme activity in male schizophrenics may be due to the presence of an endogenous irreversible inhibitor or a genetically determined variant of MAO B. Future studies will use genetic approaches to seek to identify a defective gene or genes which could be associated with (e.g., a risk factor) or cause schizophrenia.

DISTRIBUTION OF MAO A AND B IN PERIPHERAL TISSUES

Although MAO A and B play a prominent role in the turnover of neurotransmitters in the brain, these enzymes are also found in peripheral tissues. To explore their distribution, immunocytochemical mapping experiments were performed in human platelets, lymphocytes, placenta, and liver (Thorpe et al. 1987). These are tissues in which activity measurements for both MAO A and MAO B had previously been reported. In our studies, MAO A was found in placenta and in liver, but was not found in platelets or lymphocytes. MAO B was visualized in platelets, lymphocytes, and liver, but not in placenta. Thus, liver cells express both forms of the enzyme. The immunocytochemical localization of MAO A and B were in agreement with previously reported activity assays in these tissues.

The different distributions of MAO A and B in tissues probably reflect independent physiologic roles of these enzymes. For example, MAO A in placenta may limit the transfer of bioactive amines across the placental barrier, thereby providing protection for the fetus. MAO B, in contrast, may provide tissue- or cell-specific protection by catalyzing the breakdown of amines that are derived from dietary or environmental sources.

DISTRIBUTION OF MAO A AND B IN PRIMATE BRAIN

In formalin-fixed monkey and human brain (Westlund, et al. 1985, 1988, 1993), positive immunocytochemical staining was observed for MAO A and B in distinct neurons throughout this tissue. Some staining was also observed in glial cells (support cells in the brain). In both species, the distribution of MAO A-positive neurons corresponded well with the sites of localization of catecholamine-containing neurons (e.g., dopamine). In contrast, the distribution of MAO B-positive neurons was identical to the distribution of serotonergic neurons (e.g., serotonin).

ROLE OF MAO A AND B IN PRIMATE BRAIN

The distinct pattern of distribution observed for MAO A and MAO B in relation to known classes of neurons may help to clarify the function of these enzymes in the brain, including their role in controlling neurotransmitter levels. The pattern of MAO distribution is unexpected, based on previous studies of substrate preference. In mitochondrial preparations of human brain, MAO B apparently does not oxidize serotonin (White and Tansik 1979). Oxidation of serotonin in serotonergic neurons would occupy only a very small fraction of the available enzyme unless serotonin concentrations rose to unusually high levels. Under normal conditions, serotonin would be taken up into storage vesicles to be conserved for physiologically activated neurotransmission. Indirect evidence also suggests that dopamine may be metabolized in humans by MAO B (Glover et al. 1977), and not MAO A, which is found in dopaminergic neurons.

These findings led us to conclude that the major role of MAO A and B in neurotransmitter-containing neurons may be to eliminate foreign amines and to minimize their access to storage vesicles. If the amine uptake system is not absolutely specific for the active neurotransmitter in each neuron, extraneous amines may have access to neurons in which they have no legitimate physiologic function. Protection at the nerve terminal level appears to be essential for the proper functioning of neurons.

IDENTIFICATION OF A PARKINSONIAN-PRODUCING NEUROTOXIN

In the early 1980s, several individuals with a history of drug addiction self-administered a synthetic heroin which caused a parkinsonian-like syndrome in some of them. The substance responsible for this effect was identified as MPTP, a powerful neurotoxin that was found as a contaminant in the heroin preparation.

Several lines of evidence support the concept that MPTP must be metabolized to yield an active toxin. Pretreatment of animals (primates) with the MAO B selective inhibitor deprenyl prevents the development of parkinsonism when challenged with MPTP (Langston et al. 1984; Cohen et al. 1984). Also, pretreatment of animals with a substrate of MAO B reduces or eliminates the neurotoxicity of MPTP (Melamed and Youdim 1985). In contrast, clorgyline (an inhibitor of the MAO A form of the enzyme) provides little or no protection from the dopamine-depleting effect of MPTP in mice (Heikkila et al. 1984). Furthermore, Castagnoli and his colleagues (Chiba et al. 1984) reported that extracts of rat brain mitochondria, which contain MAO, oxidized MPTP to a pyridinium species, MPP^+. We confirmed these studies by showing that preparations of pure human MAO B oxidize MPTP to MPP^+. MPP^+ has been identified as the major metabolite of MPTP in primate brain (Markey et al. 1984), and MPP^+ is taken up into dopamine-containing neurons in the substantia nigra via the major dopamine uptake system (Javitch et al. 1985).

The substantia nigra is the region in brain that makes dopamine, the neurotransmitter needed for normal movement. Thus, MAO B plays a critical role in converting the neurotoxin MPTP to MPP^+, which in turn is taken up and destroys cells in the substantia nigra.

CLONING AND SEQUENCING OF MAO A AND B

Despite the differences between MAO A and B in substrate and inhibitor preference, immunological properties, and localization, the true identity of their fundamental nature was unresolved until we isolated the DNA clones that encode these enzymes and determined their nucleotide and deduced amino acid sequences (Bach et al. 1988). The MAO A and B proteins consist of 527 and 520 amino acid residues with subunit molecular weights of 59,700 and 58,800, respectively. Comparison of these sequences shows that these enzymes have very high sequence identity (approximately 70 percent), but different amino acid residues occur at the same place throughout the polypeptide chains. This finding indicates that MAO A and B are derived from separate genes.

Cloning and nucleotide sequencing studies in other laboratories and by us have yielded the deduced amino acid sequences for human liver MAO A and B (Bach et al. 1988), human placental MAO A (Hsu et al. 1988), bovine adrenal MAO A (Powell et al. 1989), and rat liver MAO A and B (Kuwahara et al. 1990; Kwan and Abell 1992; Ito et al. 1988). Direct amino acid sequencing of one-third of bovine liver MAO B has also been achieved (Powell et al. 1989). Comparison of these proteins shows high sequence identity among each enzyme type (A or B) across species (human, bovine and rat). This information is useful in helping to identify functionally significant regions of the MAO molecules because such regions will be conserved in many species.

A NEW TREATMENT FOR PARKINSON'S DISEASE

Based on the findings that MPTP is activated by MAO B, which is located in specific subsets of brain cells and that MAO A and B are different proteins, Tetrud and Langston (1989) treated fifty-four patients diagnosed with early stage Parkinson's disease with deprenyl, a MAO B specific inhibitor. They found that this drug slowed the rate of disease progression by 40–83 percent as measured by five assessment scales, including motor examination, staging, stop-second test, activities of daily living, percentage of normal function, and depression. Subsequent studies of over eight hundred subjects (Parkinson Study Group 1989) confirmed these findings. Thus, fundamental work on the sequence and function of the MAO enzymes fortuitously led to a new useful treatment of a severe debilitating neurological disorder.

FUTURE DIRECTIONS

Our nucleotide and amino acid sequencing work has put to rest the long controversy over the fundamental difference between MAO A and B by showing that these enzymes are different proteins derived from different genes. This knowledge now sets the stage for determining the three-dimensional structure of these enzymes so that novel drugs (inhibitors) can be designed to treat neurological and psychiatric disorders such as Parkinson's disease, where MAO B is the target, and depression, where MAO A is the target.

Current interest in MAO A has been intensified by the discovery of a defective MAO A gene, due to a mutation in the DNA in some members of a Dutch family who exhibited abnormal aggressive behavior (Brunner et al. 1993). This finding is highly significant because it directly links a specific faulty component (a neurotransmitter-degrading enzyme) in the brain with an alteration in normal behavior. Frequently, when one mutation in a particular gene is identified, many others are subsequently found. I speculate that such mutations could be associated with behavioral disorders other than abnormal aggressive behavior because of the complexity of the nervous system and the likely multifactoral causes of the major psychiatric disorders. Consequently, continued examination of MAO A in diverse patient populations should prove to be fruitful.

Interest in MAO B has also been sparked by the identification of an alternate form of MAO B in patients with Parkinson's disease (Kurth et al. 1993). This finding suggests that an inherited variant MAO B gene may be associated with a genetic predisposition for Parkinson's disease. These and additional studies of subjects with this variant MAO B gene may be useful for identifying individuals who are at increased risk for developing Parkinson's disease.

MAO A and B are the targets of drugs that are currently used to treat depression (MAO A inhibitors; Da Prada et al. 1989) and Parkinson's disease (MAO B inhibitors; Tetrud and Langston 1989). To date, none of the available drugs is totally satisfactory. Some of these drugs (e.g., parnate, which is used for depression) do not distinguish between MAO A and B, and some can produce life-threatening side effects such as hypertensive crisis. In order to design new drugs that have greater selectivity and efficacy for these diseases, it is necessary to elucidate structurally functional regions of MAO A and B, including their active sites. Since the amino acid sequences of these proteins are now known and structural information is forthcoming, the future holds the promise that novel drugs will be developed for these and other neurological and psychiatric disorders.

ACKNOWLEDGMENT

We wish to express our deepest appreciation to George Kozmetsky, Director of the IC^2 Institute, for his generous support and continuing encouragement on our work during the past eight years.

REFERENCES

Bach, A.W.J., Lan, N. D., Johnson, D. L., Abell, C. W., Bembenek, M. E., Kwan, S-W., Seeburg, P. H., and Shih, J. C. (1988). "cDNA Cloning of Human Liver Monoamine Oxidase A and B: Molecular Basis of Differences in Enzymatic Properties." *Proc. Natl. Acad. Sci.*, 85: 4934–4938.

Brunner, H. G., Nelen, M., Breakefield, X. O., Ropers, H. H., and van Oost, B. A. (1993). "Abnormal Behavior Associated with a Point Mutation in the Structural Gene for Monoamine Oxidase A." *Science*, 262: 578–580.

Chiba, K., Trevor, A., and Castagnoli, N., Jr. (1984). "Metabolism of the Neurotoxic Tertiary Amine, MPTP, by Brain Monoamine Oxidase." *Biochem. Biophys. Res. Commun.*, 120: 574–578.

Cohen, G., Pasik, P., Cohen, B., Leist, A., Mytilineos, C., and Yahr, M. D. (1984). "Pargyline and Deprenyl Prevent the Neurotoxicity of 1-methyl-4-phenyl-1,2,3,6-tetrahydropyridine (MPTP) in Monkeys." *Eur. J. Pharmacol.* 106: 209–210.

Da Prada, M. D., Kettler, R., Keller, H. H., Burkard, W. P., and Haefely, W. E. (1989). "Preclinical Profiles of the Novel Reversible MAO-A Inhibitors, Moclobemide and Brofaromine, in Comparison with Irreversible MAO Inhibitors." *J. Neural. Transm.*, 28, 5–20.

DeLisi, L. E., Wise, C. D., Bridge, T. P., Rosenblatt, J. E., Wagner, R. L., Morihisa, J., Karson, C., Potkin, S. G., and Wyatt, R. J. (1981). "A Probable Neuroleptic Effect on Platelet Monoamine Oxidase in Chronic Schizophrenic Patients." *Psychiatry Research*, 4: 95.

Denney, R. M., Fritz, R. R., Patel, N. T., and Abell, C. W. (1982). "Human Liver MAO-A and MAO-B Separated by Immunoaffinity Chromatography with MAO-B-Specific Monoclonal Antibody." *Science*, 215: 1400–1403.

Endicott, J., and Spitzer, R. L. (1978). "A Diagnostic Interview: The Schedule for Affective Disorders and Schizophrenia." *Archives of General Psychiatry*, 35: 837.

Fritz, R. R., Abell, C. W., Denney, R. M., Denney, C. B., Bessman, J. D., Boeringa, J. A., Castellani, S., Lankford, D. A., Malek-Ahmadi, P., and Rose, R. M. (1986). "Platelet MAO Concentration and Molecular Activity: I. New Methods Using an MAO B-Specific Monoclonal Antibody in a Radioimmunoassay." *Psychiatry Research*, 17: 129–140.

Glover, V., Sandler, M., Owen, F., and Riley, G. J. (1977). "Dopamine Is a Monoamine Oxidase B Substrate in Man." *Nature*, 265: 80–81.

Heikkila, R. E., Manzino, L., Cabbat, F. S., and Duvoisin, R. C. (1984). "Protection Against the Dopaminergic Neurotoxicity of 1-methyl-4-phenyl-1,2,5,6-tetrahydropyridine by Monoamine Oxidase Inhibitors." *Nature*, 311: 467–469.

Hsu, Y.-P. P., Weyler, W., Chen, S., Sims, K. B., Rinehart, W. B., Utterback, M., Powell, J. F., and Breakefield, X. O. (1988). "Structural Features of Human Monoamine Oxidase A Elucidated from cDNA and Peptide Sequences." *J. Neurochem.*, 51: 1321–1324.

Ito, A., Kuwahara, T., Inadome, S., and Sagara, Y. (1988). "Molecular Cloning of a cDNA for Rat Liver Monoamine Oxidase B." *Biochem. Biophys. Res. Commun.*, 157: 970–976.

Javitch, J. A., and Snyder, S. H. (1984). "Uptake of MPP$^+$ by Dopamine Neurons Explains Selectivity of Parkinsonism-Inducing Neurotoxin, MPTP." *Eur. J. Pharmacol.*, 106: 455–456.

Johnston, J. P. (1968). "Some Observations upon a New Inhibitor of Monoamine Oxidase in Brain Tissue." *Biochem. Pharmacol.*, 17: 1285–1297.

Kochersperger, L. M., Waguespack, A., Patterson, J. C., Hsieh, C. C. W., Weyler, W., Salach, J. I., and Denney, R. M. (1985). "Immunological Uniqueness of Human Monoamine Oxidases A and B: New Evidence from Studies with Monoclonal Antibodies to Human Monoamine Oxidase A." *J. Neurosci.*, 11: 2874–2881.

Kurth, J. H., Matthias, C. K., Poduslo, S. E., and Schwankhaus, J. D. (1993). "Association of a Monoamine Oxidase B Allele with Parkinson's Disease." *Ann. Neurol.*, 33: 368–372.

Kuwahara, T., Takamoto, S., and Ito, A. (1990). "Primary Structure of Rat Monoamine Oxidase A Deduced from cDNA and its Expression in Rat Tissues." *Agric. Biol. Chem.*, 54: 253–257.

Kwan, S.-W., and Abell, C. W. (1992). "cDNA Cloning and Sequencing of Rat Monoamine Oxidase A: Comparison with the Human and Bovine Enzymes." *Comp. Biochem. Physiol.*, 102B: 143–147.

Langston, J. W., Irwin, I., Langston, E. B., and Forno, L. S. (1984). "Pargyline Prevents MPTP-Induced Parkinsonism in Primates." *Science*, 225: 1480–1482.

Markey, S. P., Johannessen, J. N., Chiueh, C. C., Burns, R. S., and Herkenham, M. A. (1984). "Intraneuronal Generation of a Pyridium Metabolite May Cause Drug-Induced Parkinsonism." *Nature*, 311: 464–467.

Melamed, E., and Youdim, M.B.H. (1985). "Prevention of Dopaminergic Toxicity of MPTP in mice by Phenylethylamine, a Specific Substrate of Type B Monoamine Oxidase." *Br. J. Pharmacol.,* 86: 529–531.

The Parkinson Study Group. (1989). "Effect of Deprenyl on the Progression of Disability in Early Parkinson's Disease." *N. Eng. J. Med.,* 321: 1364–1371.

Powell, J. F., Hsu, Y.-P. P., Weyler, W., Chen, S., Salach, J. I., Andrikopoulos, K., Mallet, J., and Breakefield, X. O. (1989). "The Primary Structure of Bovine Monoamine Oxidase Type A." *Biochem. J.,* 259: 407–413.

Robinson, D. S., Davis, J. M., Nies, A., Ravaris, C. L., and Sylvester, D. (1971). "Relation of Sex and Aging to Monoamine Oxidase Activity of Human Brain, Plasma, and Platelets." *Archives of General Psychiatry,* 24: 536.

Rose, R. M., Castellani, S., Boeringa, J. A., Malek-Ahmadi, P., Lankford, D. A., Bessman, J. D., Fritz, R. R., Denney, C. B., Denney, R. M., and Abell, C. W. (1986). "Platelet MAO Concentration and Molecular Activity: II. Comparison of Normal and Schizophrenic Populations." *Psychiatry Research,* 17: 141–151.

Sullivan, J. L., Coffey, C. E., Sullivan, P. D., Taska, R., Mahorney, S., and Cavenar, J. O. (1980). "Metabolic Factors Affecting Monoamine Oxidase Activity." *Schizophrenia Bulletin,* 6: 308.

Tetrud, J. W., and Langston, J. W. (1989). "The Effect of Deprenyl (Selegiline) on the Natural History of Parkinson's Disease." *Science,* 245: 519–522.

Thorpe, L. W., Westlund, K. N., Kochersperger, L. M., Abell, C. W., and Denney, R. M. (1987). "Immunocytochemical Localization of Monoamine Oxidases A and B in Human Peripheral Tissues and Brain." *J. Histochem. and Cytochem.* 35: 23–32.

Westlund, K. N., Denney, R. M., Kochersperger, L. M., Rose, R. M., and Abell, C. W. (1985). "Distinct Monoamine Oxidase A and B Populations in Primate Brain." *Science,* 230: 181–183.

Westlund, K. N., Denney, R. M., Rose, R. M., and Abell, C. W. (1988). "Localization and Function of Monoamine Oxidases A and B." *Neurosci.,* 25: 439–456.

Westlund, K. N., Krakower, T. J., Kwan, S.-W., and Abell, C. W. (1993). "Intracellular Distribution of Monoamine Oxidase A in Selected Regions of Rat and Monkey Brain and Spinal Cord." *Brain Res.,* 612: 221–230.

White, H. L., and Tansik, R. L. (1979). "Characterization of Multiple Substrate Binding Sites of MAO." In Singer, T. P., von Korff, R. W., and Murphy, D. L., eds. *Monamine Oxidase: Structure, Function, and Altered Functions.* New York: Academic Press, pp. 129–144.

Wyatt, R. J., Potkin, S. G., Bridge, T. P., Phelps, B. H., and Wise, C. D. (1980). "Monoamine Oxidase in Schizophrenia: An Overview." *Schizophrenia Bulletin,* 6: 199.

14

Drugs as Probes for Intrinsic and Protein-Induced Bending of DNA

Laurence H. Hurley and Daekyu Sun

One of the most important problems in contemporary science today is discovering how human cells regulate their growth and reproduction. While it is clear that this is a complex system, how the many biochemical components such as proteins and nucleic acids interact together to realize this control is poorly understood. In the project described in this chapter, a small molecular weight molecule is used as a probe to determine the importance of DNA bending as an architectural feature of control processes.

(+)-CC-1065 is a biologically potent small molecular weight molecule that reacts with DNA in a well-defined manner to bend the helix by about 30 degrees. In this chapter we describe the use of (+)-CC-1065 to determine the sites of protein-induced bending of DNA. The application to two proteins is described: Spl, a transcription factor involved in control of gene expression, and Mu transposase, a protein involved in recombination.

This chapter reports a summary of results from recent studies of protein-induced bending of DNA, using a small molecular weight probe that is also a potent antitumor agent. This chapter is written from the standpoint of the utility of these findings for pharmaceutical research that provides a possible explanation for the potent biological effects of these drugs and also provides a molecular tool for examining protein-induced bending of DNA. These results have utility for society as well as science, because a knowledge of how these drugs interact with DNA has led to the development of three new anticancer agents which are currently being evaluated in patients for their anticancer activity.

INTRODUCTION

Bending of DNA double helices can be either induced or intrinsic. Intrinsic bends occur as a direct consequence of DNA sequence and, as such, are built into the DNA. Induced bends, on the other hand, occur when an external force imposes the bending on a normally straight helix. The external force may be imposed by a protein, such as the transcriptional factor TFIID; a nuclesome; or in select cases, a small DNA binding ligand, such as (+)-CC-1065. Intrinsic bends are most commonly associated with A-tracts and have been the subject of extensive structural analysis (Hagerman 1990).

The possibility has recently been raised of the functional importance of bent DNA, because of the surprising ubiquity of inherently curved DNA segments in biological systems (Zahn and Blattner 1987; McAllister and Achberger 1989; Travers 1990; Hagerman 1990). In addition, it was recently reported that DNA–protein interactions can be attenuated by the presence of intrinsic sequence-dependent DNA curvature (Shatzky-Schwarz et al. 1992).

(+)-CC-1065 (Figure 14.1) is an extremely potent antitumor antibiotic produced by *Streptomyces zelensis* (Hanka et al. 1978). (+)-CC-1065 reacts with double-stranded DNA through N3 of a reactive adenine, forming a covalent adduct (Figure 14.2) that overlaps a 5-bp[1] region in the minor groove (Swenson et al. 1982; Hurley et al. 1984; Scahill et al. 1990). (+)-CC-1065 consists of a CPI subunit (subunit A in Figure 14.2) and two repeating pyrroloindole subunits (subunits B and C in Figure 14.2) attached via amide linkages that are approximately 15° out of plane, providing the drug molecule with a right-handed twisted banana shape (Chidester et al. 1981). The CPI subunit contains the DNA reactive cyclopropane ring that alkylates N3 of adenine when it binds within certain reactive sequences (Reynolds et al. 1985).

The covalent linkage sites between (+)-CC-1065 and DNA have been determined (Hurley et al. 1984; Scahill et al. 1990), and the predominant tautomeric species of the covalently modified adenine is the doubly protonated 6-amino form, with the additional positive charge delocalized over the entire adenine molecule (Lin and Hurley 1990). A consensus sequence analysis of the (+)-CC-1065 bonding sites on DNA reveals that there are two subsets of DNA sequences 5'-PuNTTA*[2] and 5'-AAAAA* that are highly specific (Reynolds et al. 1985). Surprisingly, the alkylating subunit alone contains sufficient structural information to encode the primary molecular basis for sequence selectivity (Hurley et al. 1988), and this subunit is also essential for antitumor activity (Warpehoski et al. 1988; Warpehoski and Hurley 1988). However, as we have previously demonstrated, the noncovalent binding interactions of the B and C subunits with DNA can modulate or fine-tune this sequence selectivity (Hurley et al. 1988) and, in the case of (+)-CC-1065, produce winding of DNA (Lee et al. 1991).

The covalent bonding reaction of (+)-CC-1065 with DNA has been proposed to involve catalytic activation of the covalent reaction between (+)-CC-1065 and DNA and to be at least partially responsible for the molecular basis for sequence selective recognition of DNA by the alkylating subunit of (+)-CC-1065 (Warpehoski and Hurley 1988; Lin et al. 1991a). In addition to catalytic activation, we have also proposed that DNA conformational flexibility is an important component of sequence recognition in the (+)-CC-1065 bonding reaction (Hurley et al. 1988).

Figure 14.1
Reaction of (+)-CC-1065 with N3 of Adenine in DNA and Products from Thermal Cleavage Reaction

Species A is the product produced by thermal treatment and species B is the product produced by thermal and subsequent piperidine treatment. The exact nature of the species generated on the 5' side of the strand break is unknown.

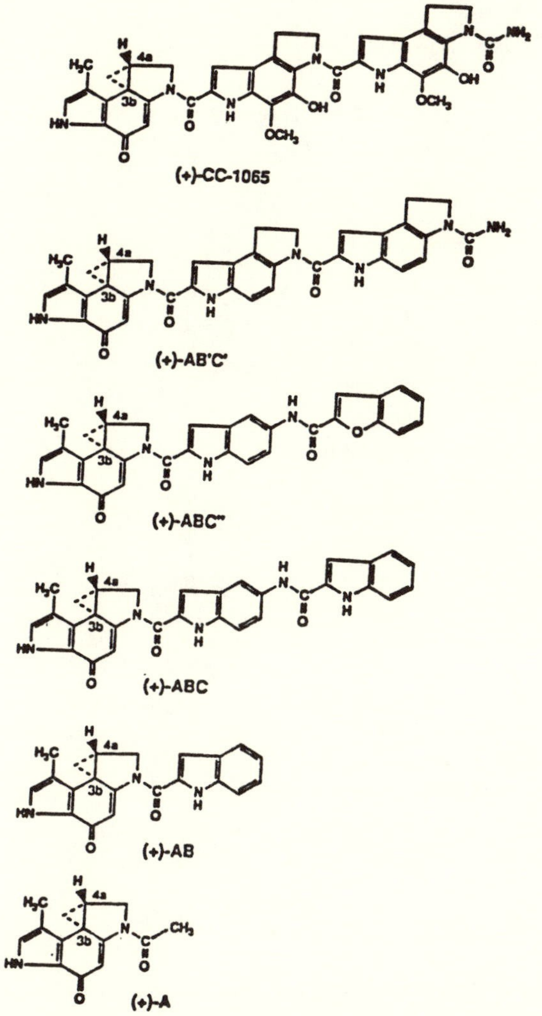

In this review, we summarize the evidence for (+)-CC-1065-induced bending of DNA, describe the structural effect of (+)-CC-1065 on intrinsic bending of DNA associated with A-tracts, and propose a truncated junction bend model for the (+)-CC-1065 entrapped/induced bending of DNA. Last, we briefly describe the application of (+)-CC-1065 as a probe of Sp1 and Mu-transposase bending of DNA.

Figure 14.2
Structures of (+)-CC-1065 and Its Synthetic Analogs Used in This Investigation

Compounds shown all have the same stereochemistry as the naturally occurring (+)-CC-1065.

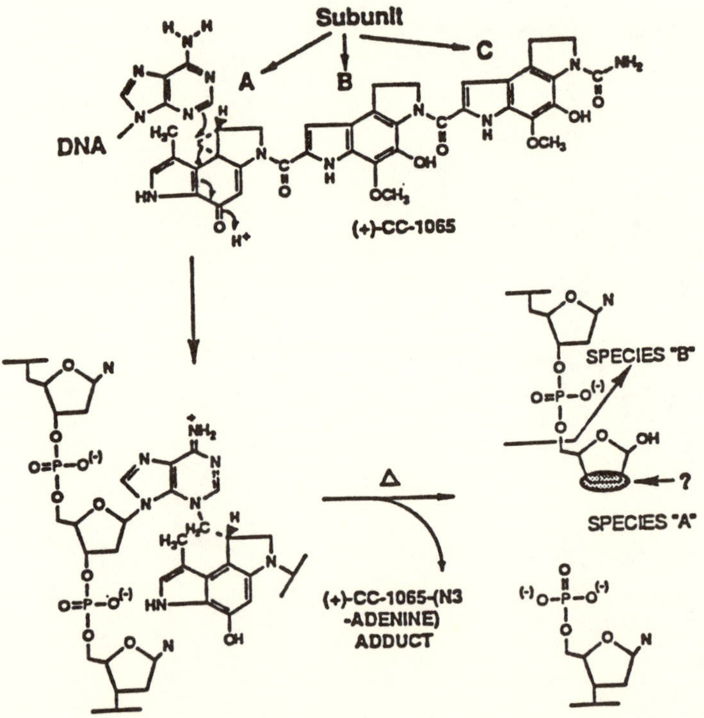

COVALENT MODIFICATION OF DNA LEADS TO BENDING OF DNA

When A-tracts occur in-phase with the helical turn, the individual bends add up to a large overall bend in ligated multimers, which shows an increasing change in R_L values (ratio of apparent size to true size) at higher molecular weight. In contrast, when A-tracts occur 180° out-of-phase with the helical turn, the bends cancel out each other, resulting in a constant change in R_L values at higher molecular weight (Koo et al. 1986). In order to study the effect of varying the distance between (+)-CC-1065 bonding sites on electrophoretic mobility, 17-, 19-, 20-, 21-, and 23-bp oligomers (Table 14.1A) were modified with (+)-CC-1065 and ligated into multimers, and their electrophoretic mobility was analyzed on an 8 percent nondenaturing polyacrylamide gel.

The autoradiogram of ligation products of non-drug-modified (C-lanes) and (+)-CC-1065-modified (D-lanes) 17-, 19-, 20-, 21-, and 23-bp oligomers is shown in Figure 14.3A. While drug-modified ligation products of 20 bp oligomers (lane 6) and 21-bp oligomers (about two times the normal helical turn of 10.5 bp) (lane 8) show considerable retardation in electrophoretic mobility compared to control ligation products (lanes 5 and 7), drug-modified ligation products of 17-, 19-, and 23-bp oligomers (lanes 2, 4, and 10) show little retardation in electrophoretic mobility compared to control ligation products (lanes 1, 3, and 9). The ratio of apparent size to true size (R_L) for each of the ligation products in Figure 14.3A was calculated and plotted against length in base pairs (Figure 14.3B). The increasing change in R_L values of ligation products of 20- and 21-bp oligomers indicates that (+)-CC-1065-induced bends are amplified as a consequence of coherent addition of in-phase (+)-CC-1065-induced bends. Ligation products of 17-, 19-, and 23-bp oligomers produce little change in R_L values because the bends are presumably out of phase. These results indicate that increasing change in R_L value is caused by (+)-CC-1065-induced bending of DNA, not by localized frictional effects of (+)-CC-1065-DNA adducts or the positive charge on the 6-amino tautomeric form (Lin and Hurley 1990) of the covalently modified adenine in the (+)-CC-1065–DNA adducts. The maximum retardation in electrophoretic mobility is achieved in 20-bp oligomers, thus indicating that the (+)-CC-1065-modified 20-bp oligomers are the most closely phased with the helical turn after drug bonding to DNA. This suggests that (+)-CC-1065 induces not only DNA bending but also DNA winding equivalent to about 1 bp per covalent modification site, because maximum bending occurs in 20-bp oligomers (2 times 10) rather than 21-bp oligomers (2 times 10.5).

In subsequent experiments using chloroquine, winding associated with the ethano bridges of the B and C subunits of (+)-CC-1065 was confirmed (Lee et al. 1991).

THE COVALENT BONDING REACTION IS RESPONSIBLE FOR THE BENDING PRODUCED BY (+)-CC-1065

Since the A subunit alone has sufficient structural information to mediate the sequence selectivity of the entire (+)-ABC molecule (Hurley et al. 1988), it was important to determine whether the covalent bonding of the A subunit to N3 of adenine is sufficient to mediate the DNA bending. A comparison of the electrophoretic mobility of ligation products modified with (+)-A, (+)-AB, and

Table 14.1
Sequences of the Synthetic Oligonucleotides Used in This Study*

A.	17bp	GAGCCATGATTACGGAT GGTACTAATGCCTACTC
	19bp	GAGACCATGATTACGGATT TGGTACTAATGCCTAACTC
	20bp	GAGACCATGATTACGGATTC TGGTACTAATGCCTAAGCTC
	21bp	GAGGACCTGATTACGGATTC CTGGTACTAATGCCTAAGCT
	23bp	GAGTGACCATGATTACGGATTCA ACTGGTACTAATGCCTAAGTCTC
B.	21-A-I bp	AAAAACCTGATTACGAGATTC TTGGACTAATGCTCTAAGTTT
	21-A-II bp	AAAAACCATGATTACGGATTC TTGGTACTAATGCCTAAGTTT
	21-A-III bp	AAAAACCATCGATTAGGATTC TTGGTAGCTAATCCTAAGTTT
	21-A-IV bp	AAAAACCATCGGATTAGATTC TTGGTAGCCTAATCTAAGTTT
C.	21-C	5' GAGGACCGGAAAAACGGATTC 3' 3' CTGGCCTTTTTGCCTAAGCTC 5'
	21-AT-1	5' AAAAAGGGCCCTTTTTCCGGG 3' 3' TTCCCGGGAAAAAGGCCCTTT 5'
	21-AT-2	5' AAAAAGGGCCCTTTTTCCCGGG 3' 3' TTCCGGGAAAAAGGGCCCTTT 5'
	21-AT-3	5' AAAAAGGGGCCCTTTTTCCGG 3' 3' TTCCCCGGGAAAAAGGCCTTT 5'

Duplexes were designed to expose three nucleotide asymmetric overhangs so as to ensure both head-to-tail ligation and to contain a unique bonding site (5'-GATTA) for drugs in the center of the sequences. (A) 17-, 19-, 20-, 21-, 22-, and 23-bp oligomers were used to study the effect of varying the distance between (+)-CC-1065 bonding sites on electrophoretic mobility and the 20 and 21 mer were also used to determine the percentage of circular *vs* noncircular DNA in (+)-CC-1065- and (+)-ABC-modified oligomers, respectively. (B) 21-A-I, 21-A-II, and 21-A-III bp oligomers were used to determine the direction and locus of (+)-ABC and (+)-CC-1065-induced bends relative to A$_5$-tract bends. (C) 21-C was used to determine the covalent modification site within the A$_5$-tract. 21-AT-1, 21-AT2, and 21-AT-3 oligomers were used to determine the locus of (+)-ABC-modified A$_5$-tract.

Figure   14.3
**(A) Autoradiogram of the Ligation Products of 17-, 19-, 20-,
21-, and 23-bp Oligomers Modified with (+)-CC-1065 on an
Eight Percent Nondenaturing Polyacrylamide Gel**

Lanes 1, 3, 5, 7, and 9 are control ligation products (C) and lanes 2, 4, 6, 8, and 10
are ligation products of 28 mM (+)-CC-1065-modified oligomers (D). Arrow heads
indicate the location of the monomer (M) and dimer (D).

**(B) Plot of R_L Values Versus Total Length of Oligomers in
bps from the Ligation Products of 17-, 19-, 20-, 21-, and
23-bp Oligomers Modified with (+)-CC-1065**

R_L values were obtained from the results of experiments shown in panel A.

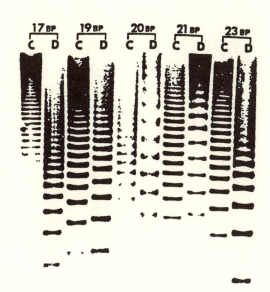

Reprinted with permission from Lee, et al., "Determination of the Structural Features
of (+)-CC-1065 that are Responsible for Bending, Winding, and Stiffening of DNA."
Chem. Res. Toxicol 4 (1991): 203-213. Copyright © 1991 American Chemical
Society.

(+)-ABC in 20- and 21-bp oligomers showed that the A subunit produced slightly more retardation than (+)-AB or (+)-ABC (Lee et al. 1991). These results, presented here as a histogram (Figure 14.4B), show that DNA bending occurs as a consequence of the covalent bonding reaction of the A subunit with DNA. Consequently, the A subunit alone has sufficient structural information to mediate the DNA bending produced by (+)-ABC. In contrast to the results with (+)-CC-1065 and (+)-AB'C' (Lee et al. 1991), (+)-ABC subunit-modified ligation products produce more retardation in electrophoretic mobility in 21-bp oligomers than in 20-bp oligomers (Figure 14.4A). This result is consistent with the suggestion made previously that the inside edge substituents of (+)-CC-1065 and (+)-AB'C' are associated with winding of DNA, since (+)-A, (+)-AB, and (+)-ABC lack these substituents.

Figure 14.4
Histogram of the R_L-1 Values of Octamers of 19-, 20-, 21-, and 23-bp Oligomers Modified with 2.8 mM (+)-A, 0.28 mM (+)-AB, and 28 mM (+)-ABC

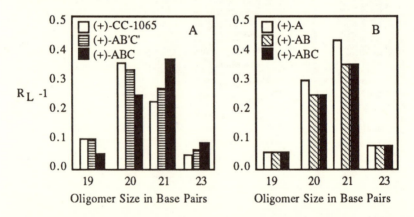

Reprinted with permission from Lee, et al., "Determination of the Structural Features of (+)-CC-1065 that are Responsible for Bending, Winding, and Stiffening of DNA." *Chem. Res. Toxicol* 4 (1991): 203-213. Copyright © 1991 American Chemical Society.

(+)-CC-1065 BENDS DNA INTO THE MINOR GROOVE BY ABOUT 14–18°

To determine the directionality of bending of DNA by (+)-CC-1065 and related drugs, and also the locus of the drug-induced bending, the four oligomers shown in Table 14.1B were used. It has been previously shown that the direction of A-tract-induced bending is in towards the minor groove, and that the center of the bend corresponds to the center of the A-tract (Koo et al. 1986; Koo and

Crothers 1988). The four oligomers I, II, III, and IV, listed in Table 14.1B, were designed to vary in distance between the center of the A-tract and the drug covalent modification site by 10, 11, 12, and 13 bps, respectively.

Nondenaturing gel electrophoresis of oligomers I, II, III, and IV (Table 14.1B) shows that modification with (+)-ABC and (+)-CC-1065 leads to increased retardation of gel mobility in comparison to non-drug-modified oligomers (unpublished results). Since oligomers I, II, III, and IV contain an A-tract that is separated by about one helical turn from the drug-bonding site, we conclude that both bends are in the same direction, for example, in toward the minor groove of DNA. A comparison of R_L values for a 5 multimer of these four oligomers modified with (+)-CC-1065 and (+)-ABC leads to some important conclusions (Figure 14.5). For (+)-ABC-modified oligomers the maximum bending occurs in oligomer III, in which 12 bp separate the center of the A-tract from the covalent modification site. This shows that optimum in-phase bending arises when one helical turn separates the center of the A-tract from the position between the two thymidines within the (+)-ABC recognition sequence (GATTA*) and consequently provides compelling evidence for the locus of drug-induced bending between two thymidines within the recognition sequence. However, for the (+)-CC-1065-induced bend, optimum bending occurs when 11 bp separate the center of the A-tract from the adjacent drug–DNA adduct site; i.e., oligomer II (Figure 14.5) produces maximum retardation. This is exactly what is expected, taking into account the earlier observation that (+)-CC-1065 induces the winding of DNA by the equivalent of about 1 bp per covalent modification and consequently reduces the bp number per two helical turns to 20.0. The overall decrease in R_L values of all oligomers modified with (+)-CC-1065 and the relatively small difference of R_L values between oligomers II and III modified with (+)-CC-1065 compared to those modified with (+)-ABC can be explained as follows. First, the overall decrease in R_L of all oligomers modified with (+)-CC-1065 relative to (+)-ABC is because (+)-CC-1065 produces a decrease in bp per helical turn between the A-tracts and consequent out-of-phase bending. Second, the relatively small difference in R_L between oligomers II and III for (+)-CC-1065 relative to (+)-ABC is because oligomer II is less out of phase compared to oligomer III, because there is one bp more per helical turn after (+)-CC-1065 modification than before. Most importantly, these results taken together show that the locus of bending is at the same site in the recognition sequence (i.e., between the two thymidines) for both (+)-ABC and (+)-CC-1065.

The estimate of bending angles in the 5'-GATTA* (A* is the covalent modification site) sequence produced by (+)-CC-1065, (+)-AB'C', (+)-ABC, (+)-AB, and (+)-A was calculated using a calibration equation for gel mobility anomalies derived by Koo and Crothers (1988). The 140 bp (heptamers of 20 bp-oligomers) for (+)-CC-1065 and (+)-AB'C', and 147 bp (heptamers of 21 bp oligomers) for (+)-A, (+)-AB, and (+)-ABC, were chosen because they are within the optimal range for the application of a calibration equation, and maximum retardation in electrophoretic mobility is achieved in 20-bp oligomers for (+)-CC-1065 and (+)-ABC' and in 21-bp oligomers for (+)-A, (+)-AB, and (+)-ABC. The sizes of oligomers, R_L values, and calculated bend angles for each compound are shown in Table 14.2. An estimate of (+)-AB- and (+)-ABC-induced bend angles (14°–18°) is smaller by 1°–2° than that of the A subunit-induced bend angle (15°–20°), suggesting that attachment of the B and C subunits to the A subunit reduces slightly the magnitude of the bending angle. (+)-AB'C' and (+)-CC-1065 apparently produce the same magnitude of DNA bending as the A subunit.

Figure 14.5
The Effect of Distances in bps between the Center of A_5-tract and the Drug Covalent Modification Site on R_L Values of 5-multimer of 21-A-I, 21-A-II, 21-A-III, and 21-A-IV Modified with (+)-CC-1065 and (+)-ABC

These oligomers were designed to vary in distance between the center of the A-tract and the following drug-covalent modification site by 10, 11, 12, and 13 bps, respectively.

  O = (+)-ABC-modified oligomers;
  ● = (+)-CC-1065-modified oligomers.

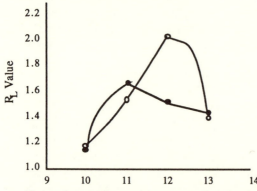

Distance between Center of A tract and Alkylation site (bp)

(+)-CC-1065 PREFERENTIALLY MODIFIES THE 3' ADENINE IN A-TRACTS

(+)-CC-1065 reacts preferentially at two conscensus sequences, 5'-PuNTTA* and 5'-AAAAA* (Reynolds et al. 1985). Significantly, in A-tracts the almost exclusive bonding site for (+)-CC-1065 is the 3'-adenine, which suggested to us and others (Koo et al. 1986) that the 3'-adenine of an A-tract has unique structural features that make it especially reactive to (+)-CC-1065. It is well known that the 3' terminal adenine junction in A-tracts has a unique structure (Koo et al. 1986; Koo and Crothers 1988; Nadeau and Crothers 1989;

Katahira et al. 1990). Confirmation of this unique reactivity of the 3' adenine in an A5 tract towards (+)-CC-1065, (+)-ABC", and (+)-ABC was shown by comparison of the reactivity of the adenines in the A-tract using gel electrophoresis (Lee et al. 1991). Overall, this result supports the junction model (Koo et al. 1986; Koo and Crothers 1988) that emphasizes the presence of a unique structure at the 3' junction of the A-tract. In addition, this implies a high level of sequence selectivity of (+)-CC-1065 and its analogs in order for them to be able to discriminate between the subtle differences in reactivity of the different adenines in an A5-tract.

Table 14.2
Calculation of DNA Bending Angles Produced by (+)-A, (+)-AB, (+)-ABC, (+)-AB'C', and (+)-CC-1065 in the 5'-GATTA* Sequence Contained in the 20- and 21-mer Oligomers Listed in Table 14.1

Compound	Size of oligomers	R_L value[a]	Bending angle, deg[b]	Optimum size for circularization, bp	Bending angle, deg, from the circularization[d]
(+)-A	21	1.310	14.9–19.8	c	c
(+)-AB	21	1.262	13.7–18.2	c	c
(+)-ABC	21	1.262	13.7–18.2	168	17.7
(+)-AB'C'	20	1.257	14.5–19.2	c	c
(+)-CC-1065	20	1.257	14.5–19.2	180	14.0

[a]R_L values were calculated from 147-bp ligation products for 21-bp oligomers and 140-bp ligation products for 20-bp oligomers.
[b]The estimate of bend angles of each compound was calculated using a calibration equation for gel mobility anomalies derived by Koo and Crothers (1988).
[c]Not determined.
[d]The bond angles of (+)-CC-1065 and (+)-ABC from the circularization experiment were determined by the method described in Husain et al. (1988).

COVALENT MODIFICATION OF THE 3' ADENINE OF AN A-TRACT WITH (+)-CC-1065 MOVES THE LOCUS OF BENDING TO THE 3' SIDE AND EXAGGERATES THE BENDING MAGNITUDE

To determine the effect of drug modification of the 3' adenine in an A5-tract on both the magnitude and locus of bending, AT-1, AT-2, and AT-3 (Table

14.1C) were modified at the 3' adenine with (+)-ABC. (+)-ABC was used rather than (+)-CC-1065 since the latter compound also produces winding of DNA (Lee et al. 1991) the equivalent of about 1 bp in addition to bending, which complicates the analysis of the results. The R_L values plotted in Figure 14.6 (filled symbols) show that in all three cases the R_L values are increased upon (+)-ABC bonding, relative to the unmodified A_5-tracts, but the R_L value of drug-modified AT-1 is increased more than that of AT-2, and that of AT-3 is intermediate between AT-1 and AT-2. Taken together, these results reveal that after drug modification the magnitude of bending is significantly increased and the locus of bending of the A_5-tract is moved about 0.5 bp to the 3' side of the central adenine in the drug-modified A_5-tract.

Figure 14.6
Plot of R_L Values Versus Total Length of Ligated Multimers in Multiplicity of Oligomers

The plots are shown for ligation products of

oligomer AT-1 (O)	oligomer AT-1 modified with (+)-ABC (●)
oligomer AT-2 (△)	oligomer AT-2 modified with (+)-ABC (▲)
oligomer AT-3 (□)	oligomer AT-3 modified with (+)-ABC (■)

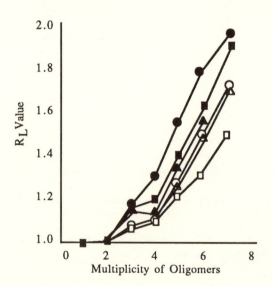

REACTION OF (+)-CC-1065 AT NON-A-TRACT SEQUENCES

Choice of the 12-mer Duplex for Detailed Structural Studies

During our initial studies designed to determine the DNA sequence specificity of (+)-CC-1065, we deliberately chose to study the early promoter region of SV40 DNA as a biologically interesting and relevant DNA target sequence (Kadonaga et al. 1986). Within this region there are two equivalent (+)-CC-1065 highly reactive adenine-containing sequences 5' AGTTA* (where * denotes the covalent attachment site) that occur as part of the two perfect 21-bp repeats (Scheme I). These repeats are part of the region of 63 bps containing the six GC boxes that are binding sites for the transcription factor Sp1.

In order to gain insight into the special reactivity of this sequence (5'-AGTTA*) to (+)-CC-1065 and deduce the structural basis for the (+)-CC-1065-induced bending of DNA, a detailed analysis of the one- and two-dimensional ^{1}H and ^{31}P NMR of the duplex (Lin et al. 1992) and its (+)-CC-1065–DNA adduct was carried out (Sun et al. 1993).

Scheme 1
The sequence and origin of the 12-mer duplex used in this study.
* The covalent bonding site of (+)-CC-1065.

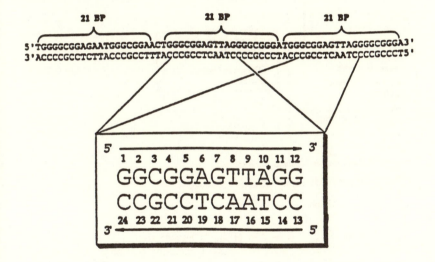

12-mer Duplex

In summary, the nonexchangeable proton (except some of the H5' and H5" protons), phosphorus resonance signals, and most of the exchangeable proton resonance signals of the 12-mer duplex were assigned by one- and two-dimensional proton and phosphorus NMR experiments (Lin et al. 1992). The 12-mer duplex maintains an overall B-form DNA with all anti base conformation throughout. Detailed examination of the 12-mer duplex by high-field NMR and hydroxyl-radical footprinting experiments reveals several local structural perturbations similar to those associated with an $(A)_n$ tract DNA duplex (Lin et

Figure 14.7
Summary Figure of the Unusual Structural Features
in the 12-mer Duplex

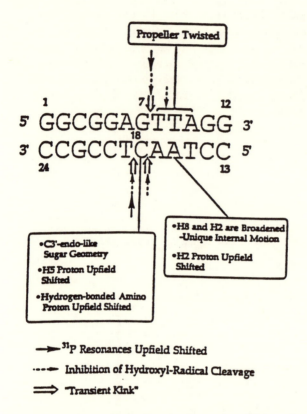

➤ ³¹P Resonances Upfield Shifted

---➤ Inhibition of Hydroxyl-Radical Cleavage

⟹ "Transient Kink"

Reprinted with permission from Lin et al., "Characterization of a 12-Mer Duplex d(GGCGGAGTTAGG)-(CCTAACTCCGCC) Containing a Highly Reactive (+)-CC Sequence by ¹H and ³¹P NMR, Hydroxyl-Radical Footprinting, and NOESY Restrained Molecular Dynamics Calculations." *Chem. Res. Toxicol.* 5 (1992): 167–182. Copyright © American Chemical Society.

al. 1992). For example, the propeller twisting between base pairs that was detected within the A·T-rich region in the 12-mer duplex is also found in DNA duplexes containing $(A)_n$ tracts. In addition, an unusual upfield-shifted aromatic resonance and compression of the minor groove is found adjacent to the 3' side of the AT-rich segment for both the 12-mer duplex and $(A)_n$ tract DNA duplex. The phosphorus resonances associated with the 7G–8T and 18C–19T steps of the 12-mer duplex, where the minor groove is narrowed, displayed unusual upfield chemical shifts. A unique local internal motion at 16A is detected at the nucleotide level. There is a pronounced local distortion centered around 18C, which is proposed to have an average C3'-endo sugar geometry. The NOESY-restrained molecular mechanics and dynamics calculations on the 12-mer sequence showed that on either side of 18C the backbone is distorted, being more compressed toward the major groove on the 5' side (i.e., at the 5'-AC/GT step) and elongated toward the major groove on the 3' side (i.e., at the 5'-CT/AG step). A summary of these unusual structural features in this 12-mer duplex sequence is provided in Figure 14.7. We propose that the propensity for a DNA sequence to adopt a bent-type structure is an important factor for the sequence selectivity of (+)-CC-1065. Furthermore, the high reactivity of this particular sequence with (+)-CC-1065 is at least in part due to the unique internal motion (i.e., conformational flexibility) and pronounced local distortion centered around 18C.

Comparison of 12-mer Duplex and 12-mer Duplex Adduct (Sun et al. 1993)

Hydroxyl-radical footprinting of the noncovalently modified strand of a 21 mer with either an unmodified or drug-modified 5'-AGTTA* sequence

A_5-tracts show a pattern of inhibition of hydroxyl-radical cleavage within the bending region (Burkhoff and Tullius 1987, 1988). The locus of bending occurs at the sites of greatest inhibition, which presumably correspond to the region of maximum narrowing of the minor groove. In comparison to the unmodified 21-Sp duplex (panel A in Figure 14.8), the drug-modified 21 mers (panels B, C, and D corresponding to (+)-CC-1065, (+)-ABC", and (+)-AB, respectively) all show an increased inhibition of cleavage to the 3' side of the covalently modified adenine. In general, inhibition occurs maximally 1 to 3 bp to the 3' side of this covalently modified bp, which is in good agreement with the locus of bending determined by nondenaturing gel analysis (see above).

Up- and down-field shifts of the A·T imino protons in the vicinity of the covalent bonding site

Up- and down-field shifts of A·T imino protons are associated with widening and narrowing of the minor groove of DNA, respectively (Lin et al. 1991b). A comparison of the exchangeable proton regions that include the imino proton of the 12-mer duplex and (+)-CC-1065 duplex adduct is show in Figure 14.9. While the imino protons for 8T·17A and 9T·16A move down-field by 0.25 and 0.77 ppm, respectively, the 10A·15T moves up-field by 2.07 ppm, the latter being indicative of base-pair opening at the covalent bonding site. These results are consistent with compression of the groove at around 8T to 9T and widening on both sides, but especially abruptly at the covalent modification site.

A TRUNCATED JUNCTION BEND MODEL FOR THE ENTRAPPED/INDUCED BENDING OF DNA IN THE (+)-CC-1065-12-MER DUPLEX ADDUCT AND AS A MECHANISM FOR SEQUENCE RECOGNITION OF DNA (SUN ET AL. 1993)

When a 21 mer containing the 12-mer duplex used in the NMR studies is ligated and subjected to nondenaturing gel electrophoresis, it does not show anomalous gel migration and therefore is unlikely to be bent (Sun and Hurley, unpublished results). However, hydroxyl-radical footprinting of the same 21-mer sequence shows inhibition of cleavage at 16A and 18C (see Figure 14.8). In addition, the proton NMR data reported here and elsewhere (Lin et al. 1992) provide further evidence for propeller twisting and corresponding narrowing of the minor groove in the A•T region between 7G–18C and 10A–15T. An unusual feature of this region of the duplex is the rapid local conformational flexibility of 16A. This local conformational flexibility is temperature dependent but is lost upon adduct formation with (+)-CC-1065 (Lin et al. 1992). We propose that this inherent conformation flexibility of the 5'-AGTTA* sequence is a contributing factor to sequence recognition by (+)-CC-1065.

Figure 14.8
Comparison of the Laser Densitometer Tracing of the Hydroxyl-Radical Footprinting of the Non-covalently Modified Strand of Oligomer 21-Sp without (A) and with Drug Modification by (+)-CC-1065 (B), (+)-ABC'' (C), and (+)-AB (C)

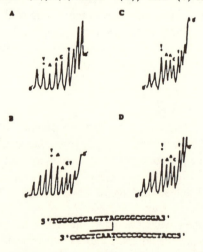

Reprinted with permission from Sun et al., "A-Tract and (+)-CC-1065-Induced Bending of DNA. Comparison of Structural Features Using Non-Denaturing Gel Analysis, Hydroxyl-Radical Footprinting, and High-Field NMR." *Biochemistry 32* (1993): 4487–4495. Copyright © 1993 American Chemical Society.

Figure   14.9
One-dimensional ^{1}H-NMR in 90% H_2O at 23 °C, Showing the Exchangeable Protons Region of: (A) the 12-mer Duplex and (B) the (+)-CC-1065–12-mer Duplex Adduct

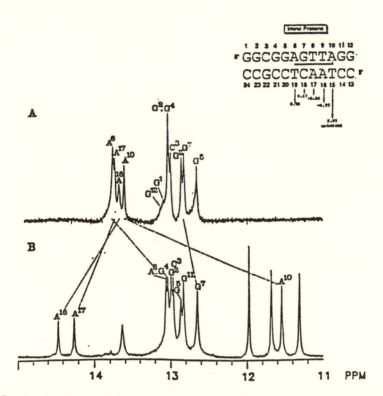

Reprinted with permission from Lin et al., "(+)-CC-1065 Produces Bending of DNA That Appears to Resemble Adenine/Thymine Tracts." *Chem. Res. Toxicol. 4* (1991): 21–26. Copyright © 1991 American Chemical Society.

Upon reaction with (+)-CC-1065, the unusual structural features of the 12-mer duplex become entrapped and exaggerated. The A·T region of the (+)-CC-1065–12-mer duplex adduct is even more highly propeller twisted than in the 12-mer duplex, and the sugar geometry of the 18C nucleotide moves more toward the C3'-endo region (Lin and Hurley, unpublished results). In addition, the kink angle at the 18C to 19T step is dramatically increased when compared with that of the same kink in the unmodified 12-mer duplex (Lin et al. 1992). These kinks create a junction around the 18C nucleotide on the noncovalently modified strand. In addition to this entrapped junction, another junction between the 9T and 10A steps on the covalently modified strand is also induced upon adduct formation. Overall, it appears that (+)-CC-1065 takes advantage of an existing propensity of this 12 mer to bend and, after covalent reaction at A10, consolidates and exaggerates this tendency. Our recent observations that (+)-CC-1065 can form an unusual covalent adduct with the guanine in the sequence 5'-AATTG* and a stable, noncovalent complex with the sequence 5'-GAATTC strongly support this hypothesis (Park and Hurley; Hansen and Hurley, unpublished observations). Based upon the junction bend model for an A-tract (Koo et al. 1986), we propose a "truncated junction bend model" for the (+)-CC-1065-entrapped/induced bend in the highly reactive sequence 5'-AGTTA* (see Scheme 2).

Scheme 2
Models for Bending of DNA. (A) The Junction Bend Model for A-tracts (Koo et al. 1986) and (B) the Truncated Junction Bend Model for the (+)-CC-1065-Entrapped/Induced Bend of 5'-AGTTA* (Sun et al. 1993)

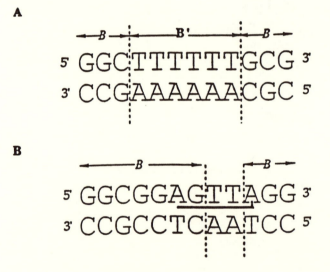

A

B

APPLICATION OF (+)-CC-1065 AS A PROBE FOR PROTEIN-INDUCED BENDING OF DNA

Transcriptional Factor Sp1

The structural details of the multimeric complex between Sp1 and the 21-bp repeat of the early promoter region of SV40 DNA have been probed by competition experiments with (+)-CC-1065, hydroxyl-radical footprinting, and circularization experiments (Sun and Hurley 1993). We have used hydroxyl-radical footprinting to probe the structural changes in DNA upon Sp1 binding to 21-bp repeats, cyclization experiment to examine Sp1-induced DNA bending of DNA, and (+)-CC-1065 as a probe for overall groove structure and reactivity after Sp1 binding to the 21-bp repeats. In hydroxyl-radical footprinting studies, the diminished cleavage of DNA backbone by hydroxyl-radical was observed in the region between each Sp1 bonding site. Generally, diminished hydroxyl-radical cleavage of DNA backbone can be attributed to either close contacts between sugar phosphate backbone and DNA binding ligand (e.g., small molecules or DNA binding proteins) or structural changes in minor groove geometry, such as narrowed minor groove due to DNA bending (Burkhoff and Tullius 1988; Yang and Nash 1989).

Our results show that upon Sp1 binding to the 21-bp repeat region, (+)-CC-1065 is still able to react in an apparently normal way at the sequence 5'-AGTTA*, which is located between two pairs of GC boxes, supporting the idea that this region does not make a close contact with Sp1 but adapts a bent DNA structure with associated compression of the minor groove. This evidence for Sp1-induced bending of the 21-bp repeats is also supported by the results of the ligation experiment using oligomers containing multimers of GC boxes, which favor circularization in the presence of saturating amounts of Sp1.

On the basis of the results of hydroxyl-radical footprinting and circularization experiments, we have shown that the six Sp1 molecules make similar contacts with their six GC boxes by interaction in the major groove to induce an overall approximate 180° curvature of the 21-bp repeats toward the minor groove of DNA. These results are used as a basis to propose a new model for the complex of Sp1 with the 21-bp repeat region (Figure 14.10).

Mu transposase

Phage Mu transposase (A-protein) is primarily responsible for transposition of the Mu genome. The protein binds to six *att* sites, three at each end of Mu DNA. At most *att* sites interaction of a protein monomer with DNA is seen to occur over three minor and two consecutive major grooves and to result in bending up to about 90°. To probe the directionality and locus of these A-protein-induced bends, we have used the antitumor antibiotic (+)-CC-1065 as a structural probe (Ding et al. 1993). Using this drug in experiments in which either gel retardation or DNA strand breakage is used to monitor the stability of the A-protein–DNA complex or the (+)-CC-1065 alkylation sites on DNA (*att* site L3), we have demonstrated that of the three minor grooves implicated in the interaction with A-protein, the peripheral two are "open" or accessible to drug bonding following protein binding. These drug-bonding sites very likely represent binding at at least two A-protein-induced bending sites. Significantly, the locus of bending at these sites is spaced approximately two helical turns apart, and the bending is proposed to occur by narrowing of the minor groove of

DNA. The intervening minor groove between these two peripheral sites is protected from (+)-CC-1065 alkylation. The results are discussed in reference to a proposed model for overall DNA bending in the A-protein *att* L3 site complex (Figure 14.11).

In summary, these studies illustrate the utility of (+)-CC-1065 as a probe for protein-induced bending of DNA, as well as for interactions of minor groove DNA bending proteins with DNA which may be masked in hydroxyl radical footprinting experiments.

Figure   14.10
A New Model for the Complex of Spl with the 21-bp Repeat Region

The model representing the plausible structure of the complex between Spl and 21-bp repeats and the interaction between 72-bp enhancer binding proteins and basal transcriptional machinery

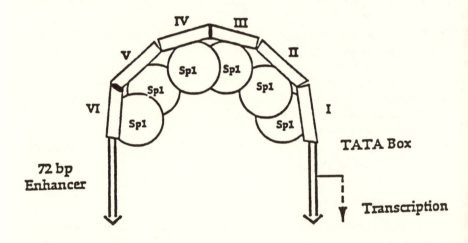

Figure 14.11
Summary of A-protein (Zou et al. 1991) and (+)-CC-1065
Interactions with the *att* L3 Site

(A) The duplex sequence of *att* L3 oligomer showing the hydroxyl-radical protection regions covering minor grooves I, II, and III and drug bonding sites (A–D) indicating the drug overlap in the minor grooves. (B) Ribbon diagram of the same region showing the proposed loci for bending into minor (m) grooves I and III by *solid squares* within base pairs. Guanine (strong) and adenine (weak) protection sites (Zou et al. 1991) are shown as *solid* and *broken* arrows, respectively. Drug bonding sites are shown as *filled bases*, and adenines showing methylation protection but not interference (Zou et al. 1991) are marked with *solid dots*. The sequence of the upper (+) strand is shown.

A

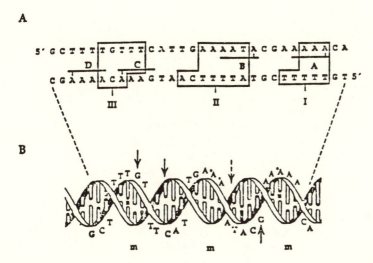

B

Reprinted from Zou, A., Leung, P. C., and Harshey, R. M. (1991). "Transposase Contacts with Mu DNA Ends." *J. Biol. Chem.* 266, 20476–20482. Reprinted by permission of the authors and the American Society for Biochemistry and Molecular Biology.

NOTES

1. Abbreviations: bp, base pair(s); CPI, cyclopropa[c]pyrrolo[3,2-e]indol-4-(5H)-one.

2. Here and throughout the manuscript, an asterisk denotes the covalently modified adenine.

REFERENCES

Burkhoff, A. M., and Tullius, T. D. (1987). "The Unusual Conformation Adopted by the Adenine Tracts in Kinetoplast DNA." *Cell* 48: 935–943.

Burkhoff, A. M., and Tullius, T. D. (1988). "Structural Details of an Adenine Tract That Does Not Cause DNA to Bend." *Nature* 331: 455–457.

Chidester, C. G., Krueger, W. C., Mizak, S. A., Duchamp, D. J., and Martin, D. G. (1981). "The Structure of CC-1065, a Potent Antitumor Agent, and Its Binding to DNA." *J. Am. Chem. Soc.* 103: 7629–7635.

Ding, Z.-M., Harshey, R. M., and Hurley, L. H. (1993). "(+)-CC-1065 as a Structural Probe of Mu Transposase-Induced Bending of DNA." *Nucl. Acids Res.* 21: 4281–4287.

Graves, D. E., and Wadkins, R. M. (1990). *Molecular Basis of Specificity in Nucleic Acid-Drug Interactions.* Ed. by B. Pullman and J. Jortner, Pullman, B., pp 177–189, Dordrecht, Boston, and London: Kluwer Academic Publishers.

Hagerman, P. J. (1990). "Sequence-Directed Curvature of DNA." *Annu. Rev. Biochem.* 59: 755–781.

Hanka, L. J., Dietz, A., Gerpheide, S. A., Kuentzil, S. L., and Martin, D. G. (1978). "CC-1065 (NSC-298223), a New Antitumor Antibiotic. Production In Vitro Biological Activity, Microbiological Assays, and Taxonomy of the Producing Microorganism." *J. Antibiot. 31*, 1211–1217.

Hurley, L. H., Reynolds, B. L., Swenson, D. H., and Scahill, T. (1984). "Reaction of the Antitumor Antibiotic CC-1065 with DNA. Structure of a DNA Adduct with DNA Sequence Specificity." *Science 226*, 843–844.

Hurley, L. H., Lee, C.-S., McGovren, J. P., Mitchell, M., Warpehoski, M. A., Kelley, R. C., and Aristoff, P. A. (1988). "Molecular Basis for the Sequence Specific DNA Alkylation by (+)-CC-1065." *Biochemistry 27*, 3886–3892.

Husain, I., Griffith, J., and Sancar, A. (1988). "Thymine Dimers Bend DNA." *Proc. Natl. Acad. Sci. U.S.A. 85*, 2558–2562.

Kadonaga, J. T., Jones, K. A., and Tjian, R. (1986). "Promoter-specific Activation of RNA Polymerase II Transcription by Sp1." *Trends Biochem. 11*, 20–23.

Katahira, M., Sugeta, H., and Kyogoku, Y. (1990). "A New Model for the Bending of DNA Containing the Oligo(da) Tracts on NMR Observation." *Nucl. Acids Res. 18*, 613–618.

Koo, H. S., Wu, H. M., and Crothers, D. M. (1986). "DNA Bending at Adenine–Thymine Tracts." *Nature (London) 320*, 501–506.

Koo, H. S., and Crothers, D. M. (1988). "Calibration of DNA Curvature and a Unified Description of Sequence-Directed Bending." *Proc. Natl. Acad. Sci. U.S.A. 85*, 1763–1767.

Lee, C.-S., Sun, D., Kizu, R., and Hurley, L. H. (1991). "Determination of the Structural Features of (+)-CC-1065 That Are Responsible for Bending, Winding, and Stiffening of DNA." *Chem. Res. Toxicol. 4*, 203–213.

Lin, C. H., and Hurley, L. H. (1990). "Determination of the Major Tautomeric Form of the Covalently Modified Adenine in the (+)-CC-1065–DNA Adduct by ^{1}H and ^{15}N NMR Studies." *Biochemistry 29*, 9503–9507.

Lin, C. H., Beale, J. M., and Hurley, L. H. (1991a). "Structure of the (+)-CC-1065–DNA Adduct: Critical Role of Ordered Water Molecules and Implications for Involvement of Phosphate Catalysis in the Covalent Reaction." *Biochemistry 30*, 3597–3602.

Lin, C. H., Sun, D., and Hurley, L. H. (1991b) "(+)-CC-1065 Produces Bending of DNA That Appears to Resemble Adenine/Thymine Tracts." *Chem. Res. Toxicol. 4*, 21–26.

Lin, C. H., Hill, G. C., and Hurley, L. H. (1992). "Characterization of a 12-Mer Duplex d(GGCGGAGTTAGG)·(CCTAACTCCGCC) Containing a Highly Reactive (+)-CC-1065 Sequence by ^{1}H and ^{31}P NMR, Hydroxyl-Radical Footprinting, and NOESY Restrained Molecular Dynamics Calculations." *Chem. Res. Toxicol. 5*, 167–182.

McAllister, C. F., and Achberger, E. C. (1989). "Rotational Orientation of Upstream Curved DNA Affects Promoter Function in *Bacillus Subtilis.*" *J. Biol. Chem. 264*, 10451–10456.

Nadeau, J., and Crothers, D. M. (1989). "Structural Basis for DNA Bending." *Proc. Natl. Acad. Sci. U.S.A. 86*, 2622–2626.

Reynolds, V. L., Molineux, I. J., Kaplan, D., Swenson, D. H., and Hurley, L. H. (1985). "Reaction of the Antitumor Antibiotic CC-1065 with DNA. Location of the Site of Thermally Induced Strand Breakage and Analysis of DNA Sequence Specificity." *Biochemistry 24*, 6228–6237.

Saenger, W. (1983). *Principles of Nucleic Acid Structure.* pp. 324–327. New York: Springer-Verlag.

Scahill, T. A., Jensen, R. M., Swenson, D. H., Hatzenbuhler, N. T., Petzold, G., Wierenga, W., and Brahme, N. D. (1990). "An NMR Study of the Covalent and Noncovalent Interaction of CC-1065 and DNA." *Biochemistry 29*, 2852–2860.

Shatzky-Schwarz, M., Hiller, Y., Reich, Z., Ghirlando, R., Weinberger, S., and Minsky, A. (1992). "Attenuation of DNA-Protein Interactions Associated with Intrinsic, Sequence-Dependent DNA Curvature." *Biochemistry 31*, 2339–2346.

Sun, D., and Hurley, L. H. (1994). "Cooperative Bending of the 21-Base-Pair Repeats of the SV40 Viral Early Promoter by Human Sp1." *Biochemistry*, 33, 9578–9587.

Sun, D., Lin, C. H., and Hurley, L. H. (1993) "A-Tract and (+)-CC-1065-Induced Bending of DNA. Comparison of Structural Features Using Non-Denaturing Gel Analysis, Hydroxyl-Radical Footprinting, and High-Field NMR." *Biochemistry 32*, 4487–4495.

Travers, A. A. (1990). "Why Bend DNA?" *Cell 60*, 177–180.

Warpehoski, M. A., and Hurley, L. H. (1988). "Sequence Selectivity of DNA Covalent Modification." *Chem. Res. Toxicol. 1*, 315–333.

Warpehoski, M. A., Gebhard, I., Kelly, R. C., Krueger, W. C., Li, L. H., McGovren, J. P., Prairie, M. D., Wicnienski, N., and Wierenga, W. (1988). "Stereoelectronic Factors Influencing the Biological Activity and DNA Interaction of Synthetic Antitumor Agents Modeled on CC-1065." *J. Med. Chem.* 31, 590–603.

Zahn, K., and Blattner, F. R. (1987). "Evidence for DNA Bending at the l Replicating Origin." *Science* 236, 416–422.

Zou, A., Leung, P. C., and Harshey, R. M. (1991). "Transposase Contacts with Mu DNA Ends." *J. Biol. Chem.* 266, 20476–20482.

Potential Agents for the Commercialization of Virus-Resistant Transgenic Plants

Maureen S. Bonness, Nilgun E. Tumer, and Tom J. Mabry

We are investigating the natural role of pokeweed antiviral protein (PAP), a protein with established antiviral properties for other plants. PAP appears to selectively enter and kill virus-infected cells by inactivating the ribosomes in that cell, thereby stopping protein synthesis and preventing viral reproduction. In our studies we demonstrated that pokeweed ribosomes are extremely sensitive to inactivation by PAP, suggesting that this protein could serve as an agent for selective cell suicide. At Monsanto Company, the gene for PAP has been cloned and transferred to tobacco and potato plants to produce virus resistant crop plants. The resulting transgenic plants (plants engineered to carry foreign genes) were found to be variably resistant to a broad spectrum of viruses. Thus, genes for antiviral proteins in uncultivated plants have potential to be used to produce virus-protected crop plants. Transgenic plants allow molecular plant breeders to generate useful genetic diversity within crop plants not possible by conventional breeding techniques.

This chapter discusses two research goals: (1) understanding the function of a ribosome-inactivating protein (RIP), a protein with antiviral properties, within a *Phytolacca* weed, and (2) development of transgenic crop plants with increased virus resistance utilizing the *Phytolacca* RIP gene. Such virus-resistant transgenic plants should lower the cost of producing crops.

This chapter concerns one aspect of the new field of genetically engineered organisms. There is no doubt that such organisms have the potential to improve the quality of life for people. However, because there are both real and imagined dangers in their use in the marketplace—and many ethical considerations as well—every step in the commercialization process must be regulated and evaluated by government agencies. But who in the federal and state regulatory agencies is qualified to regulate and evaluate the long-term safety of new organisms with new properties and new commercially valuable products? Federal policy decisions in this field are critical not only to future scientific achievements but also to commercial developments in this field.

The ability to create transgenic plants has created a revolution in plant biology. Transgenic plant technology allows molecular plant breeders to generate useful genetic diversity within crop plants that could not be generated by conventional breeding techniques. The force that drives research on transgenic plants is the immense commercial potential of the transgenic products, which could some day include innovations such as insect-resistant cotton plants, naturally decaffeinated coffee beans, or grains that can be irrigated with sea water.

We are investigating the natural role of pokeweed antiviral protein, a protein with established antiviral properties for other plants. PAP appears to selectively enter and kill virus-infected cells by inactivating the ribosomes in that cell, thereby stopping protein synthesis and preventing viral reproduction. In our studies we demonstrated that pokeweed ribosomes are extremely sensitive to inactivation by pokeweed antiviral protein, suggesting that this protein could serve as an agent for selective cell suicide. The group of coauthor Nilgun Tumer at Monsanto Company has cloned the gene for pokeweed antiviral protein and transferred it to tobacco and potato plants to produce virus-resistant crop plants. The resulting transgenic plants were found to be variably resistant to a broad spectrum of viruses. Thus, genes for antiviral proteins in noncultivated plants have the potential to be used to produce virus-protected crop plants.

POKEWEED ANTIVIRAL PROTEIN

Pokeweed antiviral protein is produced by *Phytolacca americana* (pokeweed), a weedy plant found on roadsides and disturbed sites in the eastern United States. When co-inoculated with a virus onto leaves of normally susceptible plants, this protein reduces the infection of a broad spectrum of viruses (Chen et al. 1991). PAP has since been shown to possess antiviral qualities for animal cells and is currently in clinical trials as a therapeutic agent against HIV, leukemia, and a number of cancers (Irvin and Uckun 1992; Zarling et al. 1990).

PAP belongs to a class of proteins called ribosome-inactivating proteins which enzymatically alter the shape of ribosomes (the cellular organelles that are responsible for assembly of proteins) (Endo et al. 1987). Only a few molecules of the antiviral protein can inactivate all ribosomes within a cell, thereby stopping protein synthesis and resulting in cell death; cell death prevents virus reproduction and thus stops the virus from spreading. PAP has the capacity to attack ribosomes from many types of organisms, including animals, plants, fungi, and bacteria (Irvin 1983). Although PAP has the potential to kill any cell to which it gains entrance, it is not readily internalized by healthy cells and is thus not a problem for most organisms. In contrast, some ribosome-inactivating proteins, such as the toxin from castor bean, readily enter animal cells and are consequently extremely toxic to people.

Pokeweed antiviral protein is hypothesized to act as an antiviral agent by selectively entering and killing virus-infected cells (Ready et al. 1986). We have been investigating whether or not this occurs in pokeweed, where the antiviral protein is sequestered in the cell wall, theoretically poised to attack virus-infected cells.

Although PAP appears to have unquestionable antiviral properties when applied to leaves of other species, it does not similarly provide protection when applied to pokeweed plants (Roberts and Selitrennikoff 1986; Stirpe 1982), and pokeweed plants are naturally susceptible to a number of viruses. Thus, the first question to be addressed was whether or not pokeweed ribosomes are inactivated by PAP. Determining the sensitivity of pokeweed ribosomes to PAP was hampered by the difficulty of purifying active pokeweed ribosomes independent of this protein, which is ubiquitous in all pokeweed plant parts. Previous efforts to purify pokeweed ribosomes by several laboratories resulted in relatively inactive ribosomes. This problem was solved in our laboratory by growing pokeweed cells in tissue culture, then screening cell lines to identify a cell line that did not produce pokeweed antiviral protein (Bonness and Mabry 1992). From this tissue culture cell line, ribosomes were purified and, through in vitro assays, the ribosomes were found to be highly active. Moreover, these pokeweed ribosomes were extremely sensitive to attack by PAP. We have also shown that the ribosomes are inactivated in the exact same manner that the antiviral protein inactivates ribosomes from other plants (Bonness et al. 1994). While these studies established that pokeweed ribosomes are sensitive to the antiviral protein (in vitro) and therefore possess the potential to serve in pokeweed as an agent for protection against viral infection, it still remains to be proven that this is indeed the natural role of PAP.

Through the advent of new technologies within plant biotechnology, an alternative strategy for testing the antiviral qualities of PAP has emerged— transgenic plants. Coauthor Tumer and colleagues at Monsanto Company genetically engineered several crop species to produce the antiviral protein. These transgenic plants can be compared with normal crop plants as well as pokeweed plants to determine the role of PAP. Moreover, if these genetically-engineered transgenic plants display increased resistance to viruses, the use of PAP represents a significant advancement, particularly because it works against a surprisingly broad spectrum of viruses.

TRANSGENIC PLANTS

Transgenic plants represent the newest breakthrough in the plant biotechnology boom. The potential of transgenic plants in basic and applied research is phenomenal. The ability to move genes between various plants, or between plants and other organisms, opens new avenues for the plant sciences. The new technologies provide a powerful opportunity for probing the organization and function of plant genomes, and for generating new crop plants with superior qualities.

It has been only two decades since the first transgenic organism, a bacterium, was produced. The economic potential of transgenic organisms has been reflected in industry's enthusiasm and investment. The first biotechnology company, Genentech, was formed in 1976, and the initial public offering by Genentech in 1980 set a Wall Street record for the fastest price-per-share increase. A year later, the initial public offering by another biotechnology giant, Cetus, set a Wall Street record for the largest amount of money raised in an initial public offering, $125 million. The technology of introducing foreign genes into plants was finally achieved for the first time in 1983. Currently there are more than forty species of transgenic plants with commercial value (Table 15.1); in addition, many more species of transgenic plants have been developed for basic research. Now, little more than a decade after the first plant was transformed, consumers are presented with the choice of transgenic produce in the market.

Table 15.1
Transgenic Plants of Commercial Interest

alfalfa	eggplant	peas
apple	flax	petunia
Arabidopsis	grapes	poplar
asparagus	horseradish	potato
barley	lettuce	rice
cabbage	lotus	rye
canola	kalanchoe	soybean
carrot	maize	strawberry
cauliflower	millet	sugar beet
celery	morning glory	sunflower
clover	muskmelon	tobacco
cotton	orchard grass	tomato
cucumber	pear	walnut
		wheat

Sources: Dandekar et al. 1993; Kung 1993; Logemann et al. 1992.

The use of transgenic plants does not always replace conventional plant breeding, although in many cases there are several significant advantages. Specific genes can be transferred while avoiding the guesswork and chance associated with breeding. "Molecular breeders" can avoid potential problems of unmasking some harmful genes as well as eliminating some desirable genes. Most importantly, the constraints of natural breeding barriers between varieties, species, and even kingdoms are dissolved. On the other hand, the technical challenges of transferring genes are not trivial, including identification of the gene, understanding its regulation of expression, and the intricacies of introducing the gene into a new host so that the gene is correctly expressed and inherited.

At present, the most promising commercial advances, all of which require the transfer of single-gene traits, have been made in five areas: virus resistance, insect resistance, herbicide tolerance, altered fruit ripening, and altered flower color. Future advances, most of which require the transfer of multiple genes, include improved nutritional quality of crops and tolerance to climatic stress such as drought, heat, cold, and salinity.

Producing crop plants that are resistant to viruses is of profound interest, particularly because we have no chemical treatments to directly protect plants from viruses. At present, most commercial virus-resistance strategies include the transfer of a gene for a virus protein into a crop plant. This seemingly odd approach—using a virus protein to reduce virus infection—was encouraged by early observations of cross-protection (plants with a low-grade infection of one virus may subsequently be protected from other infectious viruses). Although the mechanism of cross-protection is not understood, it appears that it involves a protein from the virus. Genes for various virus proteins—including proteins that comprise the viruses' outer coats and proteins that are involved in virus reproduction—have been experimentally introduced into crop plants. For example, transgenic tobacco plants now produce the coat protein of tobacco mosaic virus (Beachy et al. 1990), and transgenic potato plants produce virus enzymes from potato virus Y. This strategy has generally been effective, although the transgenic plants are usually resistant to only a very limited number of viruses.

TRANSGENIC PLANTS PRODUCING POKEWEED ANTIVIRAL PROTEIN

The fact that PAP is a general inhibitor of virus infection makes it an ideal candidate for developing virus-resistant plants. With the goal of acquiring broad spectrum virus resistance, PAP was selected by a number of research groups for gene transfer into crop plants (Lin et al. 1991; Hartley and Lord 1993). In September 1993 researchers from Monsanto Company reported the successful transfer of the gene for pokeweed antiviral protein into crop plants and described the subsequent antiviral trials (Lodge et al. 1993).

The PAP gene, after being isolated and cloned from pokeweed cells, was put into a series of bacteria, one of which (*Agrobacterium*) was used to infect and transmit the antiviral protein gene into the chromosomes of tobacco and potato cells. Cells from these crop plants that produced PAP were selected, were grown in tissue culture, and eventually whole plants were regenerated from these cells. The resulting plants were checked to determine the quantity of pokeweed antiviral protein produced.

Frequencies of successful incorporation of the antiviral protein gene into the crop plants were initially very low. However, when a variant form of the protein, containing two amino acid changes, was used, the incorporation frequencies were much higher. These experiments suggested that the variant form was less toxic to cells than the normal antiviral protein. The ribosome inhibitory activities of the normal and the variant antiviral protein were similar, indicating that the differences observed in the toxicity of these proteins were not due to differences in their ribosome inhibitory properties.

Transgenic plants expressing either the normal or the variant antiviral protein were obtained. A range of concentrations of the antiviral protein were found in the transgenic plants, although even the high producers synthesized PAP at levels far lower than pokeweed plants. In general, plants that expressed high levels of the normal antiviral protein were sterile and transgenic plants that expressed high levels of the variant antiviral protein showed growth reduction and mottling, while plants that expressed low levels of the wild type or variant antiviral protein appeared normal.

Finally, when the transgenic plants were challenged with a variety of viruses, it was found that they were protected from a broad spectrum of viruses. This exciting discovery established the potential of pokeweed antiviral protein for producing virus-resistant transgenic crop plants.

We do not yet understand the mechanism of virus resistance. Does the antiviral protein work directly on the virus or does it work on the host cell? Must the antiviral protein inactivate ribosomes in order to convey virus resistance? How does the antiviral protein enter plant cells? Is the antiviral protein (particularly the variant form) processed differently in the transgenic plants? Can we regulate production of antiviral protein in transgenic crop plants (that is, how much antiviral protein is produced in which plant part)? Do pokeweed cells contain an "antidote" to this potentially lethal protein? These are the questions we are presently investigating in tandem: Mabry's group is investigating the activity of PAP in pokeweed itself, while Tumer's group is working with the transgenic crop plants.

CONCLUSION

The advent of transgenic plants offers bold new opportunities for commercial applications as well as for researchers investigating basic plant biology. We are presently investigating antiviral properties of pokeweed antiviral protein. Transgenic crop plants that produce PAP have been developed, and it has been shown that these transgenic plants show degrees of resistance to a remarkably broad array of viruses. Since there are no antiviral compounds available within modern agricultural practices, there is great potential in agriculture for such a broad-spectrum antiviral agent. In addition to the development of transgenic crops, we continue to conduct research into the mechanism of antiviral action of pokeweed antiviral protein—a protein shown to also have potential antiviral therapeutic value for humans.

ACKNOWLEDGMENTS

Some of the work described here was supported at the University of Texas at Austin by the National Institutes of Health and the Robert A. Welch Foundation.

REFERENCES

Beachy, R.N., Loesch-Fries, S. and Tumer, N.E. (1990). "Coat Protein-Mediated Resistance Against Virus Infection." *Annual Review of Phytopathology*, 28: 451–474.

Bonness, M.S. and Mabry, T.J. (1992). "Tissue Culture of Endod (*Phytolacca dodecandra* L'Herit): Growth and Production of Ribosome-Inactivating Proteins." *Plant Cell Reports*, 11: 66–70.

Bonness, M.S., Ready, M.P., Irvin, J.D. and Mabry, T.J. (1994). "Pokeweed Antiviral Protein Inactivates Pokeweed Ribosomes; Implications for the Antiviral Mechanism." *The Plant Journal*, 5: 173–183.

Chen, Z.C., White, R.F., Antoniw J.F. and Lin, Q. (1991). "Effect of Pokeweed Antiviral Protein (PAP) on the Infection of Plant Viruses." *Plant Pathology*, 40: 612–620.

Dandekar, A.M., McGranahan, G.H. and James, D.J. (1993). "Transgenic Woody Plants." In (eds. S. Kung and R. Wu) *Transgenic Plants*. San Diego: Academic. 2: 129–151.

Endo, Y., Mitsui, K., Motizuki, M. and Tsurugi, K. (1987). "The Mechanism of Action of Ricin and Related Toxic Lectins on Eukaryotic Ribosomes. The Site and the Characteristics of the Modification in 28S Ribosomal RNA Caused by the Toxins." *Journal of Biological Chemistry*, 262: 5908–5912.

Hartley, M.R. and Lord, J.M. (1993). "Structure, Function and Applications of Ricin and Related Cytotoxic Proteins." In D. Grierson, ed., *Biosynthesis and Manipulation of Plant Products*. London: Blackie. pp. 210–239.

Irvin, J.D. (1983). "Pokeweed Antiviral Protein." *Pharmaceutical Therapeutics, 21*: 371–387.

Irvin, J.D. and Uckun, F.M. (1992). "Pokeweed Antiviral Protein: Ribosome Inactivation and Therapeutic Applications." *Pharmaceutical Therapeutics, 55*: 279–302.

Kung, S. (1993). "Introduction: From Hybrid Plants to Transgenic Plants." In S. Kung and R. Wu, eds., *Transgenic Plants*. San Diego: Academic. 2: 1–12.

Lin, Q., Chen, Z.C., Antoniw, J.F. and White, R.F. (1991). "Isolation and Characterization of a cDNA Clone Encoding the Anti-Viral Protein from *Phytolacca Americana*." *Plant Molecular Biology*, 17: 609–614.

Lodge, J.K., Kaniewski, W.K. and Tumer, N.E. (1993). "Expression of Pokeweed Antiviral Protein Leads to Broad Spectrum Virus Resistance in Transgenic Plants." *Proceedings of the National Academy of Science*, 90: 7089–7093.

Logemann, J., Jach, G., Tommerup, H., Mundy, J. and Schell, J. (1992). "Expression of a Barley Ribosome-Inactivating Protein Leads to Increased Fungal Protection in Transgenic Tobacco Plants." *Bio/Technology*, 10: 305–308.

Ready, M.P., Brown, D.T. and Robertus, J.D. (1986). "Extracellular Localization of Pokeweed Antiviral Protein." *Proceedings of the National Academy of Science USA*, 83: 5053–5056.

Roberts, W.K. and Selitrennikoff, C.P. (1986). "Plant Proteins that Inactivate Foreign Ribosomes." *Bioscience Reports*, 6: 19–29.

Stirpe, F. (1982). "On the Action of Ribosome-Inactivating Proteins: Are Plant Ribosomes Species-Specific?" *Biochemical Journal*, 202: 279–280.

Zarling, J.M., Moran, P.A., Haffar, O., Sias, J., Richman, D.D., Spina, C.A., Myers, D.E., Kuebelbeck, V., Ledbetter, J.A. and Uckun, F.M. (1990). "Inhibition of HIV Replication by Pokeweed Antiviral Protein Targeted to CD4[+] Cells by Monoclonal Antibodies." *Nature*, 347: 92–95.

Index

About the Contributors

CREED W. ABELL ("The Role of Basic Research in Developing New Treatments for Parkinson's Disease") received B.S. degrees in chemistry from the Virginia Military Institute (1956) and Purdue University (1958), respectively, and then obtained his Ph.D.degree in Oncology from the University of Wisconsin (1962). He joined the faculty at the University of Texas at Austin in 1986 after serving as director of the Division of Biochemistry, Department of Human Biological Chemistry and Genetics, at the UT Medical Branch in Galveston, Texas for eight years. Dr. Abell has served on several national committees for the evaluation of NIH-funded basic research. He currently holds the Henry M. Burlage Centennial Professorship of Pharmacy, UT-Austin.

Dr. Abell's work focuses on the characterization of monoamine oxidase A and B (MAO A and B), enzymes found in the brain that play a role in the metabolism of neurotransmitters. Both enzymes have been implicated in several neurologic and psychiatric disorders, and MAO B is believed to play a causative role in idiopathic Parkinson's disease. Dr. Abell's present work includes cloning, sequencing, and expressing genetically engineered forms of MAO A and B in order to understand their molecular and functional properties. His work led to the isolation of the first known monoclonal to MAO B (Denney et al., *Science* 215, 1400, 1982) and to elucidation of the nucleotide and amino acid sequences of MAO A and B (Bach et al., *Proc. Natl. Acad. Sci.* 85, 4934, 1988). Results of current studies together with information on the secondary and tertiary structure of MAO A and B could lead to new drug designs for the treatment of neurological and psychiatric disorders

VICTOR L. ARNOLD ("A Two-Stage DEA Approach for Identifying and Rewarding Efficiency in Texas Secondary Schools") is Associate Dean for Graduate Programs in the Graduate School of Business, the University of Texas at Austin. He also is Professor of Management and holds the Rex A. Sebastian/Dresser Industries Professorship. Dr. Arnold has had extensive experience in strategic management at the federal and state levels of government. His research interests are public policy and strategic management.

DONDE P. ASHMOS ("Diversification Strategy, Strategy Change, Performance and State-Defined Risk: Some Longitudinal Evidence") is an Associate Professor of Management at the University of Texas at San Antonio and is an Associate of the IC^2 Institute. Dr. Ashmos received her Ph.D. in Strategic Management from The University of Texas at Austin in 1988. Her research interests are in the area of strategic decision making, strategic change, organization design, and healthcare management. Dr. Ashmos has published in such journals as *Academy of Management Review*, *Journal of Applied Behavioral Sciences*, *Health Services Research*, *Interfaces*, and *Human Resource Management*. While at UT-Austin, she won an award for excellence in teaching, and at UT-San Antonio she has won the College of Business Outstanding Research Award. Dr. Ashmos also provides management training for Apple, Bell Helicopter, Hailburton Services, and other companies.

INDRANIL R. BARDHAN ("A Two-Stage DEA Approach for Identifying and Rewarding Efficiency in Texas Secondary Schools") is a Ph.D. candidate in Management Science and Information Systems in the Graduate School of Business at The University of Texas at Austin. His primary research interests are in productivity analysis, competitive benchmarking and logistics planning. Other research interests include evaluation of trends in healthcare policies and practices to identify and evaluate efficiency of healthcare systems and analyses of medical information.

MAUREEN S. BONNESS ("Potential Agents for the Commercialization of Virus-Resistant Transgenic Plants") is a Postdoctoral Research Assistant in the Department of Botany, the University of Texas at Austin. Her dissertation work involved the study of pokeweed antiviral proteins. She is currently investigating the biosynthetic pathway of phytoalexins from cactus cultures.

PATRICK L. BROCKETT ("Using Computer Intensive Technologies to Aid Insurance Regulators: Early Detection of Insolvency and Fraud") is Professor of Finance and Actuarial Science and Paul V. Montgomery Centennial Fellow in Actuarial Science at the Graduate School of Business, and Senior Research Fellow at the IC^2 Institute of the University of Texas at Austin. His major research interests include actuarial science, mathematical models in business and finance, applied probability in operations research, insurance and risk management, decision analysis, survival analysis and reliability theory with time-dependent covariates, finance and economic theory, and statistics applications. Dr. Brockett has been president of the Austin chapter of the American Statistical Association, and is associate editor of the book review section of the *Journal of the American Statistical Association*. He has been a consultant for the Austin Police Department and an East Austin community development project as well as a volunteer for United Action for the Elderly.

PING CHEN ("Instability, Complexity, and Bounded Rationality in Economic Change") is a Research Associate at the Ilya Prigogine Center. After graduation from the University of Science and Technology of China, he worked in the Chinese Academy of Sciences before coming to the United States. His interest in economic sciences was stimulated by his early efforts in China's reform and by Ilya Prigogine's evolutionary view of physics. He has been working with Prigogine since 1981 and got a Ph. D. in physics in 1987 from the University of Texas at Austin. He is an Adjunct Associate Professor at the Center for Management Science in Peking University and a founding fellow of Chinese Economists Society, a member organization of AEA (American Economic Association).

JAMES M. COLLINS ("Diversification Strategy, Strategy Change, Performance and State-Defined Risk: Some Longitudinal Evidence") is an Assistant Professor at the University of Alaska, Fairbanks, and is an Associate of the IC^2 Institute. Dr. Collins has a bachelor's degree in sociology from Illinois State University and a master of Business Administration and a Ph.D. in Strategic Management from the University of Texas at Austin. His current research interests are focused on the problems of risk conceptualization and measurement , corporate research and development and strategic management, and the transfer of technology in rural environments. With Timothy Ruefli, he is the coauthor of the forthcoming book *Strategic Risk: A State-Defined Approach*.

WILLIAM W. COOPER ("A Two-Stage DEA Approach for Identifying and Rewarding Efficiency in Texas Secondary Schools") is the Nadya Kozmetsky Scott Fellow of the IC^2 Institute and Foster Parker Professor of Financial and Management (Emeritus) in the Graduate School of Business of the University of Texas at Austin. Author or coauthor of more than four hundred articles and seventeen books, Professor Cooper has been a consultant to nearly two hundred business firms, and government agencies, and a dozen universities. Holder of the prestigious John von Neumann Theory Medal, jointly awarded by the Institute of Management Sciences and the Operations Research Society of America he also holds the Outstanding Accounting Educator Award of the American Accounting Association. He is a Fellow of the Econometric Society and the American Association for the Advancement of Science. A recipient of honorary degrees from Ohio State and Carnegie Mellon Universities, his main interest is in modeling management and social processes.

G. EDWARD GIBSON, JR. ("Needed Innovations in Capital Expenditure Planning") is an Assistant Professor of Civil Engineering in the Construction Engineering and Project Management program at the University of Texas at

Austin. His research interests include pre-project planning, construction productivity, electronic data management, and automation and robotics. Dr. Gibson teaches undergraduate courses in contracts, liability, and ethics, as well as engineering economy and project management. He teaches graduate-level courses in project information management systems, project finance, and total quality management. He received his Ph.D. in Civil Engineering from Auburn University and holds an M.B.A. from the University of Dallas. Dr. Gibson has several years of industry experience and is a registered professional engineer in Texas.

BOAZ GOLANY ("The Competitiveness of Nations") is the Associate Dean of the Industrial Engineering and Management Faculty at the Technion-Israel Institute of Technology. He received his primary and secondary education in Haifa, Israel. He spent four years of active duty in the Israeli Defense Forces and has been with the reserve forces of the IDF since then. He graduated from the Officer Corps program with distinction and later became a Major in the IDF. He has a B.Sc. (summa cum laude) in Industrial Engineering and Management from the Technion (1982) and an interdisciplinary Ph.D. from the Business School of the University of Texas at Austin (1985). He was awarded the Naor Prize of the Israeli Operations Research Society in 1982 and the Yigal Alon Fellowship from the Israeli Education Ministry in 1986. In 1991, he was a recipient of the Technion Academic Excellence Award. Dr. Golany has published over forty papers in academic and professional journals and books. His publications are in the areas of industrial engineering, operations research and management science.

Dr. Golany has served as a consultant to various companies and agencies in Israel and the United States. In the United States, he has been actively involved in various operations research projects in the military milieu, including the Tactical and Strategic Air Commands of the U.S. Air Force, the Training and Doctrine and Recruiting Commands of the U.S. Army, and the Recruiting Commands of the U.S. Navy and Marine Corps. He has been a consultant to MRCA Information Services and The Magellan Group in Austin since 1985. There, he has participated in efficiency improvement projects for commercial enterprises such as Coca Cola, KFC, and BankOne as well as government agencies such as the Texas Department of Transportation and the Ohio Department of Education.

In Israel, he has been a consultant on inventory-control issues to several companies in the oil industry and in particular, to the Israeli Refineries Ltd. He has been active in various professional societies including The Institute of Management Science (in the United States) and the Israeli Operations Research, where he served as the Treasurer in 1989-1992.

LINDA L. GOLDEN ("Using Computer Intensive Technologies to Aid Insurance Regulators: Early Detection of Insolvency and Fraud") holds the Zale Corporation Centennial Professorship in Business and is Chair of the

Department of Marketing Administration in the College and Graduate School of Business at the University of Texas at Austin. She is also a Senior Research Fellow of the IC^2 Institute. Dr. Golden has published extensively in marketing, consumer behavior, and quantitative methods. Her publications have appeared in journals such as the *Journal of Consumer Research, The Journal of Marketing Research, Management Science,* the *Journal of Official Statistics,* and the *Journal of Mathematical Sociology.*

ALOK GUPTA ("Pricing of Services on the Internet") is a Ph.D. candidate in the Department of Management Science and Information Systems at the University of Texas at Austin. He got his undergraduate and masters degrees in engineering from IT, BHU, India, and the Pennsylvania State University, respectively. His research interests include real-time estimation and pricing of externalities in large network simulation of physical systems, and applications of mathematical programming. At present he is working with Andrew B. Whinston and Dale O. Stahl on his dissertation, temporarily titled "Estimation of Priority Prices for Achieving Stochastic Equilibrium in Networks with Negative Externality and Is Applications." He is a member of ORSA and TIMS.

LAURENCE H. HURLEY ("Drugs as Probes for Intrinsic and Protein-Induced Bending of DNA") is George H. Hitchings Professor of Drug Design and Head of the Laboratory for Drug Design, Drug Dynamics Institute, College of Pharmacy, University of Texas at Austin. He was born in 1944 in Birmingham, England. He received his B. Pharm. (Honors) in 1967 from Bath University (United Kingdom) and his Ph.D. (Medicinal Chemistry) in 1970 from Purdue University, where he studied under Professor Heinz G. Floss. He completed an honors degree specializing in Pharmacognosy at Bath and was the recipient of the 1970 Dean Jenkins Award for the outstanding graduate student at Purdue University College of Pharmacy and Pharmacal Sciences. During his graduate studies, he was awarded a David Ross Fellowship from Purdue University. In 1970 he joined Professor James Kutney's group in the Department of Chemistry at the University of British Columbia as a postdoctoral fellow.

In 1972 he was appointed Assistant Professor at the University of Maryland School of Pharmacy; in 1977, he became Associate Professor; and in 1979, Professor. He joined the Drug Dynamics Institute in the College of Pharmacy at the University of Texas at Austin in 1981 and was appointed Professor of Medicinal Chemistry. He was Head of the Division of Medicinal Chemistry from 1983 to 1985. Since September 1985, Dr. Hurley has served on the graduate faculty in the Chemistry Department of the University of Texas.

Dr. Hurley's research interests are in the area of the mechanism of action of antitumor antibiotics. His work has been published in numerous journals, such the *Proceedings of the National Academy of Science* (USA), *Journal of Biological Chemistry, Nature, Science, Biochemistry, Journal of the American Chemical Society, Journal of Medicinal Chemistry, Accounts of Chemical*

Research, Journal of Antibiotics, Cancer Research, Biochemical and Biophysical Acta, and *Chemical Research in Toxicology.*

Dr. Hurley has served as principal investigator on over thirty research grants, including awards from the National Institutes of Health, National Science Foundation, Research Corporation, the Welch Foundation, and a number of pharmaceutical companies. In 1984 he was given an Outstanding Investigator Award from the National Cancer Institute, which supports his research program at a level of about $450,000 per year over a period of seven years. Since 1975 Dr. Hurley has been invited to give presentations at universities and pharmaceutical houses both in the United States and abroad. He has also participated as a speaker in numerous symposia, including chairing symposia on "DNA as a Target for Drug Action" and "DNA Sequence Specificity of Antitumor Agents."

Dr. Hurley is a Fellow of the American Association for the Advancement of Science and a member of the American Chemical Society, American Pharmaceutical Association, Academy of Pharmaceutical Sciences, American Association for Cancer Research, American Society for Pharmacognosy, and the Chemical Society of Great Britain. He has been a consultant to a number of pharmaceutical companies and now serves as a member of the editorial boards of the *Journal of Medicinal Chemistry, Journal of New Anticancer Drugs, Chemical Research in Toxicology,* and *Anticancer Drug Design* and is editor of *Advances in DNA Sequence Specific Agents.* Dr. Hurley has served as a grant reviewer for the National Institutes of Health (Member and Chairman, Bioorganic and Natural Products Study Section, 1984-1988), the National Science Foundation, and a number of private donor research award committees. He is a recipient of the 1988 George Hitchings Award in Innovative Methods in Drug Design, the 1989 Volwiler Research Achievement Award from the American Association of College of Pharmacy, and he was named a 1988 Distinguished Alumnus of Purdue University School of Pharmacy and Pharmacal Sciences.

SAU-WAH KWAN ("The Role of Basic Research in Developing New Treatments for Parkinson's Disease") is Senior Research Scientist in the College of Pharmacy and the Institute for Neuroscience at the University of Texas at Austin. She received her Ph.D. degree in Biochemistry from McGill University in Montreal, Canada. Her long-range goal is to understand eukaryotic gene regulation and expression. She has focused on selected genes in the nervous system, such as those that encode monoamine oxidase A and B and dopamine receptors. These proteins play vital roles in neurotransmitter function and have been implicated in neurological and psychiatric disorders.

DAVID B. LEARNER ("A Management System for Monitoring and Analyzing the Productivity of Armed Forces Recruiting") has been President of MRCA Information Services since 1974. Previously Dr. Learner was chairman of the Applied Devices Corporation and Vice President for Research at the advertising firm BBD&O. He serves as a director of several corporations, and is on the advisory boards of the University of Texas Foundation and the University of Georgia's Graduate Marketing Program.

Holder of the Ph.D. from Ohio State University, Dr. Learner was adjunct Professor of Management at Carnegie Mellon University. He is a Senior Research Fellow at the IC^2 Institute at the University of Texas. He is author or coauthor of numerous publications in marketing and advertising research. Throughout his career he has encouraged academic-business liaison and the application of research in business situations. He has been honored with the McKinsey Foundation Award and the Advertising Industry Award for outstanding contributions.

TOM J. MABRY ("Potential Agents for the Commercialization of Virus-Resistant Transgenic Plants") is a Professor of Botany, College of Natural Sciences, the University of Texas at Austin. Dr. Mabry's research interests include *Phytoalexins* (the antibiotics of plants), antitumor agents and neurotoxins from plants, flower pigments, including the betalains, and the production of specialty chemicals from plant tissue cultures and cell suspensions. Dr. Mabry joined the UT-Austin faculty in 1962 following a postdoctoral fellowship at the Organic Chemistry Institute of the University of Zurich in Switzerland. Chairman of the UT-Austin Botany Department from 1980 to 1986, he has been a Guggenheim Fellow at the Plant Biochemistry Institute of the University of Freiburg, an Alexander von Humboldt Senior Scientist awardee at the Cell Biology Institute of the University of Heidelberg, and president of the Phytochemical Society of North America. In 1986 Dr. Mabry received the award of the American Chemical Society for the Application of chemistry to food and agriculture.

His activities include organizing symposia, "Plant Biotechnology: Research Bottlenecks for Commercialization and Beyond" in 1987 and "Commercializing Biotechnology in the Global Economy" in 1989. Dr. Mabry is author or coauthor of more than five hundred research papers and ten books.

MARY MOORE ("Telemedicine: Its Place on the Information Highway") is currently a Title 11B doctoral fellow in the Graduate School of Library and Information Science at the University of Texas at Austin. She also serves as a Senior Research Associate in the Center for Research on Communication Technology and Society. She was curriculum developer and evaluation specialist for MEDNET, a project of Texas Tech University School of Medicine (November 1989-August 1992). Among her current or recent assignments are: evaluation consultant, Texas Department of Health; research associate on reviews of research in DHCP and IAIMS project programs, and a research consultant to the School of Nursing on meta-analyses of the study of the impact of managed care on patient outcomes. Ms. Moore's dissertation, currently in progress, centers on technology adoption factors in telemedicine. In 1993 she was winner of two research awards from AT&T for her research project and report on "Secrets of Success in Telemedicine Projects."

FRED YOUNG PHILLIPS ("A Management System for Monitoring and Analyzing the Productivity of Armed Forces Recruiting") is Research Programs Director and Judson Neff Centennial Fellow at the IC^2 Institute of the University of Texas. Dr. Phillips is a Senior Lecturer on the university's Marketing and Economics faculties and Associate Director of UT's Center for Cybernetic Studies.

Until 1989 he was a Vice President at MRCA Information Services, a company that has led the market research industry in innovation for fifty years. His responsibilities at MRCA included corporate management and planning, consulting project management, and the design of advanced methods and applications for consumer panels. One of these was DYANA™, the market research industry's first interactive computer inquiry system for data-based consumer research.

Dr. Phillips's professional achievements and expertise are in market research, technology marketing, new product development, and strategic and innovative business use of computers. His contributions in operations research include "Phillips' Law" of longitudinal sampling, and the first parallel computing experiments with Data Envelopment Analysis.

In 1992 he was co-recipient of a three-million-dollar grant from the Air Force for the study of Japanese technology management practices. In 1993 he won support from the United Nations and from university innovation centers in six countries for an International Year of Technology Commercialization to occur in 1999. As Research Programs Director, he has brought many other federal, state, and foundation grants to the IC^2 Institute.

Dr. Phillips has been a consultant to such organizations as Texas Instruments, Tandem Computers, Frito-Lay Inc., the Association of Home Appliance Manufacturers, and the Office of Naval Research, and he serves on several boards of advisors and boards of directors. He is a member of the Institute of Management Sciences, the Information Industries Association, the Western Regional Science Association, and the American Marketing Association. He has been honored with a National Science Foundation Fellowship in Industrial Engineering and the Toyota Fellowship for Economics Research. Recently he was an invited speaker at the Advertising Research Foundation's Leaders' Forum, at the Western Regional Science Association Presidential Panel, and at the Innovation Workshop of the Wharton School of Business at the University of Pennsylvania.

Dr. Phillips attended the University of Texas and the Tokyo Institute of Technology, earning the Ph.D. at Texas (1978) in mathematics and management science. He has held teaching and research positions at the Universities of Aston and Birmingham in England, and at the General Motors Research Laboratories and St. Edward's University. He is author or coauthor of many publications in operations research and marketing, and editor of two recent books for managers, *Thinkwork: Working, Learning and Managing in a Computer-Interactive Society* (Praeger 1992) and *Concurrent Life Cycle Management: Manufacturing, MIS and Marketing Perspectives* (IC^2 Institute of the University of Texas at Austin, 1990). He is a founder and member of the Advisory Board of the Austin Software Council.

ILYA PRIGOGINE ("Instability, Complexity, and Bounded Rationality in Economic Change") is the Director of the International Solvay Institute of Chemistry and Physics in Brussels, Belgium, and the Ilya Prigogine Center for Studies in Statistical Mechanics and Complex Systems, the University of Texas at Austin. He is an Ashbel Smith Professor of Physics and IC^2 Institute Fellow at UT-Austin. He won the Nobel Prize in 1977 for his work on nonequilibrium physics and chemical reaction. He was awarded the title of Viscount by the King of Belgium and Commandeur de la Légion d'Honneur of France in 1989 and has received twenty-two scientific prizes. He is the member of fifty-eight academies and scientific societies, including the National Academy of Sciences, USA, and the Academy of Sciences of Russia. He has received twenty-five Doctor Honoris Causas degrees.

WALT W. ROSTOW ("The Austin Project, 1989–1994: Interim Report on an Ongoing Innovation") was born October 7, 1916, in New York City. He received a B.A. degree from Yale University in 1936; and a Ph.D. from Yale in 1940; he attended Balliol College, Oxford, England, 1936-1938, as a Rhodes Scholar.

His career as an educator began in 1940 when he became an instructor of economics at Columbia University. During World War II (1942–1945) he served as a Major in the OSS. After the war Dr. Rostow joined the State Department as Assistant Chief of the German-Austrian Economic Division. He later returned to teaching, as the Harmsworth Professor of American History, Oxford University, England, 1946-1947.

In 1947, he became the Assistant to the Executive Secretary of the Economic Commission for Europe. He returned to England in 1949 to spend a year at Cambridge University as Pitt Professor of American History. From 1950-1961, Dr. Rostow was Professor of Economic History at the Massachusetts Institute of Technology, and from 1951-1961 he was also a staff member of the Center for International Studies, MIT.

In January 1961, President Kennedy appointed Dr. Rostow as Deputy Special Assistant to the President for National Security Affairs. He served in that capacity until December 1961, when he was appointed counselor of the Department of State and Chairman of the Policy Planning Council, Department of State. In May 1964 the president appointed him to the additional duty of United States Member of the Inter-American Committee on the Alliance for

Progress (CLAP), with the rank of Ambassador. He served in these latter two capacities until early 1966, when President Johnson called him back to the White House as his Special Assistant for National Security Affairs, where he remained until January 20, 1969.

In February 1969, Dr. Rostow returned to teaching at the University of Texas at Austin, as Professor of Economics and History. Dr. Rostow is the Rex G. Baker, Jr., Professor Emeritus of Political Economy.

Dr. Rostow received the Order of the British Empire (honorary , military division) the Legion of Merit, and the Presidential Medal of Freedom (with distinction). He was a member of the Board of Foreign Scholarships, January 1969 to December 1971.

Dr. Rostow is the author of over thirty books, the latest of which are *Theorists of Economic Growth from David Hume to the Present, With a Perspective on the Next Century* (1990), and the third edition of *The Stages of Economic Growth* (1990).

JOHN J. ROUSSEAU ("A Management System for Monitoring and Analyzing the Productivity of Armed Forces Recruiting") is a Research Scientist at the Center for Cybernetic Studies at the University of Texas at Austin. Formerly, as Senior Research Scientist for MRCA Information Services, he was responsible for the development and implementation of advanced quantitative models as potential information products, and for the design of integrated business data and analysis services. He has B.Sc. (1969) and M.Com (1970) from the University of Birmingham (United Kingdom) and an interdisciplinary Ph.D. from UT-Austin. He has held teaching and research positions at the Universities of Birmingham and Aston in England, the University of Texas at Austin, General Motors Research Laboratories, and Southern Methodist University; and he has been a consultant to a number of private companies and academic research centers.

His publications have been in the areas of applied economics, game theory, information systems science, operations research, and management science.

TIMOTHY W. RUEFLI ("Diversification Strategy, Strategy Change, Performance and State-Defined Risk: Some Longitudinal Evidence") is Professor of Management and former chair of the Department of Management at the Graduate School of Business of the University of Texas at Austin. An expert on corporate strategy and its quantitative dimensions, he has performed extensive data-based analyses of the relative strategies of U.S. versus Japanese firms in electronics and other industries.

DALE O. STAHL ("Pricing of Services on the Internet") brings a unique set of credentials to this research. In 1969 and 1970, he received B.S., M.S., and Engineering degrees from the Massachusetts Institute of Technology in the field of Electrical Engineering, with research experience in computer science and neural nets. In 1981, he received his Ph.D. from the University of California at Berkeley in the field of Economics with a focus on mathematical economics. Since then he has held positions at Duke University, M.I.T., Boston University, and Tilburg University in the Netherlands. He has published thirty-four articles in the top economics journals in general equilibrium theory, dynamics and stability theory, and game-theoretic approaches to price determination.

BEN G. STREETMAN ("Interdisciplinary Research in Materials and Devices for Electronics and Photonics") is Professor of Electrical and Computer Engineering and Director of the Microelectronics Research Center at the University of Texas at Austin and holds the Dula D. Cockrell Centennial Chair in Engineering. His teaching and research interests include semiconductor materials and devices, radiation damage and ion implantation, molecular beam epitaxy, transient annealing, deep level impurities and defects in semiconductors, and multilayer heterostructures. After receiving the Ph.D. from the University of Texas at Austin (1966), he was on the faculty (1966-1982) of the University of Illinois at Urbana-Champaign. He returned to UT-Austin in 1982. In 1989 he was chosen to receive the Education Medal of the Institution of Electrical and Electronics Engineers (IEEE). In 1987 he was elected to membership in the National Academy of Engineering and in the same year received the AT&T Foundation Award of the American Society for Engineering Education (ASEE). In 1981 he received the Frederick Emmons Terman Award of the ASEE, and in 1980 he was elected Fellow of the IEEE. He serves on the Administrative Committee of the IEEE Electron Devices Society and has served on the IEEE Device Research Conference Program Committee (1975-1982), including service as Program Chairman (1981) and Conference Chairman (1982). He serves on the Executive Committee of the Electronics Division, Electrochemical Society, and is a Divisional Editor of the *Journal of the Electrochemical Society*. He serves on the NAS/NAE/IoM Government-University-Industry Research Roundtable Council, and is chairman of the Working Group on New Alliances and Partnerships: Enhancing the Utilization of Scientific and Engineering Advances. He serves on the Science and Technology Advisory Council for ALCOA, and on several other panels and committees in industry and government. He is the author of the book *Solid State Electronic Devices* (Prentice-Hall 1972, 1980, 1990), and has published more than one hundred and eighty technical articles. Twenty-four students of electrical engineering and physics have received their Ph.D. degree under his direction.

DAEKYU SUN ("Drugs as Probes for Intrinsic and Protein-Induced Bending of DNA") received his B.Pharm. in 1984 from Sung Kyun Kwan University and his M.S. degree in 1986 from KAIST, both in Seoul, Korea. From 1986 to 1989 he worked as a research scientist at the Genetic Engineering Center, KAIST, in Seoul. He entered the University of Texas at Austin in 1989 and received his Ph.D. degree in 1992. His Ph.D. dissertation was nominated for a

University Dissertation Award. He is currently employed as a Postdoctoral Fellow in the College of Pharmacy at UT-Austin.

During his years as a graduate student and postdoctoral fellow at UT-Austin, Dr. Sun has published approximately eighteen papers.

GERALD L. THOMPSON ("The Unreasonable Effectiveness of Management Science for Solving Management Problems") is IBM Professor of Systems and Operations Research, and has been on the faculty of the Graduate School of Industrial Administration of Carnegie-Mellon University since 1959. He received a B.S. degree in electrical engineering from Iowa State University, an S.M. degree in mathematics from MIT, and a Ph.D. degree in mathematics from the University of Michigan. His research is in the areas of game theory, mathematical programming—especially structured integer programming, mathematical economics, market game theory, mathematical control theory, differential games, scheduling theory and applications, manpower planning, electrical power generation and distribution systems, and management sciences applications. He has been author or coauthor of numerous books and research papers which have appeared in various mathematics, operations research, economics, management sciences, and electrical engineering journals. He has consulted for a number of industrial firms and has lectured at various institutes and programs in the United States and Europe. Recent publications include: (with S. Sethi) *Optimal Control Theory: Management Science Applications* (with A. Sethi); "The Pivot and Probe Algorithm for Solving a Linear Program" (with J. Teng); "Optimal Pricing and Advertising Models for New Product Oligopoly Models" (with J. Aronson); "A Survey on Forward Methods in Mathematical Programming;" and a DOE Report on *Needs, Opportunities and Options for Large Scale Systems Research.*

STEN THORE ("The Competitiveness of Nations") is the Gregory A. Kozmetsky Centennial Fellow in the IC^2 Institute of the University of Texas at Austin. He is a senior research scientist at the university. He teaches in the departments of economics (economic change and creativity) and aerospace engineering (the commercialization of space technology). He is a faculty member of the new Executive M.Sc. program in the Commercialization of Science and Technology that the IC^2 Institute will be teaching in Washington, D.C., starting in the spring of 1996.

Since Dr. Thore joined the IC^2 Institute in 1978, he has been working on resource and supply systems modeling, industry logistics, and the economics of high technology. His most recent publication is *The Diversity, Complexity, and Evolution of High Tech Capitalism,* Kluwer Academic Publishers, Boston 1995, which addresses a fairly wide audience of business people and economists. Earlier he published a monograph entitled *Economic Logistics: The Optimization of Spatial and Sectorial Resource, Production, and Distribution Systems* (Quorum Books 1991), and a textbook entitled *Computational Economics: Economic*

Modeling with Optimization Software (Scientific Press 1991, coauthored with G.L. Thompson of Carnegie Mellon University).

Dr. Thore has authored or coauthored nine books and more than eighty research papers. His recent contributions include the development of a new constrained least squares regression technique (with applications to productivity change in the manufacturing sector), stochastic formulations of data envelopment analysis (with applications involving the comparison of the efficiency of capitalism and state socialism), the pricing of heterogeneous goods (such as high technology products with many consumer attributes), and several studies of the cost-effectiveness and competitiveness of the U.S. computer industry.

Before coming to Texas, Dr. Thore held a chair in economics at the Norwegian School of Economics and Business Administration in Bergen. At that time he specialized in the optimization of bank funds management, financial intermediation, and the flow-of-funds. On various sabbatical leaves, he was a visiting professor at Northwestern University, Carnegie Mellon University, and the University of Virginia.

Dr. Thore holds the degree of *filosofie doktor* from the University of Stockholm, Sweden. He was a founding member and the first chairman of the Norway Chapter of The Institute of Management Sciences. He is a naturalized U.S. citizen; he is also an honorary citizen of the state of Texas. He is listed in *Who's Who in the World*.

RICHARD L. TUCKER ("Needed Innovations in Capital Expenditure Planning") is the C. T. Wells Professor of Project Management and Director of the Construction Industry Institute at the University of Texas at Austin. He is a native Texan, and has his bachelor's, master's, and doctoral degrees from the University of Texas.

Dr. Tucker has been a project engineer for Engineering Science Consultants in Austin, served on the faculty and was Associate Dean of Engineering at the University of Texas at Arlington, and also served as Vice President for Research at Luther Hill & Associates, a Dallas contractor. For the past several years, he has served as a consultant in project management and construction productivity improvement to owners and contractors.

In 1983, Dr. Tucker led an effort by both industry and academia to form an institute that would be dedicated to improving the cost effectiveness of the U.S. construction industry through research and development. That effort led to the formation of the Construction Industry Institute (CII). CII is now recognized as a national forum for construction R&D, and Dr. Tucker serves as the Institute's director.

Dr. Tucker is a registered professional engineer, and has authored numerous publications and served on many technical committees. Among his many honors, he has been awarded the first Peurifoy Award for Construction Research (1983) and is an honorary member of the Moles. He was recently recognized as the recipient of the Joe J. King Professional Engineering Achievement Award by the College of Engineering at the University of Texas at Austin.

NILGUN E. TUMER ("Potential Agents for the Commercialization of Virus-Resistant Transgenic Plants") is a professor at the AgBiotech Center, Rutgers University. Her research concerns the development of transgenic plants that have increased agricultural value, in particular virus-resistance. Prior to going to Rutgers, Dr. Tumer was a group leader at Monsanto Company. She is an author of seven patents for virus-resistant plants. She received her Ph.D. in biochemistry from Purdue University and her B.A. in chemistry from Agnes Scott College.

KEHONG WEN ("Instability, Complexity, and Bounded Rationality in Economic Change") is a Post Doctoral Fellow at the Ilya Prigogine Center. In 1982 he entered the Modern Physics program of the University of Science and Technology of China. After receiving the Bachelor of Science degree in 1987, he came to the University of Texas at Austin through the CUSPEA program directed by Professor T. D. Lee. He first worked on simulation of complex chemical reactions, then shifted his focus to applying nonequilibrium statistical physics and nonlinear dynamics to economic problems such as business cycles and stock market dynamics. He received his Ph.D. in physics from the University of Texas at Austin in 1993. Ongoing research includes studying the development strategy of China's economic reform from the point of view of economic self-organization.

ANDREW B. WHINSTON ("Pricing of Services on the Internet") is a professor in the MSIS Department, Computer Science Department, and in the Economics Department at The University of Texas at Austin, where he is also a fellow of the IC^2 Institute, Director of the Center for Information Systems Management, and holds the Hugh Roy Cullen Centennial Chair in Business Administration. He received his Ph.D. in management from Carnegie Mellon University in 1962. He served as an Assistant Professor at Yale University from 1961 to 1964 in the Department of Economics and the Cowles Foundation for Research in Economics. In 1964 he joined the faculty of the Economics Department at the University of Virginia as an associate professor and was later appointed as professor in the Business School at Purdue University with a joint appointment in Computer Science.

Professor Whinston has been a principal investigator on contracts from the National Science Foundation, Office of Naval Research, and Army Research Office as well as on numerous grants from companies such as Apple, NCR, IBM, and Shell Development. He is also the editor-in-chief of the journals *Decision Support Systems* and *Organizational Computing*, and an associate editor of most of the academic journals in the information systems field. He has coauthored over two hundred and fifty articles in such journals as *Management*

Science, Information Systems Research, Operations Research, America Economic Review, ACM Transactions on Database Systems, Econometrica, Review of Economic Studies, Journal of Economic Theory, Southern Economic Review, Bell Journal of Economics, Journal of Public Economics, and *Journal of Combinatorics* and coauthored sixteen books.

His current research is concerned with the potential of prices in engineering an improvement in the performance of Internet. In collaboration with Dale Stahl and Alok Gupta, price adjustment mechanisms are proposed and a stimulated behavior of the Internet as an economy is studied. Another ongoing research topic is the specification of software agents on the basis of a rational search mode: an agent learns the preferences of the owner and carries out the search for a service or product across large-scale databases. In general, Whinston is pursuing several topics that involve the economics of information systems and computational economics.

Professor Whinston was recently named as the Distinguished Information Systems Educator in 1994 by the Data Processing Management Association.

JOHN M. WHITE ("Interdisciplinary Research in Materials and Devices for Electronics and Photonics") received a Bachelor's degree in chemistry from Harding College in Searcy, Arkansas, in 1960. He attended graduate school at the University of Illinois, where he held a Woodrow Wilson Fellowship (1960-1961), a Robert F. Carr Fellowship (1961), and a University Fellowship (1961-1964). His research with Aron Kupperman at Illinois and at the California Institute of Technology focused on the reaction of photochemically produced monoenergetic deuterium atoms with hydrogen molecules. White received the Ph.D. in chemistry in 1966.

In 1966 he joined the faculty at the University of Texas at Austin as assistant professor. He was promoted to full professor in 1976 and served as chairman of the Chemistry Department from 1979 to 1984. White was named Norman Hackerman Professor of Chemistry in 1985. He currently directs the Center for Materials Chemistry at UT.

Harding University named him their Distinguished Alumnus in 1985. The following year, he was named the first Outstanding Alumnus of Alpha Chi, a national honorary society. In 1989 White received a Humboldt Foundation Senior Scientist Award in support of a sabbatical leave at the Fritz-Haber Institute in Berlin, where he worked with Gerhard Ertl. He was the recipient of the 1990 ACS Kendall Award in Surface and Colloid Chemistry.

White is a longtime visiting staff member at Los Alamos National Laboratories, a principal editor of the *Journal of Materials Research* and advisory editor for *Chemical Physics Letters,* and a member of the editorial boards of *Applied Surface Science, CRC Critical Reviews in Surface Chemistry,* and *Surface Science.* He belongs to the American Chemical Society. the American Vacuum Society, and the Materials Research Society. His research interests include surface and materials chemistry, the dynamics of surface reactions, and photoassisted catalytic reactions. He has published over three hundred articles in referreed journals.

FREDERICK D. WILLIAMS ("Telemedicine: Its Place on the Information Highway") is a communications professor, researcher, and author. He is director of the Center for Research on Communication Technology and Society at the University of Texas at Austin, where he occupies the Mary Gibbs Jones Centennial Chair in Communication. He served as founding dean of the Annenberg School of Communications at the University of Southern California between 1972 and 1985. His publications include some seventy-five articles and thirty-six books.

Williams' most recent books on topics relating to communications technology include Research Methods and the New Media (with R. Rice and E. Rogers; Free Press 1988) and Measuring the Information Society (edited; Sage 1988). Recent textbooks include the second edition of *The New Communications* (Wadsworth 1988) and *Technology and Communication Behaviour* (Wadsworth 1986). Professional management books include *Innovative Management using Telecommunications* (with H. Dordick; Wiley 1986); *The Executive's Guide to Information Technology* (with H. Dordick; Wiley 1984). Popularly written trade books include *The Communications Revolution* (New American Library 1984) and *Growing Up with Computers* (Morrow 1984), the latter cowritten with his wife, Dr. Victoria Williams.

XIAOHUA XIA ("Using Computer Intensive Technologies to Aid Insurance Regulators: Early Detection of Insolvency and Fraud") graduated from Zhejiang University, Hangzhou, People's Republic of China, in 1983, receiving a B.S. in Computer Science and Engineering. He worked as an assistant lecturer at Zhejiang University for four years and also as a computer engineer. From 1988 until 1992, he was an assistant to the Dean of Academic Affairs, responsible for the development of curricula and instructional technology and instructional evaluation. For one year, he worked as an engineer in the technology management and quality control department at Wenzhou Electronic and Instrument Corporation in Whenzhou, Zhejiang.

He has developed several management information systems for a regional taxation agency and for the Dean's Office of Academic Affairs at Zhejiang University. He has published several articles in Chinese.

Mr. Xia entered the Ph.D. program in Management Science at The University of Texas at Austin in the fall of 1992 and is currently a doctoral candidate. His research interests are neural networks and their algorithms and applications and applications, of operations research models in finance, especially in risk management and insurance.